the government of the United Kingdom

THIRD EDITION

GWENDOLEN M. CARTER

Northwestern University

HARCOURT BRACE JOVANOVICH, INC.
New York   Chicago   San Francisco   Atlanta

The contents of this volume are reprinted from
Major Foreign Powers, Sixth Edition,
by Gwendolen M. Carter and John H. Herz.

Copyright 1949, 1952, © 1957, 1962, 1967, 1972,
by Harcourt Brace Jovanovich, Inc.

All rights reserved. No part of this publication may be reproduced or transmitted in any form or by any means, electronic or mechanical, including photocopy, recording, or any information storage and retrieval system, without permission in writing from the publisher.

Cover painting by Benedict Umy

ISBN: 0-15-529647-7

Library of Congress Catalog Card Number: 76-181534

Printed in the United States of America

contents

INTRODUCTION   2

1

THE BRITISH PEOPLE AND THEIR POLITICS   3

1. The Challenge to Great Britain	3
2. The Island and the People	5
3. The Economy and the State	19
4. Organs of Political Opinion	22
5. Britain in a Period of Change	29

2

THE BRITISH POLITICAL HERITAGE   30

1. Historical Background	30
2. The British Constitution	37
3. British Political Ideas	46

3

BRITISH PARTIES AND ELECTIONS   53

1. The Character of the British Party System	53
2. How the Parties Are Organized	57
3. Elections	73
4. Effectiveness of the British Party System	85

4

THE BRITISH PARLIAMENT   89

1. The House of Commons: Its Members	90
2. The House of Commons: Organization	94
3. The House of Commons: Its Work	99
4. The House of Commons: Lawmaking	106
5. The House of Commons and Finance	111
6. The Private Member's Influence	113
7. The House of Lords	117
8. The Future of Parliamentary Reform	120

5

THE BRITISH CABINET, PRIME MINISTER, AND MONARCH 121
1. The Cabinet 121
2. The Prime Minister 129
3. The Monarch 131

6

THE BRITISH ADMINISTRATION: NATIONAL AND LOCAL 134
1. The Range of Public Responsibilities 134
2. The Structure of Administration 134
3. Local and Regional Government 145
4. The Public Service 151

7

ENGLISH LAW AND COURTS 163
1. English Common Law 163
2. Judges, Juries, and Officials 166
3. The Courts 171
4. Judicial Control of Government Officials 177

8

GREAT BRITAIN AND THE WORLD 180
1. The Commonwealth of Nations 180
2. International Relations 190

CONCLUSION 194

BIBLIOGRAPHY 195

INDEX 219

charts and maps

The United Kingdom of Great Britain and Northern Ireland	7
Survey of Self-Assessment on Class Basis	16
Elite Response of Importance of Press	26
Where Influence Lies	26
Structure of the Conservative Party	61
Structure of the Labor Party	68
Geography of a Typical British Election, 1959	74
Accuracy of the Polls, 1945–64	76
Accuracy of the Polls, 1966	76
Accuracy of the Polls, 1970	76
Map of the General Election, 1970	83
The National Results, 1945–70	84
The House of Commons, 1945–70	91
Occupation of Elected MP's, 1970	92
Floor of the House of Commons	98
Local Government Areas as Proposed by the Redcliffe-Maud Commission, 1966–69	147
Local Government Areas Proposed by Conservative Government, February 1971	149
Court System of England and Wales	172
The Commonwealth of Nations	182–83

The
government
of the United Kingdom
of Great Britain
and Northern Ireland

Introduction

Throughout the twentieth century Great Britain has been the strongest and most reliable ally of the United States; equally, the United States has been Britain's most powerful support. Whatever differences in attitude and approach have existed—and there have been many—the bonds of self-interest, history, and sentiment have been too strong to allow the rupture of their often cited "special relationship." As Great Britain now moves to assume a place within the European Common Market, however, new questions arise about the character and strength of that relationship. How much did it depend on Great Britain's position as a world power rather than a European one? Will the Atlantic alliance be complementary to or be replaced by a British orientation that looks south and east rather than west? What will be the effect on foreign affairs of Britain's inevitable concentration on adjusting its economic and political alignments to a more Continental role?

Bismarck said long ago that the most significant fact for the twentieth century would be that Americans speak English. British institutions, English literature, law, and education have had a deep and persistent effect on American life. The advanced British social welfare system and radical approaches to the care of the environment have unfortunately had less impact in this country. The old stereotype of the British as a highly conservative people perpetuating the past through their lords and castles and their colorful royal ceremonies is a technicolor screen, which tends to conceal the active experimentation by means of which the British are seeking new ways to cope with the manifold problems of a highly industrial, urbanized society. There is much for Americans to learn from British attempts and even failures to master the most pressing problems of our day—such as poverty, pollution, color prejudice, and discrimination—for it is in these areas that we, too, are struggling to find solutions.

In the chapters that follow there is abundant material on the British heritage of history and ideas; the explanation of why one of the two major political parties of supposedly staid Britain is called Labor and was founded on a socialist creed; the ways in which the British are seeking to make the workings of their legislative body more efficient and responsible; how powerful the prime minister is in practice in comparison with the president of the United States; the structure and operation of the nationalized enterprises, which manage one-fifth of British economic life; the character of English law and courts, which have so direct a relationship to our own legal system; and the changing orientations of British foreign policy. In all these areas, the British have raised basic questions as to whether institutions and policies are fulfilling the purposes of the British people and adhering to the high standards of democracy they prize. In learning about contemporary Britain, its problems and its efforts to wrestle with them, we not only can learn about a great country, which in the nineteenth century was the world's leading power, but also can gain constructive perspective on our own current issues and how to tackle them.

1
The British people and their politics

1 THE CHALLENGE TO GREAT BRITAIN

The British[1] people today face great challenges: to revitalize their economy; to adjust to their changed position in world affairs; to devise new political techniques in response to defects in traditional institutions; to respond constructively to increasing regional self-consciousness in Scotland and Wales and to the strains caused by postwar colored immigration; and to find new ways, as they have in the past, to resolve the conflicts and tensions that are endemic in a mobile industrial society. The external reputation of the British people for steadiness and sanity tends to conceal from outsiders the widespread questioning of standard values and of institutionalized ways of acting that pervades British society. The British are making persistent, although occasionally contradictory, efforts to cope with these challenges. But the process is a painful one, and the tensions manifest themselves in angry outbursts from time to time at the character or the slowness of change.

Great Britain was long one of the world's great powers and is the one whose institutions have been most widely copied in other countries. Both the Conservative and Labor parties have been reluctant, therefore, to restrict their country's international role despite its unstable balance of payments and lessening influence in international crises. Both parties sought when in office during the sixties to secure entry to the Common Market, although both contain sharp internal divisions of opinion on this European orientation. Labor has led in stressing the need to reduce the outlay on military expenditures and to concentrate more on the welfare of the people of the British Isles. The Conservatives have also reluctantly conceded the need for retrenchments in overseas commitments, especially east of Suez. Thus it is the extent and timing of withdrawals, rather than fundamental orientations, that divide the parties in the field of international relations.

The second great issue in British politics—which revolves around the dimensions and character of what is called "the welfare state"—creates more clear-cut differences between the parties. At issue is the degree to which the power and resources of the government should be used to create a more egalitarian society. In

---

[1] *British* in this section refers to the inhabitants of the United Kingdom, although properly the term can be used also to refer to persons in other parts of the British Commonwealth and empire. *Great Britain* and the *United Kingdom* will be used interchangeably, although, strictly speaking, Great Britain includes only England, Wales, and Scotland.

Northern Ireland, it should be noted, differs from the other parts of the United Kingdom in that its population is represented in a legislature of its own in Belfast, as well as in the British Parliament. The partition of Ireland, which dates from 1921, divides the island between the homogeneous Catholic Irish Republic, which occupies most of its territory, and Protestant-dominated Northern Ireland in its northeastern corner, which has home rule inside the United Kingdom. Sporadic violence between Protestants and Catholics in Northern Ireland, particularly since 1969, has led to the presence of British troops to maintain order. (For more details on this situation, see Chapter 8, Section 1.)

part the approach to securing this objective has been through state-supported institutions like schools and hospitals, but it involves also a more equitable distribution of wealth, largely through taxation. The Conservatives, who place primary emphasis on individual initiative and the enterprise of the capitalist class, believe that economic health requires trade union reform and restraint in wage increases. Although they are committed to extend aid to those groups in society who cannot provide for themselves—that is, the aged, ill, infirm, children, and unemployed—they also aim at lower taxation to encourage active entrepreneurship inside and outside the country. The Labor party, as an article of faith, is primarily committed, on the other hand, to the well-being of the working class and to a basic egalitarianism to be secured through using state instrumentalities to create conditions for its realization. Although in practice the orientation and behavior of the leaders of both parties are less far apart than these contrasts might suggest, there are distinctive differences in policy decisions, depending on which party is in office.

Both British parties believe strongly in personal rights and the rule of law. They believe that individual freedom must be combined, however, with effective government, and that open discussion should be organized through channels that protect minority rights but facilitate majority action. Although class, regional, and, now, color distinctions complicate the process of reaching decisions and responding to them, both parties are dedicated to the effective use of parliamentary institutions (although possibly reformed and revitalized) in their search for constructive answers to complicated and delicate issues. With all the ferment of change, convention still maintains its hold. Although Britain's future is difficult to calculate, the ways in which it has surmounted crises in the past lends support to the faith that it will do so again.

THE IMPORTANCE OF BRITAIN FOR OTHER COUNTRIES

British political machinery and experience have long had unusual importance for other countries, for no people in modern times have been more fertile in the invention and adaptation of political institutions. Wherever men of British descent founded new governments in the last century and a half—in Canada, Australia, and New Zealand—they carried British institutions with them. Moreover, such countries as India, Kenya, and Jamaica, when they became independent, adapted British forms and institutions. On the continent of Europe almost every democracy has been strongly, if not always happily, influenced by the British example. The person who understands British government has a standard, therefore, by which to measure many of the world's democracies.

SIMILARITIES WITH AND DIFFERENCES FROM THE UNITED STATES

The British government, moreover, is sometimes held up as an example for Americans to imitate. Some of its more ardent admirers, it must be confessed, value it for different and even conflicting reasons, and some of them seriously misunderstand its character. Yet not infrequently the American people are urged to scrap some part of their constitutional machinery or political practices in favor of the British equivalent.

It is all the more important, therefore, to understand the extent to which the two countries are comparable. The sharing of a common language and of common cultural, legal, and political traditions often encourages the assumption that the political outlook and conduct of the two countries must also be similar. Both nations take it for granted that peoples who are not "Anglo-Saxon" will differ from them in attitude and policy, but each is subject to a peculiar irritation when it finds its standards disregarded by the other. There is shrewdness in the comment that Great Britain and the United States are divided by their common language.

There are, in actuality, important political differences between the two countries, differences that stem in large measure from dissimilarities in geography, economic structure, class divisions, way of life, and inherited political ideas and institutions. Anyone who is to understand British politics, therefore, must first of all know something about these differences.

2 THE ISLAND AND THE PEOPLE

THE ISLAND

The fact that Britain is an island has long conditioned British attitudes. Only twenty-two miles of water separate the southeast shore of England from the European continent—and plans are under consideration to build a connecting tunnel—but for many generations those few miles gave the British people the feeling of security that the Atlantic and the Pacific, until recently, gave Americans. Today, air warfare and nuclear armaments have destroyed any such idea. If the Channel helped to prevent Hitler's armies from conquering Great Britain, it could not keep the Allies from successfully invading occupied France, and it could not keep German planes and rockets from devastating many heavily populated centers on the British island.

Yet there are certain ways in which the earlier protective role of the Channel still influences British politics. During the critical centuries when Continental states developed great standing armies that became instruments of autocratic government, the British were relatively free from any corresponding threat. The British army, as the saying goes, was a navy; and a navy was hardly an asset in putting down popular resistance to royal authority on land. Security from invasion made it possible, in the seventeenth and eighteenth centuries, for the British to develop and consolidate free institutions of government at the very time that their neighbors across the Channel were submitting to absolute monarchy. Thus, although the Channel today has lost much of its defensive importance, the free institutions that it protected continue to exist.

Commercial and military position

Great Britain's geographical position has been important in another respect. So long as the Mediterranean was the chief path of trade, the island suffered commercially from its location on the fringe of the European world. But once America was discovered, the new trade routes turned the island into a center of world commerce. Great Britain pioneered the industrial revolution. Favorable conditions for importing raw materials and exporting manufactured goods made it the workshop of the world. Partly through the resulting capital accumulation, Great Britain became, too, the world's greatest banking center. If the island had remained purely agricultural, its population would necessarily have been small; but the profits from its industry, shipping, and worldwide investments made it easy to import the food and resources necessary to support a population larger than that of more self-sufficient France.

Great Britain's dependence on sea power encouraged its acquisition of key points on the world's trade routes: Gibraltar, at the mouth of the Mediterranean; the Falkland Islands, off the southern tip of South America; Cape Town, in southern Africa; and Singapore, dominating the route around Southeast Asia. Overseas settlement in areas that became Canada, Australia, New Zealand, and South Africa formed the core from which developed the modern British Commonwealth of Nations. During the nineteenth century the British navy, unmatched in strength, provided a condition of security that is often called the "Pax Britannica," which made possible an exchange of goods and services that helped both these overseas areas and Great Britain itself. Widely scattered other countries, like India, Malaysia, and Nigeria, where the British once governed diverse peoples very different from themselves in race, traditions, and conditions of life, have moved through self-government to independence since World War II but still associate themselves with Great Britain through the Commonwealth. These vast international connections brought Great Britain power, prestige, and wealth, and stretched its communication lines around the world.

Today this very dependence on foreign trade constitutes both a military and an economic liability. Because of its relative poverty in raw materials other than coal, Great Britain relies heavily on outside sources to maintain its factories; it needs oil from the Middle East, rubber from Malaysia, nickel from Canada, iron ore to make the steel with which to produce the locomotives and heavy machinery that form so substantial a part of its exports, and much besides. Although a proportion of its foreign investments have been reestablished since the days they were liquidated to pay the costs of two world wars, Great Britain must earn most of the money for food and raw materials by selling in foreign markets—often, as in the United States, in the face of protective tariffs. Fourteen to twenty percent of its gross national product (GNP) is exported, compared to 4 percent for the United States.

Since Great Britain remains predominantly a processing economy, failure to maintain its imports and exports can be disastrous. Both the United States and the Soviet Union have vast resources and markets at home; in an emergency they could support themselves to a considerable extent. But to Great Britain such an emergency might mean strangulation. Thus, whereas the United States and the Soviet Union, in military terms, think first of all of security from attack against the homeland, Great Britain must also think of the equally fatal effect of any serious interference with its commerce with distant lands. Moreover, failure to compete economically could also mean a kind of death by attrition.

Climate and size

Another geographical consideration of great political importance is the smallness of the British island and the evenness of its climate. Great Britain (not including Northern Ireland, which has an area of 5,244 square miles) has an area of only 89,041 square miles, as compared with 3,022,387 for the continental United States. The island is twice the size of Pennsylvania but a little smaller than Oregon. Moreover, the major portion of its population (which by mid-1971 was about 55.5 million) is concentrated in a relatively small area, since in the north and west (including most of Scotland and Wales) the country is hilly or mountainous. The climate, however, is remarkably even. There is somewhat more rain in the west than in the east and somewhat more sun in the east, but the winters tend to be mild, the summers cool, and the rainfall fairly well distributed throughout the year. There is nothing to compare with the great range of climate and the vast distances that encourage the distinctive outlook and individuality of different American regions. On the contrary, the great bulk of the people live within a few hours' train or motor ride of London, and the same newspapers can be read on the same morning throughout the island.

As a result, the Englishman is more likely than the American to think in exclusively national terms. Both in Scotland and in Wales there is a strong local consciousness, recently reflected in regional parties (see Chapter 3, Section 2), although the national parties win the seats in general elections. However, less than one-sixth of the British population is Scottish or Welsh. In England itself, where the overwhelming majority of the people live, there is little particularist feeling. There is considerable interest in local history and in regional variations in landscape, architecture, and dialect, but this interest is not reflected in a distinctive political feeling. Political parties can use the same literature and emphasize the same principles in Somerset as in London or Norfolk or Yorkshire.

Great Britain's relative homogeneity and compactness have an important political consequence. In American politics little is more significant than the extent of political decentralization. Not only do sections of the country have distinct characters of their own, but each state has a complete government. The most important political organizations in the United States are state and local rather than national. No American party can win a national election unless it carries several of the great sections, and every party platform represents a compromise of rival sectional interests. Votes in Congress often run along sectional rather than party lines, and even the nominations for national office must take geography into account: if the presidential nominee comes from the West, the vice-presidential nominee must come from the East or the South.

In England, in contrast, no one cares whether a party's leaders come from Durham or Devon or Essex. Unlike American practice, candidates for the legislature do not need to be residents of the constituencies for which they stand. Historically, the smallness of the island simpli-

THE ISLAND AND THE PEOPLE

THE UNITED KINGDOM OF GREAT BRITAIN AND NORTHERN IRELAND

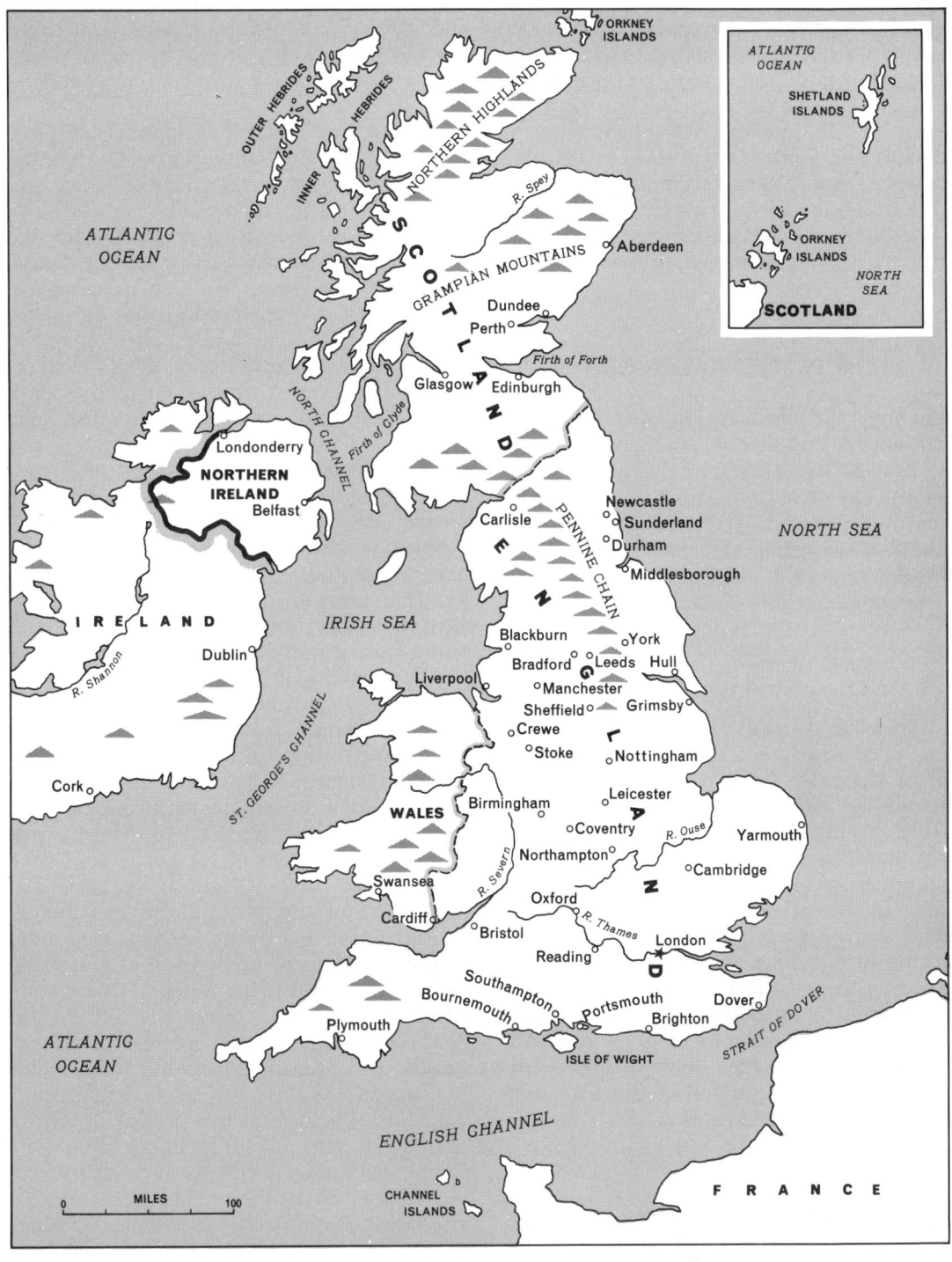

fied the task of centralizing the government; and governmental centralization, reinforced by ease of transportation and communication, has fostered a well-integrated political and economic life. Apart from the strong sectionalism in Northern Ireland (accentuated by recent violence) and the marked self-consciousness in Scotland and Wales (which leads to demands for some devolution of governmental responsibilities), the most important political issues in Great Britain are not primarily regional in character; parties are free to plan in national rather than local terms.

THE PEOPLE: NATIONALITY

In origin the inhabitants of Great Britain are both ancient and diverse, for the early history of the island is, almost to the point of monotony, one of invasion, conquest, and settlement by different peoples coming from a great variety of geographical areas. In later years Shakespeare could hail the "silver sea" surrounding the British isle and serving it

> . . . in the office of a wall,
> Or as a moat defensive to a house
> Against the envy of less happier lands.

But in prehistoric and early historic times, the seas often acted as a highroad bringing invaders and visitors from far places as the airways do today.

The first historical knowledge we have of the inhabitants of the island comes from a time when most of Great Britain was inhabited by Celts. By reputation they were a folk of imagination and quick intelligence, though somewhat lacking in discipline and emotional restraint; and even today there is an amusing tendency to attribute any marked strain of individuality or lyricism in English writing, or any "un-English" political excitement among the masses of the people, to a survival of this Celtic element in the national character.

For a time, from the first to the fifth centuries, England and a part of Scotland were under the control of the Romans; but apart from their famous roads, a number of ruins, and some place names, few direct traces of Roman influence have survived. With the withdrawal of their legions early in the fifth century, the island was left open to the inroads of various Germanic peoples: Angles, Saxons, Jutes, and, later, Danes. As the invaders penetrated westward, it was only on the fringes of Wales, Cornwall, Cumberland, and western Scotland that the Celts continued to predominate.

The last great invasion of England took place in 1066, when the Normans gave the country, for a time, a ruling class which was French in customs, language, and manners, but which was not numerous enough to make fundamental changes in the composition of the population. Since that time there has been no successful invasion of the country. Moreover, except for the Celtic fringes of Wales (where about 30 percent of the people speak Welsh) and of Scotland (where a few Highlanders speak Gaelic), the Irish immigrants in a few large cities, and a wartime infiltration of Poles and central Europeans, the population of Britain was long exceptionally uniform in language, religion, and way of life.

Since World War II, however, the British have confronted a color and immigration problem that bears on their Commonwealth relations and their economic situation, as well as on their population structure. Immigrants from the West Indies and the Indian subcontinent had brought Great Britain's colored population to an estimated 1.2 million by mid-1969. (By 1985, the specialized British Runnymede Trust estimates, there will be fewer than 3 million colored people in Britain, two-fifths of them born there.) Although the 1969 figures represent only 2.7 percent of the population—compared to the black 11 percent in the United States—the same problems of discrimination in housing and employment have been apparent in the urban areas, where they are most numerous. So, too, has the intensity of local bitterness against them, reflected in or whipped up by the inflammatory speeches of Enoch Powell, a Conservative, who has been termed "a George C. Wallace with an Oxford accent."

In 1962, for the first time in British history, restrictions were placed on immigration from Commonwealth countries—a move that roused ill feeling in some of the new countries of that association (see Chapter 8, Section 1). Moreover, progressively tightened restrictions have followed under both Labor and Conservative governments. Although parallel acts have been passed prohibiting racial discrimination in "places of public resort" (comparable to the public accommodations section of the Civil Rights Act of 1964) and establishing a Race Relations Board that can investigate cases of discrimination, the problems remain. But whereas color was an election issue in a few local areas in 1964, despite strong official party disapproval, it has played only a minor role in scattered constituencies in subsequent elections.

Immigration into Great Britain needs to be considered in a broader context than the color issue suggests. The present population includes an unusually high proportion of young people up to fifteen years of age and older ones over sixty-five. Because of lower birth rates in the early 1950s (repeated from 1964 to 1969), no net growth in the labor force can be foreseen before 1975, particularly since there will be a sharp drop in 1972 when the school-leaving age is raised. In contrast, because of the different American postwar pattern in births, there will be 35 percent more eighteen-to-twenty-four-year-olds in the United States in 1975 than in 1965. Moreover, according to the Organization for Economic Cooperation and Development (OECD) estimates in 1969, the likely growth, including immigration, in the active population in the United States between 1965 and 1980 will be nearly 30 percent, with comparable increases in France and Switzerland. In Britain, West Germany, Italy, and Sweden the active population, in contrast, will probably be not much, if at all, larger in 1980 than in 1965.

On balance, net postwar emigration from Great Britain—which varied between nineteen thousand and sixty-three thousand during the five years from 1965 to 1970—has balanced net immigration (now limited to under thirty-five thousand a year). On these projections, the British population may appear to be reaching stabilization, which will comfort those who have been alarmed about overcrowding Britain's available land space. But those concerned to expand production may look with envy on the annual intake into economically prosperous West Germany of hundreds of thousands of temporary foreign workers from its European partners and perhaps one hundred and fifty thousand into France. Britain, too, will face comparable inflows when it joins the Common Market, for although Commonwealth immigration need not be affected, Britain will have to provide free entry to workers from its new European partners. Thus the population issue is far from settled. Much more study is needed of the relation between size of population, extent of skills, industrial expansion, housing, and the other services for its people to which Great Britain is committed.

THE PEOPLE: RELIGION

Religion has had a greater influence on British politics than most of the British themselves realize. It is politically important, for example, that there is no great religious division and that, as a whole, the island's people are overwhelmingly Protestant. A few of the oldest and noblest families are Catholic, and recent immigration from Ireland has added significantly to this church's adherents in the poorest and least influential sections of society; but altogether under 10 percent of the population in the United Kingdom are Catholic (compared with 20 percent of the population in the United States). Thus there is no basis whatsoever for a Catholic political party such as those that have existed in France, Italy, and other countries.

Of greater political significance is the division that exists within the Protestant church. At present, about 70 percent of the people of England are, at least nominally, adherents of the Church of England, that is, the Anglican Church, which corresponds to the Episcopal church in the United States; about 20 percent are so-called Nonconformists, who are generally Methodists (700,000), Baptists, Congregationalists, or Presbyterians. In Scotland, however, the mass of the people belong to the Presbyterian church, which is the Church of Scotland, and in Wales most belong to Nonconformist denominations.

The Church of England

Because it is an established church, the Church of England is to a certain extent involved in politics. Its head is the monarch, and representatives of the Church sit in the House of Lords and help to make the law of the land. Anglican clergy performed the ceremony of crowning the present queen; it is they who open Parliament with prayer. The highest members of the clergy are, in effect, appointed by the Crown, on the nomination of the prime minister. Despite numerous Church commissions set up since 1870, of which the latest reported in December 1970, they have not found ways for the Church to have more freedom in determining its own affairs. The greatest concern is that the creed of the Church of England is established by parliamentary statute and may be changed only by parliamentary action.[2]

More important than the present state of the establishment, however, is the historical influence of the opposition between the Church of England and Nonconformity. Authority in the Church of England, as just noted, traditionally has come from above, and it was natural for those accustomed to authority in the Church to support it in the state. Thus there has been a marked tendency for at least those of the upper class who are Anglicans in religion to be Conservatives in politics. And the Conservative party still considers itself, to some extent, the special defender of religion and the interests of the Church.

Nonconformist influence

English Nonconformists, in contrast, have tended to be critical of state authority ever since their persecution in the seventeenth century.[3] The Congregationalists (who still call themselves "Independents") and Baptists practiced a peculiarly loose and individualistic form of church organization. Authority rested in the congregation, not in a clerical hierarchy, and members were free at any time to withdraw and form new churches. Such ideas, when applied in the political sphere, are closely related to those in the American Declaration of Independence (both denominations, of course, colonized New England) and provide grounds for questioning the legitimacy of any authority not based upon consent. Throughout the nineteenth century the Liberal party, with its emphasis on personal liberty and the limitation of state authority, drew its strongest support from these churches. Today there remains a large Nonconformist element in the Labor party.

It is still possible, in several important respects, to trace the influence of Nonconformity upon British politics. In the first place, the Nonconformists' demand for toleration of different religious ideas and organizations led naturally to insistence on respect for different political ideas and parties. In addition, Nonconformity is the source of the "Nonconformist conscience" (a first cousin of the "New England conscience"), which has come to be shared by a large section of the Anglican Church and which expects the conduct of the government, in foreign as in domestic policy, to be moral and Christian. For example, there was a vast outpouring of indignation within Great Britain itself against Eden's use of force in the 1956 Suez crisis and deep concern at the Conservative decision in 1971 to sell arms to South Africa.

Yet if the Nonconformist heritage has had an idealistic influence upon British politics, it has also had an intensely practical one. In some Continental Protestant churches, political action has always been suspect, but the British churches have encouraged a general interest and participation in politics. It used to be said in the nineteenth century that every Nonconformist chapel was a recruiting station for the Liberal party. When the Labor party was founded, it was no accident that its party organization combined local democracy with a high degree of centralization, for many of its early leaders were themselves Methodist or Baptist lay preachers who could place both their eloquence and their practical knowledge of organization at the disposal of the new party.

In addition, the Nonconformist churches made their chief appeal to people in the lower

---

[2] Since it often happens that the prime minister is not himself an Anglican, there results an odd situation (and one which many Anglicans dislike) under which the highest clergy of the Church may be nominated by a Welsh Nonconformist like Lloyd George, a Presbyterian like Balfour or Bonar Law, or even—to achieve the ultimate in doctrinal incongruity—by a Unitarian like Neville Chamberlain. Moreover, many members of Parliament are Nonconformists, Jews, Catholics, or members of no church at all. In 1927 and 1928, changes in the Prayer Book of the Church of England, requested by the representative bodies of the Church, were refused by Parliament partly because of the votes of Nonconformists and even—to the scandal of the devout—of one Parsee.

[3] Although the Methodists, whose religious activity began in the eighteenth century, preached a doctrine of obedience and submission to state authority, they organized vigorous political action on such issues as prison reform and abolition of the slave trade.

classes whom the established Church failed to reach. In countries such as Russia or France or Germany, where the church tended to identify its interests with those of the upper classes, it was natural to regard the church as an ally or tool of an oppressive state, an instrument for keeping the exploited in subjection. But in England the lower classes had a church of their own that was itself to some extent oppressed by and critical of state authority. Accordingly, there was no need, in attacking political injustice, to attack religion as well. On the contrary, religion played an important part in fostering both the trade union and the socialist movement in Great Britain. And since it is difficult to be both a Christian and a believer in the extreme doctrine of class war, religion contributed to the moderation as well as to the idealism of the Labor party.

Today all the British churches cooperate in programs of social betterment, and some of their most eminent members are advocates of radical economic reform. The vote on church union between the Anglicans and the Methodists failed in mid-1969 only because the Anglican lower clergy did not support it to the necessary 75 percent, but the efforts go on both in England and Wales. Moreover, by his formal visit to the Pope in 1965, the Archbishop of Canterbury supported the idea of wider associations, which are one of Britain's greatest needs.

POLITICAL CULTURE

In way of life, as in nationality and religion, the British people are exceptionally homogeneous. The sentimental American still likes to think of England as a "green and pleasant land" of villages, churches, and country houses, and the tourist still prefers a visit to the Lake Country or Stratford-on-Avon to an acquaintance with Manchester or Glasgow. But the unromantic fact is that Great Britain is heavily urbanized and industrialized; its population is one of the densest of any Western country. Whereas the United States has some 57 people to the square mile, the United Kingdom as a whole has 607, more than ten times as many, and England and Wales have 837, that is, nearly fifteen times as many. This density, coupled with intense industrialization in certain centers like Birmingham, Manchester, and indeed the whole of the "black country," and of other urban conglomerations, has led to a high degree of urbanization, reaching 80 percent in England and Wales and 70 percent in Scotland (the latter the same degree as in the United States). The British stress on industry has resulted in a very heavy proportion of urban workers compared to those still on the land. Only 3.2 percent of the British working force is in agriculture (in the United States it is 6.7 percent), while 46 percent work in industry, mining, and the like (compared to 40.9 percent in the United States). Thus, whereas the proportion of urban workers to farmers in the United States is six-and-a-half to one, in Great Britain there are fourteen urban workers to every farmer. This latter situation, as we shall see, has a massive impact on the class and party systems.

But while occupation, urbanization, and industrialization are strong conditioners of political attitudes, they are not the only ones. The British class structure, which has long been the basic fact of British society, also reflects other factors such as tradition, education, behavior, manner of living, and, although to a decreasing extent, accent. Above all, the class structure and its impact rest on social self-perception.

Traditionally, the British class structure made its sharpest line of demarcation not between the aristocracy [4] and the middle class (as has so often been the case on the Continent) but between the upper middle and the lower middle class. The most important factor in determining who fell on which side of the line used to be education, which in turn was determined not only by financial standing but also by inherited traditions, sense of values, and habit.

EDUCATION

Prior to the Education Act of 1944, fees were imposed for secondary school education, and most children dropped out at fourteen, at the

[4] In Great Britain, a title ordinarily descends only to the eldest son, while the rest of the children of a nobleman become "commoners." Thus a person may be closely related to a number of peers without having a title himself, and the distinction between the aristocracy and the upper middle class is blurred.

end of elementary education, with no chance to enter schools that would prepare them for college and relatively little preparation for a job. The educational system thus tended not only to perpetuate the class structure but also to stratify the opportunities for employment.

Moreover, educational opportunities were further limited by the predominant position of the private preparatory schools (comparable to the private elementary schools in the United States), which had a virtual monopoly over entry to the great public boarding schools such as Eton and Harrow (called "public" because they are not run for private profit, though they are entirely or mainly independent of state aid or control, and are, in fact, like the American private preparatory schools), to which students normally go at thirteen. Only 5 to 10 percent of the schoolboy population entered the preparatory schools and the great public boarding schools, but the great majority of this group went on to a university, particularly to the most ancient and distinguished British universities, Oxford and Cambridge. Although Oxford and Cambridge accounted for about one-quarter of all the university students in England and Wales before the war, only a small percentage of their prewar undergraduates had attended the state elementary schools, although half of the students at other British universities were trained at such schools.

Moreover, in contrast to the United States only a relatively small proportion of British youth attended college. With a population three times as large, the United States had twenty times as many students in colleges and universities in 1939 as had Great Britain (1 million as compared with 50 thousand). It is true that socially and intellectually the American college, at least in the first two years, is more akin to a British secondary school than to a British university and that vocational and professional training in Great Britain is handled in other types of institutions. Also, in proportion to the total population, the number of university students in Great Britain had doubled since 1900. Nonetheless, only a relatively small minority of one in a thousand enjoyed higher education in prewar Britain.

Britain extended free compulsory education up to the age of fifteen with the 1944 Education Act. But the gap between the children of the middle-class and working-class families tended to be perpetuated by the division between the academically oriented grammar schools, which required success in the eleven-plus examinations for entry, and the modern schools to which went the children who did not achieve this standard. Labor bitterly attacked this division and urged its replacement by a system of comprehensive schools combining grammar, technical, and modern school sections. These schools thus include a broad range of courses that provide much the same educational base for all and thus aid social mobility. The Conservatives, traditionally protective of the middle class and also concerned for academic excellence, resisted the change during their period of office from 1951 to 1964; Labor attempted to institute it on a national scale in 1965. Since the responsibilities for public education are divided between local authorities and the national government, the issue has been a complex and often divisive one. Local authorities could choose between six major types of organization for comprehensive education, and the choice and implementation of the plans have been affected by local conditions, the party orientation of the particular local council, and the pressures of teachers' groups.[5] The end result in many areas, however, has been a widespread transformation of British secondary education.

A unified, free system now extends through age sixteen (raised from fifteen in 1972), and free tuition and mandatory grants (average £276 [$622] a year) are provided for all students taking first degree (undergraduate) courses, high-level nondegree courses, and teacher-training courses. Introduction of testing for aptitudes in place of the eleven-plus examinations, much more coeducation, use of team teaching and of educational television are comparable to the more creative innovations in American secondary education. At the same time, a much higher proportion of those educated at public schools, followed by those who graduate from grammar schools, continue to go to the university than is the case for those attending comprehensive schools.

[5] Paul E. Peterson, "British Interest Group Theory Reexamined: The Politics of Comprehensive Education in Three British Cities," *Comparative Politics* (April 1971), pp. 381–402.

The number of universities has expanded to forty-five, all of which are privately run but receive block five-year government grants (paid in annual installments) through an independent body, the University Grants Committee, on the basis of their requirements and plans. Prospective candidates for most universities apply through the University Central Council on Admissions instead of directly to individual universities, so their applications can be passed on to their second choice if they fail to be accepted at their first. (Just under sixty thousand were admitted in 1971 out of over one hundred and fifteen thousand candidates.) Moreover, local technical colleges draw an increasing number of those graduating from secondary schools.

To widen opportunities for higher education, the Labor government instituted an educational experiment known as the Open University, which is a unique blend of a correspondence course, television and radio broadcasts, individual tutoring, and additional facilities at 250 study centers throughout the country. Founded by Royal Charter in June 1969, the Open University's first academic year started in January 1971 with 25,000 students enrolled in its basic course, thereby doubling Britain's university enrollment of first-year students. The Open University has its own center in Milton Keynes in North Buckinghamshire, with a staff of some 350 academics and administrators, while other staff members are located in different parts of the country. It concentrates its efforts on preparation for the B.A. degree in arts or in science, which can be taken through its facilities in a minimum of three years, although most students will take longer. Each student has a tutor, must take an annual written examination, and must attend a two-week summer school. Costs, both to the students and the government, are low compared to conventional study. Thus the Open University vastly enlarges the possibilities for pursuing higher education in Britain, capitalizing on the relative smallness of the country's area in comparison to population and bringing high-quality training within much easier reach of those already employed or otherwise prevented from pursuing regular, full-time study.

British higher education in conventional institutions was evaluated in 1971 by the University Central Council on Admissions as well as by the Department of Education and Science and the local associations that provide the students' grants. Arguments in support of raising grants are that the drop-out rate among British students is one of the lowest in the world, that graduates are produced rapidly, gauged by international standards, that the cost per graduate student is among the least expensive anywhere, and that a high proportion of students are studying science and technology. Over 40 percent of those admitted to the university still come, however, from the top 15 percent of professional homes in Britain. As a consequence, the children of unskilled and skilled workers have somewhat less chance of a university education in Britain than in most other Western European countries. Nonetheless the educational changes that have been instituted in the postwar period have brought the system considerably closer to the goal of equality.

SOCIAL SECURITY

Another striking change in British life has resulted from the extension of "welfare state" responsibilities, which rest on the premise that the weaker members of society must be protected from the worst effects of economic pressures in integrated, industrialized, modern society. Between 1906 and 1911, almost thirty years before comparable American action (although not as early as in Germany), the British government had instituted a "New Deal" that provided national health and unemployment insurance for some groups, noncontributory old age pensions, a national system of unemployment exchanges, and free meals for school children. Piecemeal extensions after World War I failed, however, to overcome the basic causes of urban poverty: interruption or loss of earning power due to unemployment or illness and more children than families could support on meager incomes. Following the famous Beveridge Plan to establish a "national minimum standard" for all, comprehensive social security schemes based on insurance were established by 1948 that covered everyone "from the cradle to the grave" (or, more jocularly, "from the womb to the tomb").

This social security program, supported by individual and employer contributions and government funds,[6] provides benefits on retirement for women at sixty and men at sixty-five, special benefits for those suffering industrial injuries, for widows, orphans, and for maternity periods and, most controversial and costly, virtually free medical and hospital care.

The British National Health Service pays doctors salaries according to certain prescribed scales (whose levels have been determined by a variety of bodies, including a special review board, but remain unsatisfactory to many doctors). Patients enroll with the doctors of their choice, who treat them without charge when they are in need. The permissible limit for a doctor's list is 3,500 patients (or 5,500 for a doctor with an assistant), but doctors claim, not surprisingly, that even national average lists of over 2,000 are much too large. Hospitals are nationalized and free (private paid care is also available) but are under decentralized control; medical and dental clinics and health centers are directed by local government authorities and executive councils whose members are nominated by the latter and by local practitioners and the department responsible for health. Prescription costs are a source of contention between Labor and the Conservatives, the former keeping them low and the latter imposing higher charges. There are also charges for eyeglasses, dentures, and wigs.

Despite the comprehensiveness of these programs, there were still half a million families with a million and a half children in serious need in 1966 and possibly as many as 5 million in 1970 below the poverty line. Trade union leaders called that year for an increase in family allowances and asserted that inadequate wages were a major cause of this poverty. Other proposals have been for minimum wage legislation, a negative income tax, or minimum income guarantees. On the other side of the ledger is the fact that the cost of social services is increasing more rapidly than is national wealth. Although a considerable percentage of the support for social security, including national health care, comes from employers and employees (contributions from both were increased under the 1967 National Insurance Act), the costs of family allowances, and particularly of the health services, heavily tax the Exchequer.

Five-and-a-third percent of the national income is spent on health services, which is far more than originally anticipated. These growing costs are partly because people live longer, there are more chronic illnesses, and there are new sources of illness that are more expensive to treat. Some criticisms of the present health service maintain that costs could be reduced through structural changes that would overcome the present overlapping between the roles of general practitioners, the hospitals, and local community services. Others stress the need for more doctors.[7] Inadequacies in current standards of subsidized care are said to be the reason why a million to a million and a half people still prefer to contribute to private health schemes. Yet infant mortality rates have been brought down from 46 per 1,000 live births in 1945 to 18 in 1969 (20.7 in the United States), and the maternity death rate from 1,260 per 100,000 births to 19 (27.4 in the United States). A 1968 survey indicated that 95 percent of the people were satisfied with the present health system, including doctors.

Inadequate housing also creates pressing social problems. Although both the Conservatives and Labor have set targets for new houses to meet the demands of an increasing population and to replace the buildings destroyed during the war or made unsafe by time, slums and overcrowding still persist. Two million existing houses have been declared unfit for human habitation, and there are even some persons who remain homeless. The two political parties have approached this problem from different perspectives. Labor has emphasized security for tenants through rent control, which it reimposed in 1964, and favors public building by local authorities for rental purposes. The Conservatives lifted most rent controls in 1957, but extensive property speculation culminating in a well-publicized scandal, and undue concentration on office and luxury building were unpalatable effects that they are unlikely to permit again. They have rescinded Labor's ban

---

[6] The small weekly family allowances for all children after the first and also war pensions are a direct charge on the Exchequer.

[7] One-half of all junior doctors in Great Britain now come from overseas, many of them from India or the West Indies—so do the nurses—and an average of four hundred doctors and ninety dentists leave Britain every year.

on selling council-built houses, however, and are once again encouraging private builders to construct houses for home ownership.

Housing relates not only to urban renewal and building but also, especially in a densely populated country like Great Britain, to the siting of industry, the building of new towns, and land use and values. Some impressive advances have been made regarding constructive land use. Fifteen new towns had been built by 1960, and a number of new national and forest parks and nature reserves have been established. Problems of compensation and of taxing increased values have bedeviled arrangements, however, with the Conservatives placing premiums on sales to private interests and Labor favoring purchases for public purposes and development charges for other interests.

Conservatives and Labor also differ in their general approaches to social welfare. Labor's egalitarianism leads it to favor across-the-board benefits and to have special concern for the needs of the working class. Labor sees social welfare as part of the vast redistribution of wealth in Britain, which it favors. The Conservatives, in contrast, believe that pensions should provide only a basic income floor below which people cannot fall; that any higher or "second floor" should be dependent on people's own income levels or on employers' insurance plans. Their special concern is for the obviously disadvantaged, the disabled, widows, and the aged, for whom higher pensions were included in their first budget. Their perspective on other social services is strongly influenced by the fact that the costs of social welfare place a very heavy charge on the national budget as well as on employers on whom they depend to improve Britain's economic position.

THE CLASS STRUCTURE IN A PERIOD OF CHANGE

What is apparent from the foregoing survey is that the British people have moved a long way since World War II in overcoming the most pressing sources of poverty and inequality. In many ways, British society has become more egalitarian than American society. Regional differences in standards of living, although they exist especially in Wales and Scotland, are less marked than in areas of the United States. Education is now provided on a more egalitarian basis, particularly since all schools must meet national standards. Social welfare extends much further than in the United States, especially in the field of health. What impact, we must ask, have these developments had on the British class structure, particularly in a time when the distinctions between classes have been under heavy attack as unwarranted and, of course, undemocratic?

Perhaps the most surprising result of recent surveys of the working and middle classes is that despite the major changes that have occurred in their conditions of life, there has been so little change in their self-perception and attitudes. A series of articles in *The Times* (September 28 through October 2, 1969) by Roy Lewis and Angus Maude, who had previously made a significant study of the British middle class,[8] coupled with the data from public surveys made in 1948 and 1969, show that approximately the same percentages regarded themselves as working class or as belonging to different sections of the middle class in 1969 as in 1948. Specifically, whereas 46 percent of the sample in 1948 rated themselves as working class, 50 percent did so in 1969; and whereas the 1948 divisions into upper middle, middle, and lower middle class found 6 percent, 28 percent, and 13 percent placing themselves respectively in those categories, 1969 found 4 percent, 31 percent, and 14 percent doing the same. The change from 2 to 1 percent of those rating themselves upper class seems generally insignificant. What is striking is that if the 5 percent who did not answer in 1948 are divided statistically between the working class and the middle class, there has been no significant change in the social self-assessment of the population during the twenty-one years in which Great Britain has been going through what most people regard as a peaceful social revolution.

This paradox suggests that far from becoming a "classless" society in which the affluent working class has merged with the middle class, British society retains most of the same class distinctions it used to have. In other words, the once popular theory of *embourgeoisement*, that

[8] Roy Lewis and Angus Maude, *The English Middle Classes*.

Survey of Self-Assessment on Class Basis

	SOCIAL CLASS SELF-DEFINITION	TOTAL	WORKING	LOWER MIDDLE	MIDDLE	UPPER MIDDLE	UPPER
	BASE: ALL INFORMANTS HAVING JOB	623	309	85	192	35	2
How satisfied are you with the sort of job you have?		%	%	%	%	%	No.
	Very satisfied	52	45	56	59	66	(1)
	Fairly satisfied	38	42	38	32	26	(1)
	Fairly dissatisfied	6	8	1	7	8	(—)
	Very dissatisfied	4	5	5	2	—	(—)
	BASE: ALL INFORMANTS	948	471	129	292	50	6
How satisfied are you with the sort of house you live in?		%	%	%	%	%	No.
	Very satisfied	47	44	44	54	52	(1)
	Fairly satisfied	34	35	37	30	32	(4)
	Fairly dissatisfied	10	10	12	8	10	(—)
	Very dissatisfied	9	11	7	8	6	(1)
	BASE: ALL INFORMANTS	948	471	129	292	50	6
How satisfied are you with the people you make friends with?		%	%	%	%	%	No.
	Very satisfied	75	73	75	81	78	(3)
	Fairly satisfied	22	24	24	18	18	(3)
	Fairly dissatisfied	2	2	1	1	4	(—)
	Very dissatisfied	1	1	—	*	—	(—)
	BASE: ALL INFORMANTS	948	471	129	292	50	6
How satisfied are you with the kind of neighborhood you live in?		%	%	%	%	%	No.
	Very satisfied	53	49	49	61	56	(1)
	Fairly satisfied	30	32	33	26	24	(3)
	Fairly dissatisfied	9	9	9	7	14	(1)
	Very dissatisfied	8	10	9	6	6	(1)

Source: Marplan Ltd., Market Research, *The Times*, September 29, 1969.

is, of all being merged into an amorphous middle class, does not hold. Even though youth from the working class may complete their advanced education, the appeal of habitual association may well counterbalance the new stimuli of academic training and a white-collar job. Moreover, since working-class families rarely have the same desire as middle-class families to have their children pursue higher education, the numbers of those who turn their back on possibilities for scholarships and university training and prefer manual labor remains considerable. Upward mobility is not difficult, although it is probably less common than generally supposed. In the Marplan survey, half of those describing themselves as lower middle class said their parents had been working class, and one-fifth of the self-styled middle class said the same. But despite the far-reaching changes in education, housing, and the rise in material standards of living, no more people appear to *feel* middle class than immediately after the war.

The strongest influence on what people feel about their "class" appears to be associations. The social pressures of the work place and trade unionism commonly counterbalance the middle-class influences operating through education and rising standards of living. A 1968 study [9] of the political attitudes and voting practices of a sample of highly paid manual workers in Luton, a prosperous and growing industrial center somewhat removed from the older industrial areas of the country, indicated

[9] John E. Goldthorpe et al., *The Affluent Worker: Political Attitudes and Behaviour*.

both a strong retention of working-class perceptions and steadfast loyalty to the Labor party.

Nonetheless, despite the high proportion of urban workers in Britain's industrial society and the 50 percent of its population whose self-perception places them in the working-class category, not all of them support the Labor party, or it would always be in office. There has always been a percentage of manual laborers who support the Conservatives, originally because of a deference pattern of behavior but more recently because they accept the Conservatives as a national, not a class party. Women are more inclined to vote Conservative than are men from the working and lower middle classes. Young people usually follow the same voting patterns as their families. Where Labor party allegiance is consistent, however, it often embodies an intensity not found among Conservatives.

The prevailing fact in British political life is the remarkable consistency with which a high proportion of constituencies return the same party to Parliament election after election and the no less consistently small margins that separate the percentage totals of votes cast for the two major parties in general elections (see Chapter 3, Section 3). Although it is obvious that governments change, the swing of the electoral pendulum may be due more to nonvoting than to changing party allegiances or the impact of new voters. British political alignments appear extraordinarily fixed.

At the same time there is no sense of a "class war." David E. Butler and Donald E. Stokes, in their comprehensive study of political change in Britain, point out that "the image of politics as the representation of opposing class interests," which was increasingly accepted in the interwar and immediate postwar periods, is not common among newer Labor voters.[10] The need for Labor to be concerned with national interests when in office or seeking it has drawn its leaders away from primary identification with class goals. Moreover, the spread of affluence into large segments of the population and the leveling effect of the mass media, especially television, has inevitably ameliorated much of the bitterness of the past and made it common to consider that the interests of all classes are compatible. Such political and social controversy as exists is largely within and between the middle classes. Its perhaps oversensitive conscience has been torn both by its sense of guilt over privilege and enforced conformity of standards and no less by its concern at the new permissiveness decreed by middle-class representatives in Parliament in such matters as homosexual practices, divorce, abortion, pornography, gambling, censorship, and the abolition of capital punishment. In addition, the character of middle-class life has changed materially, for this is the first generation to be almost wholly without regular paid domestic service, especially on a live-in basis. The horizons of middle-class mothers have necessarily shrunk; they have less time to devote to "good works," and, in particular, much less time for local government activities.

Probably the most noticeable impact of social change on occupation has been the replacement of the independent entrepreneur by the salaried professional manager. Family businesses and new small businesses appear to be on the way out due to heavy taxation and to the ability of big business to absorb promising concerns. Owner-occupied farms are similarly being sold or sometimes fragmented to pay the bills on the rest. It is easier to leave securities to one's children than to pass on a business or a professional partnership, although even the former process suffers from heavy estate and capital gains taxes. Nonetheless, the middle class seems satisfied with its prospects for increased salaries and higher standards of living. Since there has been no noticeable shortening of professional training courses, the waiting period for ultimate prosperity is often considerable, but those in the professions, such as doctors, teachers, airline pilots, have turned, and generally effectively, to trade union techniques in bargaining with the government, which provides their livelihood.

INTEREST GROUPS

It once was thought that interest or pressure groups scarcely existed in Great Britain, and certainly not to the degree they do in the

---

[10] David E. Butler and Donald E. Stokes, *Political Change in Britain: Factors Shaping Electoral Choice*, pp. 115–17.

United States. The crucial difference between the operation of pressure groups in the two countries, however, is neither their numbers nor their effectiveness, but the way they operate. The purpose of an interest group is obviously to secure the most favorable conditions possible for its members by urging their case where support may be decisive. In the United States, it is natural, therefore, for interest groups to exert pressure directly on individual congressmen, who are far less bound by party discipline than their opposite numbers in Great Britain. American pressure groups also work on and with the administration at every level from the president through the bureaus, but because Congress has control over appropriations, they naturally focus a great deal of their attention there.

In Great Britain, the distribution of effective power within the political system leads to different tactics. Pressure is focused on the executive and administrative departments, because they are the locus of decision-making. Disciplined parties mean that it is not the individual members of Parliament but the Cabinet and Shadow Cabinet who are the effective molders of policy. In as far as interest groups focus their attention on political parties, it is rather on their central offices than on the parliamentary parties. But above all, as we shall see in Chapter 6, interest groups work with and through the administration, which to a very large degree is entrusted with instituting and supervising the broad social and economic policies that have been transforming much of the character of British life. The British are neither so concerned about delegated legislation nor so suspicious of organized group pressures as are Americans. On the contrary, they welcome an open relationship between the representatives of special interests and the government bureaucracy, making provisions in numerous instances for official representation of such interests in advisory committees or for engaging them in formal negotiations, as with the National Farmers' Union in the government's annual price review.

A striking illustration of the operations of group politics is provided by Harry Eckstein's detailed study, *Pressure Group Politics: The Case of the British Medical Association*. Whereas less than half those eligible belong to a British trade union, 80 percent of all doctors are members of the British Medical Association (BMA). Although it has undertaken more of a broad public relations campaign since his study (which was first published in 1960), the BMA has followed the general pattern of exerting its chief influence on whatever administrative department is responsible for health. Unlike some other British pressure groups, like the National Farmers' Union itself, the National Union of Manufacturers, and the Federation of British Industries, all of which were long (and rather too obviously for their own initial effectiveness with Labor) aligned to the Conservative party, the BMA has studiously avoided identification with either political party. As far as Parliament is concerned, the BMA can depend on presenting its point of view through those MP's who are doctors, a normal way in the British system (see Chapter 4, Section 1) for voicing the views of special interests. Occasionally, as when the government had decided to ban the manufacture of heroin, the BMA managed to create enough back-bench pressure to have the measure withdrawn. Its chief activities, however, are concentrated in the administration, where, by mutual consent, the BMA is consulted on almost every departmental decision. Only on the very tricky issue of doctors' salary ranges has the government been forced to take the matter out of the range of departmental decisions, but its review bodies' recommendations have not avoided more or less open public negotiations.

The fact that the government and the BMA have disagreed sharply on the issue of doctors' pay does not obviate the accepted value for the political process of pressure group activities. The BMA, like other interest groups, provides a wealth of information both on practical details and on desires. Moreover, pressure groups, as Eckstein points out,[11] perform two significant general and in a sense divergent functions: both an integrative function, by organizing objectives into "manageable ranges of alternatives for action"; and "a 'disjunctive' function,"

---

[11] Harry Eckstein, *Pressure Group Politics: The Case of the British Medical Association*, p. 162. For an important reexamination of Eckstein's thesis on group politics, see Peterson, "British Interest Group Theory Reexamined," *Comparative Politics* (April 1971), pp. 381–402.

by keeping specific needs and demands visible within what might otherwise be too low a common denominator of aggregated interests that have been sieved through the funnels of two disciplined political parties.

The growing participation of government in economic life, with the concomitant closeness of its relations with organized producers, has also helped to stimulate industrial and trade associations. Concentration has gone further in industry than in commerce, the two being organized separately. By the 1950s, 90 percent of the larger firms and 76 percent of the smaller ones belonged to one or another of the thirteen hundred industrial trade associations. World War I had seen the formation of the Federation of British Industries (FBI, British style) and the National Union of Manufacturers (NUM). Another "peak" organization is the Confederation of British Industry, whose two hundred and seventy affiliates negotiate with 70 percent of the worker population. The FBI now represents six-sevenths of all industrial concerns employing more than ten workers. Some thirty or forty associations, each covering a total industry, seek with varying success to coordinate their interests when they consult with the relevant government department. Where there are a number of big producers, as in chemicals and motor cars, coordination is much easier to secure than when many small firms are involved. In comparison with industry, commerce is more dispersed, although the Association of British Chambers of Commerce (ABCC), founded in 1860, now has over a hundred constituent chambers, with some sixty thousand members. Many retail merchants who are not within the ABCC belong to the National Chamber of Trade.

Concentration of trade unions is no less striking. The Trades Union Congress (TUC), founded in 1868, has never had a rival, nor has it ever experienced a split such as that between the CIO and the AFL. By 1894, the TUC already represented 65 percent of all unionists and had a million members; by 1970, it represented almost all the more than nine million registered trade unionists. It should be noted, however, that the TUC can rarely act effectively as a unitary body. Its members are divided among over six hundred unions, but two-thirds of these are in the eighteen largest unions, just over half in eight unions, each of which has over a quarter of a million members, while the Transport and General Workers Union has just over a million and a half members.

Because of the special relation of the unions to the Labor party, both as constituent members and through their own sponsored MP's, much of their influence is exerted through the party. Even so, the TUC, like the big trade and producers' associations, maintains constant and close relations with the executive, both ministers and civil servants. Like other organized producers, trade unions share in the rough structure of functional representation that exists side by side with parliamentary representation, mainly through advisory committees. In addition, however, an almost constant series of less formal contacts goes on through visits and phone calls. What Samuel Beer calls "an intricate system of bidding and bargaining" proceeds constantly, linking parties and administration to the major interest groups of the country.

3 THE ECONOMY AND THE STATE

THE ECONOMIC PROBLEM

The most serious problems facing the British today are economic. Wage inflation, a plethora of strikes, low output per man compared, for example, to the United States, the lowest increase in industrial production of any highly industrialized country, and a sharp decline in Britain's share of manufactured exports are sources of worry to whatever government is in office. Great Britain remains heavily dependent on its overseas trade, which amounted in the mid-1960s to about 14 percent of the GNP. There was substantial growth in its share of world trade thereafter, and a large invisible surplus continued from the carrying trade, services abroad, and investments overseas. Moreover, the Labor government transformed what had been an annual deficit rate of £800 million in the balance of payments into an annual £600 million surplus, largely as a result of the 1967 devaluation of the pound. But the devaluation in itself, although essential and probably overdue, created internal strains from which Britain is still suffering.

The impact of devaluation on the British people was sharply to check the growth in their personal standard of living, since the immediate effect was to raise prices. Temporarily, demands for comparable increases in wages were restrained by the wage freeze Labor had imposed, but as soon as these restrictions were removed, there were widespread demands for rises in pay. At the same time, however, firms were suffering from decreases in profits and therefore reluctant either to expand production or to increase pay. Unemployment grew, wage demands and strikes, both official and unofficial, took place, and inflation was stimulated by the interaction of rising prices and increased wages.

The special dilemma that the Conservatives confront is that their program of checking trade union wage demands, which they see as the major cause of Britain's galloping inflation, accelerated unemployment, particularly in certain areas of the economy, to a degree that threatened explosive social and political pressures. The Conservatives oppose wage and price freezes (such as the Labor government imposed in 1966 but subsequently modified radically under trade union pressure) and have tried, by psychological and other pressures, to keep wage increases, especially in nationalized industries, to progressively lower percentage advances. (Wages rose 7.5 percent in 1969 and 13 percent during the year ending August 1971.) But following prolonged strikes by the dock workers, electrical workers, and postal workers (the latter patiently endured by the public), the government found itself confronted with recommendations by independent boards that exceeded the levels it had set. Moreover, moral pressure on private industry to hold down wage increases failed in the main because employers in capital-intensive industries preferred to yield substantial wage increases rather than risk strikes. At the same time that this process was continuing, unemployment was mounting to nearly one million by the end of 1971, by far the highest total since 1940. Although calculations vary as to relative levels of unemployment in Great Britain and the United States, it appears that they have been approximately the same, varying between 4.5 and 5 percent of the working population.

The Conservatives' projected "hard line" with business inefficiency has, in practice, also been bent. Although bankruptcy at Rolls-Royce met an initial cold response, the government quickly nationalized part of the huge concern and subsequently offered substantial underpinning of costs to enable Rolls-Royce to fulfill its American contract for TriStar engines. The United States Congress in August 1971 approved a government guarantee of 250 million dollars in bank loans for the Lockheed Aircraft Corporation, the American company concerned, thereby rescuing the TriStar contract for Rolls-Royce engines.

The Conservative government puts particular emphasis on individual initiative to stimulate the economy. It has reduced the corporation tax and the standard rate of income tax (after deductions and exemptions), the latter in such a way as to benefit those with higher incomes. It eliminated the selective employment tax (SET) in 1971. This tax was introduced in 1966 to raise revenue, particularly from the construction and service occupations, which previously paid lower taxes than did industry, and by this means also to induce workers to shift to manufacturing. The SET was particularly disliked by business because of the extensive paper work involved. Its removal led to claims of some lowering of prices, but on the whole it appeared that the benefits were not passed on to the consumers. Subsequently, the purchase tax was reduced. The Conservative government plans ultimately to shift much of its indirect taxation to the value-added tax (VAT), which is used widely in Common Market countries. The base of VAT is the total income originating from the enterprise and its profits but without reference to the cost of the raw materials it uses. The theory is that VAT is imposed on the contribution a firm makes to the national income, and it is left to the individual firm to determine on what basis the tax shall be estimated. If the product is exported, the tax is returnable, making it a way of subsidizing exports. Like SET, VAT requires complicated administration both by business and by the government.

The Conservatives have also sought to save money by cutting subsidies and increasing charges for health and welfare services, except for the very poor and for cultural facilities. Prescriptions and dental work cost more, free milk is now provided in schools for a smaller age group, museums must charge admission fees, and food costs will rise if and when agricultural subsidies are reduced. These policies have naturally led to sharp criticisms from Labor.

Many British economists believed that more drastic cutting of indirect taxation, coupled with government pump-priming to achieve a 5 percent growth rate within two years, was necessary to break, or at least much reduce, the interacting cycle of price and wage increases that was stimulating the disturbingly high rate of inflation. The Trades Union Congress, although worried about unemployment, was not prepared to hold back wage demands unless the economy improved. Moreover, although the Conservative government was ready in 1971 to enter the Common Market, there were obvious disadvantages to doing so in a period of recession. But confronted with a still more serious problem of how to turn recession into growth without unduly adding to the inflationary spiral, the Conservatives chose not to institute a wage and price freeze such as President Nixon imposed in August 1971 but to depend on appeals for wage restraint and tax cuts to stimulate consumer spending, investment, and employment.

It is commonly believed by the British that they are the most heavily taxed people in the world. According to a report of the Organization for Economic Cooperation and Development (OECD), however, Britain came only sixth in 1968 among OECD's fourteen member states, which are the most developed outside the Communist world. But if social security contributions are omitted, Britain moves into third place, along with the Scandinavian countries, and is one of four in which taxes take more than one-third of the national income. Britain is also one of five OECD countries in which private individuals contribute more than 30 percent of the national income in taxes. Moreover, indirect taxes in 1968 were taking 19 percent of the British national income. Most interesting is the fact that British companies are among the most lightly taxed in the world, if social security taxes are taken into account, paying less than half what companies are taxed in France, Holland, and Japan, and not much more than half what American companies pay. In addition, British companies get considerable sums returned in investment grants. It seems difficult to maintain, therefore, that the tax burden on British companies is what has been holding them back.

The crucial problem appears to be the productivity of labor. A hundred years ago Britain's real product per head was the highest in the world. Up to 1939, it was second only to the United States. By late 1970, however, Britain had slipped to thirteenth place among Western countries, with the United States at the top, followed by the three Scandinavian countries, Canada, Australia, New Zealand, Germany, France, the Netherlands, Belgium, and Switzerland. The reason is that, although Britain's postwar rate of growth was higher than in earlier periods, it has not used modern technology and improved productivity to the degree that Germany, France, Italy, and Japan have. Labor tried to stimulate industrial training and encourage more mobility of workers, but the problems still remain.

There appear to be many reasons for this development. Trade unions have resisted modernization, soft Commonwealth markets offered easy access after the war but expanded less quickly as these countries industrialized, management has been less aggressive than in other countries and less skillful in handling fast growth where it has occurred, technical education has still lagged behind classical studies, the "brain drain" has robbed Britain of some of its best talent, and taxation, with its heavy burden on higher income groups, may have been discouraging. Moreover, concern for the balance of payments has led to stop-and-go government policies and deflationary programs that have acted as a curb on growth from time to time.

There are different ways of evaluating a satisfactory economic situation in any given country.

Growth in GNP is commonly regarded as the norm. But to ensure that all people live well above the poverty level may be still more desirable. Britain's welfare state seeks to ensure a basic standard of living that will not be dragged down by sudden emergencies such as illness, unemployment, or industrial injuries. Social and economic stability may be preferable to rapid growth. Yet it is also clear both from the industrial ferment in Britain in the last few years and from the general sense of malaise in regard to British institutions and performance, internally as well as externally, that the British are not satisfied with conditions as they are. Yet the obvious signs of dissatisfaction such as strikes, slowdowns, and the bitterness caused by the provisions of the Conservatives' Industrial Relations Act (not unlike the American Taft-Hartley Act), which seeks to regulate collective bargaining and union behavior, may in themselves impede whatever efforts are made to tackle the causes of inflation and of Britain's relatively slow industrial growth. Thus the need to break out of the cycle of largely self-defeating efforts to improve conditions, to find more constructive ways to restore mutual confidence, and to stimulate cooperative efforts to work toward broadly accepted goals.

4 ORGANS OF POLITICAL OPINION

POLITICS AND PUBLIC OPINION

In studying the politics of any country, it is important not only to understand the nature of the social, economic, and other divisions of the population but to discover what organs of public and political opinion are available for the expression of these interests.

Experts still disagree about the exact meaning of *public opinion,* but no one today challenges the fact of its importance. In democracies it has long been assumed that governments ought, in general, to do what their people want them to do. And even in dictatorships the rulers, far from ignoring public opinion, have become proficient in the art of molding and manipulating it. In every modern country, regardless of form of government, the press, radio, and television are political weapons of tremendous power, and few things are so indicative of the nature of a government as the way in which that power is exercised.

THE PRESS

In a democracy like Great Britain's, the press has three major political functions: to provide channels of communication for news and views; to inquire into and criticize governmental and privately run affairs, so as to keep the public informed and alert (a role that gives it the title of "the fourth estate"); and to represent different positions on public issues of the day, so that citizens have the necessary facts and arguments out of which to form opinions. To perform these functions, it is necessary to have a variety of publications reflecting different points of view but, hopefully, with a common commitment to presenting the news as cogently and impartially as possible.

The assumption behind the special role the press is expected to play is that information and arguments represent power. Later on in Chapter 4 we shall discuss the way in which debates in Parliament are presented to the public, for only if these debates receive publicity will they fulfill the role of public education for which political representation is designed, and only if the public is prepared for new issues and new problems will it be able to influence its representatives before it is too late. There is a very special responsibility on the media, not only the press but also radio and television, to keep the public continuously alerted to all aspects of public issues.

In some countries the government interferes with the press to such a degree that news is immediately suspect. On this score, the British have had little ground for complaint. In the years before World War II, when the Conservatives were in power, there were occasional complaints that certain officials had tried to influence the press, the radio, and even newsreels in an attempt to prevent the publication of inconvenient news items or distasteful opinions. There was no open censorship, but tactful suggestions might be made to editors, reporters, or proprietors; and since proprietors often were Conservative in sympathy, and since editors and reporters might conceivably be reluctant to antagonize officials upon whom they were dependent for information, the suggestions may have had some influence.

During the war, the government acquired extraordinary authority under the Emergency Powers (Defence) Act of 1939 (not unlike its predecessor, the Defence of the Realm Act, 1914) to prohibit publications that were likely to cause serious public disorder or to promote disaffection. But these powers were exercised, on the whole, with laudable restraint and ended soon after the war.

The structure of the British press

Both the 1947–49 and 1961–62 Royal Commissions on the Press were concerned not with the influence of government on the press but with the growing concentration of private ownership. The few vast publishing empires, it was suggested, might use their power to control the ideas and information reaching a large section of the British public or to influence the government itself. Unlike newspapers in the United States, the typical large morning newspaper in Great Britain has a national as well as a local circulation, which combined is far larger than that of any single American newspaper. This is partly because of the differences in size of the two countries but also because the British read more newspapers proportionately than any other people in the world.

Although the consensus now is that there are no longer "press barons" who act as Lord Beaverbrook and Lord Northcliffe did in the 1920s and 1930s when they used their papers to further their own strong political views, it is important to take a careful look at the contemporary structure and trends in the British newspaper world. A recent study [12] points out that the total circulation of national newspapers has slipped from a peak in the 1950s, but that the number of daily newspapers has increased from nine to ten, although the number of Sunday newspapers went down from eleven in 1937 to eight since 1961. Total circulation figures for both types of papers, however, remained constant in the 1960s. So have those of provincial morning papers (eighteen in number) and evening ones (down from seventy-four to seventy-one) and Sunday newspapers (constant at five), but these now sell below the 1947 level. London evening papers shrank from three in 1947 to two by 1961, and their combined circulation continues to fall.

These gross statistics should be broken down into a distinction between "quality" papers—*The Daily Telegraph*, *The Guardian*, *The Times*, and *The Financial Times*—and "popular" papers—*Daily Mirror*, *Daily Mail*, *Sun* (formerly the *Daily Herald*), *Daily Sketch* (which closed in 1971), and *Morning Star* (until 1966, the *Daily Worker*). It becomes apparent, then, that the shrinkage in circulation is in the popular papers. In contrast, the quality papers have increased dramatically in sales, although, of course, their circulation totals are much smaller. Five out of every six adults in Britain reads one or more newspapers. Readership is generally counted as three times circulation.

Within this complex, the increasing concentration of ownership is evident—the total sank from fourteen in 1947 to ten in 1967. Moreover, the Daily Mirror group (International Publishing Company, IPC) increased its holdings of national dailies and Sunday papers from nineteen in 1947 to forty-three papers in 1966; Beaverbrook Newspapers, from sixteen to twenty; News of the World Organization reduced its number from nineteen to sixteen; Daily Mail and General Trust rose from thirteen to twenty-five. This trend is also understandable. It costs a prohibitive amount to start a newspaper, and many do not run at a profit. Indeed, only three national newspapers were making a profit in 1967. Revenue comes from sales and from advertisements. Quality newspapers get more than twice as much from the latter (especially classified advertisements) as from sales; popular papers make a third

---
[12] Colin Seymour-Ure, *The Press, Politics and the Public: An Essay on the Role of the National Press in the British Political System*.

to a half times as much from sales as from advertisements. It is not surprising that the trend is toward the ownership of papers of both types in a single hand or concern, so as to balance revenues and costs against each other. More important is the question: Does this concentration of control provide the public with only slanted or partial presentation of the news?

The most important issue here is one of political partisanship. Those newspapers showing a Conservative bias in the 1966 election included six dailies—*The Times, The Daily Telegraph, The Financial Times, Daily Express, Daily Mail,* and *Daily Sketch* (merged into the *Daily Mail* in 1971)—and four Sunday papers—*The Sunday Times, Sunday Telegraph, Sunday Express,* and *News of the World*—with a joint estimated readership of 31.5 million. Those that had an anti-Conservative bias were four dailies—*The Guardian, Daily Mirror, Sun,* and *Daily Worker*—and four Sunday papers—*Sunday Mirror, The Observer, Sunday Citizen,* and *People*—with an estimated readership of approximately 33 million. In the event, of course, the Conservatives were handsomely defeated in that election.

It may be assumed that most readers take the newspaper that corresponds to their own political preferences. In general this seemed the case in 1966 except in regard to the *Daily Sketch,* which Seymour-Ure suggests would be "the natural paper of that electorally important person, the Working Class Tory,"[13] whereas, in practice, the voting intentions of its readers registered in 1964 were heavily Labor and Liberal. What seems obvious in any case is that partisanships tended to cancel each other out or, to put it in other terms, that there was a very wide range of publications pointing out the merits of each side and equally publicizing flaws in the other.

All those persons with large press holdings necessarily look on them as ways of making a profit. Lord Beaverbrook asserted in 1947, however, that his prime objective was a political rather than commercial one. Lord Thomson maintains he is mainly interested in making money, and he appears to be much more typical than Beaverbrook of most proprietors today. The Monopolies Commission reported in 1966 that "the Thomson Organisation has in practice given its editors a great deal of freedom."[14] The Economist Intelligence Unit, after a searching investigation the same year, concluded that *The Sunday Times* and the *Daily Mirror,* both of which had proprietors who were more politically committed than Lord Thomson, were models of "efficient management," whose proprietors set the general lines of policy for editors but left details to them. It is also noticeable that well-known columnists and cartoonists seem to enjoy complete liberty in expressing their own positions on issues, regardless of whether or not they conflict with those of management.

In 1970, the press provided adequate, if rather dull, coverage of the election. Although the campaign generated much less excitement than in 1966, the wavering course of the public opinion polls introduced a helpful element of suspense (see Chapter 3, Section 3). Those papers supporting the Conservatives, in particular the *Daily Mail, Daily Sketch, The Daily Telegraph, Daily Express, The Sunday Times, Sunday Express,* and *Sunday Telegraph,* indicated their positions rather earlier than did the Labor supporters, the *Daily Mirror, Sun, The Guardian, Sunday Mirror, News of the World,* and the *People,* but neither group was as uncritical either of the policies or of the leaders on its preferred side as in previous elections. *The Times* ultimately came out for the Conservatives; *The Observer* endorsed neither. Problems with the economy received greatest attention, with the Tory-supporting press exploiting it fully, while those endorsing Labor were more defensive. From June 10 to 13, less than a week before polling day, there was a newspaper blackout as a strike stopped the publication of all national newspapers. Thus the dependence on television coverage became even greater than usual, but unlike 1966, when the press tended to regard television as a competitor, this time it saw television as complementary to itself.

The press had gone through some significant changes in ownership and approach between the

---

[13] Seymour-Ure, *The Press, Politics and the Public,* pp. 54–55.

[14] Seymour-Ure, *The Press, Politics and the Public,* pp. 115–16.

1966 and 1970 elections. *The Times* had passed into Lord Thomson's organization in 1967, been redesigned, and had increased its circulation 60 percent, although it was still not making a profit. The *Sun* (formerly the strongly Labor oriented *Daily Herald*) had been sold to the Murdoch interests and transformed into a popular tabloid without any apparent ideological commitment, although it was strongly pro-Labor and anti-Powell in 1970. The most striking changes affected the IPC publications. Their colorful and opinionated chairman, Cecil King, had been ousted in 1968, and two years later the *Daily Mirror*, with the rest of the huge IPC publications, was taken over by the Reed paper and publishing group. Thus concentration continued but with some shifts in personnel, which emphasized the business aspects of newspaper publishing.

Evaluating the effect of press coverage in the 1970 election, Colin Seymour-Ure suggests that it helped to "integrate" the campaign by providing a national focus.[15] In its search for an issue, the press tended to focus on the difficulties of the British economy, thereby attacking Labor at its weakest point. Overall, the press was pro-Conservative, even though not optimistic. But since the press almost universally expected a Tory defeat, it can hardly be said that it contributed much to the Conservative victory.

To safeguard the freedom of the press and to combat abuses of it, the first Royal Commission on the Press had recommended the establishment of a General Council of the Press. In July 1953, a council of twenty-five members, nominated by editors, journalists, and managers, began to respond to specific complaints against newspapers and tried to determine standards in controversial issues. Its annual reports show a keen concern for public as well as professional interests. In response to urging from the press for more publicity on local government affairs, the council succeeded in securing an act sponsored by a member of Parliament, which went into effect in June 1961. In 1963, it strongly criticized the imprisonment of two journalists who had refused to reveal their source of information in the Vassall spy case. In 1971, it censured Lord Arran for the intemperate language he used in the *Evening News* toward the Arabs in commenting on the Middle East. Publicity is its best means of exerting influence.

The influential press

Of particular importance, as we have suggested, is the influence wielded by several national dailies of quality. Among these papers are the Conservative *The Daily Telegraph*; *The Financial Times*, which is widely read by business people; and the liberal *Guardian*, formerly *The Manchester Guardian*, which has an international reputation for the excellence of its news and editorial comment that is ably supported by its weekly airmail edition for overseas.

The Times of London, however, is the most powerful of the island's newspapers. Its readers include the most eminent people in Great Britain: government officials, politicians, judges, diplomats, scholars, clergymen, officers of the army and navy, and the well-educated classes in general. Its reporting is noted for reliability and completeness, if not for liveliness; and, especially in foreign affairs, its reputation for reflecting or even anticipating government policy gives it an almost official tone. One of its most famous features is "Letters to *The Times*," which may provoke a national debate as effectively as might a speech in the House of Commons.

In addition to these daily papers and to *The Sunday Times* and *The Observer*, certain weekly periodicals wield great influence. This is particularly true of *The Economist* (nonpartisan and widely read abroad as at home), the *Spectator* (moderately Conservative in tendency), and the *New Statesman and Nation* and the *Tribune* (which speak for Labor groups). Such publications indulge in discussions of ideas and issues, and it is in these periodicals, rather than in the daily press, that new and unorthodox ideas can best win a hearing. Their readers are, as in the case of *The Times* and *The Guardian*, men and women who themselves influence opinion and legislation; such publications, therefore, often

---

[15] Seymour-Ure, "Fleet Street," in *The British Election of 1970*, by David E. Butler and Michael Pinto-Duschinsky, pp. 231–58.

Elite Response to Importance of Press
(In Percentages)

READ REGULARLY	
The Times	67
The Daily Telegraph	43
Financial Times	26
The Guardian	20
Daily Express	19
Daily Mail	12
Daily Mirror	4
The Sun	2
None of these	3
Not answered	1
Wrote in others	1

Usefulness of Daily Newspapers
(In Percentages)

	INTERNATIONAL NEWS	PARLIAMENT	COMMENT	THE ARTS	COMMERCE/ INDUSTRY
The Times	61	62	51	46	39
Daily Telegraph	32	30	30	20	17
The Sun	*	*	1	*	—
Daily Mirror	*	1	2	*	*
Daily Mail	1	2	5	*	1
The Guardian	14	17	21	16	5
Financial Times	10	6	11	12	44
Daily Express	2	3	7	*	1
None of these	1	1	2	5	2
Not answered	9	9	10	19	16

* Less than 0.5%.

Where Influence Lies
(In Percentages)

"VERY INFLUENTIAL"	
BBC	52
Parliament	42
The Press	40
Trade Unions	33
Civil Service	23
The Monarchy	15
The Church	2

	VERY INFLUENTIAL	FAIRLY INFLUENTIAL	NOT VERY INFLUENTIAL	NOT AT ALL INFLUENTIAL	UNDECIDED	NO ANSWER
The Church	2	18	55	23	1	2
The Monarchy	15	39	30	13	1	2
Parliament	42	40	12	1	1	3
BBC	52	39	6	1	1	1
The Press	40	47	9	1	1	1
Trade Unions	33	42	18	3	2	2
Civil Service	23	30	24	15	4	3

Source: The Times, October 1, 1971.

exert a greater influence on politics than do newspapers with many times their circulation.

RADIO AND TELEVISION

Important as the press is in providing news and discussion, the growth of radio and particularly of television provides powerful means of capturing public attention. But while private enterprise predominates in the publishing field in Great Britain, radio broadcasting remained a government monopoly until the Conservatives introduced commercial broadcasting in 1971. Television followed the same path until late in 1955.

The British Broadcasting Corporation (BBC), a public corporation established in 1927 and financed by individual license fees, still provides most radio programs, but it has long since been outstripped in the television field by commercial television. The latter is organized in a very different way in Great Britain from the way it is organized in the United States. In 1954, the Independent Television Authority (ITA) was established for an initial ten-year period—subsequently extended to 1976—to own and operate transmitting stations; the cost is met by private companies that provide programs, own the production studios and equipment, and reap the profits of advertising. The role of ITA is to see that programs report the news accurately (in practice they have done so more attractively than has the BBC), preserve reasonable impartiality in controversial issues, and do not violate good taste.

As a channel of communication, television has particular importance as "the most pervasive, most trusted, and . . . most potent" of the mass media.[16] Its use raises special questions: Should journalists and producers be free to direct public attention to the issues *they* feel are politically important? If so, how can a balanced presentation of different points of view be secured? If not, what controls or safeguards should be instituted and by what bodies? For if it is vital for the press to provide a wide variety of approaches to the news it purveys, is it not still more important that television does the same? And whereas television in the United States operates through a variety of networks and local stations (which, however, may all be insensitive to minority and radical positions), British television has a far more limited range of programs and thus, one might feel, a more concentrated political impact.

The most careful study of these issues, particularly as they are related to a general election, has been made in the book *Television in Politics: Its Uses and Influence*, whose authors, Jay G. Blumler and Denis McQuail, deliberately set out to analyze their findings for the 1964 election in the perspective of an earlier study of the effect of television in the election of 1959. The latter study had concluded that its impact was relatively negligible. Major changes had occurred, however, between the two elections in the attitudes of political parties, and especially of the Labor party, regarding the use that could be made of television to secure voter support. As Richard Rose has commented, the 1964 general election saw "in duration, expense, and expertise the biggest propaganda campaign in twentieth-century British politics." [17] It was in that election that television came into its own as the most important of all means of political communication.

The principle of providing free radio and television time to political parties at election time is well established. In 1964, and again in 1966 and 1970, the ratio of free time allotted to the Labor, Conservative, and Liberal parties was five to five to three, respectively. Originally provided in fifteen minute doses, party broadcasts were limited in 1970 to ten minutes in response to viewer reactions, and thirteen broadcasts were held: five Labor, five Tory, and three Liberal. (Minor parties feel, legitimately, that they are discriminated against.) The parties were similarly given these allocations of time on radio. In 1970, the same general rules imposed by the parties were adhered to as in earlier post–1959 elections: no live audiences (because of rowdiness at speeches in 1959), no Sunday programs, and full consultation as to speakers and choice of constituencies for surveys. Television is also expected to main-

---

[16] Jay G. Blumler and Denis McQuail, *Television in Politics: Its Uses and Influence*, p. 3.

[17] Richard Rose, *Influencing Voters: A Study of Campaign Rationality*, p. 14. (See especially Chapter 1.)

tain impartiality in matters of party controversy and to refrain from editorializings.

In 1964, Harold Wilson had sought a face-to-face debate, but the Conservatives had refused; in 1966, Heath sought such a debate but Wilson refused unless the Liberal leader was included as an equal participant, which the Tories rejected because it appeared to put them on the same plane as the Liberals; in 1970, Wilson again ruled out a confrontation with Heath. Although the three leaders appeared once on the same broadcast, there was no debate. But despite the absence of this dramatic approach, the leaders of the two major parties inevitably attract the greatest attention in every election, and necessarily at the expense of coverage for other parties.

Although the 1970 election caught television unawares, with ITA, in particular, already booked on prime time with presenting the World Cup series, the general conclusions reached by Blumler and McQuail in their study of the impact of television in the 1964 election appear to hold. Their findings indicated that the high levels of political viewing in 1964 were chiefly motivated by a desire for information, particularly the desire to learn more about political developments that might affect the viewers' own lives. The Blumler-McQuail study also showed that only a few sought help in deciding how to vote, and that most had already made up their mind on this issue before campaigning began and did not change. If viewing during the 1970 campaign did have an effect, it was probably to the advantage of the Conservatives, who had worked out an integrated and attractive campaign series, whereas Labor, conscious of how much of its film prepared for the 1964 election campaign had not been used, decided on virtually impromptu appearances, whose effects were often messy.

It is not only in politics, however, that the impact of radio and television is felt. Widespread public demand for an external agency somewhat comparable to the Press Council to review specific complaints against BBC radio or television programs led to the appointment early in 1972 of three distinguished independent individuals to form the Programmes Complaints Commission. Its jurisdiction is limited to complaints where "a viewer, listener or organization continues to feel aggrieved after receiving a BBC explanation." The effect of its judgments, which must be publicized by the BBC in print or on the air, depends on public and agency reactions. Many people hope, therefore, that in the long run the commission will acquire more authority, both to review standards of taste for programs (e.g., violence on the screen) and to recommend restitution where damage has been proved.

ADEQUACY OF THE ORGANS OF INFORMATION AND OPINION

The press, radio, and television in Great Britain offer suggestive contrasts both with each other and with the corresponding institutions in the United States.

If one takes as a standard the number of channels for different views, for free discussion, and for reliable information, then the great American advantage is that there are many more such channels. While British national newspapers have tended to drive local papers out of business, most American cities still have daily newspapers of their own, making it easier for different regional views to be expressed. Yet even in the United States the growth of the chain newspaper has restricted this independence, while the decline in the number of cities with competing dailies is even more serious. Thus, while there are more daily newspapers in the United States than in Britain, there are many towns where the reader cannot choose among papers that reflect differing political outlooks.

In contrast, the great advantage of the British press is that the major—and even some minor (e.g., the Communist)—political movements in the country have their views expressed in organs of national circulation and that anyone on the island can choose among several, widely different national newspapers. The great disadvantage, shared in the United States, is that the extraordinary expense of starting and maintaining a newspaper means that the presentation of rival views in daily and Sunday papers depends on proprietors and a limited number of editors.

In theory, radio and television should in both countries provide notable instruments for political information and expression. Yet in the United States, although there is more independence and diversity of ownership and a freer expression of opinion on controversial issues, the influence of advertising agencies and sponsors restricts the amount of time devoted to public affairs, while political comment tends to be one-sided and conservative. Yet the British have also not found the way to take full advantage of these media.

To make the organs of information and opinion contribute helpfully to an enlightened public opinion is, in fact, no simple task. To place control in the hands of private owners is often to give a disproportionate voice to conservative political groups. To place control in such public organizations as political parties, cooperatives, trade unions, or business associations may give a wider representation to divergent views, but such organizations are likely to be even more one-sided than private owners in their presentation of the news. To place supervision and control in the government, quite apart from any danger inherent in official control of the sources of information, may be to achieve impartiality in reporting at the expense of the most fertile kind of political discussion and argument. To place control in the sort of trusteeship under which *The Times*, *The Guardian*, and *The Observer* used to be published provides greater personal freedom for editors and writers, but there was a possibility (happily avoided) of deterioration through lack of competition.

Increasingly it is suggested that the best solution lies in the simultaneous existence of a variety of forms. Thus the competition of privately owned publications and commercial television can act as a spur to those owned by public bodies or by trusteeships, while the existence of the latter can provide a check on the accuracy and completeness of the former.

5 BRITAIN IN A PERIOD OF CHANGE

In almost every aspect of life the British are seeking new relationships and forms of action. This process of change reflects an oppressive sense of dissatisfaction with a society that is falling short of its ideals of justice, humanism, fraternity, and beauty. The aim of those who promote change is to reawaken a sense of destiny in Britain and determination to achieve it. World War II had called forth almost superhuman efforts to withstand bombing and the threat of invasion. The immediate postwar period saw the creation of the welfare state. But there are now questions in some quarters as to whether welfare aid is not more of a burden than a benefit, and whether efforts to achieve social harmony have not sapped initiative. Conversely, there is fear that a concentration on individual self-interest may undermine personal standards of conduct and divide society more sharply into the well-to-do and the less favored. To some degree these opposed positions reflect the philosophies of the Conservatives and Labor, but the issues go more deeply than in party politics. These issues, as in the United States, revolve around the basic question: What are the overriding values that society and government should use as guides in making their decisions?

The chapter that follows gives a more complete picture of the historic foundations of British institutions, ways of acting, and formative political ideas. Thereafter, the dynamic element in British government, the political parties, will be analyzed, as well as the ways in which they operate within the legislature and the functioning and power of the executive. In the sections on the national and local administration, law and the courts, and finally foreign affairs an account will be given of government in action seeking to promote the public good internally and externally in response to the political actions of the elected representatives of the people. After this broad survey we will return again to the issues raised in this chapter and in the Introduction to the study of Great Britain, in an effort to provide some clearer guidelines to the likely course of British politics and life.

2
The British political heritage

1 HISTORICAL BACKGROUND

Few things are more perplexing to the outside observer than the British habit of preserving the form of inherited institutions while modifying their spirit and their function. Other great countries, such as France, Germany, and Russia, have altered their political systems openly, deliberately, and violently. But in Great Britain, with only one important interruption, political innovation has taken place within a framework of continuity. In some instances, notably the evolution of the Cabinet system, change came about gradually through the blend of chance and expediency. The essential background to this development, however, the assertion of Parliament's power vis-à-vis the monarchy, required a civil war and the Revolution of 1688. Thereafter, inside this structural balance there grew up not only a Cabinet government exercising the still existing powers of the Royal Prerogative but also the modern two-party system, which steadily tilted the balance of power between the two chambers toward that one, the House of Commons, which is popularly elected. At the same time, the process of evolution that curbed its power left virtually untouched the membership of the so-called upper house. Thus the anachronism of a second chamber based largely on the hereditary principle continues to exist in Great Britain's highly structured and socially minded modern democracy. In a period like the present when calculated change is being proposed in almost every aspect of British life, it is particularly important to be aware of how change has taken place in the past and of the framework within which it is being sought for the future.

ORIGINS OF THE PARLIAMENTARY SYSTEM

The origins of the British Parliament often are traced to ancient Anglo-Saxon times when a council known as the Witenagemot (or Witan), whose composition and powers are still a matter of debate, used to be called together to advise the English kings. With the Norman Conquest in 1066 the Witan disappeared; but William the Conqueror, while concentrating greater power in his own hands than the Saxon kings had known, summoned a *Magnum Concilium* (Great Council) at regular intervals. At such times, according to *The Anglo-Saxon Chronicle*, the greatest men in England were with him: "archbishops, bishops, and abbots, earls, thegns, and knights." In the intervals between these meetings, a smaller *Curia Regis* (King's Court, or Little Council) remained to advise the king. The practical work of administration was carried on by the royal household.

In contrast to the kings of France, whose

authority continued to be challenged and limited by powerful nobles who commanded the allegiance of their tenants, William instituted a system of land tenure according to which the first loyalty of every landholder was to the king and not to a local lord. From an early period, therefore, England attained a degree of political centralization far greater than that on the Continent. Yet institutions of local government which had originated before the Conquest continued in existence and provided a limited experience in self-government.

It was William's great-grandson, Henry II (1154–89), whose reign (which followed a period of anarchy) marked the next great advance in English government. Traveling or itinerant justices now fostered the growth of a law common to all the land. Moreover, the grand jury was used for accusation and was followed by the jury of verdict, which replaced the earlier methods of trial by ordeal, battle, or compurgation.

EARLY LIMITATIONS ON ROYAL AUTHORITY

If it was due to the strength of Henry II that an orderly and firm governmental authority was established, it was due to the weakness of his son John (1199–1216) that this authority was limited by Magna Charta (the Great Charter), the most famous if not the most effective of those restraints on political authority that are the essence of constitutionalism. Subsequent tradition has transformed into a charter of English liberty what was primarily a guarantee of the specific rights of English barons. Yet certain articles—such as the famous provision (Article 39) that no free man might be arrested, imprisoned, dispossessed, outlawed or exiled, or harassed in any other way save by the lawful judgment of his peers or the law of the land—lent themselves to a far broader interpretation and application than their sponsors imagined. The document was not democratic in any modern sense, but it reiterated the principle that the king was not unlimited in power and that abuses of power might be resisted. The legend that was subsequently attached to Magna Charta made it a powerful instrument for liberty.

THE GROWING SPECIALIZATION OF FUNCTION

With the passage of time, there was a tendency for judicial or administrative business, which required the continuous attention of some governmental body, to fall to the lot of the *Curia Regis*. As the amount of business increased and the members of the *Curia Regis* became more highly skilled and specialized, such subdivisions as the Courts of Exchequer, Common Pleas, King's Bench, and Chancery, which were the forerunners of the modern court system, split off from it. More purely administrative work was left to the royal household, to such institutions as the Exchequer and the Secretary of State, which developed out of it, and to the main core of the *Curia Regis*.

Somewhat later the *Curia Regis* itself developed into what was known as the Permanent Council; it was within this body that, in the fifteenth century, the Privy Council, a smaller and more efficient body, grew up and eventually assumed the powers of its larger and more unwieldy parent. In turn, a still smaller entity never defined in law, the Cabinet, grew up within the Privy Council in the eighteenth century. Today the Cabinet still formally legitimizes its acts through the Privy Council, although in practice it is the Cabinet that makes executive decisions.

THE RISE OF PARLIAMENT

The *Magnum Concilium* (Great Council) of the kings of England was a meeting of the great nobles and ecclesiastics of the kingdom, somewhat resembling a modern House of Lords. From time to time, however, and generally for the purpose of winning popular consent to the levying of new taxes, kings would summon representatives of the lesser gentry, who were too numerous to attend in person. In 1213, King John, in need of money, commanded the presence of four "discreet knights" from each county, and in 1254 (at a time when the Great Council was coming to be known as Parliament) Henry III, also in need of money, summoned two knights from each county. In 1265, Simon de Montfort, who had led the barons in a temporarily successful revolt against the king, summoned a Parliament to which were invited not only two knights from each shire but two burgesses from each of those boroughs (towns) known to be friendly to his party. And although, with the reestablishment of King Henry's power, this practice was temporarily abandoned, the famous Model Parliament, held in 1295 by Henry's son, Edward I, included burgesses as well as knights, clergy, and barons.

At this time the privilege of attending Parliament was commonly regarded as a mixed blessing. Far from demanding the privilege as a right, people looked upon it with understandable apprehension, both because the journey to Parliament was expensive, uncomfortable, time-consuming, and, on occasion, dangerous, and because those summoned to Parliament were summoned to increase their own taxes. Thus attendance at Parliament was compulsory rather than the result of any demand for the right of representation. The lesser gentry and the burgesses were ordered to attend when they became prosperous enough to attract the attention of a government ever eager for new sources of revenue.

For a time Parliament met in three groups or estates: one for the nobility, one for the clergy, and one for the commoners. The lesser clergy, however, eventually withdrew; the higher clergy (who were themselves great nobles) met with the nobility; and the lesser barons or knights (who often were the younger sons of the nobility) sat with the commons, thereby helping to prevent the growth of a sharp political cleavage between the nobles and the middle classes, such as occurred in France. By the end of the fourteenth century, the system of two chambers, one for the lords and one for the commons, had taken shape. Moreover, early in the fifteenth century it came to be understood that proposals for grants of money should originate in the House of Commons and then win the approval of the Lords, an arrangement which, by centering the power of the purse in the House of Commons, enormously enhanced its authority.

During this period Parliament also acquired certain legislative powers. Earlier, individual commoners had had the right to present petitions to the king asking for redress of grievances, and eventually the Commons presented such petitions as a body. Successive kings discovered that it was easier to persuade Parliament to grant new taxes if the petitions were granted first, and laws began to be enacted by the king at the request of the Commons and with the assent of the Lords. However, not until early in the fifteenth century did the laws always coincide with the terms of the petitions. Henry V (1413–22) agreed that nothing should be enacted that changed the substance of the petitions; and during the reign of his successor, Henry VI (1422–61), the formula came into use which is still followed: statutes are made "by the King's most excellent majesty by and with the consent of the Lords Spiritual and Temporal, and Commons, in this present Parliament assembled, and by the authority of the same."

TUDOR ABSOLUTISM

Much of the fifteenth century was occupied by those struggles between rival factions of the nobility known as the Wars of the Roses. The ultimate victor in this conflict, Henry VII (1485–1509), was the first of the Tudor dynasty, a line of energetic monarchs who gave the country the firm and orderly government it wanted and so enhanced the authority of the king that the period is often referred to as that of "Tudor absolutism." Partly because of the effectiveness of the great nobles in killing one another off, Henry succeeded in concentrating great power in his own hands. Parliament during his reign was the servant of the king rather than an independent force, and the real center of governmental activity was the Privy Council, a group of advisers chosen by the king and drawn from the middle classes rather than from the great nobility. Under the Tudors, too, greater authority in local government was given to country gentlemen (rather than nobles), who served without pay as justices of the peace and acquired both the political experience and the sense of public service that have been outstanding virtues of the British upper classes.

Although the power of Parliament declined under Henry VII, the struggle between Henry VIII (1509–47) and the Roman Catholic

Church increased Parliament's prestige, not because Parliament failed to act as a docile instrument of the king but because the king made so much use of it as an ally in the struggle. Thus the "Reformation Parliament," which sat from 1529 to 1536, acquired a political experience and importance and enjoyed a degree of freedom of speech that set powerful precedents for later times. It was this Parliament that passed the legislation completing the breach with the Church of Rome and making the king the supreme head of the Church of England.

During the dozen years that intervened between the governments of Henry VIII and his daughter Elizabeth I (1558–1603), Edward VI (1547–53), a Protestant, and Mary (1553–58), an ardent Catholic, reigned over a country torn by religious controversy and plagued by bad government. Elizabeth, however, reestablished the Anglican Church of her father, with a ritual resembling that of the Catholic Church but with a creed that was more definitely Protestant than that of the church of Henry VIII. During her reign England came to identify itself with Protestantism in opposition to the Catholicism of its bitter enemy, Spain.

Elizabeth's government, like that of her father and grandfather, was firm and orderly, and it commanded the overwhelming support of public opinion. By this time members of the House of Commons, far from considering their duties a burden, had come to take pride in their growing political influence and to act with greater independence. Toward the end of Elizabeth's reign, the members (particularly those who were Puritans, that is, belonged to the extreme Protestant wing of the Church of England) increasingly indulged in criticism; it was evident that, although the devotion of the Parliament to the queen was very great, a tactless successor might find this body a source of serious opposition to his will.

THE LIMITATION OF ROYAL AUTHORITY

Elizabeth's successor, James I (1603–25), the first of the Stuart kings, was sufficiently tactless to precipitate precisely such opposition. Already king of Scotland, James I became ruler of the entire British island, although it was not until 1707, under Queen Anne, that the Act of Union formally united the two countries.[1]

In his native Scotland, James had already found the Calvinistic (Presbyterian) form of Protestantism far too democratic for his tastes; and the rapid growth of Puritanism in England provoked his opposition for similar reasons. His firm belief in the divine right of kings conflicted sharply with Parliament's conception of its own authority. From 1611 to 1621, with the exception of a few weeks in 1614, James actually ruled without any Parliament at all; and, when finally he was obliged to summon a new Parliament, its vigorous criticism led him quickly to dissolve it.

Far from ending with James's death, royal quarrels with Parliament grew more bitter. Charles I (1625–49) dissolved his first two Parliaments in rapid succession and resorted to highly unpopular forced loans in the absence of financial grants from that body. When Parliament was again summoned, in 1628, a Petition of Right (which ranks with Magna Charta as a charter of British freedom) was drawn up, asserting the ancient liberties of the kingdom and denouncing royal abuses of power. Charles was forced to accept this document.

Eventually, however, quarrels between the king and Parliament's Puritan members resulted in the Civil War which lasted from 1642 to 1649. In this struggle, which reflected a social as well as a political and religious cleavage, the majority of the peers, the Anglicans, and the Catholics supported the king; the majority of the townspeople and the Puritans supported Parliament; and the landlords and country gentry divided themselves between the two parties. In 1649 the defeated king was executed, and in 1653 Oliver Cromwell, who as leader of the victorious parliamentary armies already held effective power, assumed the title of Lord Protector under the only two written constitutions England has ever had, the Instrument of Government (1653) and the Humble Petition and Advice (1656). Yet Cromwell, like his royal

[1] Wales had been added to the Crown by Edward I in 1284, and the fact that the Tudor dynasty was Welsh in origin later helped to reconcile Wales to this union. But Scottish and Welsh nationalism are still political forces (see Chapter 3, Section 3).

predecessor, repeatedly disagreed with and dissolved Parliament, and his death in 1658 led quickly to the restoration of the monarchy with Charles II (1660–85) as king. The Instrument of Government vanished, the Anglican Church was reestablished, and all Nonconformists suffered serious restrictions upon their religious and civil rights.

In appearance Charles accepted the supremacy of Parliament; and although he disagreed with it from time to time and secretly longed for absolute power, controversy was never pushed to the point of endangering the throne. Charles's brother and successor, James II (1685–88), was less discreet. Even before his accession large numbers of "Petitioners" asked that he be barred from the throne because of his adherence to Catholicism, while "Abhorrers" of the petition upheld his right to the succession. Once he had become king, however, James's efforts to restore the Catholic Church enraged both Nonconformists and Anglicans (including many of the Abhorrers), and his quarrels with Parliament precipitated the Glorious Revolution of 1688, which drove him from the throne and transferred the crown to his daughter Mary and her husband William, Prince of Orange.

At the time of their accession, the quarrel between king and Parliament was finally settled. Parliament, in the famous Bill of Rights of 1689, listed the practices that had caused trouble during the previous half-century and forbade their revival in clear and unequivocal language. The legislative authority of Parliament was assured, the king was forbidden to levy any tax or impost without parliamentary consent, the regular convening of Parliament was guaranteed, and certain individual liberties were specifically confirmed. A few years later, in 1701, the authority of Parliament over the Crown was established beyond all doubt when the Act of Settlement deliberately changed the order of succession to the throne, passing over the Catholic descendants of James II and providing that James's daughter Anne (1702–14) should be succeeded by the German, but Protestant, House of Hanover. British sovereigns, unlike those in certain Continental states where the official religion was that of the ruler, henceforth had to belong to the established church of their people.

THE RISE OF THE CABINET

The reigns of the first two Hanoverian kings, George I (1714–27) and George II (1727–60), marked a further, if less dramatic, decline in the royal power as authority passed into the hands of the Cabinet, a small group of leading ministers who advised the king.

It had long been apparent that the Privy Council was too large and unwieldy a body to conduct public business, and smaller groups had already been used for the purpose of guiding legislation through Parliament. However, so long as the Stuart monarchs remained on the throne, they maintained their right to choose their own ministers and to change them at will. Both William and Anne continued to choose their Cabinet ministers and to meet with them regularly, but it was obvious that their relations with Parliament were better when the Cabinet had the confidence of Parliament. Thus began the practice of choosing ministers who shared the same general views—and the views of the majority of the members of Parliament. There was no change in the law, but the dependence of the ministry upon the king lessened; at the same time, its dependence upon Parliament increased.

The first two Georges took a greater interest in Hanoverian affairs than in British. Far from trying to expand the Royal Prerogative, they let slip some of the powers that William and Anne had been careful to maintain. And since they had trouble understanding both the English language and English politics, they gave up the practice of presiding over meetings of Cabinet ministers.

From 1721 to 1742, both Cabinet and Parliament accepted the leadership of Sir Robert Walpole, who was First Lord of the Treasury and Chancellor of the Exchequer and who was in fact the first British "prime minister," a title that did not come into general use until much later.[2] When, in 1742, Walpole lost the support of the House of Commons, he resigned his office, an act which implied that the survival of a ministry depended not upon the favor of the king but upon the acquiescence of Parliament. George III (1760–1820) tried, with some success, to recover the lost ground; but growing

[2] This title was first used officially in the Treaty of Berlin, 1878, but not in a statute until 1917.

opposition in Parliament (as indicated by its famous resolution of 1780 that "the influence of the Crown has increased, is increasing, and ought to be diminished") and the insanity of the king during the last decades of his reign put an end to the effort.

THE RISE OF PARTIES AND OF DEMOCRACY

The growth of political parties in England was as gradual and unintentional as other changes in the government, but no change was of greater importance. Before the seventeenth century rival groups of nobles might contend for power, as in the Wars of the Roses, and there were adherents of different religious principles, but there were no political parties in the modern sense. The division in the Civil War, however, between the aristocratic, Anglican Cavaliers who fought for King Charles and the middle-class, Puritan Roundheads who supported Parliament reflected a difference in religious and political principles as well as economic interests that prepared the way for future party alignments. With the Restoration of Charles II there appeared a clearer difference between the greater part of the land-owning gentry (the Tory squires), who upheld the authority of the king and the Anglican Church, and the alliance of powerful Whig nobles with the Nonconformists and the mercantile classes —a difference paralleling that between Abhorrers and Petitioners. When James II opened his attack on the Anglican Church, however, the Tories were torn between loyalty to the king and loyalty to the Church; some joined the Whigs in inviting William and Mary to take power, while others remained unreconciled to the change. Thus the Glorious Revolution, for a time, had the curious effect of making Whigs rather than Tories the chief support of the monarch on the throne, although not of monarchy as an institution.

The eighteenth and early nineteenth centuries witnessed almost incredibly long periods of office, first for the Whigs under the first two Georges and later, with one brief interruption, from 1783 to 1830, for the Tories. But it is still more important to be aware that these two nascent political parties represented virtually the same interests. As feudal restrictions on economic development were swept away during the seventeenth century, the way was opened for vast economic expansion. Capitalist agriculture, leading to the enclosure movement and the loss of independence of the English peasant, produced efficient and rich returns from the land. Parallel to this development went economic expansion overseas by commercial interests. Each process worked to the other's advantage and drew both land-owning and commercial classes into each other's spheres. The result was a massive interpenetration that has stamped their character ever since.

Reform of the suffrage

Although the principle of the supremacy of the House of Commons had been clearly established, that house was far from being a widely representative body. Property qualifications fixed in the fifteenth century still determined the vote in many areas, while the failure to redistribute seats in accordance with movements of population resulted in the growth of "rotten boroughs" (which had lost most of their population but retained their original representation) and "pocket boroughs" (which were under the control of landed proprietors who frequently sold the right to represent the borough in Parliament). Thus, in the Scottish constituency of Bute, only one of the fourteen thousand inhabitants had the right to vote, and he was therefore in a position to elect himself unanimously to Parliament. The constituency of Old Sarum had no residents at all, and Dunwich had sunk beneath the sea, but each was still represented in Parliament. In contrast, large towns grew up that had no representation.[3]

As the industrial revolution created a large class of well-to-do businessmen who were eager for a greater share of political power, agitation for reform increased. Yet those in Parliament clung tenaciously to power; and it was not until a Whig government came into office, late in 1830, that popular agitation met with a favor-

---

[3] When Americans, in the years before their Revolution, complained of "taxation without representation," it was pointed out that English communities too were taxed without having any parliamentary representation. The argument that relevant interests were represented, that is, of merchants, hardly appealed to either side.

able parliamentary response. Even then it was necessary to dissolve the House of Commons and hold a new election before a safe majority could be found for the bill reforming Parliament. The House of Lords continued its resistance until the king threatened to appoint enough new peers to assure a majority for the bill.

The Great Reform Act of 1832 did not increase the electorate drastically (about half a million men, mostly drawn from the upper half of the middle class, gained the right to vote), but it did away with the worst inequalities of the old system. Most of the rotten and pocket boroughs were eliminated; the representation of the smaller communities was consolidated or lowered; and new or increased representation was given to the large ones. But the climax of the evolution begun in 1832 was only reached in 1885 with the series of acts on representation (1867 and 1884), corrupt and illegal practices (1883), and redistribution and registration (1885) that established the constitutional principle that representation must approximate population. In 1918, the decisive advance in this regard was made when the vote was finally given to all male citizens age twenty-one and over and, with important qualifications, to women of thirty and over. In 1928, the suffrage was extended to women on the same basis as men. Thus by stages reaching over nearly a century, the British achieved universal adult suffrage.

Change in party character

The original increase in the number of voters had relatively little effect upon the political system. During the first part of the nineteenth century, both parties continued to draw their support from the well-to-do classes, and many members of these relatively informal groupings were intimately related through family and social ties. Even in policy, lines tended to be blurred. The Whigs were somewhat more willing to accept mild electoral reform; but many Tories were in agreement with them, and in 1867 they "dished the Whigs" by themselves, introducing the legislation that extended the right to vote. In fact, the Tories (who were, at this time, identified with the land-owning rather than the manufacturing element) were somewhat more willing than the Whigs to support measures of social reform, such as restrictions on the exploitation of women and children in industry.

In the meantime, however, the working class, bitter at the hardships of rapidly growing industrialization, had made its own efforts to create change and failed. In 1819, it mounted a nascent national political campaign and was repressed. Working-class agitation was part of the ferment that led to the reform movement in 1831–32, but labor failed to share its returns. For a decade Chartism sought ineffectually to extend the franchise. Thereafter, while Continental socialist parties were taking form under the spur of Marxist philosophy, a period of profound disillusionment and even apathy marked the British working class. The British Social Democratic Federation, formed in 1884, had no appreciable effect in extending its Marxist concepts to labor. When the latter began seriously to organize at the turn of the century, it was to protect itself against the restrictions on trade union organization implicit in the Taff-Vale decision. Once the Labor party began to penetrate into Parliament, however, it grew rapidly to become the predominant representative of the working class.

The Labor party formed a distinctively new feature in the British party system. Both the Conservatives (as the Tories were now called) and the Liberal party (as the Whigs were now named) had grown up *inside* Parliament and subsequently reached out for extraparliamentary organization following the 1867 electoral act. The Labor party sprang from the grassroots *outside* Parliament and used its extraparliamentary organization to reach into the legislature to influence the uses of political power.

Even before the Labor party emerged as a political force, however, the established parties had developed all the characteristic features of the modern political party: representative constituency associations coordinated by a national organization; an annual conference; a central party headquarters, destined to become ever more powerful; party election manifestos; and the special role of the party leader in an electoral campaign. The latter factor was accelerated in the last quarter of the nineteenth century by the fact that both the Conservatives and Liberals possessed exceptionally able and popular leaders, Disraeli and Gladstone, who in themselves came to symbolize to the voters the spirit of their respective parties. As voters were increasingly influenced in choosing their representatives by party leaders, policies, and organization, the party began to assume its modern role of link through Parliament between people and government.

By the time the Labor party became a factor in the political scene, sharp divisions over Irish home rule led the Conservative and Liberal parties to draw apart once more into more distinctive groupings. The old nobility had moved, almost without exception, into the Conservative party. The latter became more stamped by land-owning interests. While it had the support of some urban middle and working classes, as it has today, its backbone was in the rural areas where the local squire and the Anglican parson exercised dominant political influence. The Liberals attracted the new and wealthy industrialists who opposed high tariffs (it had been the growing industrial middle class that successfully secured the abolition of the Corn Laws in 1846) and also government interference in industry. It was also supported in the main by the Nonconformist middle classes and the majority of those workers who had the right to vote.

But with Labor's rapid growth in working-class popularity, the Liberals increasingly lost members at both ends. Although there were periods in the nineteen twenties when none of the three parties could win a parliamentary majority, there was a strong tendency for the wealthy industrialists and merchants to switch their allegiance to the Conservatives, while the working class found the Labor party the most effective advocate of its interests. Thus the Liberals became a minor party, and the British political scene resumed its traditional form of a two-party system: Conservatives and Labor.

Reform of the House of Lords

The successive extensions of the franchise also brought a fundamental change in the position of the House of Lords. So long as the House of Commons remained unreformed, the influence of the Lords was very great, and it was not unusual for the majority of the members of the Cabinet, including the prime minister himself, to be members of that chamber. But as the right to vote was widened, so grew the prestige of the House of Commons as the spokesman of the electorate. Leadership in the Cabinet came to rest with men who could win elections and who were likely to be members of the House of Commons. Moreover, the opposition of the Lords to many of the political, social, and economic reforms accepted by the House of Commons led to increasing irritation; and when, in 1909, a struggle broke out over the Lords' financial powers, the way was prepared for the Parliament Act of 1911, which enabled the House of Commons, by complying with fairly rigorous conditions, to pass even nonfinancial legislation over the Lords' veto.

Thus, through a series of changes that worked themselves out over long periods of time, the British government developed from a highly centralized monarchy into one of the most advanced democracies in the world.

2 THE BRITISH CONSTITUTION

FORM AND FACT

The gradualness of this evolution, and the British habit of retaining traditional forms despite radical changes in the position of power, produced two characteristics of the British constitution that confuse most Americans: there is no single place in which the constitution as a whole is clearly and definitely written down, and those provisions of the constitution that do exist in writing often differ markedly from actual constitutional practice. A foreigner who reads the American Constitution will be misled about certain political practices (he will find, for example, no mention of judicial review, the cabinet, or political parties, and the electoral college will seem much more important than in fact it is), but in general he will find a not too inaccurate outline of the structure of the American government. In Great Britain, however, the form and the fact of the constitution sometimes seem to have very little to do with each other. Walter Bagehot could write, for example, in the introduction to the 1872 edition of his classic book *The English Constitution*, that Queen Victoria possessed the constitutional power to:

> . . . disband the army . . . ; she could dismiss all the officers, from the General Commander-in-Chief downwards; she could dismiss all the sailors too; she could sell off all our ships of war and all our naval stores; she could make a peace by the sacrifice of Cornwall, and begin a war for the conquest of Brittany. She could make every citizen in the United Kingdom, male or female, a peer; she could make every parish in the United Kingdom a "university"; she could dismiss most of the civil servants; she could pardon all offenders.

Yet any ruler who used his constitutional powers in this way, contrary to the advice of his prime minister and Cabinet, would find the entire country denouncing him for the unconstitutionality of his action. Nor is the confusion lessened by the fact that no law provides either for a prime minister or for a Cabinet. The fact is that, unlike the American, the British constitution is not a definable body of fundamental and mostly written rules. Rather, it is, as a parliamentarian has said, "a blend of formal law, precedent, and tradition." It is similar to the American Constitution, however, in that it consists of the rules that affect the working of governmental institutions. These rules are found in part in statutes but can be fully understood only through an examination of the institutions and procedures to be described in the following chapters.

CONSTITUTIONAL SOURCES

Great documents

Among the sources from which the constitution is drawn are, in the first place, certain great charters, petitions, and statutes such as Magna Charta, the Petition of Right, the Bill of Rights, the Act of Settlement, the Reform Act of 1832, and the Parliament Act of 1911. Most of these were acts passed by Parliament, but a document such as Magna Charta is considered to be part of the constitution simply because it represents a great landmark in national history, much as though Americans considered the Declaration of Independence and the Emancipation Proclamation to be part of their Constitution—as, indeed, they are part of the living tradition of American government.

The distinguishing thing about most of these charters and statutes is that they were the products of constitutional crisis and that they contain the terms of settlement of those crises. In the life of any great country certain issues arise that, like the controversy over slavery in the United States, cut to the foundations of the political system. In Britain, once such an issue has been definitely settled, either by the victory of one party or by a definitive compromise, the British consider that settlement part of their constitution. In spirit this practice is not unlike the addition of the Thirteenth, Fourteenth, and Fifteenth Amendments to the American Constitution at the end of the Civil War. But in Great Britain, since there is no written constitution to amend, the settlement generally takes the form of a law that looks like any other law passed by Parliament. What makes it a part of the constitution is the context of constitutional struggle within which it originated, as in the case of the Great Reform Act of 1832 or the Parliament Act of 1911, and the fact that it shapes the character of some part of the governmental machinery.

Important statutes

In addition to these more spectacular charters and statutes, there are certain other statutes that are significant, not because they mark the conclusion of a great constitutional struggle but because they deal with subjects of such intrinsic importance as to place them automatically in a category above ordinary law. Into this category, for example, fall the laws extending the right to vote.

None of these laws aroused the excitement that characterized the Reform Act of 1832, but any attempt to repeal them would now be regarded as an attack upon the basic constitutional principle of universal suffrage. Yet, whereas in the United States the granting of the suffrage to women was embodied in a formal amendment to the Constitution, electoral reforms in Great Britain have been made through the process of ordinary legislation.

While electoral laws have a particular relevance to the extension of political democracy, it is worth noting at this point that two significant areas of British government that have been completely transformed by statute are local administration and the public service. The former agencies of local administration, the justices of the peace and corporations of long established towns, became obsolete in the early nineteenth century. They were originally replaced by *ad hoc* agencies, but subsequently a structure of elected councils was set up that was more suitable for the period of representative government. Since then, many local services, like the provision of education and hospitals, have become part of integrated national systems.

The development of the British public service, which plays a vital role in government, was similarly the result of legislation. In sharp contrast to Continental countries, especially France and Prussia, where a highly centralized bureaucracy became the instrument of monarchical power, the supremacy of Parliament over the king kept the British public service in a disorganized and ineffective state until the mid-nineteenth century. Thereafter, it was shaped into a career service, steadily assuming more and more functions with the growth of "big government."

The long-range impact of these two developments has been great. The elective character of local institutions and recruitment by merit in the civil service may be ranked with electoral reform as basic principles of the constitution. But it is important to be aware at the same time that the growth of government functions, the far-reaching impact of administrative decisions, and the discretion inevitably vested in the hands of members of the bureaucracy have made it difficult to maintain the supremacy of Parliament and Great Britain's cherished "rule of law." Many of the new devices introduced in recent times, like the parliamentary commissioner (the ombudsman, see Chapter 4, Section 3), are efforts to safeguard the rights of individuals in the face of the ever-growing role of government and of fears lest it abuse its power.

Judicial decisions

A third important source of constitutional principles is to be found in court decisions. In interpreting the provisions of the charters and statutes that are part of the British constitution, judges have, to some extent, defined and developed its meaning much as the Supreme Court has clarified and expanded the provisions of the American Constitution. Even more significant, however, is the fact that some of the most important principles of the British constitution are principles of the common law —that is, principles not established by any law passed by Parliament or ordained by the king but rather established in the courts through the use of decisions in individual cases as precedents for decisions in later cases. The first decisions often were based on common customs or usages; as these decisions "broadened down from precedent to precedent," there grew up a body of principles of general application that is looked on as a bulwark of British freedom and an essential part of the constitution. The right to trial by jury and the writ of habeas corpus (which prevents a person being held in prison without trial) both developed in the courts of common law.

Today, according to the common law, the British subject has full freedom to say or write anything he pleases so long as it is not slanderous, libelous, seditious, obscene, or blasphemous; and public meetings may be disbanded only if the assembly becomes riotous or seems likely to commit a breach of the peace or a crime of violence. For the most part, such limitations do not constitute a serious interference with political liberty. *Blasphemy* and *obscenity* have little application to politics, and considerable latitude is given to strong political language before *libel* or *slander* can be invoked. *Sedition*, however, has at times received an unpleasantly broad and vague application, and the leeway that the police enjoy in determining what is a "breach of the peace" has aroused considerable concern. Indeed, as we shall see, there have been proposals that the civil rights that are embodied in the American Bill of Rights should receive statutory reinforcement in Britain.

The conventions of the British constitution

Fourth, and most difficult for Americans to understand, is that part of the British constitution that depends on custom or convention. These conventions ordinarily are not embodied in written laws and thus are not enforceable in the courts. Moreover, since they constantly grow and change and adapt themselves to new circumstances, it is difficult to say at any moment exactly what they are. As our study of the growth of Parliament and the Cabinet has shown, such conventions usually originate in practices that are followed for the sake of convenience. But if such practices are followed for a long enough time, the person who departs from them will be denounced for the "unconstitutionality" of his action.

One of the accepted conventions of the unwritten constitution is that if a government resigns, the monarch shall ask the leader of the opposition to form a new government. Another (as the Preamble to the Statute of Westminster, 1931, declares) is that a law affecting the succession to the throne or the royal title shall require the assent of the Parliaments of the overseas members of the Commonwealth as well as of the United Kingdom. Although there is no recourse to law if these conventions are disregarded, such an action would be a profound shock to the public. Similarly, if a minister publicly disagreed with governmental policy and yet refused to resign his portfolio, or if the monarch refused to dissolve the House of Commons on the request of the prime minister or refused to sign a particular law, there would be a popular reaction at least as strong as that which greeted President Roosevelt's plan to modify the composition of the Supreme Court. So pervasive is the loyalty to constitutional practices, that such a course of action seems unthinkable. In this sense, the protection of the constitution is in the hearts and minds of the people.

There are, however, more practical sanctions. The conventions of the constitution exist because they serve a real purpose. To violate them is often to make the government itself unworkable. If, for example, the queen began to act independently of the Cabinet, the Cabinet itself would resign, and the House of Commons would undoubtedly refuse to give its support to any new Cabinet—if, indeed, any members could be found to join such a Cabinet. The British government works only if the Cabinet and the House of Commons are in accord and if the queen follows the advice of the Cabinet. To depart from these rules in any important respect is to interfere with the whole machinery of government.

If a convention of the constitution is violated, it can, of course, be enacted into law. For example, it was long assumed that, through lack of use, the House of Lords had lost its power to reject any financial measure passed by the House of Commons. In 1909, however, the House of Lords rejected the famous Lloyd George budget that threatened the economic interests of many of the peers by placing heavy taxes on land. The Liberal party, which controlled the House of Commons at this time, denounced the Lords' action as a breach of the constitution and succeeded, after a bitter struggle, in winning the passage of the Parliament Act of 1911. This act made it impossible for the Lords to delay money bills for more than one month. In this way, the written law restored a violated constitutional convention.

Such developments should not be difficult for Americans to understand. In the United States few constitutional practices are more important than the action of the Supreme Court in holding acts of Congress unconstitutional when they conflict with the Court's interpretation of the Constitution. Yet one may read the American Constitution through without finding any statement granting this power to the Court. Nonetheless, it has by now become so established a part of the American form of government that only the most extreme reactionaries would think of challenging it. The practice has become part of the living constitution if not of the written one. Similarly, it was once maintained that the custom of having no president serve for more than two consecutive terms had become an unbreakable precedent. In 1940, in fact, when President Roosevelt ran for a third term, his opponent, Wendell Willkie, actually charged that he was acting unconstitutionally

—thereby using the word in its British rather than its American sense. The subsequent Twenty-second Amendment to the American Constitution, which limits the president to two terms, indicated that the convention was more firmly rooted than it at first seemed to be.

Sometimes a practice may be a matter of usage rather than of convention. During the greater part of the nineteenth century the prime minister was at least as likely to be a member of the House of Lords as of the House of Commons. However, as the House of Commons gained prestige with the extension of the right to vote and with the curtailment of the power of the House of Lords, it became increasingly inconvenient to have the chief spokesman of the Cabinet in the House of Lords when the Cabinet's fate was being decided in the House of Commons. From 1902 on, prime ministers were regularly chosen from the House of Commons. What may well be the decisive precedent was established in 1923 when the king, in appointing a new prime minister, passed over the most prominent Conservative, Lord Curzon, and appointed Mr. Stanley Baldwin.[4]

Later it was suggested that the same development was taking place in connection with the important post of Foreign Secretary. Here, too, there was a disadvantage in having a subordinate official explain and defend foreign policy in the House of Commons; the precedent seemed to be building up that only a member of the House of Commons might hold the post. In this case, the expectation proved premature, for Prime Minister Chamberlain appointed Lord Halifax to the position, and in 1960, despite protests, Prime Minister Macmillan chose Lord Home as Foreign Secretary. In 1970, Prime Minister Heath also chose him to be Foreign Secretary, but since he had renounced his peerage in the meantime, Alec Douglas-Home is now in the House of Commons.

Because British government is party government—that is, carried on by whatever organized group has received majority support at the polls—it has been increasingly felt that the election returns should not only designate which party shall assume the responsibilities of governing but should also control, both negatively and positively, the program that it undertakes while in office. This view has given rise to what is called the "mandate convention," which assumes that the government should institute radical changes only if the electorate has passed on them at a general election. This view was a matter of considerable controversy after the Labor party's victory at the polls in 1945. It was noticeable, however, that the Conservative majority in the House of Lords, in the years immediately following 1945, approved bills instituting such measures as nationalization, with which it was out of sympathy, on the ground that Labor had received a mandate from the electorate. Moreover, when the Labor government decided in 1947 to reduce the length of time the Lords could hold up legislation, its action was bitterly attacked as a violation of the mandate convention, since this measure altered the balance of power between Lords and Commons and had not been submitted to the electorate. It is clear from subsequent developments that the mandate convention is not yet finally established. The frequency of references to it, however, indicates a growing effort to establish some voters' control over major governmental decisions.

CONSTITUTIONAL PRINCIPLES

We can now sum up the most important principles of the constitution.

The first of these is the *fusion of powers*, which means that the monarch must always take the advice of the Cabinet, and the Cabinet must always have the support of the House of Commons. According to this principle there can never be in Great Britain the kind of prolonged disagreement between the executive and the legislature that has occurred so often in the United States. In the latter, as we well know, it is not at all unusual for the president to veto legislation passed by Congress or for Congress to refuse to pass legislation recommended by the president. This is particularly the case when, as in President Nixon's first term, the president belongs to one party and the majority of congressmen to the other.

In Great Britain, such disagreements are im-

---
[4] The fact that Mr. Baldwin was more acceptable to the rank-and-file of his party than Lord Curzon and the lack of representation of the Labor party—the official opposition—in the House of Lords may well have been the decisive reasons for the action; popular belief in the official interpretation, however, soundly established the precedent.

possible. Before the days of disciplined parties, it might have been a debatable point whether Parliament controlled the prime minister and Cabinet, or whether the prime minister and Cabinet controlled Parliament. No one contested, however, the principle that they must work in agreement. Today there is no chance that the House of Commons would vote against an important measure sponsored by the Cabinet or pass a bill opposed by the Cabinet. Thus, in sharp contrast to the United States, the executive and the legislature in Great Britain never follow conflicting policies.

It is easy to misunderstand the nature of this fusion of powers. Even Bagehot suggested that it meant that the Cabinet is merely a committee of the working majority of the House of Commons. On the contrary, although there is no formal separation of executive and legislative powers in the British parliamentary system corresponding to the somewhat artificial division in the American system, there is a very real distinction between the Cabinet and Parliament. In fact, the key to the British system of government is the continuously maintained balance between the Cabinet's executive and legislative initiative and the consideration of legislation by Parliament. The Cabinet, or "government," makes appointments, summons Parliament, initiates and organizes the legislative program, decides on dissolutions, all without consulting Parliament. In so doing, it uses the inherent power of the Crown (which it represents), a power vast in extent and still not wholly defined in scope. Through this power, and the strength resulting from a well-disciplined party, the Cabinet provides positive and effective direction of affairs. The function of Parliament is not to weaken or supersede this leadership but to make sure that there is full consideration by the public, as well as by its own members, of all the issues introduced by the government before it gives them its formal consent.

A second and closely related principle is the *supremacy of Parliament*. Supreme legal power in Great Britain is exercised by Parliament (the House of Commons, the House of Lords, and the sovereign), which according to the old saying can do everything but make a woman a man and a man a woman. In contrast to American practice, there is no judicial review in the sense of testing the constitutional validity of laws, and there is no complicated process of constitutional amendment. The veto power of the titular executive has lapsed through nonuse, and the king will accept any measure passed by the two houses of Parliament. No court would dare to hold an act of Parliament unconstitutional, and, theoretically, Parliament itself can change the constitution at any time simply by passing an ordinary law. Thus, it is sometimes pointed out that Parliament could, quite legally, extend its own term of office forever, depose the king (who would have to sign the warrant), turn England into a republic, make Buddhism the established religion, or restrict the right to vote to women of seventy years old and over.

Yet merely to say this is to point to the absurdity of the idea. Parliamentary supremacy is exercised in the spirit of responsibility, and responsibility is to the nation as a whole, not just to the majority in Parliament. There is a strong sense of "the rules of the game." Profound psychological checks and self-restraints commonly come into operation when substantial changes affecting the functions and balance of institutions are under consideration. Devices such as all-party conferences and royal commissions, which will be considered in Chapter 4, can be used to analyze proposals introducing legislation. Thus, although Parliament is legally supreme, it acts with responsible self-restraint.

Theoretically, there is a major difference between the American concept that legal authority vests ultimately in the citizens, who confer it temporarily on the president and on Congress, and the British concept that legal authority inheres in Parliament and in the Crown (whose authority is now exercised by the Cabinet). According to the British concept the British Parliament and Cabinet are two coequal, interrelated elements, each possessing and exercising an independent authority, not, as in the United States, an authority merely delegated by the voters.

But the distinction should not be pushed too far. Although *legal authority* rests in the Cabinet (using the authority of the Crown) and in Parliament, *political power* resides in the British people as it does in the American people through their right to vote for the representatives and government of their choice. Perhaps the greatest practical importance of the distinction regarding the ultimate seat of legal authority in the two countries, therefore, is in the attitude of the elected representatives: in the United States, members of the House of Representatives are likely to look on themselves as delegates from their constituencies; thus only the president and, to a lesser degree, the Senate represent the whole country. In Great Britain, on the other hand, members of Parliament, particularly the ministers, accept a primary loyalty to act on behalf of the country as a whole.

A third important principle is the distinction between the king as a person and *the Crown as an institution*. Regardless of the personal qualities of the individual, the institution of monarchy is the object of great respect, both because of its antiquity and because of the ceremony and pageantry of which it is the focus. Whatever changes may take place behind the governmental façade, the Crown continues to symbolize the stability and durability of British institutions and to command the loyalty of the British people.

In form, the powers of the Crown are very great. Every action of the government is carried out in its name. It is the Crown that makes appointments and assents to laws, that makes treaties and commands the armed forces. The not wholly defined prerogative powers inhering in the Crown can be used during emergencies. Moreover, as noted, *legally* the ministers derive their authority from the Crown and in this sense are responsible to it. But to say that the Crown has these powers and position is very different from saying that the monarch can make use of them independently. On the contrary, as we have been pointing out, the ruler may exercise these powers only on the advice of his ministers, who, of course, are responsible *politically* to Parliament and the electorate. In short, the powers of the Crown are always used as the Cabinet, supported by Parliament, wants them to be used.

Finally, one of the fundamental principles of the constitution is the *rule of law*, according to which the government and its agents, as well as individual citizens, are subject to laws that are definite and known in advance and that can be modified only by act of Parliament. Thus, no citizen may be punished unless he has been found guilty of violating the law in a trial before a regular court whose procedure safeguards him against arbitrary conviction. Similarly, the courts will protect the citizen against government officials who interfere with his rights contrary to law. Thus both government officials and private citizens are equally subject to one body of law and one system of courts.

As in the United States, the courts are the primary protectors in Great Britain of what we call "civil liberties": freedom of speech, freedom of association, freedom of assembly, and freedom from arrest and imprisonment "except," as Magna Charta stated it, "by judgment of his peers or by the law of the land." Historically, the common-law courts have been vigilant to stop the government from exercising arbitrary power. As noted, the courts devised the writ of habeas corpus centuries before Parliament passed the Habeas Corpus Act in 1679. They are still entrusted with the task of seeing that executive authorities do not exceed the powers entrusted to them and do not deviate from the strict procedures under which they should act. Yet it is no longer accepted unquestioningly that they are adequate to this task.

ARE CIVIL LIBERTIES ADEQUATELY PROTECTED?

There are two special reasons for doubts regarding the adequacy of current procedures for protecting civil liberties in the United Kingdom. The first is that while most people continue to act within the known and traditional boundaries of freedom of opinion, speech, and action, there are an increasing number of individuals and groups that operate out of a different cultural context and feel that they have rights that are inadequately or condescendingly protected. Many students and "hippies" obviously feel outside the established consensus but so also do radicals on the right, such as working-class Powellites.

This universal problem, experienced also in the United States and on the continent of Europe, is felt with particular sensitivity in Great Britain because of its long history of expanding liberties through eliminating restrictive laws, like those hampering trade union activity, and illiberal institutions, like the Lord Chamberlain's theater censorship. Indeed, a series of liberalizing statutes was passed under the Labor government in the late 1960s relating to abortion, homosexuality, and divorce, while capital punishment was abolished. Yet there are still nonconforming groups that feel restricted. A particular problem caused by some of those outside the present consensus is, of course, that their freedom to act impinges at certain points—as with the Powellites—on the rights and even safety of others.

The second and more widespread concern focuses on the steady encroachment on individual liberties by big government and by the administration in implementing parliamentary statutes. In a debate on the subject in the House of Lords on June 18, 1969, cogent reasons were given why human rights now need more protection in Britain than in the past: the concentration of power in the central government, especially in the executive; the growth of the administrative structure and the need for remedies in case of administrative abuse; the increasing invasion of privacy and use of computors to store information about individuals (a practice recently challenged in the United States when it was disclosed that army sources had been collecting such material concerning some distinguished political figures as well as dissidents).

A perennial cause of concern has been the executive discretion of the Home Secretary. Its use early in 1970 to deport Rudi Dutschke, a radical student leader who had been active in West Berlin but was then studying at Cambridge University after convalescing from a bullet wound suffered two years before, was hotly criticized. So, too, was the fact that the evidence on which the decision was based was presented to the tribunal in secret.

Probably the most serious abridgment of human rights by a British statute was the Commonwealth Immigration Act 1968, which, in response to fear of a massive population movement, withdrew the right of entry to the United Kingdom from citizens of Asian origin living in Africa. In response, one of the rights proposed for legislation is the right to a valid passport, and another is the right of all citizens to entry to and residence in the country.

As an alternative to the Right of Privacy Bill, which had been introduced in Parliament, the Labor government at the beginning of 1970 appointed a committee, under the chairmanship of the Right Honorable Kenneth Younger, to "consider whether legislation is needed to give further protection to the individual citizen and to commercial and industrial interests against intrusions into privacy by private persons and organizations or by companies and to make recommendations." Legislation for this purpose and to safeguard specific civil rights might be like our Bill of Rights, which simply states rights possessed by the American people and leaves it to the courts to determine in a particular case how to test whether the relevant law violates them or not, or the rights might be defined in the legislation. Such a statute could be entrenched—that is, given a superior status that demands a special procedure for amendment or rescinding—but in the light of the long-established British practice of regarding certain legislation as of constitutional importance, it seems unlikely that such an unusual step would be taken.

However the British settle this problem, it is clear from American experience that legislation can perform only part of the task of protecting civil liberties and human rights. What remains crucial is the attitude of ordinary citizens, and of the police, toward civil liberties. Anyone who has listened to the explosive utterances of orators at Hyde Park Corner and watched their orderly audiences realizes the value of such safety valves. The story of the London bobby listening to a particularly inflammatory speech and finally drawling, "All them as is going to burn down Buckingham Palace make a line on this side," is fortunately also not untypical. Such an atmosphere, where it exists, remains the best protection of civil liberties, although it may well be aided by written guarantees.

THE VALUE OF THE CONSTITUTION

Admirable as are the principles of the British constitution, Americans, and occasionally the

British themselves, may be troubled by a number of questions that are variations on a single theme: with a constitution that is, in part, so vague and that can be changed so easily, either through the imperceptible development of custom or by the passage of an ordinary act of Parliament, how can anyone be sure that constitutional principles really will be maintained in times of special stress? In the United States the Constitution can be formally amended only by a long and complicated process, and Americans occasionally question the usefulness of the much-heralded rule of law if Parliament can change that law at any time.

As already pointed out, however, Parliament does not change the law lightly or without careful consideration. There is, in fact, a very real restraint upon its authority, although a different kind of restraint from that to which Americans are accustomed. The first defense of the constitution lies in the force of tradition and public opinion rather than in a court or a difficult process of amendment. The members of Parliament, like most Englishmen, have been brought up to believe in discussion, in the rights of individuals and minorities, and in the need to preserve the essential character of the constitution. It is true that the same forces act in defense of the American Constitution, but in the United States there is more of an inclination to leave this defense to the Supreme Court. Yet there is something to be said for a system that makes it clear that the maintenance of the constitution is the responsibility of the people themselves.

Despite the current concern in Great Britain regarding the protection of civil rights, it would be hard to prove that they are any less secure in Great Britain than in the United States. If the Supreme Court of the United States has an excellent record for the protection of civil liberties, there have been times when, by its own confession, it has lapsed. Moreover, it takes a long time and a good deal of money to carry a case to the Supreme Court, and by the time a decision is rendered it may be too late to remedy the damage. Humble people, who are the most likely to be oppressed, may not even be able to raise the necessary money.

One advantage of a written constitution, it is sometimes said, is the greater ease with which the ordinary citizen may detect an infraction of its provisions. The lines are more distinctly drawn; it is not so hard to tell when someone steps over the boundary of constitutional prohibition; and there is a tangible statement around which public opinion can rally. Yet in fact many issues touching civil rights seem far from clear until after the judges have ruled on them.

Another claim is as debatable. The difficult process of amendment, in the case of the American Constitution, may give the public a longer warning about a contemplated change, a greater opportunity to think matters through, and even a margin of time in which to change their minds and recover from transitory hysteria. But the very difficulty and complexity of the process constitute an invitation to circumvention. It is so hard to get an extremely controversial amendment adopted that constitutional flexibility—particularly in the extension of the government's economic powers—has come to depend on the willingness of the Supreme Court to render a broad interpretation of constitutional wording rather than upon a deliberate decision of the electorate to change these words. Here, too, there is something to be said for a method of change whereby amendments may be made in a straightforward manner in sufficient time to meet the essential needs of a changing society, yet without sacrificing the considerable thought and discussion of their implications.

In any event, the ultimate defense of any constitution, whether written or unwritten, whether equipped with elaborate defense mechanisms or with none at all, must lie in the watchful concern of its people. In their alertness and use of constructive imagination, the British have at least as good a record as Americans.

3 BRITISH POLITICAL IDEAS

To understand the attitudes of a people as well as the political programs of particular groups, it is necessary to know the political ideas that have claimed their allegiance, for nowhere is it more true than in politics that ideas are both the forerunners and the outcome of action. In the course of the past hundred years, three great currents of ideas have competed for the political allegiance of British citizens. In the middle of the nineteenth century the principal contenders were conservatism and liberalism. Today they are conservatism and socialism. But although liberalism has declined as an independent force, its successful rivals have absorbed a significant portion of its content. As a result, it is impossible to understand contemporary politics in Great Britain without some familiarity with all three currents of thought.

BRITISH CONSERVATISM

In Great Britain, as in every other country, the natural tendency of conservatives is to like traditional institutions and political principles and to regard any far-reaching innovation with suspicion, if not distaste. Established institutions, they think, rest upon the safest of all foundations: that of experience. To desert them is to abandon oneself to the uncharted seas of theorizing and speculation. Although change may be necessary at certain times, it is not necessarily a good thing in itself, and thus it should be carried out in such a way as to preserve as many as possible of the inherited institutions.

There are certain differences between British and American conservatives, however, that result from differences in the institutions they have inherited. Where American conservatives are devoted to a constitutional system that places strong restraints upon the government, British Conservatives trace their descent from the Tory party, which once stood for the authority of the Crown against parliamentary limitation. Although British Conservatives have long since come to accept the supremacy of Parliament, the fact that for so many generations the upper classes controlled Parliament encouraged a greater willingness to uphold the authority of the state than seems natural to American conservatives.

The influence of Burke

Somewhat paradoxically, the man who has had the greatest influence on Conservative thought, Edmund Burke (1729–97), considered himself a Whig. He defended the rights of the American colonists at the time of the Revolution, and he was devoted to the principles of the Glorious Revolution of 1688. To Burke, however, these revolutions had been fought in defense of the established constitution and the inherited rights of Englishmen. This was a very different view from the affirmation of natural rights of the American Declaration of Independence, for Burke believed that men possessed only those rights that had evolved through history; thus Englishmen, wherever they were, had rights not possessed, for example, by Frenchmen.

The French Revolution of 1789 seemed to Burke to have an entirely different character. Its leaders frankly proclaimed their intention of destroying or remolding such time-honored institutions as the monarchy, the aristocracy, and the established church; they proclaimed their belief in the power of reason to create new institutions and to remedy ancient injustices. To Burke, human reason seemed but a weak and fallible guide in comparison with the lessons of tradition and experience. If new circumstances required changes in the inherited constitution, Burke wanted them to be made within the spirit of that constitution and with as little modification as possible of its inherited form.

Burke viewed society as living and growing well beyond the lifetime of any individual or generation and linking the past, the present, and the future. Society, he said, is a contract, not to be lightly entered into like "a partnership agreement in a trade of pepper and coffee, calico or tobacco . . . and to be dissolved by the fancy of the parties." And he added: "It is to be looked on with other reverence. . . . It is a partnership in all science; a partnership in all art; a partnership in every virtue, and in all perfection. As the end of such a partnership cannot be obtained in many generations, it becomes a partnership not only between those who are living, but between those who are living, those who are dead, and those who are to be born." In such a perspective, whose essential character is accepted by most conservatives today, the purpose of change is to preserve the balance of institutions, both public and private. The way in which the British constitution has adapted itself to new conditions meets the conservative ideal of continuity, which embodies distrust of changes based on "theory" but also forceful and often creative responses to circumstance.

Modern conservatism

It has been typical of the best of Conservative leaders, such as Benjamin Disraeli (later Earl of Beaconsfield, 1804–81) and Winston Churchill (later Sir Winston, 1874–1964), that they have known when to yield to the demands of a democratic and industrial age. By making concessions before the accumulated pressure and irritation became too great, they not only retained a strong popular following but were able to make reforms in their own way, thus preserving much of the traditional order. Further, they were often able to determine the direction and the extent of the changes.

This adaptability to new circumstances has been easier for British than American conservatives, because the former have had no objection to state activity and have rejected both the doctrine of the right of the individual against the state and any belief in inalienable natural rights. Today, Conservative spokesmen regard certain principles, sacrosanct to American free-enterprise conservatives, as the core of the "liberal heresy." Partly because of this adaptability, partly because of the long, slow development of the British constitution, partly perhaps because the British tend to be empiricists rather than theorists, much of the conservative approach has deeply permeated British thinking and ways of action, even those of the Labor party.

Imperialism

In the late nineteenth century, Conservatives became identified with another doctrine: imperialism. Earlier in the century many Englishmen, disillusioned by the loss of the American colonies and preoccupied with the industrial transformation at home, took little interest in the nation's overseas possessions. Disraeli himself could say in 1852 that "these wretched colonies will all be independent too in a few years and are a millstone around our necks." The empire continued to grow, but it grew, according to the famous phrase, "in a fit of absence of mind."

During the last third of the century, however, there was a remarkable change in the attitude both of statesmen and of the people as a whole. It was Disraeli who made Queen Victoria Empress of India and, with farsighted shrewdness, acquired for Britain the predominant control of the new Suez Canal, which so greatly shortened the route to India, Australia, and Hong Kong. As the economic competition of other countries developed, the possession of empire markets gained in significance. Moreover, the idea of empire began to appeal to those leading monotonous lives in bleak industrial cities. The acquisition of an empire became a source of pride.

The doctrine of imperialism, justified by its supporters as embodying a sense of responsibility for the development and welfare of subject peoples, was at its best a benevolent paternalism, but all too often took the form of exploitation. Most imperialists thought of national profit and power before they thought of colonial welfare. Even when most responsible for those they governed, imperialists enjoyed a feeling of superiority that could not easily be reconciled with a spirit of democracy.

At first there were many Liberal as well as Conservative imperialists, but with the passage of time Liberals increasingly denounced the acquisition of territory by conquest and demanded greater rights for colonial peoples—a stand in which they were joined by the new Labor party. In contrast, Conservatives tended to resist the transfer of imperial power and the postwar transformation of the dependent Asian and African empire into part of a multiracial Commonwealth, but here, as elsewhere, they ultimately yielded to circumstances and helped to direct its final stages.

BRITISH LIBERALISM

The influence of Locke

To the average American, the most familiar ideas in British politics are those associated with some of the early Whig thinkers. In particular the writings of John Locke (1632–1704), who wrote in defense of the Glorious Revolution of 1688, influenced the leaders of the American Revolution and found their way into the popular political vocabulary of the time. Thus, much of the American Declaration of Independence is simply a restatement of Locke's principles.

Locke taught that all men are naturally equal; that they possess a natural right to life, liberty, and property; that governments are voluntary associations formed to protect these rights; and that governments should be so organized and limited as to prevent an abuse of their powers. To that end Locke advocated a separation of powers between the executive and the legislative branches of government, and he denied the right of a government to injure the lives or property of its subjects, to tax or take property without consent, to delegate to other agencies powers granted it by the people, or to rule by arbitrary decree instead of by laws duly enacted by Parliament. If a government violated these principles, Locke believed that the people had the right to recall their grant of power and to set up a new government.

Much of the divergence between political thinking in Great Britain and the United States today can be understood in terms of the degree of rejection or acceptance of Locke's ideas. In the United States the success of a government founded upon these principles has seemed sufficient proof of their validity; but in late eighteenth-century Great Britain, Locke's belief in natural rights and the right of revolution came to be identified with the excesses of the French Revolution and the Reign of Terror. While British Liberals (and, today, many British Conservatives) continue to believe in limited government, Liberal reforms would have been long in coming to Great Britain if they had had no other intellectual foundation than a belief in natural rights.

The Utilitarians

The man who, more than any other, provided a fresh basis for Liberal political action, Jeremy Bentham (1748–1833), was a Tory in origin. He had even less use than Burke for the doctrine of natural rights, for in his view the aim of government was not to protect men's "rights" but to promote "the greatest happiness of the greatest number," with each individual counting like every other. Every governmental policy was to be judged by its "utility," that is, by its tendency to increase human pleasure and to decrease human pain. Bentham worked out elaborate tables by which such utility could be judged; the policy that resulted in the greatest happiness was the policy to be followed.

There was nothing intrinsically democratic in this theory, except its emphasis on equality: but since Bentham was convinced that men are fundamentally selfish, he felt that only a government of the people would look out for the interests of the people.

The result was that Bentham, for reasons very different from those of Locke, came to some of the same conclusions. He did not think that men are equal because of a law of nature, but he did think that each man's happiness is as important as that of any other. Using this criterion, he subjected the inherited institutions of his time to a devastating rational analysis and advocated sweeping changes in such institutions as the electoral system, the law, the penal system, and the poor law.

Bentham's influence on the course of British Liberalism was prodigious. In place of the discredited school of natural rights, he offered a new program of practical political reforms that made a strong appeal to the common sense of the British people and that, it is sometimes said, helped to save Great Britain from the kind of violent revolution that afflicted the Continent. His influence, however, also helped to separate the main current of British Liberalism from the main current of American democratic thought. Whereas Americans continued to believe in the existence of individual rights beyond the power of government and in the necessity of separating and balancing powers in order to control the government, Bentham saw no need to check government so long as it was promoting the happiness of the majority of the people. His "greatest happiness" principle provided a strong basis for popular government and majority rule, even at the expense of minority rights. Moreover, where many American liberals long clung to the idea that that government is best that governs least, Bentham and his followers (the Utilitarians or Philosophical Radicals) logically were bound to uphold governmental action aimed at the elimination of human misery. Thus Benthamite Liberals welcomed social welfare programs long before such programs became part of the creed of American liberals.

Economic liberalism

Bentham himself did not foresee to what extent his ideas could be used to justify governmental action. In economic affairs, paradoxically, he accepted the teaching of Adam Smith (1723–90), who believed that there is a natural harmony of economic interests, and that men, if not interfered with by the government, will unconsciously promote the interests of the community at the same time that they consciously promote their own.

According to Smith, the community pays its highest rewards to those who provide the services it most desires; and, since each individual wishes to earn as much money as possible, he will do exactly those things that the community wishes him to do. As a result, the government does not need to, and indeed ought not to, interfere with the economy but should limit itself to national defense, the protection of life and property, and the building of certain public works too costly for private individuals to undertake.

In the early part of the nineteenth century there was no apparent conflict between the ideas of Bentham and those of Smith. Merchants and industrialists supported the Liberal party as the agent of laissez faire and free enterprise at the same time that radicals supported it as the advocate of a broader suffrage and other democratic reforms. The advance of the industrial revolution and the growing demand for economic reform strained this happy partnership. Factory owners were bitterly opposed to many of the reforms that other Liberals advocated enthusiastically as the most effective way of promoting human happiness and eliminating human misery.

The influence of Mill

To some extent this conflict in Liberal ideas was personified in the life of John Stuart Mill (1806–73). Mill's father, James Mill, had been one of Bentham's most able and intimate disciples, and John Stuart Mill himself grew up in the citadel of Benthamite ideas. As a young man, however, he began to question certain of Bentham's teachings. In particular, he placed greater emphasis upon the worth of the individual personality, and he thought the great objective of society to be not the happiness of the individual but his growth and development. Better, he thought, to be Socrates dissatisfied than a satisfied pig. Thus society should aim at the cultivation of those qualities that are peculiarly human and that distinguish men from animals: before all else the power to think well and to think for oneself.

Such a goal led Mill to be suspicious of any state activity that would limit the freedom of the citizen or reduce his self-reliance. At the same time, however, Mill was well aware of the existence of economic abuses that only the state could remedy. In his famous essay *On Liberty* (1859) he tried to draw a distinction between those actions of the individual that concern only himself, with which the state ought not to interfere, and those actions likely to affect or harm others, which the state may control or prohibit. Thus the state might intervene to prevent the adulteration of goods or to force employers to provide healthful working conditions.

Mill also came to believe that political reforms of the sort advocated by many Liberals —the extension of the suffrage, and the reform of the law and of Parliament—although desirable in themselves would not produce a good society unless accompanied by far-reaching economic reforms. The fundamental problem of society, he wrote in his *Autobiography*, was "to unite the greatest individual liberty of action with a common ownership in the raw material of the globe and an equal participation of all in the benefits of combined labor." Thus Mill had, in fact, become a socialist in ideal—although a reluctant socialist who believed intensely in individual self-reliance and in freedom of thought and expression and who wished to combine this freedom with social and economic equality. He did not try to say in any detail how this change was to come about, but apparently it was his hope that through education and experience men might come voluntarily to "dig and weave" for their country as well as to fight for it.

Today British Liberalism is still struggling with the problem of how to reconcile individual liberty with social welfare. Many of the merchants and industrialists, who used to provide the party with its financial strength, have gone over to the Conservatives, and Conservative leaders often appeal to the rest of the Liberals to follow that example. Yet it is increasingly common today to hear Conservatives using the old Liberal slogans of individual freedom from government control.

Many Liberal voters have also turned to Labor—in some instances not because they approved of socialism in principle but because Labor's concrete program of social reform appealed to idealistic elements within the Liberal party. Moreover, as the Liberal party itself weakened, a vote for Labor often seemed the most effective way of voting against Conservatism and imperialism.

Today the Liberals, more than any other party, concern themselves with the protection of individual liberty. But they combine this devotion to liberty with what they call "a radical programme of practical reform." Thus it is characteristic of the present attitude of the party that Lord Beveridge, the sponsor of the famous Beveridge Plan for security "from the cradle to the grave," was one of its conspicuous leaders.

BRITISH SOCIALISM

Toward the end of the nineteenth century, as we have seen, the issue of economic reform was replacing political reform as the subject of greatest political controversy. To many reformers the obvious way of bringing about change was direct economic action by trade unions and consumers' cooperatives. But there were also those who believed that only political action could remedy economic and social injustice. Among them some, like H. M. Hyndman and the Social Democratic Federation, were under the influence of Karl Marx and believed that reform would come through class warfare and revolution. Others, like the members of the Independent Labor party, placed greater emphasis on winning seats in Parliament and local councils and concentrated on an ethical and democratic appeal which, in the Nonconformist tradition, had great influence on the British workingman.

The Fabians

Some of the most influential ideas, however, were those of the Fabian Society, which was founded in 1884. Unlike Marxist socialists, the Fabians opposed the doctrine of class warfare and advocated a policy of planned gradualism. As the saying went, they substituted evolution for revolution. But evolution must be urged along the correct path. Their motto was, "For the right moment you must wait, as Fabius did most patiently when warring against Hannibal, though many censured his delays; but when the time comes you must strike hard, as Fabius did, or your waiting will be in vain, and fruitless."

The membership of the Fabian Society has never exceeded a few thousand, but among its members have been men and women of the greatest ability and influence: George Bernard Shaw, Sidney and Beatrice Webb, H. G. Wells, Graham Wallas, Ramsay MacDonald; and in more recent years, Harold Laski, G. D. H. and Margaret Cole, R. H. Tawney, Leonard Woolf, Clement Attlee, and Hugh Gaitskell. When the Labor party came into power in 1945 and introduced its massive program of nationalization, the Fabian membership included 229 members of Parliament, several Cabinet ministers, and the prime minister himself. And if one hears little of the Fabians these days, and much more of the antidoctrinaire attitudes and impact of Harold Wilson, this fact does not undercut the long-term, creative effects of the Fabian Society.

The aim of the Society, as stated in 1896, was "to persuade the English people to make their political constitution thoroughly democratic and so to socialize their industries as to make the livelihood of the people entirely independent of private Capitalism." Its method, in Shaw's words, was to give up "the delightful ease of revolutionary heroics" for the "hard work of practical reform on ordinary parliamentary lines." By raising wages, shortening hours of work, providing security in old age, ill health, and unemployment, and promoting public health and safety, they hoped to destroy or to reduce some of the worst evils of modern industrial society. By taxing inheritance, ground rents, and income from investments, they hoped to reduce the outstanding economic inequalities. And by increasing public ownership, local as well as national, of public utilities such as gas, water, electricity, and public transport, they hoped gradually to extend the amount of public ownership, to gain experience in the public management of property, and to prove the efficiency and practicability of such management. What was at first done on a small scale and in individual instances could eventually be expanded, they thought, into a completely socialized society.

The outstanding achievement of the Fabian Society was its influence on public opinion inside and outside the Labor party. The brilliant scholars, writers, and speakers who served the Society presented the results of their research and experience in a vivid and effective way. Fabian pamphlets and Fabian lectures reached and influenced large numbers of people, especially in the middle classes, who would have been antagonized by talk of revolution and bored by theory but who could be convinced by hard facts and common sense. The Labor party itself had particular need of these clear and penetrating analyses of domestic, colonial, and foreign affairs with their far-sighted proposals for policies to achieve the ends the party sought. Coming late to the political scene and into a milieu shaped for centuries by others, Labor would have remained at a serious disadvantage both inside and outside Parliament without the intellectual resources the Fabians provided. More than any other group, it was the Fabian Society that gave the practical cast to British socialism that distinguishes it from the more doctrinaire socialism of the Continent.

In 1900, some of the trade unions, the Social Democratic Federation, the Independent Labor party, and the Fabians formed the organization that later became the Labor party and is today the political arm of British socialism. As a result, it is characteristic of British socialism that there is no one orthodox school of thought. Rather, a variety of ideas and many types of people are found within its ranks. Instead of formulating a rigid ideological program to which all must adhere, there has been a willingness, in a typically British way, to avoid ultimate theoretical issues while agreeing upon and striving for immediate concrete goals.

The notable achievements of the post–World War II Labor government in making Great Britain more "socialist"—the nationalization of major industries, the creation of the national health service, and the reconversion of the economy from war to peace—left fewer specific goals around which to formulate programs. Hugh Gaitskell, whose optimistic rationality envisaged social evolution proceeding by stages, held the party to a middle way that attracted a wide spectrum of middle-class as well as working-class support. Although the Harold Wilson administration has been criticized for not moving Britain to a more egalitarian society, it must be admitted that socialist thinking these days appears more characteristic of certain intellectual and upper middle-class groups than of its traditional working-class base. The New Left of Trotskyites, Maoists, anarchists, and student "radicals" is looked on askance by the Old Left, which divides its energies between its traditional role inside the party and specific outside issues, like child poverty, saving the environment, or antiapartheid movements. Some of this energy rubs off on the Labor party, which remains more "progressive" in objectives than the Conservatives and more effective than the Liberals.

In a period of relative affluence, the similarities between political parties tend to become more prominent than the differences. Yet British Conservatives under Edward Heath are raising questions about the scope of public ownership and of social services that no Labor administration would consider. It is to Labor's advantage that the Powellites' center is within the Tories. The class base of each of the two major parties has not noticeably shifted. None of these differences is so great as to provoke more than sharp debate within a political system equally accepted by both. Yet however marginal the differences between the two major parties may appear to be, each under pressure still reflects the ideas and forces out of which it came.

3
British parties and elections

1 THE CHARACTER OF THE BRITISH PARTY SYSTEM

Without an understanding of the character and functions of British parties, the most important aspects of British politics would seem inexplicable. It is the parties that aggregate the vast variety of aspirations and demands of every section of the British populace. It is the parties that articulate these demands in understandable principles and programs and that recruit teams of potential officeholders that are pledged to support these principles and programs. At all times, the voluntary associations that we call parties serve as links between individuals and groups on the one hand and the processes of government on the other, focusing and even creating demands through their promises and performance, as well as responding to government actions or opposition demands.

Thus in the infinitely complex and continuous interactions of interests and pressures within modern Britain, political parties play an indispensable role. They reduce alternatives to manageable dimensions. Moreover, through identification and discipline, they support the fusion of authority in the hands of persons who are at one and the same time Cabinet, parliamentary, and party leaders. By these means, political decision-making is kept visible and responsive as well as effective.

Let us now take a few steps back to some simpler statements on the purpose and role of political parties. Everyone agrees that in a democracy the government ought in general to do what the people want it to do, and everyone agrees that the government should be led by men whom the people themselves have chosen. But it is easier to say this than to discover a workable way of determining what the people want. The ordinary citizen, acting alone, is comparatively helpless when it comes to drawing up a complete program for his government. He lacks the time, the information, and the practical experience to work out the solution to political problems for himself, and as an individual he is too unimportant for the government to care very much what he may think. If he wants to influence the policy of his government, his best resort is to join with others who share his general views, to work out a common program with their help, and to run candidates for office who are pledged to put this program into effect.

This work of uniting, of organizing, and of agreeing on candidates is characteristic of political parties in all democracies. For those citizens who want to participate actively in politics, parties provide the natural channel for action. For the rest of the community, they offer a choice of candidates and policies. The ordinary voter, instead of having to determine his personal attitude on every issue, has the far easier task of deciding which of two or three broad programs suits him best. And the party that wins the favor of the largest number of voters, ideally at least, proceeds to carry out the program the voters have approved.

But if this is the ideal function of political parties, it must be admitted that it is a function often performed half-heartedly or badly. Many men in any country join and work for a political party not so much because of their devotion to its public aims as because of their desire for personal power and the material advantages of office. Some parties may even be so organized as to impede rather than encourage political action by the ordinary voter. Thus, in judging the degree of democracy in and the effectiveness of any party system, it is necessary to ask several questions:

Does it offer the mass of the people a meaningful and an adequate choice both of policies and of leaders?

Do the parties respond to the needs of the people and the country, are they flexible enough to allow for change, and are they responsive to new ideas, programs, and groups?

Is the internal organization of the parties sufficiently democratic to provide a channel for active political participation by the rank-and-file of the membership, not just in promoting the victory of the party, but in determining its policies and choosing its leadership?

Does the party system assist the process of arriving peacefully at a settlement of controversial issues, or does it exacerbate the differences among the different elements in the community?

Is the party system an effective instrument for carrying out the judgment of the voters once they have made a choice of parties?

SIMILARITIES IN TWO-PARTY SYSTEMS: GREAT BRITAIN AND THE UNITED STATES

In more ways than is commonly believed, the British party system is like the American. In both countries political parties are large, popular organizations that try to win public office in order to promote policies in which they believe and also to enjoy the material privileges that go along with office. In both countries, ordinarily, there are two large parties. Although in Britain the Liberals have managed to maintain a foothold of representation in Parliament since their decline after World War I, and regional parties occasionally emerge, there is no such division of votes and representation as is common in France and in Germany. Thus British and American voters can generally count that their votes will result in a clear-cut majority in the legislature for one major party or the other, although coalition and even minority governments have not been unusual in Great Britain in this century.

It would ordinarily be argued, however, that the division between parties in Great Britain has a different class basis from that in the United States. It is true that party loyalties in Great Britain have deep historical, social, and family links that do much to explain the persistence of party allegiances. But it is also true that the ultimate purpose of a party is to win an election. Thus when there are only two major contestants for office, each must strive to command as wide a spectrum of support throughout the country as possible. Thus while Labor maintains its dominance in mining, steel, and the docks, the Conservatives attract not only the fast-disappearing traditional working-class Tory, with his tradition of deference, but also the workers in new industries and in white-overall and white-collar industrial occupations.[1] These facts support the notion that the social solidarity of the working class is no longer necessarily reflected in its patterns of voting. Conservatives remain relatively strong in rural areas, but Labor has bitten into some of them. Labor's social-welfare emphasis appeals to most of those in need, but Conservative support among retired persons is particularly strong. Labor commands a strong hold on the professional classes, but both Conservatives and Liberals take their share.

It is thus becoming less true that it is easier to guess a man's political allegiance in Great

---

[1] In a 1960 sample of five hundred working-class men and women, who by industry, trade union membership, sex, age, and membership in employer-run superannuation schemes matched the total adult working-class population of Great Britain, only 56 percent said they were working class, 40 percent described themselves as a middle class, and the remaining 4 percent refused to consider themselves part of any class group. Thirty-eight percent of those describing themselves as working class, and 16 percent of those calling themselves middle class, supported Labor. Twenty-two percent of those who described themselves as working class, and 24 percent of those calling themselves middle class, supported the Conservatives.

Britain from his social status than it is in the United States. The Conservatives have a built-in base of support among the upper classes and the wealthy, but it is clear that in the United States the Republican party also secures a disproportionate share of the votes of the more prosperous. Organized labor and minority groups generally support the Democrats, although the trade unions have no such organic relation to either party in the United States as they have to Labor in Britain. The less prosperous professional groups in the United States tend to be as staunchly loyal to the Democrats as they are to Labor in Britain.

A close examination of British parties reveals that, in practice, there may be as wide differences *within* a particular political party as there are *between* them. The stereotypes of both British and American political parties tend to stress the differences between the extreme wings of each of the contestants—right-wing Conservatives or Republicans contrasted with left-wing Laborites or Democrats—but the degree of consensus on policy in the middle or median points of the major parties on both sides of the Atlantic is often no less striking. It may even be the case that over such issues as the welfare state or international involvements, the differences in the basic positions of the Democratic and Republican parties have been wider apart than those of Conservatives and Labor. In further trans-Atlantic comparisons, Labor is more egalitarian in philosophy than the Democrats; the Conservatives have a more philosophical basis for their commitment to hierarchy than have the Republicans. Thus Labor is more oriented to the interests of the working classes than are the Democrats, although less so under Wilson than in previous periods; while the Conservatives are probably only rarely more to the right than the Republicans. What is essential in evaluating both British and American parties—and particularly the former, since British parties have so long been pictured in the United States as being poles apart—is that in both countries the parties are different coalitions of ideas and interests, that neither of these parties is nearly as homogeneous as ordinarily supposed, and that there is more overlap in their spectrum of opinions, support, and policies than is generally realized.

DIFFERENCES BETWEEN BRITISH AND AMERICAN PARTIES

The differences that exist between British and American parties are largely organizational and relate to structural factors in the two countries: the single-member districts, the unitary as compared to federal form of government, and the parliamentary in contrast to the presidential system. A noticeable result is in the degree of *centralization*. In the United States, power rests (if at all) with state and local party organizations, and no man can remain a leader of a national party unless he has the support of these organizations. Between elections, in the United States, the national party organizations almost disappear. Furthermore, the turnover at all levels of the American party organization is high. Thus diffuse organization characterizes the American party system, whereas there is much greater permanence in British party organization. A further striking difference is that in the United States, the congressional and presidential parties are far from being the same, while in Great Britain the national organization of each party is concerned only with a single election which determines both the representation in Parliament and the executive. Moreover, although American parties are increasingly concerned with national issues and personalities, the British have a much longer tradition in this regard.

This tendency is encouraged by the smallness of the country and the relative homogeneity of its population. In the United States, as we know, parties must appeal to a great variety of clashing sectional, class, and social interests, and they cannot appeal too wholeheartedly to one without antagonizing the rest. The party that concentrates on the labor vote, for example, may lose the farmer and the middle classes. The party that devotes itself to the industrial East will irritate the West and the South. Any precise commitment to one group may mean a loss of votes from others. No party can win unless it has the support of a combination of groups and sections, and party programs tend to reflect this diversity. It is true that the Republicans emphasize business interests and the value of a balanced budget and are suspicious of the expansion of federal control, while the Democrats identify themselves with social-welfare programs and do not hesitate to use national powers, financial and other, to aid underprivileged groups. This difference between the American parties has at times been sharper than that between the British, all of which accept the social welfare state. Nonetheless, both Republicans and Democrats attempt to appeal to all groups in the community, a factor in the somewhat surprising coalitions that occasionally appear.

British parties are as eager for victory as are American, but their job is somewhat simpler. Sectionalism is less important, although the Scots and the Welsh have distinctive needs and demands and so do certain areas in the north of England. In general, however, the focusing of national life in and around London is paralleled in party organization.

DISCIPLINE

In Great Britain, the attitude and voting of members in Parliament is largely predictable from their party alignment, but this is not the case in Congress. Americans are accustomed to the idea that politics makes strange bedfellows, and in the past they have accepted without much question the alliance of conservative southerners with urban radicals in the Democratic party and the combination of eastern captains of industry with midwestern farmers in the Republican. But one of the recurrent patterns of American politics has been the alignment in Congress of Republican and Democratic conservatives against Republican and Democratic liberals. In neither party have party leaders been able to impose discipline in congressional voting on their nominal followers.

There was a time, during the first part of the nineteenth century, when British parties also were strange and somewhat loose alliances and when advocates and opponents of free trade, imperialism, and progressive social legislation could be found within the ranks of both the Conservative and Liberal parties. This was a time, however, when comparatively few citizens had the right to vote and when, although the sources of their wealth might be different, all voters were drawn from the same well-to-do class. Members of Parliament could be acquainted personally with a large proportion of their electors and hold their seats on the basis of personal rather than party loyalties. There was little need for elaborate political organization.

Even after the Reform Act of 1832, many seats continued, to all intents and purposes, to be pocket boroughs of wealthy landholding or commercial families; and although some attempt was made to organize parties on a more popular scale, they continued to be somewhat unstable alliances of members of Parliament united on personal grounds rather than mass organizations of people bent on promoting some common policy.

It was the extension of the right to vote in 1867 and later years that sharply modified the system. Once the mass of the people could participate in elections, it was no longer possible for the parliamentary candidate to know most of the electors personally. He needed an organization to reach them, and he had to have money to pay for it. But he had no patronage of his own at his disposal, and, unless he was a very wealthy man in his own right, he inevitably turned to the national party for help. In the years after 1867, therefore, both of the large parties were obliged to build up organizations, and by the time of the Conservative electoral victory of 1874 it was clear that political success largely depended on the appeal of the party's program and leader and the effectiveness of the party organization. This was particularly true for Labor when it entered the party arena, for only by solidarity could it hope to match the greater resources of the older parties.

The building of effective party organizations had a far-reaching if unintentional consequence. Once the candidate for Parliament became more dependent for his success on the work and money of the organization than on his own efforts, his personal independence was restricted. If he voted frequently against the party's leaders on important issues, he could hardly expect their organization to support him in the next election. Yet he could not win the election, in most instances, without such support. The result is that the ordinary member of Parliament does not vote against the leaders of his party with the casualness that characterizes much congressional cross-voting in the United States. The member of Congress is mainly dependent on local support and represents local interest, and these interests may disagree with the national leaders or be indifferent to certain national issues. Although there have always been elements of disaffection in each of the major political parties in Great Britain, and split voting on issues of conscience or conviction, ==members of Parliament commonly vote in support of positions assumed by their leaders.==

To follow so closely their party's leaders and program, as British MP's commonly do, would appear intolerable to the average member of the American Congress. The latter likes to think of himself as capable of making up his mind on each issue as it arises and of voting as he thinks right, regardless of his party leader or even of his party platform. To him the behavior of British MP's destroys an element of personal freedom essential to democracy.

Some members of Parliament would agree with this analysis. But others among them would undoubtedly point out that the freedom of the member of Congress is sometimes purchased at the price of party irresponsibility. The president may well find that he uses votes from the opposition party in order to carry through a program or policy on which his own party is split. Thus it is more difficult to place responsibility for particular decisions, at least as far as Congress is concerned. But in Great Britain the voter knows that if the Conservative party is successful in an election, it will have the power to carry out its program; and the same is true of a Labor victory.

Moreover, as we well know, it is quite possible to have a Republican president at the same time that Congress contains more Democrats than Republicans. Not only was this the situation in 1968 when Richard Nixon was first elected president, but it remained so after the congressional elections in 1970. Such a situation is, of course, impossible in Great Britain where the prime minister achieves the country's highest office not because votes have been cast for him directly, or through a special electoral college as in the United States, but because his party has more members in the House of Commons than has any other party. The prime minister and his parliamentary party are thus tied together in Great Britain in a way unknown in the United States. Congressional candidates may be elected "on the coat-tails" of a popular president but this fact may make little difference to how faithfully the congressman votes for "his" president's policies. In Great Britain, as we have noted several times, it is the exception for the MP to break party lines, since he knows that his party's appeal and leaders have been major factors in securing his election, and that future elections may depend on party solidarity.

2 HOW THE PARTIES ARE ORGANIZED

British political parties are among the largest in the world. Nearly one-quarter of all those eligible for the franchise belong to one or another of the political parties. The Labor party can boast of by far the largest number, something over seven million, most of them affiliated trade union members, but in the early 1960s some eight hundred thousand in constituency organizations. The Conservatives count nearly three million, an unusually high total for a right-wing party. One-fifth to one-quarter of those who customarily vote Conservative are members of the party's organization, whereas only about one-thirteenth or one-fourteenth of those who normally vote Labor are enrolled as individual members. Many Labor supporters, of course, are enrolled through the unions. The big increase in the number of individual Labor members came at the end of the war, just before and after the major electoral success of 1945. The Conservatives with a mammoth effort trebled their membership in the late forties and early fifties.

The next section describes the formal extra-parliamentary structure of individual British parties and also indicates organizational developments between the elections of 1966 and 1970. In this way it will be possible to gain a better understanding of the character of the parties, how they work in and out of office, and what is involved in preparing for an election.

THE CONSERVATIVE PARTY

The Conservatives pride themselves on being a national party, drawing support, as they do, from all segments of society, and standing for social order, modernity, and individual initiative. For the past century, they have distinguished themselves in promoting compromises and concessions in response to changing conditions that have eased and helped to reconcile the conflicts of different classes in British society. The party is not based on dogma but on principles so broad as to be capable of the widest possible interpretation. A clear indication of this breadth of principle is that Enoch Powell, whom Heath expelled from the Conservative shadow cabinet (the party leadership while in opposition) in 1968 for an inflammatory speech on immigration, still campaigned for the Tories in 1970.

Although committed to social welfare—which they differentiate sharply from socialism—Conservatives maintain that the state should only do for individuals what they cannot do adequately for themselves. Thus the party is dedicated to limited government to the degree that is possible in a complex industrial world. Its leaders believe that while the state can establish the framework for a good life, individuals and groups should develop their own ways to realize it.

Conservatives take special pride in traditional institutions—the monarchy, Parliament, and law—but they also look on them as efficient instruments of modern society that should constantly be subjected to scrutiny and open to change. They accept public ownership (as with BBC) when convinced it is the most practical expedient to meet a specific need. Edward Heath's particular concern for efficient administration is rooted in the Toryism of Disraeli, Pitt, and Peel. Never "little Englanders," Conservatives view foreign policy primarily as a means of advancing and protecting British interests. Policies toward the Soviet Union or South Africa are looked on, therefore, from the perspective of aiding trade or ensuring peace rather than of standards derived from the character of their regimes. This explains the Heath government's attitude to the sale of arms to South Africa.

The Conservatives thus combine breadth of philosophy with some hard-headed notions about government and policies. They appeal nationally but continue to believe in a natural hierarchy of ability, if no longer officially in a hierarchy of birth and status. Thus they counterpoise to Labor's emphasis on egalitarianism what they believe to be a more natural, and therefore more lasting, view of society based on the differences in men's capacities, energies, and achievements.

The party structure

Historically, the Conservative party came into existence *inside* Parliament and only subsequently reached outside for electoral organization. This is the reason why the constituency units are known as associations. These associations tend to function like clubs. In middle-class districts, where the Conservatives are strongest, it is often "the thing to do" to belong to the local Conservative party organization, just as it is to belong to other accepted social groups. While the associations are open to all who care to participate, their middle-class leadership provides a flavor, which may not appeal to the less well-to-do in the community.

Active constituencies have a hierarchy of leaders, a few at the top in the constituency offices and others holding posts in the association's component sections, the ward branches, and women's and youth groups. Formal decisions are taken in the constituency's Executive Committee, which includes representatives of all such groups, but since that body includes about fifty or more members, it elects a smaller group known as the General Purposes Committee, which generally makes the decisions. The key decision, of course, is the selection of the candidate, and it is this small group that exercises paramount influence in this matter as well as all others.

Manual workers are almost entirely absent from local Conservative leadership—as, indeed, they are also from Conservative benches in

Parliament—although they will form a substantial proportion of the voters in a constituency. In Greenwich, for example, a 1950 survey found that lower-income groups formed 60 percent of the voters but only 9 percent of the leaders. National headquarters deplores the over-representation of the middle class in constituency organizations and their general apathy in performing an integrating role within their segments of society. It made strong, but relatively unsuccessful, efforts between the two elections to persuade constituency associations to become more representative and also to modernize their organization, particularly in the cities. It had more effect in getting the local associations to raise more money and to pay higher salaries to the professional party agents who carry much of the responsibility for organizing campaigns. It is largely due to these efforts that the number of agents remained as high in 1970 as in 1966.

In the past, local Conservative associations had tended to choose candidates who could pay their own campaign expenses and contribute heavily to party funds. In 1948, however, sensitive to the charge of being the party of wealth, the Conservatives had accepted the far-reaching recommendations of the Maxwell Fyfe Committee on Party Organization that candidates should be relieved of all election expenses and that contributions to party funds by the local MP or a candidate should be restricted to £50 or £25, respectively. Although Conservatives commonly spend twice as much on a campaign as Labor does, financial resources, paradoxically, now play a less important role in the selection of Conservative candidates than of Labor candidates.

Despite their potentially greater resources, the Conservatives found themselves in urgent need of raising funds after the 1966 election. Through a national appeal from the autumn of 1967 to early 1969, they succeeded in raising £2.25 million ($6 million), over £.75 million ($1.8 million) of it from local associations. Nonetheless, although this response once again balanced the Conservative budget, it did not permit spending in the 1970 election on the scale of 1964. Thus while the Conservatives had some financial advantage in the election, they had to depend heavily for success on efficiency, morale, and intraparty communications.

Party machinery

The Conservative party machinery is divided into two almost autonomous structures: one of them is democratic, the other autocratic. The *democratic* organization is the National Union of Conservative and Unionist Associations, which is a federation of the constituency associations and the eleven areas and Scotland into which they are grouped. The *autocratic* organization is that of the party proper, which the party leader controls. He appoints the party chairman (from 1967 to 1970, Anthony Barber, subsequently Chancellor of the Exchequer), the officers, the honorary treasurers, the deputy chairman, who is the chief professional executive and is responsible for the coordination of the work of the Central Office and the Research Department, and the two vice-chairmen, who are responsible for candidates and the women's organization, respectively. The two organizations, although retaining separate identities, interact continuously at both national and area level, a situation epitomized by the fact that the director of organization, the senior of the three directors of Central Office departments, is honorary secretary to the National Union and directly in charge of the Area Offices of the Central Office.

THE NATIONAL UNION   The most prized reward for an ardent volunteer worker in the Conservative party is to be chosen as a delegate to the annual conference of the National Union. Conservatives often claim that their organization is more democratic than that of the Labor party because their constituency units have more autonomy, because each constituency organization has equal representation at the annual conference, and because their representatives to the conference are "free to speak and vote according to their consciences." But the corollary to this equality and freedom is the relative lack of influence, let alone power of the conference and, indeed, of the National Union as a whole. The conference, in particular, with its four thousand or more participants is a rally of the faithful, more concerned with politics than administration. In the past, its hundreds of resolutions and wide-ranging discussions had not even been attended by the party leader until they were over, and he then appeared to give a prepared speech often unrelated to what the delegates had been discussing. Since 1965, however, Heath has made it a practice to attend during the debates of the conference, answering even sharp comments from the floor, and speaking to those points most at issue in the minds of conference members.

The official top decision-making organ of the National Union, the Central Council, with its 3,000 members, who are mainly appointed by constituency associations, is much too large to be effective, and so, in practice, is the Executive Committee, which has 150 members. Thus the real work is done by the General Purposes Committee of 54 members chosen from the executive. Both these latter organizations are primarily elected from below, but the leader and chief whip sit ex officio in both, and some seats are reserved for representatives of the parliamentary party and the party organization and for a few selected members. A further link between the National Union and the party organization is the Advisory Committee on Policy, which similarly includes representatives from the National Union, the parliamentary party, the party organization, and selected members. Technically, the Advisory Committee on Policy, at present under the chairmanship of the deputy leader of the party, is directly responsible to the leader of the party and is serviced by the Research Department, whose director is ex-officio secretary.

The smaller and higher the organ, the lower the percentage of party workers. Jean Blondel reported in 1963 that while party workers held 80 percent of the seats on the Executive Committee, allocated carefully to represent the variety of interests in the constituency associations, and 67 percent on the General Purposes Committee, only 36 percent—that is, eight out of twenty-two—of those on the Advisory Committee on Policy.[2] Parliamentary members held their highest proportion of members on the latter body, and the chairman of the 1922 Committee of Backbenchers sits on all three bodies. Selected members were held to strengthen the party bureaucracy on the Advisory Committee on Policy and the party workers on the two chief National Union committees.

The selected members provide the closest approach to representation of supporting interests within the Conservative structure, making a sharp contrast to the Labor party organization's heavy official representation of associated groups, especially the trade unions. At the same time, all those on national organs of the Conservative party are looked on as representing groups or bodies with distinctive interests: the hierarchy of the National Union, the parliamentary party, and Central Office at one level, and also a wide variety of subgroups representing different areas of the country as well as women, young Conservatives, trade unionists, frontbenchers and backbenchers. Thus, whatever their power, they provide the means by which the leader can keep in touch with all sections of the party and through them learn the currents of opinion in their constituencies.

THE CENTRAL OFFICE   The party leader, as we have seen, controls the Conservative Central Office (32 Smith Square) and appoints the chief officials of the party bureaucracy. This centralization of authority within the party proper provides the leader of the Conservative party with great power and also great responsibility. Confronted with a decline in organization and a generally dispirited party after the electoral defeats of 1964 and 1966, Heath and his officials had three major organizational tasks: to bridge the divisions that had developed between the shadow cabinet and the backbenchers, between MP's and the constituency associations, and between local standard bearers and the electorate. In addition, there was great need to meet a threatening financial situation and to adopt more modern electioneering techniques, particularly those using market research.

Their "quiet revolution," even though not fully realized, met a number of visible needs. New top officials, particularly with the appointment in 1967 of Anthony Barber as party chairman, stimulated Central Office efficiency and forged closer bonds with the centrally appointed area chairmen and some eighty key or

---

[2] Jean Blondel, *Voters, Parties, and Leaders: The Social Fabric of British Politics*, p. 118.

HOW THE PARTIES ARE ORGANIZED

Structure of the Conservative Party

LEADER

Formulates party policy
Appoints all principal officials
When in opposition chooses the shadow cabinet
Holds office without need for reelection

ADVISORY COMMITTEE ON POLICY

22 Members

GENERAL PURPOSES COMMITTEE

54 Members

PARLIAMENTARY PARTY

Conservative Members of Parliament: Commons and Lords

(Backbenchers are organized into 1922 Committee)

Executive Committee of National Union

Channel of contact for leaders with party membership
Occasionally makes studies
Nominates officers of National Union
Meets monthly

150 Members:
Leader and principal party officials
Representatives from provincial area councils

Central Office

National Union of Conservative and Unionist Associations Annual Conference

Acts only in advisory capacity
Has no policy-making authority

Eligible to attend:
Members of the Central Council
2 additional representatives from each constituency
Election agents and organizers

Central Council

Governing body of National Union and can amend its rules
Mainly a ceremonial organization
Meets twice a year

3,000 Members:
Leader and principal party officials
Conservative MP's and prospective candidates
Executive Committee members
4 representatives from each constituency organization
Representatives from central organizations and provincial area councils

Local Constituency Units and Associations

"critical" constituencies where the electoral outcome might not be sure. There was a major expansion of the Research Department, which is particularly important when a party is in opposition and thus without civil service help. Bureaucratic expenses were cut and moderately successful financial campaigns carried out. Confronted with the possibility of reduced business contributions under new Labor legislation requiring their disclosure, special appeals were made to the constituencies, and regional teams toured the country in search of support—"eighteen months of eating for the Party," one participant called it.[3] Moreover, party accounts were published for the first time. A redrawn Central Office list of recommended parliamentary candidates (customarily prepared after each election) was openly aimed at bringing younger, more broadly representative members into Parliament, a party objec-

[3] David E. Butler and Michael Pinto-Duschinsky, *The British General Election of 1970*, p. 97.

tive since Maxwell Fyfe's reforms, proposed in 1948. A special committee examined all aspects of the profession of party agents and recommended higher salaries for these key figures in electoral activities. Technical advice was sought on how best to capitalize on the free radio and television time allowed parties. Moreover, market research techniques were heavily drawn on, particularly, as we shall see, during the 1970 election campaign to keep Mr. Heath constantly abreast of the impact of particular issues upon the voters.

THE PARLIAMENTARY CONSERVATIVE PARTY
Within the parliamentary Conservative party, the leader commonly has the same overriding personal power that the formal organization of the party provides him, but he is subject to much more ultimate restraint. Unlike the Labor leader, the Conservative leader chooses his own shadow cabinet when out of office. When the party is in power, Conservative ministers do not even attend the meetings of Conservative backbenchers. The leader alone determines how the party whip is to be used or whether a member is to be expelled from the party. Moreover, the formulation of party policy is officially the leader's prerogative.

Yet the name given to the meeting of Conservative backbenchers, the "1922 Committee," carries a moral that few Conservative leaders can overlook. It was the famous Carlton Club meeting of Conservative MP's in October 1922 that led to the downfall of Austen Chamberlain, leader of the Conservative party in the House of Commons. The organization of private (that is, non-officeholding) Conservative MP's into the 1922 Committee followed almost immediately thereafter. Contrary to Labor party practice, ministers may attend the meetings of this group only by invitation. This is true also of the specialized committees of the Conservative parliamentary party, which have no fixed personnel, as is common with Labor. Thus there is a significant degree of organization among the Conservative private members that exists apart from ministerial direction and influence. And while the 1922 Committee is the parliamentary equivalent of the National Union—that is, it is a sounding board of sentiment, not a policymaker—the leader can remain such only if he retains the confidence of his parliamentary members. This fact explains the apparent paradox that three Conservative leaders, Austen Chamberlain, Neville Chamberlain (to make way for Winston Churchill's leadership in 1940), and, although less obviously, Sir Alec Douglas-Home in 1965 have found themselves compelled to give up their office.

Although Sir Alec Douglas-Home lost the basic confidence of his party in his ability to win a future election, he established two important innovations: the presence of the leader throughout the annual conference (although, as we have seen, Heath was the first to implement the practice); and a formalized procedure for the selection of the Conservative leader. Secrecy and agreement on a particular individual by certain Conservative "notables" (sometimes called "the magic circle" or "country house politics" or, more elegantly, the "customary processes of consultation") had played a disproportionate and subsequently bitterly criticized role in the selection of both Macmillan in 1957 and Douglas-Home in 1963.

The new procedure, approved by the national Union Executive and other relevant agencies, was formally announced in February 1965 and was thus available, after Douglas-Home's subsequent resignation, for the election of Edward Heath later that year. It is similar, although not identical, to the procedure used by the Labor party. In the event that there are more than two candidates, although this has never yet happened, Labor has an eliminating ballot in which all members of the parliamentary Labor party can vote. The decisive contest is between two names, as in Wilson's hard-fought and closely won battle with George Brown for the election in October 1963.

The Conservative procedure, followed only when a new leader is needed, provides for three ballots, with the voting limited to Conservative MP's in the Commons. The chairman of the 1922 Committee of backbenchers directs the process. Nominations are published, although the names of proposers and seconders remain secret; to win on the first ballot a candidate needs to get both an overall majority and 15 percent more of the votes than any other candidate, a stiff hurdle. On the second ballot, fresh nominations are required (providing scope for further consultative processes), but an overall majority is sufficient. If a third ballot is needed, a preferential voting system is used to bring the new leader a decisive majority. Once this crucial stage of selection has been completed, the choice is presented to the traditional party meeting in Church House, numbering 1,076 persons in 1965, made up of Conservative members of the Commons and Lords, candidates for election, and the nonparliamentary members of the National Union Executive. Although in a fifty-year period the name proposed to this final party meeting has never been challenged, the process would begin all over again if such were to happen.

In practice, the new Conservative process for selecting the leader worked smoothly and quickly following Home's resignation on July 22, 1965. The first ballot results were as follows: Heath, 150 votes; Maudling, 133; and Powell, 15. Both Maudling and Powell withdrew, and Heath was unanimously accepted at the traditional meeting on August 2, 1965. Not only had the Conservatives used a new and open process for choosing their leader, but Heath was the first Conservative in over forty years not to become both party leader and prime minister at virtually the same moment. The subsequent defeat of his party in 1966 and its opposition role in Parliament confronted him with greater difficulties in reknitting the party's unity and developing its forward look than faced his predecessors. Only with the Conservative victory in 1970 did Heath come fully into his own.

THE LABOR PARTY

The Labor party, founded to advance the purposes of the working class and still committed to its interests, also thinks of itself as a national party. Harold Wilson's goal has been to establish Labor as the dominant ruling party in Great Britain in place of the Conservatives. By edging Labor's policies into the middle, he sought to continue the combination of working- and middle-class support that had brought the party its dramatic victory in 1966.

Although both Labor and the Conservatives strive to appeal to a broad spectrum of support, there remain basic differences between them in philosophy and approach. These differences revolve around egalitarianism versus hierarchy. Labor believes in equality of treatment, equality of respect, and the equal right of each person to happiness, security, and fulfillment. Where the Conservatives believe men should be free to rise to the limits of their abilities and opportunities, and are suspicious of attempts to legislate greater social equality, Labor's objectives are to abolish gross inequalities in the distribution of wealth, the continuing and pervasive inequalities in the treatment of persons resulting from class (identified by accent, schooling, occupation, and type of home), and inequalities in power. The Conservatives resist the extension of government intervention both because it results in an unwieldy bureaucracy and because it tampers with the existing order of society and thus appears to them harmful and inherently likely to fail. Labor, in contrast, calls on the power of the state to levy taxation in the interests of the masses, to provide services for all, especially through public expenditures on schools, hospitals, and welfare, to control prices, and to regulate commerce. In particular, the two parties may not differ as widely when in office as these distinctions suggest, but their basic impulses are different as are the motives behind their calculated policies.

Confronting the electorate in 1970, Labor had the advantages of office and the choice of a precise date at which to test their fortunes but the handicap of a succession of economic and political difficulties since its 1966 electoral victory. The continuing and worsening balance-of-payment crisis, unsolved by increased taxation, had led in November 1967 to the devaluation of the pound against which the Labor government had struggled, probably for too long. Rhodesia's unconstitutional, unilateral declaration of independence, solved neither by bargaining nor by sanctions, had damaged Britain's reputation in the Commonwealth and the United Nations. Labor's application to join the Common Market had been even more peremptorily refused by President de Gaulle than the earlier application by the Conservatives. There was continued and severe tension between the Labor government and the trade unions over prices, wages, income policies, and formal and informal strikes. The effort to solve the situation through the Trade Disputes Bill of 1969 had roused such strong party and trade union opposition that it had to be abandoned. But on the more positive side, and probably the cause of Labor's much improved standing in opinion polls and the borough (town) elections in the spring of 1970, a healthy balance-of-payments surplus had appeared at last and, less desirable, a round of wage increases to balance continued heavy taxation and the rising cost of goods.

The Labor party's fortunes in the constituencies had followed fairly closely the national situation. From 1966 to 1969, there was a sharp decline in party membership in the constituencies, which brought the membership probably as low as 300,000 by the spring of 1970, well under half of what it had been several years before. The number of constituency parties with more than 2,000 members fell from 68 in 1966 to 23 in 1969. The number of full-time party agents sank in the same period from 204 to 146. In all these respects, improvement was noticeable as national morale rose, but Labor's organization, never so efficient as that of the Conservatives, was still lagging far behind by the time of the election campaign. In part, this was also due to Harold Wilson's playing down of the electoral role of Labor's national organization and to the party's extraordinarily complex, not to say cumbersome, structure.

Party structure

The Labor party's organization is one of the most complicated designed by the mind of man. From the time of its foundation the party has been composed of a number of autonomous organizations that have allied themselves for political purposes; in allotting each organization its appropriate representation in the general framework and in balancing the different, and sometimes jealous, groups against one another, simplicity and clarity of structure were early casualties.

Four types of organization have combined to make the Labor party: socialist and other societies composed for the most part of intellectuals and professional men; trade unions; cooperatives; and local and regional organizations of the Labor party.

SOCIALIST AND OTHER SOCIETIES In the first group are the Fabian Society, the Socialist Medical Association, the Jewish Socialist Labor party, and the National Association of Labor Teachers. In numbers these organizations are very small, and the terms of membership in the party now make it impossible for them to develop programs and policies of their own. In the past, however, as the history of the Fabian Society has indicated, they had a distinguished part in the development of the party's philosophy, and their research facilities and professional services still contribute new ideas and useful reports.

TRADE UNIONS The most striking feature of Labor party membership, at least to an American, is the predominance of trade unionists. The long alliance between the Labor party and the bulk of British trade unions traditionally rested on a deeply felt identity of interest and on mutual confidence. Trade union participation in politics has always been looked on as subsidiary to collective bargaining, and its importance to the unions varies in proportion to the effectiveness of the party in furthering their interests.

As long as Ernest Bevin and Arthur Deakin controlled the mammoth Transport and General Workers' Union (TGWU), which casts one-sixth of the votes at Labor party conferences, the three major unions acted as a homogeneous and loyal group, automatically supporting the policies of the National Executive Committee (NEC). But beginning in the late fifties, trade unions have become much more divided in their allegiances. Frank Cousins of the Transport and General Workers' Union and Jack Jones, who succeeded him in 1968, are well to the left in political orientation and have not hesitated on occasions to throw their weight against Harold Wilson and other parliamentary leaders in the annual conference and in the National Executive Committee. Moreover, the struggle between the Labor government and the unions over the Trade Disputes Bill of 1969 brought their relations to a low point.

This has been a matter for great concern because the unions furnish the bulk of the Labor party's membership and also more than 80 percent of its annual income. Faced with a substantial deficit after the 1970 election, the Labor party naturally turned to its surest source of financial support, the trade unions. Through a curious, partly personal, partly union arrangement, a so-called political levy goes automatically from each worker's wages into his union's political fund unless the worker signs a statement opposing the contribution. (In 1927, following the general strike of the year before, the Trades Dispute Act required workers to volunteer to pay the political levy. The Labor government reversed the process in 1946.) The fee up to 1971 (amounting to seven and a half pence or ten cents) is less than half that paid by individual constituency members. The Labor party hopes to double or even nearly triple the size of the political levy to enable it to maintain a healthy financial situation in the years to come. The process for approval, however, is as complex as are most changes within the Labor party structure. The National Executive had already taken the necessary first step by March 1971 in approving talks with the unions; the latter must then be approached individually by party leaders; and whatever figure is agreed upon is then taken to the party's annual conference.[4] Thereafter, many of the unions themselves will require constitutional changes before the levy can be raised, and this process requires a rules revision conference. Labor's need for more funds, therefore, will not be met quickly.

Oddly enough, each union can decide the number of its members on whom to pay affiliation fees to the party. Since votes at the annual party conference depend on how many affiliation fees are paid (one vote for every five thousand paid-up members), union leaders must decide between their desire for votes and for funds for their own election budgets.

Union election budgets are particularly important for those unions that sponsor their own parliamentary candidates. Union candidates[5] generally stand for relatively safe seats, and in 1970, 112 of their candidates won out of the 137 seats they contested. (In 1966, they had elected 132 out of 138 candidates.) The Mineworkers secured the largest share, 20, but the Transport and General Workers' Union took 19, and the Amalgamated Union of Engineers and Foundrymen (AEF), 16. Twenty other unions shared in union-sponsored parliamentary representation. Trade unionists have only rarely been influential MP's, because they are often selected more as a reward for past services than for their brilliance or eloquence. The left-wing leadership of the TGWU and AEF had little effect on their choice of candidates. The Wilson Report after Labor's defeat in 1955 criticized the unions for not contesting or at least supporting campaigns in marginal seats, but the smaller number of union-sponsored MP's resulted from the general decline in Labor's representation, not from particularly difficult constituencies.

THE COOPERATIVES The cooperatives have been a disappointment to Labor. Nearly two out of every three families belong to societies engaged in cooperative trading and manufacturing. Their active support could represent an enormous addition to the party's strength, both in money and in membership. But only the Royal Arsenal Cooperative Society, one of the oldest and largest of cooperative societies, has affiliated with the Labor party at the national level, though the London Cooperative Society (LCS), urged by their left-wing Young Chartist group, was considering affiliation in 1971. The cooperatives have had a political party of their own since 1917—the Cooperative party—and the LCS is its largest society. Although this party has refused to affiliate nationally with the Labor party, it has an electoral arrangement with it to run candidates as "Cooperative and Labor" in thirty constituencies. Although this limit is maintained, the National Executive of the Labor party has agreed that in addition to the fifteen seats won in 1970, the Cooperative party in the future can contest three Labor-held seats "if vacancies occur," and four in "favorable constituencies," if it will also

---

[4] Affiliation fees amounted to £306,939 ($736,653) in 1970, of which the trade unions had contributed £272,145 ($653,148) and local Labor parties only £33,729 ($70,949). Faced with an estimated deficit by mid-1971 of £153,000 ($357,200) and a projected deficit of £398,000 ($955,200) by 1975, the NEC requested the annual conference in September 1971 to provide substantial increases in both membership and affiliation fees to increase the income of Transport House to £1,000,000 ($2,400,000) over the next five years, so as to wipe out the deficit and greatly improve central party organization.

[5] It is a party rule that every Labor candidate must belong to a union appropriate to his occupation, if there is one, but this affiliation is often merely nominal.

fight eight in "difficult constituencies." With these concessions, the Cooperative party hopes to increase its representation in the House of Commons to twenty-two. MP's who carry this designation normally vote with the Labor party, although they did not do so over SET (see Chapter 1, Section 3). Although the arrangement does not seem conducive to an enthusiastic relationship, it appears to be the best possible for both sides under present circumstances.

LOCAL ORGANIZATION: THE CONSTITUENCY PARTIES   If the trade unions provide most of the membership and the money, the Labor party's local organizations provide most of the energy and do most of the work. Membership in these organizations is open to anyone who formally accepts the party's program by signing a membership card and paying a small monthly fee. Some people who already belong to the party by virtue of their membership in trade unions or socialist societies also enroll as individual members of the constituency organizations.

The most energetic, the most sincere, and the most ideologically inclined are likely to be found within the constituency members. It is the party militants who collect the party's dues, sell and distribute its literature, organize entertainments and bazaars in order to raise money, and do the hard work of electioneering. Perhaps two-fifths of those enrolled in Labor party organizations can be termed activists, a considerably higher proportion than in Conservative associations. At the same time, far from all Labor party members are left-wing socialists, although there are proportionately more of that disposition among party members than among Labor voters. The proportion of manual workers among Labor voters and Labor party members appears about the same.

Like the Conservatives, the structure of local parties (which are broadly grouped into eleven regions) includes both a large organization that technically makes the decisions and a much smaller body that actually does so. The larger body, called by Labor the General Management Committee, not only has representatives of the wards and women's and youth groups but also of the trade unions and other affiliated organizations. The more effective Executive Committee is composed, as with the Conservatives, of members elected by the larger body. The leaders of local Labor organizations are drawn more from the middle class than this class's proportion among members would indicate, and the same is now true of representation in Parliament. But there is much less of a gap in attitude between these leaders and those members who are manual workers than is found in Conservative associations, for the principles of equality and solidarity still extend throughout local Labor organizations. The old alliance between workers and intelligentsia is reflected in most Labor constituencies, with those white-collar workers who have not renounced their ties with manual workers acting as a bridge between the latter and the teachers who form a heavy proportion of Labor's local middle-class activists.

It used to be said that a major source of tension within the Labor party was between the socialist radicals in the constituency parties and the basically conservative trade union. Since left-wingers took over two of the largest unions, the TGWU and AEF, some of the resolutions and apparently also the voting at the annual conference have been as much to the left from these sources as from the constituencies. The sharpest differences in policies, in fact, have been between those backed by the parliamentary leadership, or by the NEC, on the one hand, and those of left-wing elements from whatever source. Wilson, in particular, has felt that the party should not only be loyal to the broad interests of the masses but also appeal to the middle class with a moderate outlook characteristic of a prosperous society. The militants, in contrast, wish to keep more of the socialist dogma to the fore. In foreign policy the moderates support the special relationship with the United States, while the militants are openly critical of what they term American capitalist imperialism and the American involvement in Vietnam. But while both groups wish to keep all channels open with the Soviet Union and Eastern Europe, neither side endorses Communist dictatorships, and there has been no disposition to join forces with the Communists in the kind of left-wing alignments experimented with in France.

Party machinery

Federal structures are always complicated and that of the Labor party is particularly so. In theory its ruling body is the annual conference, which leads to the claim that policies endorsed by the conference and by the NEC, which the conference elects, should be binding on the parliamentary party. This claim results from the historical evolution of the party, which, unlike that of the Conservative party, originated *outside* of Parliament and extended its activities into that body to secure the power to implement its policies. (Strictly speaking, the name "Labor party" belongs to the mass membership outside Parliament but includes those inside who are correctly entitled "The Parliamentary Labor party.") But, in practice, all the conventions of the parliamentary system thrust the ultimate decision-making authority into the hands of the parliamentary party and its leader whom Labor MP's, and not the conference, elect. Thus the leader of the parliamentary party becomes automatically leader of the party. There is also a National Council of Labor with trade unions, cooperatives, NEC, and MP representation, but it plays only a minor advisory role.

The conference and the NEC have certain powers, however, that have never been challenged. A two-thirds majority of a card vote at the annual conference can determine "what specific proposals of legislative, financial or administrative reform shall be included in the Party programme" (Clause V of the Labor party constitution). In November 1968, the NEC decided that when government policies differed substantially from conference resolutions, the relevant ministers should be requested to explain why. Moreover, the Parliamentary Committee of Labor MP's must meet with the NEC to decide what items are to be included in the election manifesto. This interaction assures expression of views of the membership party and transmittal of information, but the decision-making remains firmly in the hands of the parliamentary party as long as it is in office.

THE ANNUAL CONFERENCE Labor's annual conference is considerably smaller in size than its Conservative counterpart, since only about twelve hundred attend, compared to the three or four thousand at the Conservative conference. The conference lasts five days, longer than the Conservatives' annual gathering, and constitutes a serious drain on the resources of the delegates.

The Labor conference has changed its role since the party has become an effective contestant for supreme political power. Prior to that time, the conference could expect to be a major factor in molding the party's national policies. Once the parliamentary Labor party became the government, however, this situation necessarily changed. Decisions on policy and tactics became the prerogatives of the party *in* Parliament, and the conference became more of a sounding board to gauge party opinion *outside* Parliament. Transport House (Labor's head office) has never been reconciled to this development, inevitable though it is when Labor is in office. After Labor lost the election in 1970 and confronted the crucial decision of whether or not to support entry into the Common Market, there was sharp disagreement as to whether it would be the conference, called into an almost unprecedented special session in July 1971, that would make that decision or the parliamentary leaders of the party. Wilson insisted, however, in preserving his own ultimate freedom of action on this issue.

The most distinctive feature of Labor's annual conference is the special position of the trade unions. They have the right to send more than half the delegates—a right rarely exercised —and to control five-sixths of the vote. This is because each of the affiliated organizations has one voting card for every five thousand paid-up members or fraction thereof, and there are seventy-nine trade unions, five socialist societies, and one cooperative society affiliated. Each organization, including the constituencies, may propose one resolution (and, later, one amendment to a proposed resolution) for discussion. The organizations know before the conference is held which issues will be taken up, and they may discuss them in advance and instruct their delegates; in this way discussion of issues in local meetings may contribute significantly to the political education of the members.

Structure of the Labor Party

LEADER
When prime minister, selects the Cabinet

CENTRAL OFFICE
Transport House

PARLIAMENTARY LABOR PARTY
Labor Members of Parliament: Commons and Lords
When in opposition, selects the shadow cabinet and annually elects leader

National Council of Labor
Acts largely in advisory capacity

21 Members:
7 members chosen by Trades Union Congress
7 chosen by Cooperative Union
3 chosen by National Executive Committee
4 chosen by parliamentary Labor party

National Executive Committee
Directs and controls the activity of the Labor party *outside* Parliament

28 Members:
Leader and deputy leader, ex officio
12 chosen by trade union delegates
7 by local party organizations
3 by socialists, professional, and cooperative delegates
5 women and treasurer chosen by the whole conference

Annual Party Conference
Considers the broad outlines of party policy
Can amend the constitution of the Labor party

Eligible to attend but no votes unless they are delegates:
Labor MP's and peers and prospective candidates
Agents
Party officials

Eligible to vote:
Delegates from trade unions, constituency and borough parties, societies affiliated with the Labor party, and federations of labor parties

Trade Unions | **Local Party Organizations** | **Socialist and Professional Societies and Royal Arsenal Cooperative Society**

It used to be that the party leadership could count on the trade union vote to swing decisions in the conference the way it wished, but, as already suggested, the large unions with left-wing leadership have used their votes several times to defeat policies that party leaders have endorsed. In 1960, the TGWU, AEF, and two other unions voted down the leaders' defense policies, a sharp indication that when the party is in opposition the support of the unions should not be taken for granted. More disturbing were two defeats in conference while the party was in office: the first in 1967 opposing the government's stand on American policy in Vietnam; and the second, and more serious since a matter of domestic policy, a demand in 1968 for the repeal of the prices and incomes legislation. While no party in office will necessarily feel bound to react to a negative vote in conference, the leaders are anxious to avoid such a public rebuff and may well temper their policies to avoid it.

THE NATIONAL EXECUTIVE COMMITTEE The National Executive Committee, whose members are chosen annually by the conference, provides leadership for the latter and also manages party affairs between conferences and directs its head office. The committee is the most powerful organ in the Labor party, outside of Parliament, and potentially it might challenge the decision-making power of the parliamentary party. In practice, however, its composition makes such a challenge extremely unlikely. Of its twenty-eight members (the parliamentary leader and deputy leader are ex officio), twelve are elected by the trade union delegates, seven by the constituency parties and federation delegates, one by the delegates of the socialist, cooperative, and professional associations, and six—five women and the treasurer—by the conference as a whole. Since the General Council of the Trades Union Congress will not allow its members to stand for the NEC, the trade union members are rarely of high distinction or influence. Most important, however, is the fact that the delegates' choices are so frequently MP's that the latter generally form a majority of the members of the NEC. Especially when the party is in office, they are naturally reluctant to put any impediments in the government's way.

The NEC is responsible for discipline within the party. It can withdraw or refuse endorsement of candidates and, in contrast to the Conservatives, Labor runs an official candidate against an unendorsed one. It can expel individuals, but on several occasions it has also welcomed back errant members it had formerly ejected. It can disaffiliate an organization, a severe penalty that results in a branch losing the financial support of the local trade unions. The NEC, working through subcommittees, also develops policy statements to be submitted to the annual conference and, as already noted, shares decisions with the relevant committee of the parliamentary party as to what goes into the party's manifesto. Beyond these specific powers, the NEC controls Labor's head office, Transport House, whereas it is the Conservative leader who has that authority within his party. Transport House is chiefly responsible for organizing and coordinating Labor party activities throughout the country, and its lack of effectiveness prior to the 1970 election was a severe handicap to Labor's electoral campaign.

THE HEAD OFFICE Not particularly good even at the time of the previous election, Labor party organization deteriorated steadily between 1966 and the end of 1968. Many old-line Labor stalwarts resisted modernization, and little had been done to respond to the highly critical 1955 report on party organization by Wilson himself. Moreover, there were tensions between Wilson and Transport House, since the latter wished to publicize the socialist principles on which the party had been founded while the prime minister preferred to emphasize specific programs in wooing the electorate. A further source of division resulted from the choice in 1968 as general secretary of the TGWU's second in command, Harry Nicholas, instead of Wilson's nominee. Moreover, while Nicholas inspired some much needed constituency enthusiasm, he never gained much reputation in his role as administrator. A scheme to recruit more constituency agents did not get under way until mid-1969 and did little more than stop the decline that had been occurring in their numbers. Despite agonized complaints about lack of money, this latter issue was less significant than the stultifying caution that kept publicity and organizational efforts at a low and unimaginative level. Not until August 1969 was a campaign committee formed. Although warned by Wilson in general terms to keep its options open, this committee appears, like Transport House itself, to have geared its program to an October election. When the June date was announced, it became, indeed, the "do-it-yourself" campaign that had been prophesied.

THE PARLIAMENTARY LABOR PARTY   Although the extraparliamentary organization of the Labor party is the major channel through which the opinions of its members can be expressed, it is the parliamentary Labor party that is the real center of power within the party. This is because only the parliamentary members of the Labor party can directly affect national policy. Moreover, it is the parliamentary Labor party that elects the party leader; if the party is out of office, it reelects him annually, commonly by acclamation.

It is worth noting that the Labor party has displayed more loyalty to its leaders and less ruthlessness than the Conservative party. Despite widespread dissatisfaction with Ramsay MacDonald's attitude toward socialist goals, it was his decision to form a national government in 1931 that precipitated the break. (The Labor party maintained a solid front against participation.) When George Lansbury in 1935 confronted an irreconcilable conflict between his party's support of sanctions over Italy's attack on Ethiopia and his own pacifism, it was his decision to resign. Despite Gaitskell's unpopular attacks on Clause IV of the party's constitution, which pledged the party to try to establish a society based on "the common ownership of the means of production, distribution and exchange . . . ," and despite his opposition to unilateral nuclear disarmament, which the party conference approved by a narrow margin in 1960, Gaitskell was reelected party leader in the unprecedented contest with Wilson later the same year.

The fact that when the party is in power its leader is the most powerful political figure in Great Britain gives him at all times an extraordinary degree of influence and authority throughout the whole party. At the same time, Labor leaders are expected to listen to criticism, both within the party as a whole and within the parliamentary Labor party, and to provide personal leadership on all occasions. Thus party leaders always attend the sessions of the annual party conference, direct discussions, and reply directly to questions. When the parliamentary Labor party is in a minority in Parliament, meetings of caucus—which is made up of all Labor members in both the Commons and the Lords—are held at least once a week to discuss and decide party policy, and these members elect the shadow cabinet that occupies the front opposition benches.

Even when the Labor party is in power, however, special care is taken to consult party members outside the Cabinet. A liaison committee composed of some backbenchers, the chief whip, the Lord President of the Council, and one representative of the Labor peers acts as intermediary between the Cabinet and the party. The parliamentary party as a whole continues to meet at least once every two weeks for policy discussions in which the prime minister and Cabinet members frequently participate.

The parliamentary Labor party can expel MP's from the parliamentary caucus (the technical expression is "to withdraw the whip" —that is, not to send notices of party meetings). The most notable dissident, Aneurin Bevan, was temporarily expelled on several occasions. But, under normal circumstances, whether the party is in office or out, unity is maintained in the parliamentary Labor party less by rewards and punishments than by the awareness that only a united party can hope to gain and maintain parliamentary power. When so serious a source of division appeared, however, as whether or not to support entry into the Common Market, differences of approach emerged to complicate, as in the early 1960s, the maintenance of unity in the parliamentary party.

THE MINOR PARTIES

In a parliamentary situation in which it is a foregone conclusion that one or the other of the two major parties will form the next government, the prospects for minor parties are depressing. Yet rarely have there seemed such good opportunities for them to command attention as after 1966. The drastic fall in Labor support in the country was reflected in their plummeting in the polls from 47 percent in 1966 to 26 percent in 1968. Among the Conservatives, dispirited by two defeats, the new leader was still largely an unknown figure.

The Liberals could be expected to be the chief beneficiaries from the apparent decline of the two major parties. Prior to the rise of Labor, the Liberals themselves had formed one of Great Britain's two major parties, and they were still capable of securing a substantial number of votes throughout the country as "the party of principle." In more limited areas, Welsh and Scottish nationalism had spawned distinctive political parties that were feeding on local discontents. On the extreme left was the perennial Communist party, although, rather surprisingly, no Maoist or New Left political movements comparable to those on the Continent. On the extreme right were dissident groups, the National Front, the British National party, and a small Labor break-away, the National Democratic party. Yet in the event, none of these parties or groups did well in the 1970 election.

The Liberal party

The Liberal party had made its best showings in the 1964 and 1966 elections with 3 million and then almost 2.5 million votes in 1966 and 12 MP's (later raised to 13). On the other hand, despite Labor's tenuous majority from 1964 to 1966, that party had made no overtures to the Liberals, and Wilson's favored middle-of-the-road stance in policies undercut the Liberal claim that the electorate should turn to them to provide a radical, nonsocialist alternative to the Conservatives. Faced with this dilemma, the Liberal leader and its best-known figure, Jo Grimond, decided to turn the party over to other hands, and in January 1967, on a badly split vote, Jeremy Thorpe, a vigorous, flamboyant, left-leaning, and opportunistic Etonian, was chosen leader.

But the party had reached the height of its limited effectiveness. It was split between its traditional semiconservative, if anti-Tory, right, its down-to-earth center, and its radical left, within which the Young Liberals' antiapartheid demonstrations against the visit of the South African cricket team earned more publicity than votes. Although the party received enough money before the election to pay off its huge overdraft and to make small contributions to some of its constituency organizations, these funds came almost exclusively from a very few donors. (The party, normally less open about its accounts than either Labor or Conservatives, let it be known after the 1970 election that 85 percent of the contributions in the previous eight months had come from fewer than twenty-five people.) Perhaps above all, their program for dispersed political power through regional assemblies, more standing select committees, a revised tax structure favoring VAT (value-added tax), workers' councils, and 50 percent of votes for workers at annual company meetings failed to provide the attractive middle ground that might have enabled the Liberals to capitalize on public discontent. The electoral returns in 1970 resulted in the loss of a large number of deposits and seven seats, and penned the Liberal victories into the narrowest areas up to that date. Although they still polled over 2 million votes, the total number continued the downward trend from the 1964 pinnacle. This trend boded ill for their future as a party with nation-wide support.

Scottish and Welsh national parties

While the Liberal party failed to capitalize on discontent with Labor policies and Conservative promises, the Scottish National party (SNP) and, to a much lesser extent, Plaid Cymru in Wales, gave dramatic political evidence of the reality of Scottish and Welsh national consciousness. The two regions differ most noticeably in the fact that the linguistic base that is so important in Welsh nationalism is not a significant feature in Scotland. In the latter region it is socio-economic arguments based on the lower standards of living there than in England and the desire for some political devolution that appear to have the strongest effect. Temporarily, the response to these parties raised doubts as to the validity of the assumption that the British party system adequately aggregates the interests of these areas with the interests of England.

Both Scotland and Wales are traditional Labor strongholds, although the Liberals have long been able to elect a few MP's in both areas. In 1966, the Labor party had reached its highest level of support in Scotland, virtually 50 percent of the vote and 46 MP's elected. The Conservatives were markedly in decline with only 20 seats and 37.7 percent of the vote. The SNP came second in the poll in only three seats, while its average vote represented under 15 percent of the total. But thereafter the SNP rapidly increased its number of local branches, which rose from 40 in 1963 to 515 in 1970. It recruited large numbers of young people, who flaunted its distinctive emblem, to reach a total of over 100,000 members in all, and it built a sound financial base largely through running lotteries. In March 1967, the SNP's American-style electioneering brought its percentage of the vote in a Glasgow by-election to 28.2; in November, it captured a presumedly safe Labor seat at Hamilton (Lanarkshire) with a voluble and attractive candidate, Winifred Ewing. The traditional parties were stunned. Labor launched a bitter attack in 1968; the Conservatives finally came out in favor of devolution; the Liberals and SNP mutually rejected the notion of electoral cooperation. In 1970, the SNP fought sixty-five constituencies but, although it polled twice as many votes as in 1966, it was already in decline. Forty-three of its candidates lost their deposits (forfeited if a candidate does not poll one-eighth of the votes cast, see Section 3), and the one seat it won was in the Western Isles. The swing to the Conservatives in Scotland exactly matched that in England.

In Wales, Plaid Cymru, with three hundred branches and a claimed membership of over forty thousand, put forward candidates in all the thirty-six Welsh constituencies. Its chief support was among teachers, professionals, and traditional religious groups, but it extended for the first time beyond Welsh-speaking groups. Plaid Cymru had greater difficulties than SNP, however, in securing wide support. The violent tactics of its extremist wing alienated many Welshmen, and the linguistic, geographical, and other divisions within Wales handicapped it in presenting a nationalist appeal. Its failures at the polls were not unexpected.

Developments in both areas and particularly in Scotland pose problems for the Conservatives and, indeed, for the British people. Should the distinctive Scottish legal system, the Scottish Office, and the Scottish Grand Committee of the House of Commons be preludes to far-reaching constitutional devolutions of power? Is their nationalism rising or diminishing? The recommendations of the Crowther Commission on the Constitution will be watched with special attention in areas increasingly self-conscious but not presently separatist in sentiment.

Extreme left- and right-wing parties

The Communist party in Great Britain has followed so opportunistic and shifting a policy that it has disillusioned many of its former supporters and remains in a weak position. It is chiefly of interest because of its efforts to infiltrate the leadership of certain unions and to place a few "crypto-Communists" among Labor MP's. In its relations with the Labor party, the Communist party has alternated between scurrilous attacks and efforts to affiliate. These efforts have invariably been rejected, and under present party rules they cannot even be considered.

The Communist party, by itself, is extremely weak numerically, although its members to some extent make up in enthusiasm and unquestioning devotion what they lack in numbers. Since the 1945 election, when the party won two seats, the Communists have not succeeded in placing a candidate in Parliament. They put up a hundred candidates in 1950, in their first and only attempt to fight an election on a national scale, between ten and eighteen in 1951–59, thirty-six in 1964, fifty-seven in 1966, and fifty-eight in 1970. All their candidates lost their deposits in 1951, 1964, 1966, and 1970, and virtually all in the intervening elections. Their percentage of votes is so small, therefore, as hardly to be worth noticing, except as an indication of discontent in one or two industrial districts.

The right-wing National Front, the British National party, and the National Democratic party, with its rightist program of national regeneration, also showed little evidence of electoral strength. The former put up ten candidates but nothing substantial in the way of a constituency campaign. Among them, these parties and a few isolated others polled just under 200,000 votes—a more substantial showing than the 38,400 of the Communists, but a bare 7 percent of the total votes cast. When the time comes to exercise their franchise, the overwhelming majority of electors in Great Britain prefer to put their votes where they may have some chance of influencing the outcome.

3 ELECTIONS

Elections are the testing points of democracy. They determine who shall govern, and they thus provide a supreme test of party appeal, fervor, and efficiency. If the party is already in office, the electorate is passing on its record. If it is in opposition, the electorate is gauging its promise. A wide variety of external factors may affect an electoral situation: the balance of payments, foreign affairs, a pay dispute, a strike, even, as in 1970, the potential disruptions during a South African cricket tour (which was canceled through government intervention to prevent disorders). There are no sure ways, it seems, of determining which of the major parties will win. And this, in itself, is what makes parties, candidates, constituencies, and central offices focus on the moment when the vote is cast, for the result, whatever the reason may be, will determine their role until the next general election.

In Great Britain, postwar elections have been decided by relatively small changes in the proportion of votes received by the two major parties. Only once in this period has the gap between these two parties been more than 7 percent. The "swing," that is, the percentage of votes moving from one major party to the other in the next election, had ranged prior to 1970 from as little as 1.1 percent to the Conservatives in 1951 to 3.1 percent to Labor in 1964. In 1970, the swing to the Conservatives, reckoned as a percentage of the two-party vote, was 5.3, the highest since the war; as a percentage of the total vote cast the swing was 4.8; and as a percentage of the registered electorate, 3.6. Yet the total percentage of the votes cast for the Tories was 46.1, whereas those for Labor amounted to 43.8, a difference of only 2.3 percent.

If one examines election returns on a constituency basis, there is even more striking evidence for the consistency of party allegiance by the overwhelming proportion of voters. A study of 453 constituencies during the four elections of the 1950s disclosed the fact that 87.2 percent of them returned the same party each time. Only 58 constituencies changed party hands at all and, still more striking, only 7 of these changed twice. Another study including the 1964 election concluded that 71 percent of all seats in the House of Commons could be regarded as "safe" for the party holding them.[6] Thus, even more than in the United States, a high proportion of elections are foregone conclusions as far as their party outcome is concerned. The determination of which party shall govern is made within one-quarter of the seats contested.

This marked stability in party voting seems to undercut the importance of party policies, programs, and leaders, and to some degree it does. Yet there are other ways than switching votes by which electors signify their dissatisfaction. Low levels of constituency activity, difficulty in securing adequate funds, and failure to go to the polls are effective means of indicating lack of enthusiasm for proposals and performance. Labor's defeat in 1970 was probably due more to diminished enthusiasm for its program, particularly after the abortive Trade Disputes Bill of 1969, than to positive efforts by the Conservatives.

ELECTION DATE

Elections in Great Britain may occur with very little warning, and British parties are therefore obliged to adopt a strategy quite different

[6] Jorgen Rasmussen, "The Implications of Safe Seats for British Democracy," *Western Political Quarterly* (1966), pp. 516–29.

GEOGRAPHY OF A TYPICAL BRITISH ELECTION, 1959

PERCENTAGE OF VOTES CAST FOR
CONSERVATIVE CANDIDATES

PERCENTAGE OF VOTES CAST FOR
LABOR CANDIDATES

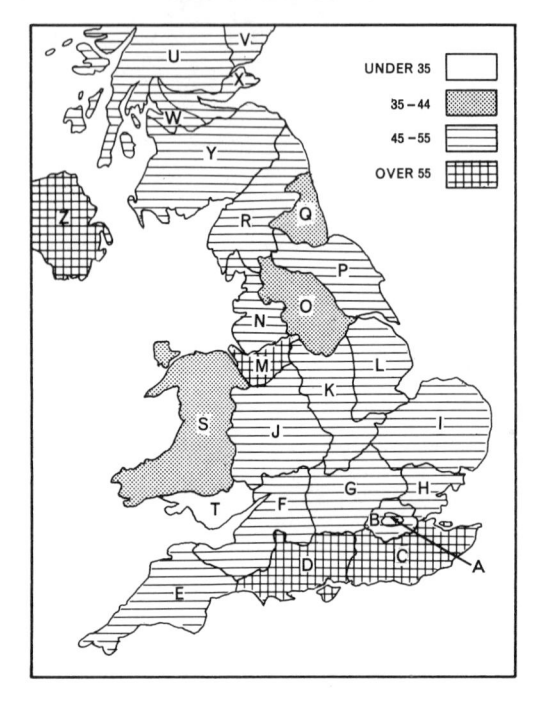

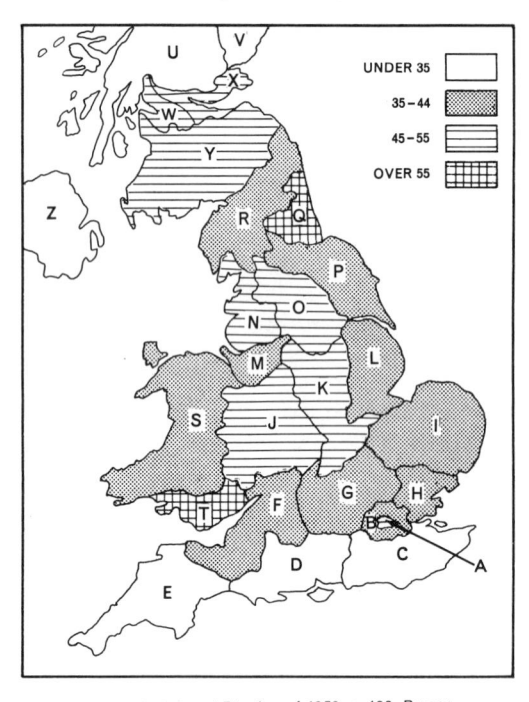

Source: The areas are those used by David E. Butler and Richard Rose. *The British General Election of 1959*, p. 190. By permission of Macmillan and Co., Ltd. and St. Martin's Press.

Important cities are in parentheses. **A** County of London **B** Suburban Boroughs **C** Southeast **D** Wessex (*Portsmouth*) **E** West of England (*Plymouth*) **F** Severn (*Bristol*) **G** South Central **H** Outer Essex **I** East Anglia **J** West Midlands (*Birmingham, Coventry*) **K** Northeast Midlands (*Nottingham, Leicester*) **L** Lincolnshire **M** Cheshire **N** Lancashire (*Liverpool, Manchester*) **O** West Riding (*Sheffield, Leeds, Bradford*) **P** East & North Riding (*York, Hull*) **Q** Northeast England (*Newcastle*) **R** Border **S** Rural Wales **T** Industrial Wales (*Cardiff, Swansea*)
SCOTLAND **U** Highlands **V** Northeast **W** Clyde (*Glasgow*) **X** Forth (*Edinburgh*) **Y** Lowlands
NORTHERN IRELAND **Z** (*Belfast*)

from that of American parties. In the United States, of course, anyone can predict the date of presidential elections for generations to come. The Constitution requires that the election be held every four years, whether it is convenient or not: candidates may announce their availability a year or more in advance, and there is active competition for delegates to national conventions in the winter and spring preceding an election. The nominating conventions themselves are held during the summer; September and October are dedicated to campaign addresses; by the time the voters make their decision early in November, they have been exposed to many months of electioneering.

In Great Britain, in contrast, the prime minister may advise the monarch to dissolve Parliament and ask for new elections any time he desires. Elections are supposed to be not more than five years apart (although because of the war there was no election in Great Britain between 1935 and 1945), but within this five-year period the prime minister has complete freedom to set the time of voting. Thus it would be perfectly possible for several elections to take place within a single year, although the cost, inconvenience, and public irritation work strongly against overfrequent elections. A prime minister with a strong majority in the House of Commons will probably wait four years. In the course of the fourth year of office, however, he and his colleagues will begin to look for favorable issues on which they can "go to the country," and when they have found such an issue and when the time seems appropriate, the monarch, on the prime minister's advice, will dissolve Parliament. Naturally, the prime minister attempts to select a moment favorable to his own party's electoral chances, but, as the 1950, 1951, 1964, and 1970 elections demonstrated, it is difficult in a complex political situation to be sure to whose advantage the time will work. In any case, except in extraordinary circumstances, the power to dissolve has only a marginal effect on the outcome of the election.

The time between dissolution and election is very short. On the eighth day (not counting Sundays and holidays) after the Royal Proclamation of Dissolution, candidates must have filed their nomination papers, and nine days after that (again excluding Sundays and holidays) the vote is taken. It is common, however, to give between twenty-eight and thirty-five days of notice of the exact date of the coming election. In 1970, Prime Minister Wilson conformed to precedent and gave thirty-one days of notice.

On May 18, Wilson went to Buckingham Palace to inform the queen of his decision to hold the election in June; that evening 10 Downing Street issued the announcement. The election date was set for June 18, 1970. Parliament would be dissolved on May 29. The official campaign would lie between those two dates.

Why did Wilson choose a June rather than an October date for the election? Was he wise to do so? Was the upswing in Labor's standing in the country, which began with the vastly improved balance of trade figures in September 1969, sufficient to reverse Labor's public image of inefficient handling of the economy? Would the rise in wage settlements in January and February 1970 result in popularity or criticism? Was the widespread public approval of Roy Jenkins' cautious, moderate budget in April 1970 the key to continued momentum toward Labor? The common belief is that Wilson finally decided on June because the opinion polls, starting with the Harris Poll of April 22, 1970, began at long last to show a Labor lead.

Wilson himself discounts this factor. He maintains that his decision resulted from the fact that the severe downswing in Labor's showing in the borough elections from 1967 through 1969 had been reversed in the spring of 1970. Labor's surprising success in the spring polls, followed by the municipal voting, were only decisive, he declares, in carrying others along with him in his decision.[7] In fact, it appears there was general agreement in the Cabinet and party that a June election was almost sure to yield a small majority whereas waiting until October might well jeopardize Labor's chance.

Opinion polls

Whatever effect the polls may have had on Prime Minister Wilson's decision on the election date—and it was widely commented at the time that if the polls became an infallible way of choosing an election date, they placed a devastating weapon in the hands of a prime minister—their failure to predict the electoral result correctly in 1970 raised many questions regarding their reliability. In earlier postwar elections they had accurately predicted the winning party even though their estimates of the percentage of votes varied considerably from the final result. Particularly after 1959, they shot into prominence as the best, indeed the only continuously available, evidence of public sentiment. From 1961 on, National Opinion Polls (NOP), a subsidiary of Associated Newspapers, had added its regular political polling to that of the Gallup Polls. Poll watching had considerable impact on both the style of the election campaigns in 1964 and 1966 as well as on the morale of the candidates. What happened in 1970?

The best experts on opinion polls, known as psephologists, agree that polling techniques were not to blame for the debacle in 1970. National Opinion Polls distributed their efforts among a stratified sample of two hundred constituencies and at two sampling points in each. Its degree of dispersion was double that used in the 1966 election. Marplan, which had the greatest errors, selected its interviewees by recognized random sampling methods. Opinion Research Center (ORC), which in the end

---

[7] Harold Wilson in *The Observer*, March 21, 1971, and *Britannica Book of the Year*, 1971.

Accuracy of the Polls, 1945–64
(Winner and Percentage Margin of Victory)

YEAR	ACTUAL RESULT (G.B. ONLY)*	GALLUP PERCENT	DAILY EXPRESS PERCENT	RESEARCH SERVICES PERCENT	NATIONAL OPINION POLLS PERCENT	AVERAGE ERROR PERCENT
1945	Lab. 9.8	Lab. 6.0	—	—	—	3.8
1950	Lab. 3.3	Lab. 1.5	Lab. 0.5	—	—	2.3
1951	—	C. 2.5	C. 4.0	C. 7.0	—	6.0
1955	C. 1.9	C. 3.5	C. 2.7	—	—	1.2
1959	C. 4.2	C. 2.0	C. 3.7	—	C. 3.9	1.0
1964	Lab. 1.9	Lab. 3.5	C. 0.8	Lab. 1.0	Lab. 3.1	1.6
Average error		2.5	2.5	4.7	0.8	2.5

* In 1951 Labor won 1.5 percent more votes in Great Britain, but the Conservatives won a parliamentary majority.
Source: The Times (London), March 9, 1966.

Accuracy of the Polls, 1966
(In Percentages)

OPINION POLL FORECASTS	ACTUAL RESULTS G.B. ONLY	GALLUP	NOP	RESEARCH SERVICES	DAILY EXPRESS
Conservative	41.4	−1.4	+0.2	+0.2	−4.0
Labor	48.7	+2.3	+1.9	+1.0	+5.9
Liberal	8.6	−0.6	−1.2	−0.3	−0.9
Average error on major parties	—	1.4	1.1	0.5	3.4
Error in forecast of Labor lead	—	3.7	1.7	0.8	9.9

Source: Adapted from David E. Butler and Anthony King, *The British General Election of 1966*, p. 175.

Accuracy of the Polls, 1970
(In Percentages)

	ORC G.B.	HARRIS G.B.	NOP G.B.	GALLUP G.B.	MARPLAN U.K.	AVERAGE OF 5 POLLS	ACTUAL RESULTS G.B.
Conservative	46.5	46	44.0	42	41.5	44.0	46.2
Labor	45.5	48	48.1	49	50.2	48.2	43.8
Liberal	6.5	5	6.4	7.5	7.0	6.7	7.6
Misc.	1.5	1	1.3	1.5	1.3	1.3	2.4
Labor lead	−1.0	2.0	4.1	7.0	8.7	4.3	−2.4
Average error on 3 parties share	1.0	2.3	2.6	3.2	3.9	2.6	—
Error on lead	1.4	4.4	6.5	9.4	12.0	7.1	—

Source: David E. Butler and Michael Pinto-Duschinsky, *The British General Election of 1970*, p. 179.

indicated a Tory victory, and Gallup Poll, which predicated a final Labor lead of 7 percent, both used quota-sampling techniques. What seems to have made the difference in reliability were how close the polls were taken to the actual date of the election—Opinion Research Center and the Louis Harris Organization, which took the latest samples, both indicated evidence of a Conservative recovery —and the kind of judgment used in adjusting the "raw" returns. The director of Opinion Research Center correctly judged that Conservative supporters were more likely to vote on election day than Labor supporters and adjusted returns in the light of this expectation. In making this judgment, he was aided by the results of 300 re-interviews, in addition to their 1,583 earlier interviews.[8]

In the future, the public may be more wary in its expectations from public opinion polls. Polls can demonstrate trends but not precise results. The polls themselves will no doubt continue their sampling of registered voters as close as possible to election day, use re-interviews more extensively, and inquire if the respondent plans to vote.

More important, however, is the evidence that the campaign itself was a crucial factor in the outcome of the election. The most intense use of polls was not by the press, although it was overloaded with their results, but by the Conservatives and particularly by Mr. Heath. Three times a day, in fact, private poll results from Opinion Research Center provided him with information on the electorate's reactions to particular issues. His confidence in the ultimate result must have been much bolstered by what he heard. For it seems apparent that there was a late swingback to the Tories in the last days of the campaign, partly perhaps because earlier doubts about Labor's ability to cope with Britain's disturbing economic situation were cemented by the announcement three days before the election of a trade deficit of 3 million pounds, a figure subsequently found to be inaccurate, partly, perhaps, because Heath's last television performance outshone the one by Wilson, or because Powell introduced the racial issue at the last moment, or maybe for some deeper reasons.

But if some factors aided the Conservatives, what caused the abstentions, presumably mainly by Laborites, that brought the voting down to 72 percent of the electorate, the lowest turnout since 1935? To gain more perspective, it is essential to examine other factors and, in particular, the party programs, the national campaigning, the constituencies, how they had chosen their candidates, who the candidates were, who could vote, how the constituency organizations marshaled their efforts to persuade and get out the voters, and what the electoral results were that put the Conservatives into power on June 18, 1970.

Party programs and national campaigning

Party programs are commonly bland documents that blur distinctions and stress generalities. Yet in 1970, there were distinctive differences between the Conservatives' well produced *A Better Tomorrow*, issued on May 26, 1970, and Labor's hastily put together *Now Britain's Strong—Let's Make Her Great to Live in*, which appeared the following day. Stressing their intention to "hand back responsibilities wherever we can to the individual, to the family, to private initiative, to the local authority, to the people," the Tories restated in contemporary terms the traditional Conservative view of a free and orderly society in which initiative, competition, and effort can maximize production to the advantage of individuals and society. In contrast, Labor maintained its emphasis on an egalitarianism in which society "must be ready to meet the basic needs of all its members," and all are protected against "economic forces they cannot control."

These differences were reflected concretely in their contrasting attitudes on national controls and supervision and on taxation. Labor

---

[8] The number of interviews used by Opinion Research Center was the smallest sample of all the polls, indicating that care in the selection of respondents is more important than their numbers, but it also proves the key role of interpretation. The size of samples in 1970 ranged from that of the ORC to *The Sunday Times* "Poll of Polls," which sampled twelve thousand people, although only relatively small increases in accuracy can be expected from samples higher than one thousand. Because of the intense public interest in polling techniques and results, the five major polls—Harris, Gallup, Marplan, ORC, and NOP—agreed in May 1970 to a new Code of Practice for opinion polls, under which each pledged to reveal full details of its methods and the composition of its samples to journalists, academics, students, other polling organizations, and political parties.

heralded a National Port Authority under which to reorganize ports and docks, a new National Freight Corporation "to cut out the old and wasteful competition between road and rail," and an Airways Board to plan for both the BOAC and BEA. The Tories declared they would "stop further nationalization and create a climate for free enterprise to expand." Further, they rejected "the detailed intervention of Socialism," which they maintained "usurps the functions of management and seeks to dictate prices and earnings in industry." Moreover, where Labor declared that "we shall ensure . . . that there is a greater contribution to the National Revenue from the rich" (a mild formulation of the wealth tax specified in their 1969 *Agenda for a Generation*), the Conservatives hinted at the introduction of the VAT, which makes goods more expensive for average consumers by adding a related tax at each point in production. And while both emphasized their commitment to social security and pensions, particularly for the elderly, the Tories maintained that "in contrast to the Labour Party, our view is that, for the great majority of people, this can and should be achieved through the expansion and improvement of occupational schemes."

Neither of these manifestos, and even less the Liberal manifesto *What a Life!*, appears to have had much impact on the electorate. What is noticeable, however, is that the Conservatives in office have moved stolidly through item after item on their program. It would have been better, therefore, if the public had paid it more attention.

In addition to the manifestos, there were national speeches in person and on television. It is conventional wisdom to believe it is national rather than local campaigns that swing elections—if, indeed, their results are determined at so late a date. More than in previous postwar elections, the national campaigns in 1970 were built around the two party leaders, Wilson and Heath. Wilson was more informal in his campaigning, but Heath loosened up as time went on and obviously also enjoyed responding to heckling. Wilson made twenty-three appearances in different parts of the country between May 29, when Parliament was dissolved, and June 17, the day before the polling; Heath made nineteen, three of them in Bexley, his home constituency. Both appeared three times on television, the first time together with Thorpe, the Liberal leader, on the BBC forum. Both Heath and Wilson held daily press conferences. Wilson's "walkabouts," making off-the-cuff speeches, achieved short-term successes, but Heath's more carefully staged public meetings had a stronger cumulative effect. Wilson appeared chiefly in the role of cheerleader, encouraging the electorate to leave problems to him and to enjoy the unprecedentedly beautiful June weather; Heath tried to awaken the public to impending dangers. Wilson said, in effect, "Trust me"; Heath said, "Change is essential." And as evidence accumulated of the rising costs of living and an unstable economic picture, these issues apparently had great impact in the constituencies, where the final decisions were to be made.

THE CONSTITUENCIES

Constituency boundaries can have a major, and perhaps decisive, influence on the outcome of an election. The British have avoided legislative "gerrymandering" by requiring periodic redrawing of constituency boundaries for England, Scotland, Wales, and Northern Ireland, each handled separately by a permanent Boundary Commission, composed of five members, mostly civil servants, and presided over by the Speaker. The objective is to provide geographical areas roughly equal in population. To an American, the prescribed number of voters in a British constituency (59,825) is remarkably small.

General reviews of constituency boundaries have taken place in 1918, 1948, 1954, and 1969. Labor is particularly sensitive to redistribution because its supporters tend to be massed in urban areas where their majorities include "wasted" votes, although, in fact, other reasons like levels of voting are probably more influential in elections. It was commonly accepted, however, that the 1948 redistribution hurt Labor's electoral prospects, and fear of this effect, coupled with the fact that it was sponsoring substantial changes in local government boundaries (see Chapter 6, Section 3) are probably reasons why the Labor government did not implement the alterations in boundaries proposed in 1969 by the Boundary Commission.

The 1948 Representation of the People Act (amended slightly in 1949) had resulted in an almost new electoral map. The total number of seats for the House of Commons dropped from 640 to 625 (largely due to the abolition of the two remaining forms of plural voting: the business premises vote and the university graduates vote [9]); only 80 constituencies retained their former boundaries; and many of the rest were so extensively redrawn as to be new in fact, if not always in name. A further review of constituency boundaries in 1954 was less drastic in results, but it led to the abolishing of 6 constituencies and the creation of 11 new ones (all in England) and brought the membership of the House up to 630.

The proposals of the 1969 Boundary Commission envisaged no less radical changes in the electoral map. They provide for 5 additional constituencies, major alterations in the boundaries of 322 of the existing 630 constituencies, and minor changes in another 38. In Greater London, it recommended reducing the 104 seats to 92, while Birmingham, Manchester, and Liverpool each lost a seat. Responding to the movement of population from the cities to suburban areas, 16 counties were to gain 22 seats in all. It was commonly believed that the effect of amalgamating city constituencies, where Labor is strong, and creating new seats in country areas, where the Conservatives get their best results, would give the latter an advantage of 10 to 20 seats.

Justifying their lack of action on the need to wait for implementation of the Redcliffe-Maud proposals for local government boundaries, which would necessarily also change those for constituencies, the Labor government only proposed changes for the London districts and nine others. Efforts by the Lords to force the government to implement the Boundary Commission's proposals met with blocking tactics that resulted in the 1970 election being fought with the old boundaries. The Conservatives, not surprisingly, passed the Boundary Commission's proposals into law in November 1970.

THE VOTER

The Labor government introduced one major change in the franchise prior to the 1970 election by lowering the voting age from twenty-one to eighteen through the 1969 Representation of the People Act. This change, which met in practice with far less enthusiasm by the group enfranchised than had been hoped, added more than three and a half years to the age span for voting, since cumbersome procedures had led in the past to a four- to seven-month delay for new voters to be enrolled on the voting register. Although the new provisions made it possible for anyone to vote from the day of his or her eighteenth birthday, new constituency registers (which the government, not the voter, as in the United States, is responsible for keeping up to date), compiled October 10, 1969, probably listed only about 70 percent of the new voters. In any case, the new voters seem not to have affected the outcome in any particular constituency. Those turning eighteen subsequent to February 16, 1970, when the new register came into effect, will be registered automatically.

THE CANDIDATE

British constituencies vary their choice of candidates between local figures, ex-MP's, or other party figures urged discreetly by the party's central office, or occasionally outsiders, since they are not required by law or custom, as in the United States, to select candidates only from their own district. Sitting MP's rarely have difficulty in being endorsed again, although private pressure may be exerted to persuade a few of the older and less desirable ones to stand down voluntarily.[10] Others may

---

[9] The business premises vote was relatively insignificant except in the City of London and a few other constituencies in the larger cities, where it has traditionally been a Conservative asset. There were 12 university seats, however, of which about half were generally held by distinguished Independents, such as Sir A. P. Herbert and Sir Arthur Salter. None of the university seats was ever held by Labor.

[10] Only seven candidates for the 1970 election—two Conservatives and five Labor—were over seventy years old (there had been nineteen in 1966, twenty-three in 1964, and thirty in 1955); one of these, S. O. Davies of Merthyr Tydfil, who was eighty-three years old, was repudiated by his local Labor party on grounds of age but won as an Independent.

seek a safer seat than available locally, a process that sometimes entails trying for acceptance in a number of places before being selected. Party members in a constituency usually favor local figures, however, and the most frequent cause of complaint against local selection committee choices in 1970 centered around this issue.

According to British election law, any citizen who is twenty-one years old or over—unless he or she falls in the oddly juxtaposed categories of peers, clergymen of the Roman or established Church, lunatics, criminals, or bankrupts—may become a candidate for Parliament by filing papers on nomination day signed by two registered voters (who are called nominators) and by eight other registered electors who "assent" to the nomination. There are no primaries, as in the United States. In practice, the decision on the candidate is made by the constituency organizations. A small subcommittee canvasses available candidates, often seeking central office advice in the process, for national endorsement of a candidate is required by the central offices for all those carrying the official party label. The two to five most promising persons are then brought before the twenty- to sixty-member selection committee—the Executive Council of the Conservative constituency association, or for the Labor party the General Management Committee—to speak briefly and answer questions. After their choice is made by ballot it is subsequently considered by a general party meeting which rarely dissents.

In 1970, most of the selection procedures within the two major parties were for Conservatives since Labor had brought in large groups of young members both in 1964 and 1966. In many cases selection of the candidate was tantamount to election, for in the five previous general elections and ensuing by-elections fought on the 1955 constituency boundaries, 470 seats had been won invariably by the same party, leaving only 160 which had changed hands. Moreover, the outcome in a number of these latter seats also seemed fairly likely. Thus, in practice, it was the selection committees rather than the electorate that chose most of the members of the 1970 Parliament, a fact that poses the same problem for British democracy as the "solid South" has done for the representative system in the United States.

Every candidate must deposit the sum of £150, the money to be forfeited if he or she does not receive one-eighth of the total number of votes cast in the election. This financial provision is intended to restrict frivolous candidacies; its effect is to place a heavy burden on the smaller parties that have relatively little chance either of electing their candidate or even saving their deposit. It may be asked, in fact, why parties and candidates facing hopeless odds continue to contest elections. The Liberals, for example, put up 332 candidates of whom 182 lost their deposits, costing the party £27,000 ($64,800).[11] But the excitement of campaigning and the sheer zest of putting forward their ideas seems enough to keep a constant supply of candidates for hopeless efforts and parties feel the need to keep their supporters alert and encouraged. Indeed, an election may be the only time that the party platform and slogans are paraded locally, and those who believe firmly in their cause find this justification enough for the effort.

Long before he files his nomination papers, an official party candidate begins to "nurse" his constituency, showing himself in public as much as possible, joining local clubs, meeting the voters, and generally making himself well known and popular. Conservative candidates, who often have considerable personal wealth, discover that every charitable organization in the constituency expects a financial contribution; and although Labor's less affluent candidates can hardly hope to win popularity in this fashion, they compensate for their handicap by the assiduity with which they visit, advise, and help the residents of the district, often becoming a combination of errand boy and father confessor whose time and services are expected to be at the disposal of every voter.

The impact of a "familiar" candidate may be considerable over a period of time. If, as has been estimated, a well-known and popular candidate may make a difference of 1 to 3 percent in the vote, this margin may be enough to swing the election. Careful observers of variations in regional or local swings from the national pattern suggest that a candidate's

---

[11] In 1970, 406 of the 1,837 candidates lost their deposits: 6 Labor, 11 Conservative, 182 Liberal, 58 Communist, 42 Scottish Nationalist, 25 Welsh Nationalist, and 82 others.

personal following is the most likely source of the difference.

THE AGENT

In addition to a candidate, a well-organized constituency has an agent, whose job it is to know the intricacies of the election law and to see that his party does not violate it, to direct the work of fighting a campaign, and, between campaigns, to build an organization and prepare the strategy for victory. During an election he is the nerve center of the party organization, assigning workers to the places where they can do the most good, watching the plans and activities of the opposing parties, sensing the feelings of the voters, discovering the greatest threats to victory in time to meet them, and generally keeping all the threads of party organization and activity in his hands. The agents are really professionals, trained by their parties and having their own professional associations. A successful agent may be promoted to a job in a better-paying constituency or in the party's central office. Candidates are dependent upon agents for advice on their campaign activities (although an occasional candidate attributes his political success to the flouting of his agent's instructions), and it is the agent who must plan meetings and arrange and supervise the collecting of signatures and the filing of nomination papers, the securing of committee rooms and meeting places, and the printing and distribution of publicity and advertising.

The extensive use of trained constituency agents has been a striking development in party organization since the war. The Conservative party has by far the largest and best-trained group of agents. In 1970, they had 439 certified agents, some of whom acted for more than one constituency. Only a small proportion of their constituency organizations, mostly in Scotland and Lancashire, had to depend on volunteers. In contrast, the number of Labor's full-time constituency agents had dropped from 204 in 1966 to 149 in June 1970. In the remaining constituencies, Labor had to depend on volunteers, a number of whom had acted as election agents in previous elections but some who were recruited at the last moment. Most Labor constituency organizations appear to have counted on the summer to prepare for the election and were thus less ready for the election campaign than were Conservative constituency organizations.

ELECTION EXPENSES

The amount of money that can be spent *in the election period* by any candidate in any constituency is limited by law, the exact figure depending on whether the constituency is rural or urban and on the number of voters it contains. Limits of expenditure were raised in 1969 from £450 to £750 ($1,800) plus 2d. per elector in county seats and 1½d. in boroughs. These limits result in astonishingly low expenditures by American standards (e.g., Edward Heath spent only $2,590 during the election period).[12] It must be noted, however, that no limit is placed on the amount of money that can be spent *before* an election is called.

In addition to the limitation on actual election expenses, there are heavy penalties, including forfeiture of election, for bribery, "treating," exerting undue influence, declaring false election expenses, and incurring expenses without the authority of the candidate or election agent (a device that prevents private persons from spending money to help their candidate, thus evading the restrictions). There are lighter penalties for paying to convey voters to the polls, publishing propaganda without an imprint, paying for music, banners, ribbons, and other marks of distinction, paying private electors for advertising, publishing false personal statements about a candidate, and disturbing election meetings. Party agents receive elaborate instructions from headquarters warning them of all the pitfalls. The services of bands may be accepted only as a free gift, and even a cup of tea at campaign headquarters must be paid for to avoid a charge of "treating."

These restrictions are intended to equalize electoral opportunities, but it is doubtful whether they serve much purpose. The funds spent by constituencies and central offices, and

---

[12] Total election expenses in 1970 for the 1,837 candidates were listed as $3,342,710, and personal expenses of candidates, like hotels and traveling, which are not subject to limitation, as $175,641. The larger electorate, due to the lower voting age plus the increase in permissible spending, increased the totals over those in 1966.

by the candidate himself outside the three weeks of the formal election period, are far more important. It is clear that the Conservatives will always have an advantage in the money at their disposal, and this cannot be removed by such rigid provisions governing expenditures in the last stages of the election. Probably only a bipartisan political fund distributed according to votes cast in the election would do so. What is more important than immediate pre-election spending is the quality of research at central headquarters and the organization and activity in the constituencies, and it was here that the disparity between the resources of the two major parties was most telling.

THE LOCAL CAMPAIGN

The foundation of the local parliamentary campaign is the canvass. It is the aim of each party to call on every voter in the district, both to give out literature and to learn, if possible, how he will vote. Elaborate and secret records are then compiled, on which the party bases its campaign. No party wastes its time on those who are going to vote for its opponent, but the parties do need to know who their supporters are so that they can be sure to get them to the polls; and they want to know who is doubtful so that they can tell where to concentrate their energy.

Much of the work of canvassing and compiling records is done by women. The Conservatives profit from the leisure of women in the upper classes; but even in the Labor party women often have more time than their husbands and are better able to find a free hour or two in the afternoon to attend meetings, work at headquarters, canvass, or collect dues. Regular meetings are held to keep them informed of current events, and such meetings may perform a social as well as an educational and political service. It is noteworthy that all parties have large women's organizations and that Labor has five seats reserved for women on its National Executive Committee, two of them in the constituency section.

The most effective events in a campaign used to be the formal meetings addressed by candidates and prominent party leaders. Political use of television and other forms of national propaganda have added a new and powerful dimension to campaigning. What has surprised both parties, however, is that far from reducing interest in meetings, television appears to strengthen it, although the older type of formal session is much less popular than more spontaneous street meetings. And if at such meetings there are fewer bands and less ornate decorations than at American party rallies, in one sense the meetings are livelier than their American counterpart. Heckling has been turned into a fine art, and the candidate must expect to be harried and interrupted by sharp, witty, and inconvenient questions. The test is often one of his good humor and presence of mind rather than of his principles, and a quick and clever response can sometimes do the candidate more good than the most carefully prepared speech.

The best picture the voter receives of the candidate's position is contained in the "election address," a pamphlet of three or four pages mailed to the voters post free. The pamphlet usually contains a picture of the candidate, a statement of the principles and issues in which he is interested, and the events that have distinguished his career. According to the post-election Gallup survey, 53 percent of the 1970 electorate said they had read at least one election address, the highest percentage since 1959. Although centrally produced literature and posters were ordered, their bulk was three times less than in the peak year of 1951 and even then had been relatively small compared to the flood of local material.

No issue appeared to dominate the campaign. Those most often mentioned were high prices, taxes, unemployment, and the Common Market (although it figured little in national campaigning). Although race relations had become more tense since 1966, and Enoch Powell provided the most striking speeches of the 1970 campaign, there were none of the racial slogans, obscenities, or bitterness that had marred the 1964 campaign. This was largely because of the determination on both sides to play down the divisive and potentially explosive immigration issue. Housing and abuse of the social services were mentioned occasionally to canvassers but few purely local issues. One candidate declared the campaign had been

ELECTIONS

MAP OF THE GENERAL ELECTION, 1970

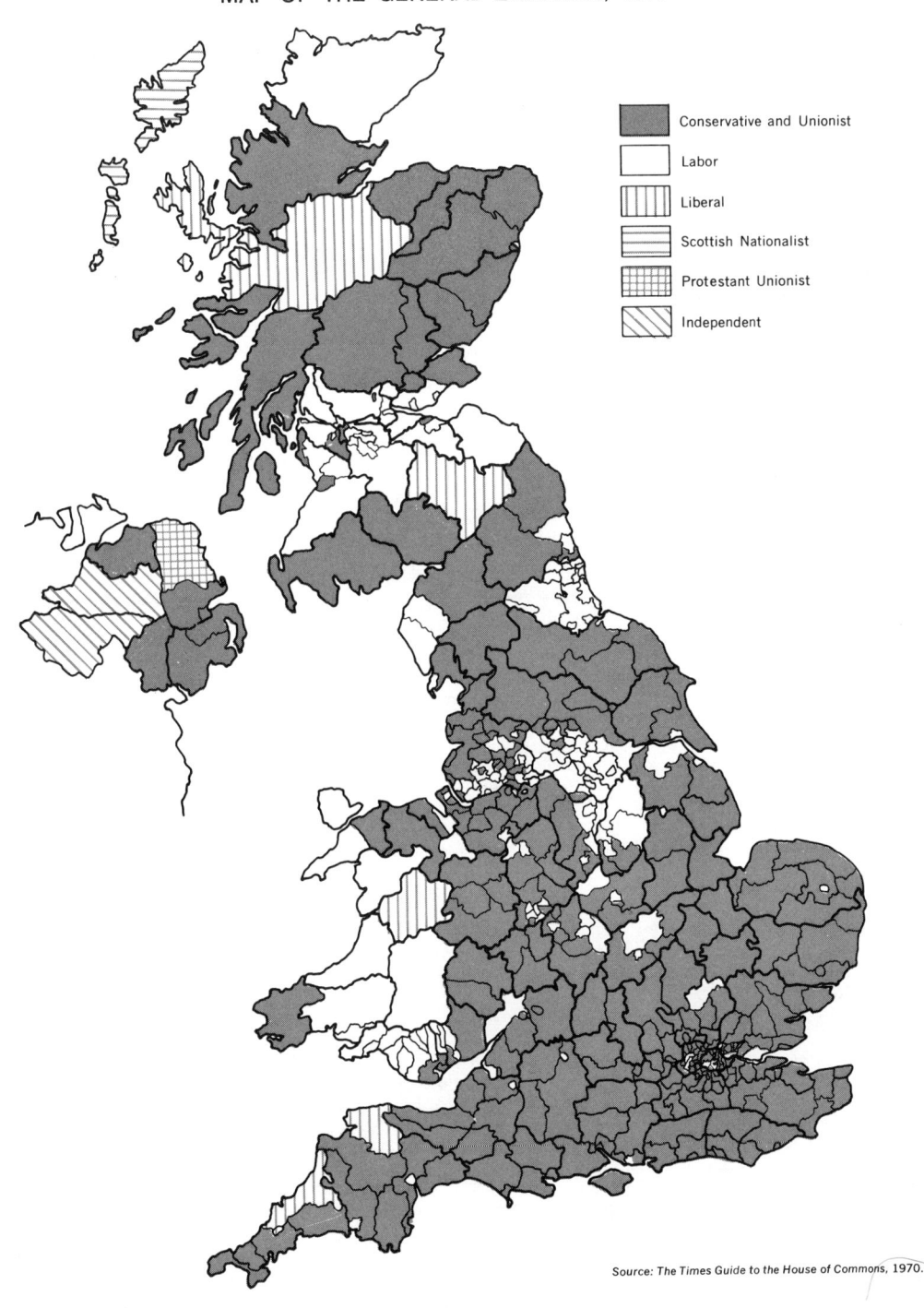

- Conservative and Unionist
- Labor
- Liberal
- Scottish Nationalist
- Protestant Unionist
- Independent

Source: *The Times Guide to the House of Commons,* 1970.

"without issues." Heath awakened only mild feelings on both sides whereas Wilson, although hated bitterly by some Conservatives, was almost universally admired for his "cleverness." One acute observer remarked: "The people wanted Wilson but not Labour, the Conservatives but not Heath." But it was Heath they got, perhaps particularly because the Conservatives had the superior organization and brought out the vote.

One place where organization had a potent influence was on the postal vote, which may have determined the outcome in at least six to eight constituencies. A wide source of dissatisfaction over the June election among Conservative voters revolved around plans for holidays abroad at that time, not in itself an adequate justification for voting by mail. Moreover, more people were eligible for postal votes in 1970 than in 1966 because the register was three months older and because the 1969 Representation of the People Act permitted postal voting for people moving within the same urban area. Although the proportion of voting by mail only rose from 1.9 to 2.1 percent, 730,000 persons were enrolled on the absent voters register, and 84 percent of these voted, 2 percent less than in 1966, but an average of 973 per constituency. Estimates are that the postal vote divided 75:25 down to 60:40 in favor of the Conservatives. In 32 seats the number of postal votes exceeded the Conservative majority, but it was probably decisive only in about one-quarter of them. Nonetheless, 6 to 8 seats form a considerable proportion of the Conservative majority of 30. Whether publicity, canvassing, and organization determined the outcome in the other 12 to 14 constituencies in which the Conversatives had the narrowest majorities is more debatable, particularly in the light of the significance of Labor abstentions.

ELECTION RETURNS

Eighty-eight constituencies changed hands in 1970, and the Conservatives made a net gain of 66 seats, both records for any postwar

The National Results, 1945–70

	ELECTORATE AND TURNOUT	VOTES CAST	CONSERVATIVE	LABOR	LIBERAL	NATIONALIST †	COMMUNIST	OTHERS
1945*	73.3% 32,836,419	100% 24,082,612	39.8% 9,577,667	48.3% 11,632,891	9.1% 2,197,191	0.6% 138,415	0.4% 102,760	1.8% 433,688
1950	84.0% 34,269,770	100% 28,772,671	43.5% 12,502,567	46.1% 13,266,592	9.1% 2,621,548	0.6% 173,161	0.3% 91,746	0.4% 117,057
1951	82.5% 34,645,573	100% 28,595,668	48.0% 13,717,538	48.8% 13,948,605	2.5% 730,556	0.5% 145,521	0.1% 21,640	0.1% 31,808
1955	76.8% 34,858,263	100% 26,760,493	49.7% 13,311,936	46.4% 12,404,970	2.7% 722,405	0.9% 225,591	0.1% 33,144	0.2% 62,447
1959	78.7% 35,397,080	100% 27,859,241	49.4% 13,749,830	43.8% 12,215,538	5.9% 1,638,571	0.6% 182,788	0.1% 30,897	0.2% 61,619
1964	77.1% 35,892,572	100% 27,655,374	43.4% 12,001,396	44.1% 12,205,814	11.2% 3,092,878	0.9% 249,866	0.2% 45,932	0.2% 53,116
1966	75.8% 35,964,684	100% 27,263,606	41.9% 11,418,433	47.9% 13,064,951	8.5% 2,327,533	1.2% 315,431	0.2% 62,112	0.3% 75,146
1970	72.0% 39,364,297	100% 28,345,678	46.4% 13,145,082	43.0% 12,179,573	7.5% 2,117,659	2.4% 672,356	0.1% 38,431	0.7% 192,577

* University seats are excluded: other 1945 figures are adjusted to eliminate the distortions introduced by double voting in the 15 two-member seats then existing.
† Including all types of Irish Nationalist.

Source: David E. Butler and Michael Pinto-Duschinsky, *The British General Election of 1970,* p. 353.

election. The Conservatives won 1 seat from the National Democrats, 5 from the Liberals, and the rest from Labor. Labor won 6 seats from the Conservatives, half of the latter's 12 by-election gains between 1966 and 1970, 2 from the Liberals, and 2 from Scottish and Welsh Nationalists. They lost 1 to Independent Labor (the elderly gentleman who refused to withdraw), and 1 to the Scottish Nationalists. Ulster Unionists lost 2 seats, 1 to a Protestant Unionist, and 1 to a Catholic Unity candidate. In sum, 542 constituencies returned the same party as in 1966, but the changes provided a Tory victory that was both surprising and decisive.

The swing in voting, even in marginal seats, showed an equally striking degree of national uniformity. No section of England and Scotland showed less than a 2.6 percent swing to the Tories. The swing was most marked in the Midlands and Leicester; lowest in rural Wales, ship-building Merseyside, Humberside, Tyneside, and most of Scotland. The Liberals, whose vote sank almost everywhere, for the first time won no seat outside the West Country, Wales, and Scotland. The Communists did worse even than usual. The Scottish and Welsh Nationalists made gains in votes only in the most remote rural areas.

On a longer-range projection, the change in the political balance between the cities and the rest of the country became still more apparent. Of the eighteen seats the Conservatives won for the first time since 1945, none were in London and only one, Leicester, was in a big city. Labor, on the other hand, held on to twenty seats—fifteen of them in London or another big city—which they had never won in the 1950s. But as in the past, both parties polled substantial percentages of votes in most constituencies.

In general, the pattern of party support continued. The Conservatives continued to secure more support from older citizens than from the young; women also tended to be more Conservative than men but by the same degree as in 1966. The middle class, including white-collar workers, continued to vote either Conservative or Liberal. But while manual workers, however affluent, remained staunchly Labor, their activists were sufficiently disgruntled as a result of Barbara Castle's 1969 Trade Disputes Bill to cut down their efforts to get out that vote.

If the defeat of a party that was ahead in the polls at the moment of dissolution was unprecedented, so had been Labor's recovery from its 20 percent deficit in the polls a year before. However much the Conservatives could cheer their victory and, in particular, their leader, the only one among them who had never lost confidence in a Tory victory, the electoral result seemed less a positive than a negative one: the lesser of two evils. The electoral future can be expected to depend even more than usual, therefore, on the voters' reactions to the Conservative record in office.

4 EFFECTIVENESS OF THE BRITISH PARTY SYSTEM

By now it should be possible to hazard certain answers to the questions asked at the beginning of this chapter.

CHOICE OF CANDIDATES AND POLICIES

In the first place, certain critics charge that the choices offered by the major British parties are narrow and unnatural. Human interests and human desires, they point out, are almost infinite in their diversity; to force them all into one of two molds is to destroy the representativeness of the system and to oblige people to vote, not in favor of a program for which they feel genuine enthusiasm, but against the program they dislike the more.

Paradoxically, other critics make exactly the opposite complaint. Extreme Conservatives and Laborites protest that the programs of the two parties, in appealing to the uncommitted voter in the middle, have become so similar that each has sacrificed its essential beliefs and made any real choice impossible. Left-wing Laborites feel that their party is too lukewarm in its socialism and makes too many concessions to the middle-class element. Thus they charge that left-wingers are compelled to vote, on election day, not for the radical program they would prefer but for a milk-and-water reformism that completely misrepresents their attitude. Similarly, many an old-line Tory of the Colonel Blimp vintage finds himself horrified at the Conservative party's acceptance of many features of a collectivist society. Yet, since there is no way in which he can vote clearly and unmistakably for the old England of the ruling classes and the vested interests, he votes reluctantly for a program in which he does not believe. Both of these groups would charge, in short, that everybody in England is obliged to accept the kind of program that appeals, in particular, to the lower middle classes.

Party representativeness

Another paradox arises when one questions the representativeness of the parties. It is the extremists and the militants—that is, voters who are not typical of the electorate as a whole—who are most likely to join a party organization. Thus the party that is most representative of its rank-and-file faces difficulties in working out a program that is representative of the community in general. In this sense, extreme democracy inside the party may be a handicap to democracy outside, and the giving of authority to a party's leaders may actually increase the representativeness of the party's program. For it is the extremists who find it most difficult to compromise and who are most willing to take a noble, unyielding, and doctrinaire stand. But the responsibilities of the party's leaders are considerably broader. They are expected to lead the party to victory, and for this they have to win the support of those who are not party members. The party members will vote for them anyway: they have nowhere else to go. It is the uncommitted voter who must be won. Thus the party's leadership is more concerned with finding a program that can attract the support of the community in general; it will stop only at that point where a loss of enthusiasm on the part of party workers will provide a counterbalancing threat to success in the election.

Intraparty organization

It is natural, however, for members of both great parties to complain about the lack of democracy in party organization: in the Conservative party, it is charged, the leader and his chosen associates make the crucial decisions, and the rank-and-file are free only to cheer and to "recommend"; in the Labor party, it is charged, trade union votes dominate the party conference. In any case, the parliamentary leader may refuse to accept its decisions. No system, say the complainants, so undemocratic in its foundations can possibly be democratic in its results.

To some extent, the Labor party has worked out more democratic procedures that the Conservative. There is more participation in local organizations. Moreover, through the mechanism of the party conference the rank-and-file have an opportunity to challenge party policy, to cross-examine party leaders, and to take part in a vigorous debate that has a powerful psychological influence. At the same time, through its predominance in the NEC, the leadership can usually prevent the party from taking action that would alienate a large number of uncommitted voters. Thus the leadership is held responsible to the rank-and-file of the party not in the sense that it is subject to their dictation but in the sense that it is forced to listen to criticism and to justify its policies. This is the case also within the parliamentary party, where backbenchers discuss issues freely and often critically with their leaders, though less so when the latter are in office.

In the Conservative party the balance is different: the personal power of the party leader is greater, and the prestige of the party conference is less, although the leadership now undergoes the kind of cross-examination and participates in the kind of debate that characterize a Labor conference. Yet, as we have seen, the parliamentary party can be ruthless in deposing a leader if he appears out of step or ineffective. Thus if immediate checks on the leader are less obvious in the Conservative party, the ultimate controls tend to be more drastic.

PARTY EFFECTIVENESS

One last paradox concerns the effectiveness of each party in responding to public demands and needs, for here too a restriction on democracy within the party may be said to contribute to democracy on a national plane. The high degree of party discipline exercised over members of Parliament and sometimes over constituency organizations can cause charges of intraparty dictatorship; yet it is only a disciplined party that can ensure the execution of the policies for which the party was put into office. Freedom for each party representative to follow his own conscience or whim may mean the failure of the party as "an effective instrument for carrying out the judgment of the voters once they have made a choice of parties."

In making the parties such an effective instrument, the two-party system performs an essential function. The voter might make a more accurate choice and one closer to his own ideas if there were a greater variety of major parties representing each gradation from reaction to revolution. But there would be no guarantee, and in fact the probabilities would be all against the possibility, that any one party would receive a majority of the seats in the House of Commons and thus be in a position to carry out its program. If no party exercises control, no party can be blamed or praised for what results. Under a two-party system, however, so long as a party is well disciplined, responsibility cannot be evaded. If a party has a clear majority, it has no excuse for not governing effectively.

PARTIES AS AGGREGATES OF GROUP DEMANDS

While it is clear that in a democratic society parties compete in the market place for consumers' votes, it should be equally clear that in what is so largely a managed economy, they also act to aggregate the demands of producers' groups and to arbitrate between their claims. We have already noted how parties may themselves create future demands through their policies, particularly since those policies are likely to create environments within which some groups fare better than others. The system thus works in a circular fashion, with parties and interest groups interacting constantly with each other. Thus parties are sometimes called "switchboards with a bias."

Interest groups are themselves significant channels of communication, without which the political system could not be truly representative or, indeed, democratic. At the same time, interest groups have different aims, objectives, and membership from political parties. Interest groups are concerned to exert pressure, not to take power; their objectives are usually sharply focused; and their membership is limited to one section of society. In the intricately constructed industrial society of the day, there are vast industrial complexes, which serve as their own pressure groups; protective organizations concerned with the interests of their members, whether these be business or labor or the professions or sport or motoring; promotional groups urging a particular cause; informal groupings such as churches, which may on occasions take an active role in a national issue like arms for South Africa; and interests that cut across these more sharply defined concerns. In focusing so directly upon party organizations and votes in this chapter, there is a danger of appearing to suggest that only parties and election time are important in the representative system, whereas the interaction between government and interest groups and between opposition parties and interest groups is continuous and essential to the health of the system. Paradoxically, the more such channels of communication bring their information and their special positions to the parties and react to their programs and policies, the more broadly representative the latter are likely to be.

CONCLUSION

By this time it should be evident that many of the criticisms made of the British party system cancel one another out and that it is impossible for this system, or any system, to meet some of the criteria of an effective and democratic system without simultaneously departing from others. In achieving a balance of the various desiderata, however, the British have not been unsuccessful. The choice presented to the voter, even if a moderate one, is clear and real, for there are significant differences between the policies and performance of the two major parties, similar though they may be in many respects. Special groups and interests, like those of the colored immigrants, however, often find it difficult to get adequate presentation of their needs, although they are increasingly calling attention to themselves. Since parties and programs attempt to attract as many voters as possible, they inevitably seek to appeal as broadly as they can, rather than to express the positions of their most militant party members. This watering-down process necessarily leads to dissatisfaction but is a consequence of broad representativeness. In neither party do the rank-and-file have direct control over the decisions of their leaders; but in both parties, channels have been developed for applying great pressure upon the leaders. And finally, the two-party system, by virtually ensuring that one party will win a majority of the seats in the House of Commons, provides that party with the effective power to govern responsibly.

4

The British Parliament

The functioning of Parliament, and especially of the House of Commons, is crucial to the relation between the British public and their government. Once an election is over, the leaders of the majority party assume responsibility as the government, become vested with vast independent powers, and are aided by a vast bureaucracy. The purpose of Parliament is to analyze the character and likely effect of the legislation it is called upon to consider, to serve as a public forum for debate on matters of national concern, and to protect individual liberties by investigating cases of injustice caused by governmental action. Through these activities, Parliament not only seeks, or should seek, to make the government defend its policies in public, but it also seeks to inform and alert the public to the implications of government policies. For the House of Commons must prepare public opinion as well as represent it. In both senses it is the essential hinge of democracy.

The working of the British political system, and particularly of the "mother of Parliaments," has long been held up as a model to other countries and, indeed, widely copied by countries of the Commonwealth of Nations. But increasingly, and especially in the past few years, both the system and the operations of Parliament have been sharply criticized. As the business of government has grown in scope and complexity, the Cabinet's control over the timetable and subject matter of parliamentary business has vastly increased. Formal opportunities for criticism have been taken over almost entirely by the opposition frontbench. Under these circumstances, there have been limited opportunities for the active backbenchers of either party to participate effectively in the parliamentary process. Their frustration and that of those who have elected them is part of the malaise that has been affecting British political life.

Much of the focus of recent attention has been on parliamentary procedures and on the need for more aid and better facilities for MP's. There has been a wealth of proposals from inside and outside Parliament that have aimed at providing more scope for individual members and more support for their efforts. More measures of reform have been introduced recently, in fact, than for scores of years. This process is far from concluded. For this reason and because it is not yet sure that all the reforms which have been introduced will be maintained, the description in this chapter of institutions like specialized committees, and even of legislative procedures must be seen to record a particular stage of change and not some assured resolution of the difficulties that caused the reform movement. Indeed, it is clear that there remains much still to change.

The efforts to reform the workings of Parliament are not unlike those that have attempted—so far without success—to crack the seniority system in the United States Congress. Both seek to make procedures more flexible and to provide younger members who have new ideas and experience with opportunities to break through traditional procedures so as to have their own direct impact on the formulation of policies. In the United States, the problem centers on the tenacious hold on the powerful committee structure by those, mostly from the South, who have succeeded in securing reelection over and over again. In Great Britain, the problem is not only the procedures as such but their reflection of the rigidities of party government and party discipline. In both countries, economic problems overshadow debates on the allocation of resources. In both, the press, radio, and, above all, television skim the cream of controversy and highlight "hot" issues before they reach the floor of the legislature. But in both countries, the legislature is the institutional center of the continuing democratic process.

It is particularly important, therefore, for Americans to understand not only the major differences between their own and British representative institutions but also the common problems that afflict them. On the one hand, the problem may be one of deadlocks, on the other that of railroading, but common to both is the sense that neither the elected member nor the electorate is having the impact on decisions that democracy assumes. The steps of change are often slow, and taken individually they may appear minute. But they represent continuing creative efforts to make the institutions of government correspond to the assumptions and purposes of democracy. As such they are vital to the health of the political process.

1 THE HOUSE OF COMMONS: ITS MEMBERS

In light of the critical comments heard so often about the "decline of Parliament" as an effective factor in the determination of policy, it might be expected that the caliber of its members would steadily decline. But such, in practice, is not the case. The prestige of being an MP in Great Britain is far higher than that of being a member of the House of Representatives in the United States. For one thing, the term of office is commonly much longer; for another, the House of Commons is the obvious center within which the drama of political action and power is played out. And although, in practice, certain committees of the House of Representatives exercise far more independent power than does any group in the British Parliament apart from the Cabinet, there is still a sense of collective importance that continues to attract to the Commons men and women of wide experience and impressive ability.

There have been many specific studies of the social, educational, and occupational characteristics of MP's in particular Parliaments. These studies tend to show that, on the whole, the representation of Labor is more diverse and, in this sense, more representative than that of the Conservatives, who continue to draw from a fairly narrow social group. The crucial feature for both is that the representative is a *party* man. Samuel Beer in *British Policies in the Collectivist Age*[1] has differentiated between four types of representation that have been characteristic at different periods: what he calls the "old Whig theory" of representing particular interests, ranks, orders, and estates; the mid-nineteenth century "Liberal" theory that representatives should be individuals who are independent of interests; the "Radical" theory of representing the people as a whole as against either individuals or interests; and the "collectivist" theory of contests between two major parties. Clearly it is the latter which now predominates.

The 630 members of Parliament elected in June 1970 nearly all came into politics after World War II, for 78 of those holding seats (49 Labor, 27 Conservatives, and 2 Liberals) had decided not to stand.[2] The age balance of

---

[1] Beer's "collectivist" theory also highlights the impact on policy of the functional representation of producers' and consumers' groups, an impact exercised very largely on the administration, which is responsible for the execution of what he sees as widely accepted general policy.

[2] On average there is a turnover of one-fifth of the membership of the House of Commons through deaths and retirements in any five-year term. Tory MP's average age forty when they enter the House, and retire about age sixty-three, after twenty-three years in Parliament; Labor MP's enter on average at forty-five years of age and remain until sixty-six, that is, twenty-one years in the House. Sixty-three MP's retired at the end of the 1966 Parliament. Only 5

The House of Commons, 1945–70

	1945	1950	1951	1955	1959	1964	1966	1970
Conservative	213	298	321	345	365	304	253	330
Labor	393	315	295	277	258	317	363	287
Liberal	12	9	6	6	6	9	12	6
Others	22	3	3	2	1	0	2	7
Total	640	625	625	630	630	630	630	630

Source: David E. Butler and Michael Pinto-Duschinsky, *The British General Election of 1970*, p. 354.

the new House did not change perceptibly, however, and its youngest member is still Bernadette Devlin, twenty-three in 1970. For the first time, no Conservative under thirty was elected, although five Labor candidates under thirty won seats. The most surprising feature of the 1970 House is the large number of MP's, 150, who had been elected for the first time—83 Conservatives, and 64 Labor, and 3 others—the largest number of new members since 1945. Twenty-one of the 48 Conservatives who had been defeated in 1966 (of whom 6 had been returned in by-elections thereafter) and 6 of those who had lost their seats in 1964 secured election.

The social profile of the Tory MP in the 1970 Parliament does not differ materially from the earlier stereotype of male, public school, and Oxford or Cambridge, comfortably well-off, and in the professions or business, although some commentators have called them a more socially minded and politically sophisticated parliamentary group. Thirty-eight members of its left-wing ginger group, the Bow Group, were elected instead of 17 in the former Parliament. They are balanced, however, by 30 members of the right-wing Monday Group, 10 elected for the first time. Moreover, a spot check after the election suggested that 33 of the new MP's were sympathetic to Enoch Powell's position on immigration.

One hundred and sixty-seven Conservative MP's have been to public school and university, and 80 to public school alone. Eton continued to provide 18 percent of all Tory MP's, only slightly less than the 24 percent in 1951, and

1970 MP's had served continuously since before the war; 7 others had experience in prewar Parliaments; and 4 had entered in wartime by-elections.

Oxford and Cambridge 52 percent, the same figure as in 1951. Forty-five percent of all Tory members are in the professions, with barristers far in the lead with 60 MP's, followed by the armed services with 24. Eighty Tory MP's are company directors and 101 in all in business, compared to 140 in the professions. Thirty-one are said to be farmers (but not whether they have large or small holdings) and 30 journalists. The working classes remain virtually invisible, with only the 2 same trade unionists (the one elected 1955 and the other in 1964) holding Conservative parliamentary seats. Among the 330 Tory MP's, 15 are women and 9 are Jews (an increase in both cases from earlier Parliaments). The vast majority of Tory members are nominal Anglicans (Episcopalians in American parlance); 13 are Catholic.

Labor representation in the 1970 Parliament, particularly among its new members, is increasingly similar to that of the Conservatives. Labor is also heavily male (only 10 women members, the smallest number since the war); 53 percent are university educated (although with a higher percentage at other universities than at Oxford or Cambridge), and 60 have been to public schools, although only 7 of these had not also gone to the university. The majority seem nominal Anglicans, although 40 Labor MP's declared they are agnostics, atheists, or humanists (designations to which no Conservative MP would admit), 31 are Jews, and 22 Catholics. Forty percent are in the professions, including 56 teachers (school through university, whereas the Conservatives number only 6), 34 barristers, and only 3 from the armed services. Only 10 percent are in business, 28 in all, among whom only 4 MP's are company directors and 10 company executives. Most notable, working-class representation has sunk from 37 percent in 1951 to 26 percent in 1970. While 112 of those elected were sponsored by trade unions, and 17 by the Cooperative party, the actual number of workingmen among Labor MP's has steadily diminished.

Of the new Labor MP's, 32 are from the professions, 11 from business, and 1 a housewife. Of the 10 who might be termed workers, 2 are railroad clerks in administrative positions and 2 are draughtsmen. Only 2 miners, 1 construction worker, and 1 seaman can genuinely be looked on as manual workers.

It is worth noting what a change in the composition of the House of Commons these similarities indicate. The rise of Labor had introduced into Parliament something of the class division that prevailed in the rest of the country. While the Conservative benches continued to look like those of the nineteenth-century House, that is, gentlemen of means who were the product of similar education and ways of life, those on the Labor benches were often manual workers who had themselves known economic hardships. Trade union representatives long continued to be drawn from such a group, but even they now display more middle-class characteristics. Thus the House has once more acquired a relative similarity in the background, training, and professions of the members on both sides, although there remain distinctively different attitudes on most issues.

Occupation of Elected MP's, 1970

	CONSERVATIVE Elected	LABOR Elected
Professions		
Barrister	60	34
Solicitor	14	13
Doctor/Dentist	6	7
Architect/Surveyor	3	2
Civil Engineer	1	2
Chartered Secretary/Accountant	6	6
Civil Servant/Local Government	12	3
Armed Services	24	—
Teaching		
University	1	13
Adult	2	10
School	6	33
Other Consultants	14	9
Scientific Research	0	5
Total	149	137
Business		
Company Director	80	4
Company Executive	14	10
Commerce/Insurance	3	5
Management/Clerical	1	7
Small Business	3	2
Total	101	28
Misc. White Collar	1	3
Private Means	4	—
Politician/Political Organizer	10	11
Publisher/Journalist	30	27
Farmer	31	1
Housewife	1	1
Student	—	—
Local Administrator	1	3
Total	78	46
Clerk	—	4
Miner	—	22
Skilled Worker	2	33
Semi/Unskilled	—	17
Total	2	76
Grand Total	330	287

Source: Adapted from Butler and Pinto-Duschinsky, *British General Election of 1970*, p. 302.

PRACTICAL EXPERIENCE

The House continues to include a wide occupational distribution, which means that many of its members have some direct personal experience with particular social institutions and aspects of the economy discussed by that body. In the American Congress most of the members are lawyers, and it is obvious that the duties of a lawyer and legislator are easily combined; but in the House of Commons less than one-fifth of the members are lawyers. Organized interests in Great Britain are not limited to attempts to *influence* members of Parliament; some of their own group *become* members of Parliament. Ronald Butt quotes the Chancellor of the Exchequer at the time, James Callaghan, in a speech of July 3, 1965, as saying he did not think of Conservative MP's in the Finance Bill debate as representing particular constituencies but "I look at them and say, 'investment trusts,' 'capital speculators,' or 'that is the fellow who is the Stock Exchange man who makes a profit on gilt-edged.'"[3] Labor has its miners and metal workers. Both sides, although in varying numbers, have teachers, doctors, engineers, and farmers. And many of these persons belong to special interest groups like the Federation of British Industries, the National Farmers' Union, the British Medical Association, and so forth. It is generally known to what interest a particular member belongs, but formal disclosure has been proposed. It does not appear, however, that the existence of such interests runs counter to party allegiance and leads to cross-voting. On the contrary, as the chancellor's comment was intended to suggest, the presence in the House of persons with special expertise and experience is welcomed. The Commons gives special attention to speeches based on such knowledge and experience, and the presence of such persons is looked on as added strength to intelligent discussion.

THE ROLE OF AN MP

Since the House of Commons is the visible expression of the principle of representation, it is important to examine the role of the MP from this angle. An MP is first and foremost a member of a party. He also has special responsibilities to his constituency. In the third place, his personal conscience may impel him to take certain stands. A British MP, therefore, must balance these three roles.

No one doubts that in the eyes of those who elected him, as well as of his party leaders, the party label predominates. To a considerable degree this involves obedience to the party whip. It may also, however, involve opportunities to influence the policies of a party behind the scenes (see Section 5). Backbench influence is commonly greater when a party is in opposition than when it is in office, but in its later years of office Labor Cabinet members, and often the prime minister, met on a regular weekly basis with the parliamentary party both to secure constituency reactions and to engage in discussions on policy. Moreover, during the same period there was increasing leniency by those in charge of party discipline, especially in the Labor party where it used to be extremely rigorous.

Increasing attention is now being given also to the role of an MP in relation to his constituency. In the first place it has been suggested by data drawn from 1955 to 1959[4] that the nature of a constituency can be correlated more closely than formerly believed with policy positions taken by MP's on certain issues. On the sensitive question of attitudes to immigration, however, responses to a questionnaire sent in March and April 1969, when correlated with voting in February 1969 on the Sandys' motion for a stricter immigration bill, seem to suggest that party position rather than constituency racial composition determine attitudes.[5]

A more important question—the role of the MP in mobilizing consent within his constituency—has been highlighted by Samuel Beer.[6] Mobilizing consent means educating constituents on those matters that are not publicized during the general election but which come up subsequently in response to changing conditions and new needs. Although unlike an American congressman a British MP is not bound by the rule of residence, it is common for him to maintain at least a center within the constituency, to perform numerous services for its members, and to keep them informed on the progress of parliamentary business, a process simpler in Great Britain because constituencies have many less members than in the United States. Beer believes, however, that the MP could do much more than he does now to provide what he calls "a more continuous, intimate interchange between authority and those subject to authority." This requires not only access by members of the governing party to the discussions on which policy is based, but also, as is continually pointed out, better facilities for understanding, explaining, and thus criticizing what government is doing. In a time

---

[3] Ronald Butt, *The Power of Parliament*, p. 461.

[4] Samuel E. Finer, H. B. Berrington, and D. V. Bartholomew, *Backbench Opinion in the House of Commons, 1955–1959*.

[5] Robert C. Frasure, "Constituency Racial Composition and the Attitudes of British M.P.'s," *Comparative Politics*, 3 (2) (January 1971), pp. 201–10.

[6] Samuel H. Beer, "The British Legislature and the Problem of Mobilizing Consent," *Essays on Reform, 1967*, ed. by Bernard Crick, pp. 81–100.

like the present when so much depends on the public's response to governmental decisions, this role of stimulating awareness of the purposes to which action is directed may well be one of the most important functions of the MP.

The third issue, of individual conscience, is far from unimportant. There are issues, like the attitude of Labor members to nuclear disarmament, which are accepted as matters of conscience. But there is also a broader range of matters, as discussed later, which is now seen to have implications for conscience. This is sufficiently sensitive both from the side of the individual member and of the whips to make it more difficult to generalize than in regard to the two other aspects of the MP's role. It should be noted, however, that the opportunity to raise questions related to civil liberties, to provoke investigations in particular cases, and to vote on such decisions as whether to return Dr. Robert A. Soblen to the United States, to which he was being extradited at the time he sought asylum in Britain, are related to personal convictions that differentiate them from more general issues of national policy.

2 THE HOUSE OF COMMONS: ORGANIZATION

CEREMONIES

The average visitor is likely to be deeply impressed by the amount of ceremonial in the House of Commons. Most afternoons at 2:30 and Friday mornings at 11:00, as the House convenes, the Speaker in wig and gown marches in solemn procession through the central hall to the chamber to the shout of "Hats off, Strangers!" With him go the chaplain in his robes and the sergeant-at-arms bearing a sword. The Speaker ascends his canopied throne, the chaplain reads the 67th Psalm and three short prayers, the doorkeeper shouts, "Mr. Speaker at the Chair," and while those members who feel less need of divine guidance stream into the room, the House of Commons begins the business of the day.[7]

This procedure is a daily event. When a new session of Parliament opens (generally once a year), there are additional ceremonies. The peers in their crimson robes and their wives in satins and tiaras assemble in their chamber, the Earl Marshal and the Lord Great Chamberlain stepping backwards precede the black and gold sword of state and the dusty red cap of state held aloft on a little stick, and the reigning monarch and royal family enter and take their seats. The Commons is then summoned to the bar of the Lords' chamber by the "Gentleman Usher of the Black Rod," an officer bearing an ebony rod with a golden tip. Here it listens to the queen read "the speech from the throne," outlining the policies for the coming session and what legislative action will be taken. In reality, of course, the speech has been prepared by the Cabinet. Nonetheless, when the Commons returns to its own chamber, it promptly passes a motion returning "humble thanks" to "Her Majesty" for her "Gracious Speech."

Before the discussion begins, one more tradition must be complied with: the House must listen to the first reading of a bill "for the more effectual preventing of Clandestine Outlawries" —not because the danger of clandestine outlawries is so great that action must be taken before the queen's message can be attended to, but as a sign that the Commons has the power in its own right to proceed with legislation without the queen's recommendation. In fact, so slight is the pressure for the bill that it is then and there abandoned, to be introduced again in identical form at the beginning of the next session. The House in the meantime moves on to debate the reply to the "Gracious Speech."

Customs of debate

During its debates the House observes certain characteristic customs. Members never address one another directly or call one another by name. All remarks are addressed to the Speaker,

---

[7] While Parliament is in session, the flag flies from the tower, and at night a light shows.

and other members are referred to as "the honorable Member for South Hackney" or the "honorable Member for Bootle" or whatever the member's constituency happens to be—unless, indeed, there is some additional distinction. Thus members of the Cabinet and of the Privy Council are referred to as "the right honorable gentleman, the Member for Limehouse," or Woodford, or Warwick and Leamington. Lawyers are "honorable and learned" gentlemen, officers are "honorable and gallant," and the sons and daughters of peers are addressed as "the noble lord" or "the noble lady."

Whenever a new member makes his maiden speech in Parliament, he humbly asks the forbearance of the House, and at the close of his speech the next speaker (who is generally a member of the opposing party) congratulates him on the success of his effort, assures him that, although he does not necessarily agree with all of it, he has listened with great interest, and expresses the hope that there will be many times in the future when the House may have the pleasure of hearing him on subjects in regard to which he has special competence. Similarly, when a new Cabinet minister makes his first speech, the next speaker for the opposition congratulates him on his appointment and on the success of his speech before he proceeds to attack the points that the minister has just made.

When the debate is over, the House of Commons also has its peculiar way of taking votes. If there is any doubt in the Speaker's mind as to where the majority lies, or if the minority demands a "division," bells are rung and the policemen in the lobbies and corridors shout, "Division." After two minutes the Speaker puts the question again, two tellers come forward from each side, and the members rise from their places and march into the lobbies. Those who vote "aye" go into one lobby, and those who vote "no" go into another. Six minutes are allowed for late arrivals from smoking room, writing room, restaurant, and corridor. Then the doors are locked, the members are identified and counted, and the tellers come forward to report the result to the Speaker, those representing the majority standing on the right facing the Speaker and those representing the minority on the left.

The case for "quaintness"

To foreigners the daily ceremonial, the pageantry of the opening session, the response to the summons of Black Rod or to the cry of "Division," the fictions concerning the "queen's speech," the exaggerated courtesy with which members are referred to may appear either quaint or ridiculous, and in either case useless. Nothing could be further from the truth. No parliament can retain the respect of its people—and indeed no parliament can transact business—if it is in constant turmoil. The ceremonial and the exaggerated deference and courtesy help to produce an atmosphere of mutual respect.

On the first day of a new Parliament, new members are warned of the conduct expected from them in the House. Ordinarily, a gesture from the Speaker is enough to quiet the House. If a disturbance breaks out, the Speaker simply rises from his seat, and the bickering members usually subside. If one of them continues to be obstreperous, the Speaker as a last resort can "name" him, and the House (including his own party) votes immediately for his suspension. But an apt comment, humor, and ensuing laughter are more common ways of keeping the House on an even keel.

This does not mean that the discussion is a lukewarm, milk-and-water affair. Courtesy and formality are thoroughly compatible with aggressiveness, sharpness, and vigor; and understatement can be as telling as overstatement. The art of the graceful taunt has been highly developed, together with the art of the witty but cutting rejoinder. Moreover, members are aware that the eyes, if not of the country, at least of the press are upon them, and when they wish to hit, they hit hard. The fact that they call one another "honorable" and congratulate one another on their delivery does not prevent the most vigorous criticism—yet it helps to keep the debate on the level of rational discussion and good humor and to prevent it from degenerating into a purposeless row.

THE SPEAKER

The smooth functioning of the House depends on the Speaker. Once the spokesman of the Commons before the monarch, the Speaker is now the regulator of debate. A major part of his function is to ensure the government efficient handling of its business. This role dates back to a famous occasion in January 1881 when the Irish members were attempting to bring all parliamentary business to a halt (not unlike a filibuster), and the Speaker on his own authority moved a closure. The following year, Gladstone introduced procedural changes that mark a watershed in the management of parliamentary affairs. Members henceforth lost their cherished right of moving the adjournment of the House in order to discuss any issue and this procedure was restricted to only those matters accepted by the Speaker as of urgent public importance. Government control of the House was assured. Other forms of closure followed, to which, however, the Speaker must agree. Since 1918, the Speaker has been empowered to select the amendments on which a vote will be taken, and in other ways he sees that government business proceeds smoothly, although with due attention to the most serious objections raised to a particular measure.

But the Speaker is also the protector of the rights of the opposition, the private member, and the public. In a recent far-reaching relaxation of restrictions, the Speaker was empowered in 1967 to determine when there is "a specific and important matter which should have urgent consideration." This provision enables the House to debate at short notice urgent foreign or domestic situations whether or not they involve ministerial responsibility.

Not only does the Speaker make such far-reaching decisions, on which he is not required to justify himself, but together with the whips he also determines who participates in a debate. The leaders of both major parties and representatives of minor parties can be expected to speak, but opportunities for backbenchers are apt to be slim. In one explanation of the order of debate the Speaker announced that:

> I have worked out a list of about 30 names covering, I hope, most interests and, geographically, most areas, but that leaves something over 70 who will be disappointed. Naturally, in these circumstances, I have had to disregard, to a great extent, the claims of maiden speeches, and I am sorry to say, too, that I have had to disregard many old Members who have not spoken yet in this Parliament, but I really could not work them in under the scheme that I have adopted.

At the same time, backbenchers naturally look to the Speaker to give them as substantial opportunities as possible. They cherish the words of Colonel Douglas Clifton Brown in 1945: "As Speaker, I am not the Government's man, nor the Opposition's man. I am the House of Commons man and I believe, above all, the backbenchers' man."

It is this view of the role of the Speaker that led to backbencher protests over the selection of Selwyn Lloyd as Speaker in January 1971 to replace Horace King, Labor's first Speaker, who had resigned because of age after performing superbly in the position from 1965 through 1970. Agreed upon mutually by both the Cabinet and the shadow cabinet, Lloyd brought a wealth of experience to the office, including continuous representation of the same constituency since 1945, Lord Privy Seal, and Leader of the House, in which latter role he showed particular sensitivity to the interests of backbenchers. But Labor backbenchers resented their own lack of consultation in the nomination, and some went so far as to nominate a startled and unwilling candidate at the last moment and finally to vote against Lloyd. He was overwhelmingly confirmed, but in the future a more open method of selection is assured.

Once selected, the Speaker rises above the parliamentary battle and breaks his ties with his own party. If a new election results in a victory for the opposition, he continues in office (in the United States he would be replaced); and he is proposed for reappointment by the leaders of the party to which he does not belong. In fact, once chosen, the Speaker retains his office until death or voluntary retirement.

For a long time, there was also a tradition that the Speaker of the House of Commons should be reelected without opposition. In 1935, 1945, and 1964, however, the Labor party, to maintain the vitality of its local constituency organization, contested the reelection of the Conservative Speaker in his own district, but with notable lack of success. The Conservatives did not contest King's seat either in 1966 or in 1970, although representatives of minor groups did so unsuccessfully. It seems, therefore, that the electorate is as determined to maintain the tradition that the Speaker should be reelected to the House as the parties have been to maintain the tradition of reappointment within the chamber.

THE WHIPS

The effectiveness of the parliamentary system is almost as dependent on the party whips as on the Speaker. It is the business of the whips of each party to keep in touch with party members, to inform them what business is coming up and when a vote is going to be taken, and to see to it that they are present to vote as their leaders want them to. The chief whip of the majority party is the parliamentary secretary to the treasury (sometimes still referred to as the "patronage secretary," although patronage is not what it once was or what it still is in the United States). Three or more lords commissioners of the treasury assist him, as do the comptroller and the vice-chamberlain of the royal household. All these officials draw a salary from the government, and there may, in addition, be a number of unpaid whips. Opposition whips work without official pay.

Reputation to the contrary, it is more important for the whips to be tactful, sympathetic, observant, and likeable than to be fierce. They must know what the private members are thinking, for the whips are the principal channel through which the party's leaders learn of the feeling of the rank-and-file. They must identify the rising young members of their party. They try to keep the members in line through good temper and reasonable appeals rather than threats and a display of force; but they also know how to suggest to the erring member the perils of party unorthodoxy. They must know what the opposition is likely to do next and what tactics will be most successful in getting business through the House with the least expenditure of energy and risk of embarrassment.

The word *whip* is also used for the notice sent to each party member listing Parliament's business for the week. If an item in this list is not underlined, there is no special reason for the member to be present; and if it is underlined only once, the matter is not very pressing. A *two-line whip*, however, means that the business is really important; and if an item is underscored three times, nothing should keep the member from voting.

Informal agreements

Gladstone once commented that the British constitution "presumes more boldly than any other, the good faith of those who work it." And it is, in fact, chiefly through voluntary and informal agreements, based on this good faith, that the House decides on its business and gets it done. What efficiency the House has is mainly the result of the ease with which the opposing parties enter into arrangements "behind the Speaker's chair" and "through the usual channels" to determine what shall be discussed, when it shall be discussed, and how much time shall be allotted to the discussion. A breakdown of this system of voluntary agreement, such as occurred over the use of closures to push through the Industrial Relations Bill early in 1971, vastly complicates the working of the parliamentary system as a whole.

Under the normal method of arranging matters informally, the whips of the opposing parties (who are the "usual channels") consult with the leaders of their parties and then with one another "behind the Speaker's chair." The opposition whips may agree to speed the debate on certain measures if the majority's leaders in turn agree to discuss certain topics in which the opposition is especially interested. Without arrangements of this sort, Parliament might have the best rules of procedure in the world and still be an outstanding failure. When a select committee of Parliament investigated the procedure on public business in 1931, the prime minister at the time, Ramsay MacDonald, told its members: "I must pay my tribute to the 'usual channels.' They are simply admirable. Whenever a reasonable arrangement can be made it is made. . . . I do not know how you could do your work in this House without the 'usual channels.'"

THE CHAMBER

If the House of Commons in action is ceremonious, it is also extremely intimate. The room in which it meets is a small one: there are seats for only 346 members on the floor, although in normal times there are somewhat more than 600 members; there is no space even for desks. At one end of the room is the Speaker's throne, and in front of the throne sit three clerks, in wig and gown, at the head of a long table holding books, documents, and two dispatch boxes. Five benches run along either side of the Speaker, the table, and the center aisle. On the Speaker's right sit the members of the majority party, with their leaders (the Cabinet ministers) occupying the front bench, which is called the Front Treasury Bench. Directly opposite them, on the other side of the table, the shadow cabinet (the leaders of the opposition) occupies the front opposition bench. There is no gradation or middle ground. One's position must be taken frankly, for or against the Cabinet.

On ordinary occasions there may be only forty or fifty members in the House (a quorum is only forty), and the front benches may be relatively empty; but at question period and for

Floor of the House of Commons

great debates members flock into the chamber, fill the seats, overflow into the gallery, and stand about the sides, lending a feeling of excitement and drama, of history in the making. This is most impressive and tends to make the speakers themselves eager to rise to the occasion.

The smallness of the House has an important influence on the nature of the debate. In such a chamber it would be foolish to engage in oratorical pyrotechnics. The members are on the same level with one another—there is no rostrum from which to harangue the assembly. If they speak from the front benches, half of their audience is behind them. If they speak from the back benches, half of the audience has its back toward them. The opposition sits only a few feet away: there is no need to shout in order to make it hear. Indeed, the leaders of either party can address one another almost in conversational tones across the table. They may, upon occasion, strike the table or the dispatch box for emphasis, or indulge in a restrained gesture, but there is little temptation to play to the grandstand. It is easy for members to make interjections, ask questions, and carry on a running debate that is serious, intimate, and not devoid of flashes of wit.

There is, in fact, a much admired and carefully cultivated "House of Commons style"— easy, casual, conversational, characterized by presence of mind and equability of temper. Occasionally, as in the case of Lloyd George or Winston Churchill, brilliance in speech will win great admiration; but in general the House prides itself on giving its attention to men who may be clumsy in their expression but who are deeply sincere or thoroughly competent to speak on the subject in hand. The rules of debate revolve around the three "r's": relevance, repetition (to be avoided), and reading (which is not permitted). The members themselves know the tricks of addressing crowds in their own constituencies, and they have no desire to listen to an eloquent windbag. The man who can impress them is the man who knows his business. No audience, in short, is a better judge of capacity and of character.

3   THE HOUSE OF COMMONS: ITS WORK

It used to be said that the principal job of the House of Commons is to make, to support, and to overthrow ministries. Strictly speaking, a ministry consists of about ninety or more offices of ministerial rank filled by members of the party that has the confidence of the House of Commons. About twenty of the most important ministers comprise the Cabinet, and the decisions of the Cabinet are binding on all ministers. The British also use the word *government* much as Americans use the word *administration* when they speak of "the Nixon administration" or a "Democratic administration." Thus, in practice, the terms *Cabinet*, *ministry*, and *government* tend to be used interchangeably.

According to Bagehot's classic work on the English constitution, "The House of Commons lives in a state of perpetual potential choice: at any moment it can choose a ruler and dismiss a ruler." Today, however, this statement has lost its meaning. With the extension of the suffrage from 1867 on and the growth of party organization and party discipline, the occasions on which the House of Commons is in a position to expel a majority government are virtually nonexistent. Only in those exceptional cases when no party controls a majority of the seats in Parliament (as in 1923–24 and 1929–31) is the ministry unstable; and even then it is not necessarily unstable, for divided opponents are unlikely to wish to force an election. Labor's slim majority between 1964 and 1966 placed its members under great strain but did not prevent it from executing major and extensive legislation. It takes a major crisis, and, indeed, a deep split within the party itself, to force the resignation of a government composed of the leaders of a party with a majority.

But this is not to say that the task of the opposition is futile. In the first place, the opposition exists to demonstrate that there is an alternative government. It must also seek to demonstrate that it is a credible alternative and that if it were in office it would be more effective, more intelligent, and more concerned for the interests of the public than the government in power. This is difficult. Action is always more newsworthy than criticism. In the crucial areas of foreign policy, defense, and the state of the pound, the opposition will be reluctant to lay itself open to the charge of "irresponsibility" by making criticisms that might damage the interests of the country as a whole. Nonetheless, Labor's attack on British policy in Suez in 1956 created a great national debate with far-reaching consequences for both parties and the allegiance of the electorate. Moreover, the opposition, if sufficiently sensitive, can capitalize on swings in public opinion, such as the discontent with austerity, which the Conservatives exploited in 1951, and the social-democratic appeal to the frustrated middle class, which helped to bring Labor into power in 1964.

The second major function of the opposition is to keep to the fore a sense of alternatives. Its criticisms may sometimes sound like caricatures of what the government considers its honest efforts to seek worthy national policies, but its role is to attack. The adversary procedure of the law courts, with its deliberate exaggeration of the strong points of both the prosecution and the defense, is also characteristic of Parliament. Indeed, one of the useful results of the need to oppose is sometimes the production of an alternative plan, as for example on immigration, that may lead to modifications in what the government decides to propose. There is no doubt that the role of the opposition is an arduous and, if long sustained, a frustrating one, but it remains at the core of what Parliament has been designed to do.

PROCEDURES FOR CRITICISM IN THE HOUSE

The organized opposition has its best opportunity to criticize governmental policy as a whole when it raises the amendment to the queen's "Gracious Speech," which is, of course, a review of the Cabinet's position and legislative plans. But it also has a further twenty-nine Opposition Days (technically called Supply Days but always used to raise questions of policy rather than the appropriation) that may now be scattered through the session and, as always, focused on any topic it wishes. Moreover, traditionally there are three two-day debates on the Consolidated Fund (of which one, by convention, is at the disposal of backbenchers to raise any subject they like). In response to appeals for more topicality of such debates, four half-days can be earmarked for debates on pressing subjects raised at no more than forty-eight hours' notice.

These guaranteed opportunities provide the opposition with 25 to 30 percent of parliamentary time. In addition, the opposition may ask for special facilities to attack the Cabinet's policy in general or to discuss some especially important issue. If the opposition "demands a day" for a *motion of censure*, the Cabinet will find time for a debate in the near future. On such occasions each side brings forth its biggest guns. The prime minister and the man seeking to take his place, the leader of the opposition, face each other in a type of direct contest for which there is no equivalent in the American system. The press and the public are both watching to render their verdicts on the relative competence of the two parties. The Speaker's power to authorize a debate on "a specific and important matter which should have urgent consideration" is yet another means of providing the dramatic spectacle of verbal thrust and counterthrust by two opposing forces, which rivets attention upon the House.

Backbenchers have their particular opportunities to raise issues on the *motion for adjournment*, commonly debated during the last half hour (10 to 10:30 P.M.) of the day's business. Originally the Speaker allocated the subjects for debate from a list submitted to him, giving preference to an individual or constituency grievance, but more recently members have balloted for all but one of these sessions.

THE QUESTION PERIOD

The most famous of parliamentary devices for securing information, publicizing government errors or omissions, safeguarding civil liberties, and keeping the administration alert and responsive are questions. A former clerk of the House has called them "the one procedural invention of the democratic age."[8] They have no counterpart in the American or in Continental legislative systems.

Four afternoons a week for the first hour (apart from prayers) of the sitting of the House of Commons, ministers give oral answers to questions that have been submitted to them in writing and in advance by a member of the House from any party, including the one in power. If he wishes, the questioner or, if called upon by the Speaker, any other member may then ask one or occasionally two supplementary questions on the spur of the moment for the minister to answer. There is thus this added element of suspense for the minister and his advisers as well as for the spectators.

Due to the great increase in the number of oral questions without any corresponding increase in the total time allocated, the only person who answers questions every week is the prime minister, who always does so at 3:15 P.M. on Tuesdays and Thursdays. These are naturally the high points of most weeks, and the press and public galleries are usually crowded at those times. Ministers have been placed on a known rotation system that brings them to the top of the list about once in five weeks.

To prevent clogging the period allocated to a particular minister, no starred question (that is, one for oral answer) can be requested more than twenty-one days ahead of his turn to answer. Even so, it is far from certain that a questioner will succeed in getting an oral answer. In 1959, there was an average of 131 questions a day on the order paper (which is printed each day and distributed to the members and visitors) of which 41 and 52 supplementaries were answered.[9] Members can also get written answers to their unstarred questions, but there is no obligation to answer a written parliamentary question on the day for which it is requested. Moreover, question time is unique in its opportunities for publicity. It comes at the start of the day's business when the House is fullest, and a striking comment may even be reported in the evening papers.

While oral answers are still by far the most desired, the cumulative effect of vast numbers of unstarred questions (for example, Ernest Marples requested sixty-eight on a single day, July 14, 1969, asking about procurement arrangements in eight different departments) can also be great. Another technique for making a special impact is for a number of members to put in approximately the same question on a particular matter. Since the answers are printed and circulated, they have considerable political impact as well as ability to shake the department concerned.

To evaluate the total effect of oral and written questions is difficult. They are, naturally, only a "spot check" on government operations. Since, however, no minister or civil servant can guess what questions will be asked during a session, the questions keep a certain tension in the administration that is useful. It is always possible for a minister in a sensitive area like foreign affairs to reply that it is not in the public interest to disclose the information requested, but this is rare. It is also possible, and indeed common, for departments like the Treasury to resist the most pointed inquiries, a good reason for the more searching investigations through the ombudsman and select committees, of which more will be said later. But with all caveats, the spectacle of the prime minister and his ministers appearing on the floor of the House to answer specific questions put by members for their own information or to publicize a complaint by one of their constituents is an impressive one. It is a major way of demonstrating the sense of public responsibility of the leaders of the government, and it is a sharp testing time for ministers, particularly new ones.

THE PARLIAMENTARY COMMISSIONER FOR ADMINISTRATION: THE OMBUDSMAN

A parliamentary question is the traditional and obvious way in which an individual can appeal through his MP against what he considers unfair or improper handling of his interests by a government department. The volume of such complaints means, in practice, however, that only those that are of genuine political importance either to individual rights or to

---

[8] Lord Campion quoted in D. N. Chester and Nona Bowring, *Questions in Parliament*, p. 269.

[9] D. N. Chester, "Questions in Parliament," *The Commons in Transition*, ed. by A. H. Hanson and Bernard Crick, p. 98.

public policy can be considered by this means. There are also other problems besides lack of time connected with questions. A minister may be uncommunicative; only the department itself has access to the files related to a particular case. The famous Crichel Down case in 1954 (described in Chapter 5, Section 1) of an arbitrary departmental action was only made the subject of an independent inquiry leading to a reversal of the decision after long and persistent nagging of the government both inside and outside Parliament.

To provide a further flexible instrument for investigating complaints against the operations of central government departments, Parliament in 1967 adapted a widely publicized Scandinavian institution known commonly as the ombudsman and officially named the Parliamentary Commissioner for Administration. The particular British form of this institution is careful not to remove from the MP the primary responsibility of seeing that his constituents do not suffer injustice at the hands of the administration. On the contrary, it is for the MP alone to decide whether the complaint is appropriate for reference to the parliamentary commissioner. Moreover, in order not to overlap with existing parliamentary powers of investigation, complaints against local government, the police, and public corporations (see discussion of select committees below) are excluded from the commissioner's purview.

As with so many British institutions, the full range of the commissioner's responsibilities and powers is still being worked out. He reports to the MP on each case referred to him and provides an annual report to Parliament on the scope of his activities. The Select Committee on Parliamentary Privilege, set up in November 1967 to examine these reports, provides a significant reinforcement of his role. Major questions regarding the exercise of his functions are whether he has the right to criticize a ministerial decision, and whether he should indicate publicly in his reports where the blame and responsibility lie for particular maladministration within a department. Both actions were originally criticized on the ground that they could undermine ministerial responsibility, and both were upheld by the select committee as being the purpose of the act which established the commissioner's office. In other words, the committee rejected the notion that ministerial accountability involves the complete anonymity of civil servants. It also implied that a thoroughly bad rule, as well as a bad decision about how to implement it, falls within the definition of maladministration, which the commissioner is empowered to investigate and determine. Yet the acceptable limits of the commissioner's decisions are still being worked out in relation to the wide range of practical situations he is called upon to investigate.

By the end of 1968, 542 MP's had referred complaints to the commissioner's office, 374 cases had been examined and the MP's provided with reports, while 727 complaints had been rejected as outside the commissioner's jurisdiction. So too were 808 written complaints received direct from the public.[10] Some of the cases, like delay with tax refunds and permission to remain in the country, resulted in the relevant department's providing compensation or finding alternative ways of meeting the request. In other words, the type of decision appears generally to be related to alleviating an individual hardship. But the fact that the resolution of such cases is made at all reflects a loosening of inflexibility in departmental rulings, which is precisely what is desired. What seems still needed is a more precise definition of what an "aggrieved person" means in terms of the statute, more freedom for the commissioner to make his own investigations without waiting for a specific complaint to be referred to him, and better reporting to the press of the investigations in particular cases. Some critics would maintain that what is needed most of all is a thoroughgoing system of administrative law on the French model (see Chapter 7, Section 4), but that seems a far from likely possibility.

THE MOVEMENT FOR PARLIAMENTARY REFORM

The establishment of the office of the parliamentary commissioner was one response to the pressure for parliamentary reform that was

[10] Geoffrey Marshall, "Parliament and the Ombudsman," *The Commons in Transition,* ed. by Hanson and Crick, pp. 123–24.

swelling during the early 1960s and reached a peak in 1966 when Labor was returned with a comfortable majority and Richard Crossman became the innovative but realistic Leader of the House. The Labor members of the 1960s were of a new type, strongly committed to the Labor movement as such but much more professionally trained and experienced than had been common in the past. Many of them had been engaged in decision-making at the local level and felt frustrated by their lack of power within Parliament. Committed to improvements in administration, education, social services, taxation, they found themselves without effective instruments of inquiry into the actual working of government machinery.

In 1966, the Cabinet approved in principle the establishment of specialized committees but on one condition: that the departments whose work they would examine should agree. In what was emphasized as "a sessional experiment," two new specialist committees were set up, one on agriculture and one on science and technology. They received the traditional power of select committees "to send for persons, papers, and records"; in addition they were given the specific authority to examine witnesses in public and, at least the second of the two committees, to employ some outside consultants. Although the "usual channels" appear to have suggested noncontroversial subjects for them to examine, in practice they plunged into highly significant issues: the nuclear reactor program, and the Ministry of Agriculture's plans for studying the effect of joining the Common Market on the British subsidy and price review system.

The pacemaker for these two specialized committees was the Nationalized Industries Committee, set up in 1955 as a result of backbench Conservative pressure to examine the reports, accounts, policies, and practices of the nationalized industries (see the fuller description of nationalized industries in Chapter 6, Section 2). The committee had proved its usefulness and become a permanent part of parliamentary machinery, but its value as a precedent was somewhat limited by the fact that it was largely confined to considering technical matters on which the government kept its hands off, and not the general issues of policy affecting nationalized industries on which the parties so sharply disagree.

Select committees have long been a means of investigating and reporting on a particular problem. In the nineteenth century, much important legislation resulted from their reports. With the growth of party divisions, the investigation of controversial subjects like the coal mines, social security, local government, population, and the civil service has been generally handed over by common consent to prestigious if often ponderous *Royal Commissions* composed of outside experts or to more flexible executive-controlled departmental committees. As with other innovative proposals of parliamentary reform, the whips have been nervous that select committees dealing with matters of public policy may undercut the responsibility and authority of the government. Thus in an era of specialization, there still remains official pressure to keep parliamentary procedure unspecialized.

The argument in support of more specialized examination of the detail of administration is, however, that under modern conditions it is no longer possible, if it ever was, to conduct government by general rules. The more government becomes involved in social and economic policies—and in Great Britain it is highly involved in the management of both— the more the citizen is affected by specific decisions. If Parliament is to scrutinize effectively the performance of government, its members must be equipped with better tools for securing information and for evaluating the specific impact of general policies. The use and disuse of select committees, and also the facilities available for MP's to secure and make use of their own information, are relevant to these facts. So also are they to Parliament's special role of keeping public opinion alert, informed, and energized, for it is not enough to have the data without the techniques of communication. The most penetrating report in the world will have no public impact if it remains buried in the files. The number of those who read the daily Hansard (the published record of parliamentary debates) is infinitesimal. If Parliament is to compete with more spectacular but less important news, it needs to use the media more effectively.

Specialized committees after 1966

The experiment of using specialized committees had a somewhat checkered but quite impressive history after 1966. A third Committee on Education and Science was set up in 1967; and subsequently committees on overseas aid and development, Scottish affairs, and race relations and immigration; the Committee on Agriculture, despite its protests, was terminated, however, in February 1969, with indications that such departmental investigations would shift fairly often; the Committee on Science and Technology has survived the change of government, and the Conservative leadership appears to have accepted the value of investigations by select committees in fields that are "noncontroversial," in the party sense. Its Green Paper of October 1970 (Cmnd. 4507) suggests retaining the subject matter of specialized committees on the nationalized industries, science and technology, race relations and immigration, and Scottish affairs, along with a Select Committee on Expenditure that would have a wider role than the former Estimates Committee, enabling it to examine the policies behind expenditures and even to question ministers on them. This is a substantial advance on the pre-1966 situation.

On balance, it seems fair to say the new specialized committees provided a more radical advance in parliamentary scrutiny of administration between 1966 and 1970 than had been anticipated or was, perhaps, appreciated. A number of useful reports were written. To a certain degree, backbenchers came into their own through this new type of check on the executive.

Yet there have also been problems to take into account. Backbenchers have complained about the heavy load placed upon them by committee assignments, with those in the new, specialized committees added to the eight standing committees to which bills are referred (see below), the committees on nationalized industries and the parliamentary commissioner, the Scottish and Welsh committees, and those dealing with the internal affairs of the House.[11] When the Finance Bill was also moved to committee instead of being taken on the floor of the House, it made a total of 629 committee assignments in 1969 being carried by about one-half the members of the House (one hundred or so government members and about forty opposition frontbench members do not serve on specialist committees, and another two hundred members rarely make themselves available). Thus the possibility exists that there will not be enough MP's available for work in the House or that attention will be drawn away from the latter.

In the second place, the committees have been inadequately staffed. The Agriculture Committee, for example, had less than half the time of a senior clerk. As Boyd-Carpenter, a prominent Conservative, pointed out in the debate on the Green Paper on select committees, November 6, 1970, the effective working of a committee depends on the provision of adequate and substantial staff.

The most disturbing problems that have developed are that the expert knowledge acquired by the members of the specialist committees has not had much impact on the House as a whole, and that the government has paid very little, if any, attention to their recommendations. Most of the committees have not had their reports debated and when the one on science and technology came to the floor in May 1968, there were only seventeen MP's present, including eleven committee members! Moreover, the government did not accept its recommendation on the organization for nuclear reactors.

Two more positive conclusions, however, can be put forward. A certain number of MP's have gained expert knowledge of the workings of departments, which they can contribute to subsequent debates. Even more important, perhaps, is the awareness within the departments of the possibilities of searching parliamentary scrutiny. In the 1970 session, the Committee on Nationalized Industries fought its way through a thicket of Treasury objections to the Bank of England itself, a striking demonstration that much more is possible than may yet have been achieved. While specialized committees may not have either the role or the potentialities their backers originally suggested

---

[11] Some perennial select committees—the Committee on Privilege and, on a more mundane level, the Kitchen and Refreshment Rooms Committee—deal with procedural or domestic matters of concern to the House itself.

and are certainly never intended to challenge the authority of the Cabinet, they have demonstrated capacities that have won respect as useful tools of parliamentary inquiry in a time of highly specialized governmental activity.

Facilities for MP's

The specialized committees have provided an institutionalized means for probing the workings of the administration, but many members, particularly of the Labor party, feel that it is even more important to provide more adequate reimbursement and facilities to enhance their competence in their jobs. Particularly surprising features of the position of a British MP as compared with an American congressman are the extraordinarily inadequate conditions of service that still persist. Only since 1964 have some small allowances for secretarial assistance been introduced; none of the two hundred odd desks for members and seventy for secretaries that are scattered around the buildings are private; there are few private rooms within the House itself where constituents can talk quietly with their members; there are no private telephones; and messages are conveyed only when the House is sitting. Travel is paid only between the MP's home or constituency and London during the session.

Above and beyond these major inconveniences is the lack of research aids in any sense comparable to those provided for Congress by the 243 (in 1966) persons employed by the Legislative Reference Service of the Congressional Library, one-half of whom are senior specialists engaged in research that is directly related to the needs and requests of members of Congress. In the Library of the House of Commons, there were only 19 graduate library clerks in 1970 who would "look things up" for MP's, of whom 12 concentrated on written replies to specific questions. The latter often arise because parliamentary questions have been returned with a note that the information is available in print; sometimes the parliamentary answer is found inadequate for the MP's needs. To a limited extent the library's research staff has also helped specialist committees, although in rare situations, as we have seen, there have been limited funds for outside experts.

These lacks of almost everything that an American tends to take for granted as necessary supports for efficient operations throw an almost unbearable burden upon those MP's who have no other means of securing them. And this, in turn, brings up the issue of compensation. MP's received no pay at all until 1911. Their salary has moved up by slow stages from the original £400 (about $1,000) to £3,250 ($7,800), the level existing since 1964. (In comparison, congressmen receive a base salary of $42,500, plus substantial allowances for assistance, and Canadian MP's, who may offer a more realistic base for comparison, receive $12,000 a year and a nontaxable $6,000 for expenses.) Thus British MP's must either have private resources, or hold another job in addition to their parliamentary work, or skimp the latter, or continuously overtax themselves. It is no wonder that most Labor and some Conservative members complain.

There is much to be said for making the job of MP a full-time one, particularly if committee work is to be increased. There is even more to be said for relating salary and expense accounts to services and facilities. Both should be linked to costs, either on a cost-of-living basis or by relating the salaries of MP's to those of some other group (in Norway they are tied to those of a sector of senior civil servants), so that Parliament is not placed in the embarrassing position, particularly in a time of financial stringency, of voting itself more money. The key point is to direct radical attention to meeting the reasonable needs of an MP to perform his function effectively. Only so can the work of Parliament itself be efficiently performed.

Publicity for the work of Parliament

But no matter how much more efficient the parliamentary instruments of investigation become, and no matter how effective the individual MP, Parliament will not perform a major part of its function unless it transmits to the public its own sense of urgency about public problems. It should also be able to identify for the public the issues around which controversy will subsequently center, which means before policy has already been determined. The great debates and, to a lesser degree, question period help to perform these functions. But as Parliament becomes more specialized in its attention to the detail of administration, there is need for carefully designed publicity that will catch the attention of the public and both alert and inform it. This is essential for "mobilizing consent" to the continuing operations of government as well as for raising necessary questions and problems likely to arise from legislation before it is too late.

The press is still probably the best forum through which such publicity can be handled. The press gallery is too small, but at least it exists.[12] But more could be done to identify in popular terms the issues being debated or analyzed if reporters were provided with reports well ahead of time, and "tipped off" on key issues. The Select Committee on Parliamentary Privilege, in its 1967–68 report, proposed that the House should take a more pragmatic view of alleged "contempts" in reporting matters under advisement. The current move to relax the operations of the Official Secrets Act, of which a British attorney general once said only half jokingly that it could cover "the number of cups of tea consumed per week in a Government department," is long overdue. This sixty-year-old law makes no distinction between security material and anything else and prohibits the receipt or publication of a government document unless an official has authorized dissemination. In the biggest Secrets case in years, however, in which *The Daily Telegraph*, its editor, and two others were prosecuted for issuing a report on the Nigerian civil war that by its critical comment on federal leadership embarrassed the Labor government, although it disclosed no matter of security, the judge in a surprise decision in early February 1971 not only cleared the defendants and ordered the government to pay costs but urged the latter to consider whether the Secrets Act had not "reached retirement age and should be pensioned off." Thus it may well be that Parliament will gradually become free of the antipublicity strait jacket that it has riveted on itself. It remains one of the cherished and legitimate boasts of the British that "secret" discussions remain secret (quite unlike those in Washington that usually hit the press almost immediately thereafter), but it seems unnecessary, and detrimental to its role of public information, that such reports and, indeed, many discussions, such as those on party policies, are kept from the public.

Television, a seemingly obvious means of linking the Commons to the public, has encountered much skepticism that is probably legitimate. If debates are to be televised, they would need to be edited for showing. Oddly enough the Lords agreed in 1967 to closed circuit television. The Commons, after more than a decade of discussion, finally resolved in December 1967 "to approve the making of sound recordings of its proceedings for an experimental period for the purpose of providing for Members specimen programmes." But there seems little disposition to expand the use of this media. Its cumulative effect might well blunt the edge of interest, except on rare occasions, rather than enhance it.

4 THE HOUSE OF COMMONS: LAWMAKING

The House of Commons has so long enjoyed the reputation of being the world's greatest lawmaking body that it may be disconcerting to most people to have given prior consideration in this chapter to Parliament's role as critic and public educator. But it is of the essence of the parliamentary system that

---

[12] As late as 1771 it was illegal to report debates in the House of Commons; to evade punishment, editors disguised their parliamentary reports under such titles as "Proceedings of the Lower Room of the Robin Hood Society" or the "Report of the Senate of Lilliputia."

Early in the nineteenth century, however, William Cobbett began to print parliamentary debates as a supplement to his *Political Register;* in 1811 the work was taken over by his printer, T. C. Hansard, who published *Hansard's Parliamentary Debates;* and today, although the government itself now publishes the text of the debates, this record still goes by the popular name of Hansard. It is an interesting commentary on British practice that the 1762 motion forbidding reports was only formally repealed in 1968.

legislation is a function of government. The positive force exercised by government, that is, by the Cabinet, is through the making of laws. Since the Cabinet controls the votes of the majority of the members of the Commons, there is no basis for doubting that public bills will be passed if the government so determines. The crucial role in public of the opposition, therefore, and in private of the government's own backbenchers, is as far as possible to use the techniques of inquiry, discussion, and opinion-forming *before* the Cabinet has fully committed itself not only to the principle but also to the details of a measure.

On average, the House of Commons spends about half its time examining bills. The Study of Parliament Group, a private group of university professors and officers of both houses, which has been making a serious analysis of the working of Parliament since mid-1964, maintains that the Commons spends too much time on legislation and too little on general debate and scrutiny of the administration. The Procedure Committee, which devoted its 1966–67 report to public bill procedure, did not agree. It did suggest, however, that more use could be made of ways in which the Commons could get into the legislative act earlier: for example, by government publishing a White Paper (i.e., a statement of proposals on a given subject) to be debated before the bill on that subject is introduced; White Papers on all major items in the "queen's speech" and special days set aside to debate them; *ad hoc* committees to consider the form of future legislation; and a willing ear to proposals by specialized committees, as with the recommendations of the Committee on Nationalized Industries regarding the form of the public corporation for the Post Office. The Procedure Committee also foresaw a further use of select committees to consider technical measures after their second reading.

In response to these dual stimuli and his own vigorous sense of realistic innovation, Leader of the House Richard Crossman introduced in the fall of 1967 a series of procedural changes in the handling of public bills (i.e., those of general importance to the country as a whole) to "streamline" the passage of legislation. Traditionally, all legislation has moved through five stages before going to the Lords for comparable stages, resolving any differences, and receiving the royal assent: a nominal *first reading*; a crucial *second reading* on the principles and purposes of the bill; a *committee stage* that deals with detailed provisions related to the agreed purpose, unlike the process in the United States where it is the crucial stage for analysis, redrafting, and even pigeonholing; a *report* stage that reviews amendments proposed in committee; and *third reading* as a whole, in which only verbal changes can be made and the bill is either passed or rejected. Under the Crossman reforms, bills can now go straight to committee for second reading and report stages unless twenty members rise in the House to object; and third readings are formal unless six members demand a debate. Since under those provisions so much can be done through committees (which will consist of between twenty and eighty members), voluntary time-tabling and use of the guillotine (see below) are now permitted.

It remains to be seen how far the Conservative government will make use of these new provisions. Contrary to the expectations of the Labor opposition, Prime Minister Heath decided to refer the controversial Industrial Relations Bill to *Committee of the Whole House*, which is the House of Commons itself sitting under a different name, with a chairman instead of the Speaker presiding, and a more flexible procedure in which motions do not need to be seconded and the same person can speak repeatedly. Formerly, all revenue and appropriation measures were considered in the Committee of the Whole, but because this procedure is so time consuming (an average of up to one-fifth of the working time of the House was spent in this procedure over a recent ten-year period), its role as the Committee of Supply was abolished in 1966, and as the Committee of Ways and Means in 1967. At the end of the latter year, Crossman forced through on a party vote the possibility of sending the Finance Bill "upstairs," that is, to a standing committee. The Conservatives bitterly opposed this procedure, however, as removing a fundamental right of individual members to criticize so vital a measure. In practice, when the "technical" aspects of the Finance Bill were sent to a standing committee in the 1968–69 session, that procedure appeared to work so smoothly as to restrict still further the publicity the Finance Bill generally secures through providing opportunities for general debate. Thus it is far from sure that in the future the Finance Bill will go to a standing committee rather than be considered in detail by the House as a whole.

SOME FURTHER LEGISLATIVE MATTERS

In considering the process of legislation, we have already described both the traditional stages for the passage of a bill and the Crossman procedural changes. In order to make the British legislative system quite clear, it will be useful at this point to differentiate between public and private bills, to describe the standing committees to which most measures are referred, to define the forms of closure that can be used to accelerate the progress of a bill, and to describe the process of delegated legislation.

Public and private bills

Public bills, as we have noted, are those of general importance; *private bills* concern a special locality or person or body of persons. A public bill can be introduced by any member of Parliament except that only a minister can introduce a money bill. If the bill is introduced by a minister it is called a *government bill*; if by a private member, it is called a *private member's bill* (not to be confused with a private bill, which has its own special procedure). Relatively few private members' bills become law, commonly not more than one major and several minor such measures in a session.

The first problem for private members' bills is to find time not already secured by the government and official opposition. Members must ballot for the privilege of introducing their bill; even if they succeed in the draw there are further problems. The member must somehow or other manage the technical job of draftsmanship, and he must act as his own floor manager—persuading enough members to attend the discussion of his bill, both on the floor and in committee, to maintain a quorum, and persuading enough members to vote in favor of it so that there will be a majority. Finally, he must be assured of the approval—or at least the benevolent neutrality—of the leaders of the majority party, for only those bills are likely to receive the approval of the House that the leaders are willing to see approved.[13]

The procedure for a private bill is quite different. Individuals or groups who desire its enactment simply file petitions with an official in each House called the "Examiner of Petitions for Private Bills" and with the government department most directly concerned. Persons whose interests are affected by the bill are notified, and when these conditions have been complied with, the bill is read a first time and ordered to be read a second time. Following the second reading, those bills that are unopposed go to a committee on unopposed bills, while the others are sent to a private-bills committee that holds elaborate hearings in which each side is represented by paid counsel, and witnesses with an interest in the bill are brought in to testify. The committee members act as impartial judges, and their report to the House of Commons is almost invariably adopted without discussion.

Regardless of whether it is opposed or not, the passage of a private bill is an expensive proposition. Both houses impose high fees related to the amount of money the bill proposes to raise or expend, and it is necessary to pay fixed parliamentary agent's fees as well as printing bills for the draft statute and the eight advertisements that must run in the local press and London *Gazette* before consideration. Thus, even if the procedure is straightforward, the cost may give a local authority pause.

Standing committees

Earlier in this chapter attention was focused on select and specialized committees, and mention has been made of the use of the Committee of the Whole House. The normal procedure

[13] These are only the major pitfalls that the private member must avoid. One can find an elaborate and grimly amusing description of the others in Sir A. P. Herbert's book, *The Ayes Have It,* which recounts the author's own difficulties in winning acceptance of a bill for divorce reform. In spite of his exceptionally good luck, it is worth noting that even one so blessed in friends and ability could not get his bill accepted without considerable assistance from the government of the day.

for legislation, however, is to go to one of the eight *standing committees*, which, to quote Bernard Crick, "are thought of as the House of Commons in miniature and not as a gathering of specialists or special interests."[14] Since 1960, there has not even been a core of members appointed to each committee. The Speaker appoints a chairman and, as required, anything from twenty to fifty members roughly in proportion to the strength of the parties in the House. Apart from the Scottish Standing Committee,[15] to which any measure exclusively concerned with Scotland is referred, and one reserved for private members' bills, there is no specialization of subject matter, although some regard is given to the interests of the members when they are assigned. Bills are referred quite arbitrarily in accordance with their position on the parliamentary timetable to whichever standing committee is ready to receive them.

Standing committees fulfill a very different role from their American counterparts. The latter each have a particular focus, for example, agriculture, education, and ways-and-means. As indicated, they provided a crucial stage in the legislative process. In Great Britain, however, a standing committee must accept the general purpose of the bill as defined in second reading and concentrate on the detailed provisions for implementing this purpose. Thus, unlike standing committees in the American system, those in Parliament are not supposed to undertake a creative consideration of the broader issues related to a particular measure, and hence they cannot call for witnesses or papers and have no research staffs. Not surprisingly, service on parliamentary standing committees is unpopular because it is time consuming and devoted to details. At the same time, the work these committees do is essential and occasionally decisive in producing a constructively framed measure.

Periodically, in the course of considering more effective means for MP's to supervise the executive, proposals are made for strengthening the committee system by making it more specialized and functional. We have seen how specialized committees have been used creatively in limited "nonpolitical" fields, but there seems little chance they would be allowed to go deeply into such topics as defense, foreign affairs, or even social security. To allow standing committees to do so is also unlikely since the executive jealously guards its prerogative in the former fields and its control over legislation in general. Some observers also feel that a proliferation of parliamentary committees to examine government work in progress, however appropriate to the separation of powers in the American system, would be dysfunctional in the homogeneous British political system in which the Cabinet and majority party are mutually supportive under normal conditions and not intended to check each other. Under these circumstances, the most constructive proposals appear to be to lower the size of committee quorums so as to provide more flexible movement of specially interested MP's from committee to committee as their subjects change. Standing committees could also usefully have more facilities, and perhaps adopt greater flexibility in concentrating on the more important provisions of a measure rather than taking up its clauses in order.

LIMITATIONS ON DEBATE

Since the demands on parliamentary time are so numerous and pressing, a variety of means have been developed to prevent filibusters and other time-consuming attempts to delay or obstruct business and thus to concentrate attention on the most important aspects of legislation. In one way or another, these means depend on the impartiality and good judgment of the Speaker, who, as we have seen, first instigated the closure, and here, as elsewhere, is the supreme regulator of the work of the House.

Of the formal devices used by the House of Commons, the most important are various forms of *closure*. Any member may at any time move that "the question be now put," and if the Speaker is willing to entertain the motion, the House of Commons must vote immediately and without further debate on the question of whether or not it desires an immediate vote on

---

[14] Bernard Crick, *The Reform of Parliament*, p. 85.

[15] There is also the Scottish Grand Committee, consisting of all members from Scottish constituencies plus ten to fifteen other members as needed to preserve the balance of parties, which pays prior attention to all matters referring to Scotland.

the subject under discussion. If at least one hundred members vote in favor of the motion, and if they constitute a majority of those present and voting, debate is halted and a final vote taken. Of course, a majority party always has one hundred votes at its disposal, and the provision would be open to serious abuse were it not for the fact that the Speaker refuses to accept such a motion until the opposition has had a fair chance to present its case.

There are several refinements of the closure procedure. A *guillotine* resolution may be adopted, as with the Industrial Relations Bill of 1971, assigning a certain amount of time in advance for the debate on a specific measure. At the conclusion of that time, regardless of where the debate stands, the guillotine falls and a vote is taken. In order to prevent such a procedure from concentrating debate on the opening provisions of a bill, the device of *closure by compartments* may be used to divide a bill into a number of sections, assign a certain amount of time to each, and arrange for the guillotine to fall as each subperiod of time elapses. In addition, through the use of the *kangaroo*, the Speaker may arrange to concentrate the debate upon those proposed amendments that are most important or most controversial, hopping over those that are of less consequence. Such restrictions are loudly deplored by ordinary members of Parliament, but the whips and the leaders of the great parties insist that only through such limitations can the parliamentary machine be made to work.

DELEGATED LEGISLATION

A further way of providing time and expertness is for Parliament to pass bills in general outline, at the same time delegating the power (in theory to a minister or ministers, in practice to government officials) to make rulings and regulations that will achieve the intent of the bill in specific cases. Thus Parliament sets the general purposes of the legislation, but expert administrators work out the technical details that Parliament has neither the time, the information, nor the skill to anticipate. If changing circumstances or unpredictable developments make certain rules inappropriate or obsolete, the administrators are free to make new regulations to carry out Parliament's original purpose, and Parliament itself need not be troubled to pass new legislation.

Such a delegation of legislative authority has obvious advantages in achieving expertness and flexibility, and every advanced industrialized country has had to resort to delegated legislation in order to prevent the legislative machinery from breaking down in the face of the volume and technicality of laws demanded by the public. The question is how to maintain adequate parliamentary control.

Since June 1944, a select committee of Parliament called the Statutory Instruments or Scrutiny Committee has considered all statutory rules and orders to decide whether they violate any of the limitations of the relevant act. Only some 3 or 4 percent of administrative rules and orders must be affirmed by Parliament; about half the others lie before the House for forty days and are then considered approved if there has been no negative prayer (that is, appeal) against them. Sometimes the House is not even aware an administrative rule is on the table unless the Scrutiny Committee makes one of its rare special reports on it. In order to determine whether it should do so, the Scrutiny Committee can call departmental witnesses to explain what has been done, but it is sharply limited in checking or criticizing such action and in asking why it has been done. Moreover, despite the fact that the committee is expected to investigate "unexpected" or "unusual" use of powers, it is not allowed to question the relevant minister, on the grounds that this is the prerogative of the House as a whole: a curiously rigid and restrictive view of ministerial responsibility.

In light of the large and probably growing use of delegated legislation, these procedures seem strikingly inadequate. There is at present no clear way of determining the extent of the rights being assigned to ministers or their departments rather than to Parliament or the courts of law. The volume of orders is so great that it is almost impossible to provide adequate scrutiny in the committee's fortnightly meetings. Moreover, delegated legislation may well affect matters of principle but the Scrutiny Committee is not allowed to discuss the merits of the matters before them. Even when it makes a report to the House, there is no automatic debate on the matter, so it is left to some individual member to raise the issue—if he wants to do so.

The distinctive American answer to delegated legislation is the regulatory commission, but in the United Kingdom it is felt that such institutions would violate the close relation between the executive and the legislature. Congress itself has no procedure for reviewing administrative orders unless special provisions are written into legislation such as the Administrative Reorganization Act of 1946, which authorizes the president to propose plans for reorganization of administrative departments or agencies. In those cases the plans are transmitted to Congress and go into effect if not rejected within a prescribed period of time. Another approach is for administrative orders to be challenged in court—a practice more common in the United States than in Great Britain—to determine whether the rule is within the delegation of power and whether proper procedures have been observed. None of these practices in either country provides adequate supervision of the use of delegated legislation, but the complexity and technicality of so much of contemporary government activity make such use inevitable.

5 THE HOUSE OF COMMONS AND FINANCE

Control over the public purse strings is the great traditional weapon of popular defense against executive tyranny, and according to constitutional custom, as reinforced by statute, this power belongs exclusively to the House of Commons. All money bills must be introduced in this House, and since the constitutional crisis of 1911 the House of Lords has had no power to reject a money bill passed by the Commons.

In practice, however, the House of Commons has yielded its financial power to the Cabinet. According to the Standing Orders of the House of Commons, the House may consider no proposal for the expenditure of money that is not recommended by the Crown (that is, the Cabinet); and any proposal to reduce expenditures is considered an indication of lack of confidence. (The so-called Supply Days, formerly hitched to proposals to cut a department's grant by some infinitesimal sum, are now openly given over to general debates on subjects chosen by the opposition.) Thus, unless the Cabinet itself is willing to propose an increase in expenditure or to accept a proposal to reduce appropriations, the budget as originally proposed is adopted unchanged. So strong is the presumption that the budget will be approved in the form presented by the Chancellor of the Exchequer that the provisions are put into effect immediately following the speech in which the chancellor "opens his budget." The chancellor and his colleagues are bound by so strong an obligation of secrecy before the delivery of the speech (in order to prevent the possibility that someone might profit from the possession of inside information) that, in the fall of 1947, even the inadvertent revealing of certain budgetary proposals a few minutes before the speech entailed the prompt resignation of the chancellor, Hugh Dalton. A graver indiscretion by James Thomas, Chancellor of the Exchequer in 1936, abruptly and permanently terminated his parliamentary career.

The consequence of this system is to ensure the enactment of an expertly prepared budget that can easily arouse considerable envy in the breasts of American officials. In the United States, as in the United Kingdom, the executive may prepare a careful plan for balancing revenue and expenditure, but the United States Congress is its own master in budgetary as in other matters. Once the president's financial proposals have been set adrift on the legislative sea, they are at the mercy of the winds of congressional prejudice and special interests. Unpopular taxes may be cut; special expenditures demanded by powerful pressure groups may be added; executive departments that have incurred congressional wrath may find their appropriations drastically reduced; and the most carefully laid plans of the administration may be disrupted. During the debates on the budget many an executive agency lives in a condition of the tensest anxiety, wondering whether it may be eliminated entirely through the loss of its appropriations—a situation that is hardly calculated to encourage able men to enter public service. And there are times when any resemblance between plans for expenditure and plans for revenue seems to be little more than coincidental.

But if Americans sometimes look at the British system with envy, it leaves open many questions about how parliamentary scrutiny and public information can be provided. These are questions to which much attention has been given in recent years. The Plowden Report (Cmnd. 1432, 1961) pointed out that as far as is politically feasible debates on finance should deal with major issues affecting the formulation of government policies. The annual economic survey presented at the same time as the budget, and debated together with the chancellor's taxation proposals, is far more useful for this purpose than the annual estimates, whose form remains confusing to most persons outside the Treasury. Moreover, White Papers in 1963 and 1966 attempted to forecast expenditures over a five-year period, and this has now become customary. Many grants, of course, like those for defense, local authorities, universities, social welfare, are already determined well in advance of the presentation of estimates. Only changes in legislation are likely to affect such areas of expenditure, and these naturally are debated in Parliament.

The use of a select committee to focus attention on public expenditure has so far been disappointing. First appointed in 1912, the Select Committee on Estimates, with its six or more subcommittees, mainly occupied itself with spot checks on administrative efficiency. It was replaced in 1971 by a Select Committee on Expenditure (as recommended by the Select Committee on Procedure in December 1968) that is "to consider public expenditure and to examine the form of the papers relating to public expenditure presented to this House." In so doing, it can also question ministers, a new development. The Expenditure Committee has a general subcommittee (sixteen members) and eight further subcommittees (nine members each) that examine the activities, estimates of expenditures, and efficiency of selected functional fields of administration dealt with by government departments, such as power, transport and communication, and housing, health and welfare. The total operations of the Committee on Expenditure are being evaluated side by side with those of other select committees to prevent both overlaps and omissions. Thus the whole structure of investigation is still in a mobile state.

While the purpose of the Estimates, and now of the Expenditure Committee, is to consider current expenditures and where possible to seek economies, that of the powerful Public Accounts Committee is to ensure that public money has neither been wasted nor used for purposes for which it was not intended. In this task, the Committee is immensely aided by the Comptroller and Auditor General with his large and expert staff, who are unique among administrative officials in being directly responsible to Parliament and not to the executive. Not only can the committee draw on the results of the continuous checking of departmental accounts by the five to six hundred members of the Exchequer and Audit Department of the Comptroller and Auditor General, but it can also examine its own witnesses. If the Expenditure Committee were provided with equal facilities, it might be able to catch some mistakes before rather than after they are committed. For example, in 1964 the Public Accounts Committee discovered that due to an underestimate of development costs of the "Bloodhound" missile, the company developing its guidance system had made what were termed "excessive" profits. Subsequently arrangements were made for repayment of substantial portions of the undue profits, but much trouble and expense would have been saved if the error had been discovered earlier. Here, as in so many places in Parliament's work, better facilities are needed to cope with the pressures of work and time.

Even if the process of parliamentary supervision of finance is so considerably improved, there still remain overriding problems connected with overall expenditures and investment and the relation of one form of expenditure to another (e.g., of social welfare and defense). In many ways these are the most important decisions a government makes, for they have a crucial impact on the country's rate of growth, level of employment, ratio of public and private advance, and, probably, international standing. Projections and economic analyses are helpful, and these are being increasingly provided. But it is debatable whether Parliament can be equipped to oversee these all-important issues, or whether any existing legislative body adequately does so.

6 THE PRIVATE MEMBER'S INFLUENCE

The combination of party discipline and effective rules of closure makes Parliament a remarkably efficient body in the sense of getting work done. And the most vaunted advantage of the British parliamentary system is its freedom from the sort of deadlock between executive and legislature that occurs so frequently in the United States. A good many Englishmen, however, maintain that the efficiency of Parliament is purchased at a high price. It is possible—as it is not in the United States—for the government to draw up a coherent and well-planned program of legislation in the knowledge that it will pass through the legislature without serious mutilation. But the immunity of such legislative proposals is possible, they say, only because the ordinary member of Parliament accepts his party's leadership and discipline.

Because of limitations on time, the average member only occasionally can introduce a bill of his own, and his chances of participating in an important debate are slim indeed. Moreover, only under exceptional circumstances does a member disregard the prescription of the party whips, and it is the exceptional issue on which the party whips have nothing to prescribe. One of those rare occasions came in 1964 when the House of Commons, on a free vote on a private member's bill to abolish capital punishment, demonstrated, as it had already done in 1956 under similar circumstances, its opposition to the death penalty. (The House of Lords, which had vetoed the measure in 1956, finally acceded in mid-1965.) Free votes were subsequently allowed on liberalizing the laws governing abortion and homosexuality between consenting adults (both introduced by private members). Only on such issues are parties apt to welcome the full exercise of individual conscience. The unprecedented Conservative party decision in mid-October 1971 to permit its members a free vote over entry to the Common Market, on which both major parties were seriously split, was made largely for tactical reasons.

THE BASES OF PARTY DISCIPLINE

There are several reasons why members normally respond to discipline. In the first place, the party member who regularly and intentionally defied the leadership of his party would almost certainly lose the support of both his local and the national party organization in the next election. Here it must be remembered that the ordinary member secures election only partially because of his own qualities and more particularly because he belongs to a particular party.

Behind the cruder weapons of party discipline, however, there are certain psychological considerations that exert a strong influence upon the private member. Thus he knows that if he votes against the policy of his party when it is in power, its chances of being returned to office at the next election will have been impaired. Nothing is more likely to shake the confidence of the electorate than a serious split in the forces of a party in Parliament. The Liberal party lost its power largely because of repeated splits in its ranks, and Labor's disastrous defeat of 1931 followed a similar cleavage in the party.

A member of a party may disagree bitterly with his leaders on one issue or even on four or five, but that is a very different thing from wanting the opposition to take over the government. If he disagrees with his own party on even 20 percent of its policies, he probably disagrees with the opposition on 90 or 95 percent. The discontented members of a party are usually those who are on the extremes furthest away from the principal opposition. Thus the most disgruntled members of the Conservative party are generally the reactionary Tories who may dislike the moderation of their own party but who turn apoplectic at the thought of bringing Labor into power; and the most dissatisfied of Labor's followers are the ones who are most radical and who would die before they would help to establish a Conservative government. Even if they disagree with their party leadership on an important issue, the knowledge that a serious defection will undermine its appeal and threaten to bring the enemy into power is enough to make most of them swallow their scruples and go into the correct lobby.

If there is an important amount of resentment in party ranks, however, concessions are likely to be made. Naturally, leaders are even more anxious to avoid an open party split than are their followers, and they will do much to avoid so dangerous a situation. Ronald Butt in his impressive study of *The Power of Parliament* has given a detailed and careful analysis of the situations between 1945 and 1969 in which Labor and Conservative backbenchers have tried to influence their parties' policies and even voted against them. While a government may feel that political advantage or sheer necessity impels it to go ahead in the face of strong backbench opposition, as with the "wage-freeze" provisions in Labor's Income Bill in 1966, it will only do so after the most serious consideration and efforts to persuade their followers to accede.

Butt maintains that Labor backbenchers have been "more ferociously insubordinate"[16] but at the same time less effective than Conservative backbenchers in influencing the policies of their leaders when the latter are in power. The Labor backbench rebellions between 1945 and 1951 were almost entirely over foreign policy, opposing the close alignment with the United States against the Soviet Union and urging a mediating role between the two. Twenty-three Labor members voted in December 1945 against taking an American loan, while forty-four abstained. In 1948, thirty of them voted against the government's Palestine Bill. Still more serious was the open opposition to the retention of conscription in 1946. On this occasion, as again in 1966 on Wilson's decision to maintain Britain's position east of Suez, the prime minister went to the unusual length of calling for a virtual vote of confidence within the parliamentary Labor party, although in general party leaders maintain that their responsibility is to the House as a whole, not simply to their own party.

Labor's open divisions over foreign and defense policies undermined public confidence in 1951 and thus contributed markedly to the Conservative victory in that year just as its divisions in the late 1950s and early 1960s over both defense and the traditional commitment to complete public ownership contributed to keeping it out of office until Hugh Gaitskell and Harold Wilson managed to reunite the party by 1963. But the backbench opposition to its foreign and defense policies from 1945 to 1951 had relatively little effect on Labor's policies. This is partly because the domestic policy of nationalization was eminently satisfactory to the rank-and-file, and because the "rebellions" were localized in a special group of Labor members. It was also because in the most serious of the revolts, that over conscription, Labor leaders had not only the support of the Conservatives but also of the bulk of public opinion.

Conservatives came into office in 1951 as a party of "national unity," but almost immediately pressures developed among their backbenchers for a more distinctively Tory policy of a free market and private enterprise. Already in April 1952, thirty-nine Conservative members signed an Early Day motion criticizing the government's delay in denationalizing steel and road haulage; within a week Prime Minister Churchill announced the intention to proceed with both. Butt attributes the establishment of the Select Committee on Nationalized Industries in 1955 to Conservative backbench pressure to secure more effective parliamentary supervision of state-owned industries.[17] Conservative backbenchers, supported by powerful industrial interests, also secured the breakup of the BBC's television monopoly and the establishment of commercial television.[18] These successes were achieved mainly, however, be-

[16] Butt, *Power of Parliament*, p. 187.

[17] Butt, *Power of Parliament*, pp. 207–08.

[18] See H. H. Wilson, "Pressures on Parliament: The Commercial TV Affair," *Politics in Europe: Five Cases in European Government*, ed. by Gwendolen M. Carter and Alan F. Westin.

cause they were limited and specific objectives that did not run counter to their leaders' major program.

The Suez crisis of 1956 demonstrates both the effect of earlier persistent right-wing nagging at Conservative leaders to preserve British interests in Egypt and the relatively slight effect of those who opposed the forcible British and French action aimed at keeping Suez an international waterway. Only eight Conservative backbenchers abstained in the crucial vote of confidence on November 8, 1956 (it may be noted that none of the eight won seats again as Conservative members), but the obvious divisions within the party both over the action itself and subsequently the withdrawal from it (principally motivated by American and Commonwealth opposition and the impact on the balance of payments) seriously shook the party. Anthony Eden's resignation due to ill health may have avoided a more forcible ouster. Butt attributes Harold Macmillan's succession as party leader and thus prime minister instead of R. A. Butler's to the fact that the latter's opposition to the Suez venture made him unacceptable to a wide spectrum of the Conservative party.

The Macmillan government proved so sensitive to backbench opinion that in 1957 it made substantial concessions to delay the impact of its Rent Bill and even withdrew its Shops Bill. In its original form the Rent Bill would have removed at the end of six months rent control, which affected some eight hundred thousand tenants. Although they favored the principle of freeing landlords from restrictions, many Conservative backbenchers feared the potential impact on their constituents of rent hikes and tabled a series of amendments at the committee stage. The press also took up the issue. Although the period of reducing rent control was then extended to fifteen months, eleven Conservatives openly abstained when the bill came to a vote.

The withdrawal of the Shops Bill is an even better instance of the effect of backbench opposition. Although organized retail interests and the unions supported the proposed lowering of the general closing hour from 8 P.M. to 7 P.M. and late closing once a week from 9 to 8 P.M., Conservative backbenchers rushed into the fray on behalf of the "small man" whose best means of competition with large chains seemed to be to stay open longer hours. Faced with their continued opposition, the bill was ultimately withdrawn. In another case, the backbench revolt in 1964 against the Conservative government's decision to abolish resale price maintenance (the climax to a long debate within the party) was marked by its unprecedented motion for rejection of the bill on February 16, 1964, and a final, somewhat unsatisfactory resolution of the issue through compromise amendments.

Yet there were also issues over which the Macmillan government refused to budge. One hundred backbenchers tabled a motion on February 9, 1961, criticizing the government's Central African policies as too much determined by African interests, but since Labor favored still more progressive policies the government persisted. A rebellion aimed at restoring corporal punishment failed for the same reason, although sixty-nine Conservatives voted against their leaders. More serious issues dividing the Conservatives were entry into the Common Market, nuclear defense (in which the party leaders accepted heavier expenditures than they would have done without backbench pressure), and the Profumo scandal, which nearly cost Macmillan the leadership of his party. Although he survived the test, he might not have done so if there had been an obvious alternative leader.

The opposition to British entry into the Common Market was powered by older Conservative backbenchers who feared it would infringe on British sovereignty and damage British and Commonwealth agriculture. They pursued a campaign inside and outside Parliament to thwart Macmillan's effort to join the EEC. On March 21, 1962, more than thirty Conservatives moved in the Commons that the government should make it clear to Common Market countries that Britain would not join without "special arrangements to protect the vital interests in the countries of our own Commonwealth partnership." There was another comparable motion on July 30, 1962. In the end, of course, it was President de Gaulle's veto that stopped negotiations, but the division on the issue within the Conservative parliamentary party ran deep. (The Party Conference voted in support both in 1961 and 1962.) Only a substantial indoctrination process under Macmillan prepared the way for the parliamentary party to later accept Heath's position on Common Market membership.

During Labor's second substantial period of office, from 1964 to 1970, the influence of its backbenchers continued, in Butt's view, to establish broad limits within which government policy could be carried on. Backbench pressure appears to have forced the renationalization of steel on which Wilson was never very keen. Effective crossbench pressure helped to shape the 1965 Race Relations Bill, while Labor backbench influence led to dropping a proposed provision for deportation of Commonwealth citizens if "public interest" so required. The Cabinet's decision in February 1968 to limit the entry of Kenya Asians through the new Commonwealth Immigrants Bill led to a storm of protest and 62 votes against it, including 35 Labor votes, and 180 abstentions. When the new Race Relations Bill extending prohibitions on discrimination in housing, employment, and insurance was proposed in April, it was at a time of considerable tension, due to a disturbing speech by Enoch Powell. But the two front benches, although pressed by their own backbenchers, maintained a tenuous accommodation with each other and with their own more extreme followers that kept the issue from becoming the subject of a party fight.

Wilson had to meet stiff criticism from his own party on maintaining Britain's position east of Suez, and he subsequently modified the policy. Another bone of contention was American policy in Vietnam, from which nearly a third of the Labor parliamentary party demanded in a formal motion that the government disassociate itself, as did the annual conference. On appeal Wilson was upheld both in the parliamentary party and in the House, although there were thirty-two Labor abstentions. Milder methods of discipline were introduced to cover more than the traditional ones of conscience, such as religion, pacifism, and so forth. On two issues in which conscience clearly was involved—the response to Rhodesia's unconstitutional declaration of independence and maintenance of the arms embargo against South Africa—many Labor backbenchers felt intensely and helped to stiffen the government's position.

The most serious quarrel between the Labor Cabinet and its followers and their union supporters came in 1969 over the bill to reform industrial relations and limit the scope and number of unofficial strikes. Fifty-three Labor members voted against Barbara Castle's White Paper "In Place of Strife" (Cmnd. 3888) and forty abstained. The Cabinet split. The government then decided on a much revised short bill to impose a conciliation period, dropping in the process a bill to reform the House of Lords, which was meeting strong opposition from backbenchers on both sides of the House. After substantial negotiations with the unions, Wilson decided in June 1969 to drop the Industrial Relations Bill in return for an undertaking by the Trades Union Congress to deal with unofficial strikes. The issue was thus left to the Conservative government, which assumed office in June 1970 with a clear mandate for an industrial relations measure that, paradoxically, was to be subjected to bitter frontbench as well as backbench objections by the Labor opposition and considerable nonofficial obstructionism.

This data on backbench influence and efforts helps to modify the traditional picture of backbenchers as "brute votes" herded into the division lobbies by the whips. It indicates the degree to which party leaders, particularly the whips, and the Leader of the House must keep in continuous touch with backbench currents of opinion and take them into account before launching a bill and even during its progress. Certain other features of the parliamentary scene should be added. When a party is in office, it must be concerned much of the time with a national as compared to a party approach to issues—hence the Conservative government's nationalization of Rolls-Royce—and its sharpest criticism may well come, therefore, from those of its own followers who cling most rigidly to party dogma. In general, backbenchers are much less likely to embarrass their leaders if the party has a slim majority, as Labor had between 1964 and 1966, than when it has a safe majority; at the same time, party leaders have to watch their votes as Wilson did in withholding the called-for measure on steel renationalization during that period because of the open opposition of two of the members of his tiny majority. Thus it is apparent that party government is not always dominant. But ordinarily there are strong resources at the command of party leaders that, as we suggested at the start of this section, commonly assure them success if they remain firm in their determination to push through a measure or a policy.

7 THE HOUSE OF LORDS

The efforts to make parliamentary procedures and the supervision of the administration more effective do not stop short with the House of Commons; they have relevance also in regard to Great Britain's anachronistic second chamber, the House of Lords. Everyone agrees that a second chamber is needed to perform certain functions, and most people would agree that the House of Lords now undertakes some useful tasks. What is not settled, however, is exactly what functions it should perform in order to complement but in no way challenge the functioning of the House of Commons and, still more difficult, what should be the membership of a reconstituted second chamber.

In November 1968, a White Paper on House of Lords reform (Cmnd. 3799)[19] proposed comprehensive and radical changes that suggest ways of ultimately resolving both issues. These proposals seek to eliminate the hereditary basis of membership; to prevent any one party from having a permanent majority, as the Conservatives have always had, and also to assure the government of the day a "reasonable" working majority; to further restrict the power of the House of Lords to delay public legislation; and to abolish the Lords' "absolute power to withhold consent to subordinate legislation against the will of the Commons." The proposed composition of the Lords for securing these objectives is a two-tier house in which there would be both "voting" and "nonvoting" members, the latter with the right to ask questions, move motions, and serve on committees but not to vote; restriction of voting and of future membership to peers of the first creation; existing peers by succession to remain nonvoting members for life (unless created life peers), but no subsequent succession to carry the right to a seat; the number of bishops to be gradually reduced from twenty-six to sixteen; and the Law Lords to be retained.

PRESENT COMPOSITION OF THE HOUSE OF LORDS

How different this body would be from the present House can easily be seen by describing its composition at the time the White Paper was issued. The overwhelming majority of its 1,062 members hold their seats not because of any popular demand for their services, nor because of any marked capacity for legislative work, nor even because of any outstanding personal achievement or intelligence (although some of the peers are extremely able and intelligent). Rather, most of the members hold their seats as the result of chance: the typical peer, who represents 90 percent of the membership, simply happens to be the eldest son of the eldest son in a chain reaching back to an ancestor who was first created a nobleman.[20]

In addition to 736 hereditary peers by succession and 122 of first creation, the House of Lords in August 1968 included 26 lords spiritual of the Church of England; 23 serving or retired lords of appeal in ordinary (the "Law Lords," whose seats are held for life and may not be

---

[19] The White Paper drew on discussions on reform of the Lords in the Joint Party Conference on the subject. Parliament No. 2 Bill, 1969, which was intended to implement the reforms, was ultimately withdrawn due to backbench opposition and obstruction from both parties and to make way for Labor's Industrial Relations Bill, which, in turn, was withdrawn due to Labor backbench and union pressure.

[20] This is less far back in many instances than commonly believed. Almost half of the peerages have been created since 1906; only one in fifteen dates from 1689; and only one in fifty from 1485. Moreover, a "boom in barons"—forty-six new peers in the last six months of 1964 to increase Labor and Liberal representation in the Lords—created an unprecedently rapid increase in numbers, although Pitt had created fifty in five years, Lloyd George a hundred and fifteen in six years, and Attlee ninety-eight in six years.

inherited); and 155 life peers and peeresses appointed under the Life Peerage Act of 1958. (Since 1963, peeresses in their own right also sit in the House of Lords.)

The greatest outcry in the past against the inevitability of hereditary succession came from rising young politicians, like Quintin Hogg and, even more strenuously, Anthony Wedgwood Benn, who long sought the right to hold a seat in the House of Commons. Finally, in 1963 the Peerage Act permitted the disclaimer of peerages, an opportunity seized by Hogg, who, somewhat paradoxically, has now returned to his peerage as Lord Chancellor. The measure also permitted the Earl of Home to become Sir Alec Douglas-Home, for a short while leader of the Conservative party and prime minister after Macmillan's resignation.

The 1958 and 1963 Peerage Acts introduced two new principles into the composition of the House of Lords, the one of additions for life only (a principle previously restricted to the Law Lords), the other of possible renunciation of peerages. Since only a relatively small minority attend regularly, a Standing Order of 1963 added the provision that if a peer or peeress did not respond to the writ of summons and take the oath within a month of the opening of the session, he or she would be considered to have applied for leave of absence and would not, therefore, be able to take part in proceedings. None of these provisions, however, has satisfactorily met the problem of designing an acceptable second chamber. The Conservatives are reluctant to give up the hereditary principle as the dominant basis for its composition, while Labor has termed the social privilege embodied in the present House an affront to democracy. Yet both parties have come to agree in general about the legitimate and desired functions of the second chamber, an approach that may ultimately result in agreement about its composition.

THE POWERS OF THE HOUSE OF LORDS

Over the years, the House of Lords has steadily lost its coordinate power with that of the House of Commons. It was early accepted that no defeat in the House of Lords could force out a Cabinet. It was also long understood that the peers should not reject or modify financial legislation contrary to the wishes of the House of Commons. When, in 1909, the House of Lords did reject the Lloyd George budget with its heavy land taxes, the resulting constitutional crisis led to the Parliament Act of 1911, which removed the Lords' power of rejecting a money bill. This act also substituted for the Lords' previous power of defeating legislation a power of delay. Henceforth the House of Commons could pass any measure over the Lords' opposition if it did so three times in three successive sessions within a period of two years. This procedure was further cut by the postwar Labor government through the Parliament Act of 1949 to two successive sessions and one year between the original second reading and the date on which the bill passed the second time. More important than these restrictions, however, is the awareness that no elected government will ever permit the nonelected Lords to throw out an important measure of legislation. As Lord Carrington, Conservative Leader in the House of Lords, said on February 16, 1967: "It has always been my view that the House of Lords will only be able to use its delaying power once"—meaning that power would be abolished forthwith.

One coequal power that the House of Lords still retains is the power to withhold consent to subordinate legislation (i.e., orders in council or ministerial order or regulation), private bills, and bills to confirm provisional orders, none of which comes within the limitations of the Parliament Acts. Although in practice this power has been a theoretical rather than practical check on the overall control of the House of Commons, Labor has proposed that it should be abolished.

THE FUNCTIONS OF THE HOUSE OF LORDS

More important to consider than its still remaining powers are those functions that are inadequately performed by the Commons and that the Lords can perform well. As early as 1918, Lord Bryce made the classic statement on such functions, of which two have become even more important today because of the pressures of time on the Commons. These two are to examine and revise bills coming from the Commons and to initiate bills on noncontroversial subjects so they are in shape for Commons' consideration. A further important function is to provide a forum for wide-ranging debate on significant, nonpartisan issues.

By far the most important part of the Lords' work concerns the task of examination and revision, for that chamber has both the time and the expertise to catch flaws and ambiguities resulting either from clumsy drafting or from the many amendments that have been inserted in a particular measure during its passage through the Commons and that the Parliamentary Counsel's Office has not had time to catch. In the unusually badly drafted Transport Bill of 1947, for example, the Lords proposed 242 amendments, 200 of which were purely drafting or agreed amendments and accepted by the Commons, while the other amendments that were forced through by the Conservative majority in the Lords were rejected in the Commons—a good indication both of the usefulness of the reviewing function and of the restraints on the power of the Lords.

In the second range of activities identified by Lord Bryce, the Lords have been particularly effective in highly technical matters, especially those concerning such subjects as law, patents, and accountancy, and in examining the existing situation in matters in which the government does not wish to become directly involved like abortion, homosexuality, and artificial insemination. The Lords also perform a sterling task in handling noncontroversial government measures, reviewing obsolete statutes, contributing to the Joint Standing Committee on Consolidated Bills, which seeks to bring into a single measure related provisions scattered through many statutes, and reviewing private bills, about half of which start in the Lords. It must also be noted that for historical reasons the House of Lords is the highest court of appeal in the kingdom (a fact considered further in Chapter 7). During its sittings as a court, however, only the nine Law Lords, the Lord Chancellor, and any members who hold or have held high judicial office take part in the proceedings.

Although, as we have pointed out, the membership of the House of Lords is so large, about fifty to eighty of those members do most of the hard, routine work that is so valuable. Perhaps another fifty join in when their special field of competence is under consideration. The life peers have added some unusually intelligent and experienced individuals to the personnel of the House (although the patronage, so common with new peerages, has also not been absent to the degree anticipated). There have also been distinguished "Lords of the first creation," like Lord Attlee, Lord Beveridge, author of the famous social insurance report, and Lord Lindsay, political philosopher and Master of Balliol College, Oxford. Some of the most useful members of the Lords are crossbench, that is, they do not take the party whip.[21] While any British government is likely to feel more at ease when it has a working majority in the House of Lords as well as the Commons, what is most needed are composition and functions that can most adequately supplement the Commons in performing those tasks to which the movement of parliamentary reform has been dedicated.

[21] In support of its proposal to abolish the hereditary basis for membership of the Lords and break its permanent Conservative majority, the 1968 White Paper pointed out that in August 1968 there were 350 peers who took the Conservative whip, compared to 115 who took the Labor whip, and 40 the Liberal whip. Taking into account attendance at more than one-third of the sittings up to August in the 1967–68 session, however, the ratios were closer with 125 taking the Conservative whip, 95 the Labor whip, 20 the Liberal whip, and about 50 no whip at all. The ratios swung the other way when the party designation and attendance of created peers—that is, life peers and those of the first creation—were considered. Figures for this group of 326 members indicated 95 Labor, 77 Conservative, 8 Liberal, and 141 without a party whip; and for those 153 who attended more than one-third of the sittings, 81 Labor, 38 Conservatives, 8 Liberal, and 26 without the party whip.

8 THE FUTURE OF PARLIAMENTARY REFORM

To implement the movement for parliamentary reform may well require much more articulation of the work of the two Houses than has been attempted so far. Such articulation would proceed from a determination of what the Lords could do to relieve the Commons of some of its current, time-consuming legislative work so the latter could devote more attention to developing informed criticism of ministerial and departmental conduct of affairs and to looking ahead to impending social and economic problems. Bernard Crick, a member of the Study of Parliament Group, in his revised second edition of *The Reform of Parliament*, has outlined a series of functions the Lords could perform in these regards. While the most active member of the House of Lords might well find that his proposals relegate them to further obscurity and a dull program, the functions build on much of their present work but carry the logic still further.

Professor Crick proposes removing all power of delay and restricting the legislative function of the House of Lords to determining the internal consistency and points of law and administration in a measure, thus making it "an upper house to and for the Commons of scrutiny and investigation" on the pattern of select committees. Standing committees of the Lords should concentrate, in his view, on subordinate legislation (which, as we have seen, gets far too little scrutiny under present circumstances), statutory powers (where the same problem exists), and the machinery of government (as proposed by Jo Grimond, then parliamentary leader of the Liberal party in a debate on the subject on November 19, 1964). In addition to having its Law Lords provide the final court of appeal, Crick suggests that the Lords have a standing committee on administrative justice, which could supplement the rather circumscribed work of the parliamentary commissioner. As far as debates are concerned, he endorses, as do all observers, the widest possible latitude to consider any subject under the sun.

Crick envisages a highly competent and experienced body of men and women working on the agreed understanding that they are taking nonpartisan tasks off the shoulders of the Commons without in any way challenging the latter's control of decisions. (He also suggests adding some salaried short-term members for particular fields.) With the basic work of inquiry and scrutiny being done on their behalf in the Lords, the Commons could concentrate on basic social and economic problems. Some movement in these directions has already been made. It is hard to deny that the end result could meet many of the criticisms that have been raised throughout this chapter *if*—and it remains a big *if*—the knotty problem of the composition of the Lords can be settled.

5

The British Cabinet, prime minister, and monarch

1 THE CABINET

The Cabinet is the apex of party government. It is invested with power through the electoral decision, which has provided its party with the majority of seats in the Commons, and it maintains its authority because of the support of that majority. It provides legislative and administrative initiative to the House of Commons, whose role, as we have seen, is to consider, criticize, and legitimize these initiatives.

Although the Cabinet is the central instrument of government, one can search the law without finding more than incidental reference to it or to its leader, the prime minister. The Cabinet, in fact, is one of the typical anomalies of British politics. Its power arises not from any formal delegation of authority but from its dominance over those who do possess legal power: the Parliament, the monarch, the Privy Council, and the permanent administrative staff.

In form the Cabinet is a group of royal advisers that grew out of the royal household and the Privy Council, much as the Privy Council itself descended from the Great Council of the Norman kings by way of the *Curia Regis* and the Permanent Council. Every Cabinet minister is appointed to the Privy Council. Since membership in the Council is for life, the Privy Council is a very large body that includes both former and incumbent Cabinet members, together with certain public servants from the civil service and military forces. In its name are issued "orders in Council," a great variety of executive orders many of which are a form of delegated legislation representing an exercise of general authority granted by act of Parliament.

HOW THE CABINET IS CHOSEN AND ACTS

If in form the Cabinet is a group of royal advisers, in practice it operates very differently. Far from having a free hand in appointing its members, the monarch must choose as prime minister the leader of the party that secures a majority in the House of Commons and the prime minister himself selects the remaining members of the Cabinet. The Cabinet exercises the prerogative powers of the Crown, such as summoning and dissolving Parliament, although the writs are issued in the name of the monarch. The speech the monarch reads at the opening of Parliament is written by the prime minister and his associates. In short, the monarchy has no independent involvement in the political process—quite likely the requirement for its continued existence.

Not only in form, but also in composition, powers, and relationship to the legislature, the British Cabinet is obviously very different from the American cabinet. In the United States, the president may choose whomever he pleases, subject to confirmation by the Senate. He may even select a member of the opposite party, as when President Nixon appointed a Democrat, John Connally, to be Secretary of Commerce in 1971, while earlier Presidents Kennedy and Johnson had a Republican, Robert McNamara, as Secretary of Defense. Few cabinet members are ever chosen from Congress, and those who are must resign their seats in Congress. While the president may pick whom he wishes to head the great departments of government, he can as easily dismiss them or ignore their advice. Moreover, no one expects the members of the American cabinet to have one common position on all issues. It is also evident that neither the president nor the relevant cabinet member can count on all members of the president's party to vote in support of the measures they recommend.

In Great Britain, however, the prime minister not only chooses all the members of his Cabinet from his own party but each must hold a seat in Parliament to be eligible for office. When Patrick Gordon Walker failed to win a seat in a specially staged by-election in 1964, he had to forfeit his appointment as Secretary of State for Foreign Affairs. Moreover, while technically the prime minister is at liberty to offer posts in his government to anyone he likes, in practice there are a considerable number of prominent party figures who virtually choose themselves. Making a Cabinet is a matter of delicately balancing the important and influential but also differing points of view and political outlooks. In this sense, the Cabinet becomes a microcosm of the party.

Despite the variety of opinions within a Cabinet, the essence of Cabinet responsibility is that, after a matter has been thoroughly explored, all shall agree to support the same policy in public. Indeed, if one Cabinet member feels strongly enough that the policy approved by the majority of his colleagues is wrong, he is honor bound to resign. If he does not do so—and it is a startling and rare occasion when such a resignation takes place—the minister is duty bound to speak in support of the collective decision and to vote in favor of it in the House. And this credo of collective responsibility extends not only to the fifteen or twenty Cabinet members who made the final decision but to all those holding one office or another through to the unpaid parliamentary secretaries, which, in practice, means nearly one-third of the total parliamentary party. The principle received concrete enforcement in 1967 when seven parliamentary private secretaries were dismissed for abstaining on May 10 on a motion to authorize British entry into the Common Market.

The convention of collective responsibility was intended originally as a means of making the Cabinet responsible to Parliament. It has become, in practice, a device for isolating and to a degree neutralizing dissatisfaction with generally agreed upon Cabinet policies, and it thus helps to keep backbenchers in check by denying them influential leadership.

Since the dogma of collective responsibility acts so forcefully to reinforce the position of the Cabinet, it is not surprising that the opposition should also attempt to secure similar solidarity behind the decisions of the shadow cabinet. While the pressures are not quite so strong when a party is in opposition, it is noteworthy that Enoch Powell was expelled from the Conservative shadow cabinet in 1968 because of a provocative speech on colored immigration.

Since a Cabinet minister is not only a member of a governing collectivity but also the head of an administrative department, he is held responsible in Parliament for its administration as well as for general policy. Parliamentary questions, the investigations of the parliamentary commissioner (ombudsman), specialized committees and debates on Opposition days, or motions for adjournment can all focus on the ill-functioning of a department or a harmful decision it has made. High civil servants cannot be cross-examined in Parliament on departmental decisions (although occasionally they are by the commissioner or a committee) and the approach must be through the relevant minister, for he is in Parliament and therefore "get-at-able." Whether evidence of departmental mismanagement leads to the resignation of a minister generally depends on whether the party is ready to stand behind the minister or to sacrifice him. In the Crichel Down case, the relevant minister, Sir Thomas

Dugdale, resigned.[1] But others have not done so. Ministerial resignations may also take place for broader reasons, for example, when the Cabinet wishes to disavow a policy, as with the Hoare-Laval Pact during League of Nations sanctions against Italy's aggression in Ethiopia, or for personal behavior, as with the unhappy Profumo case.

THE MEMBERSHIP OF THE CABINET

The prime minister decides the size of his Cabinet and, within certain limits, determines which departments shall be represented in it. Since World War II, Cabinets have averaged between eighteen and twenty-three members, much larger than the Churchill war Cabinet of six to eight members, who were freed of departmental duties and met almost daily. Despite subsequent appeals to separate planning and administrative functions in the interests of efficiency, postwar Cabinets continue to include both. Thus, in addition to the prime minister, the central figure, a normal Cabinet includes the Chancellor of the Exchequer, the Foreign and Home Secretaries, Lord Chancellor, the Ministers of Defense, Labor, and Agriculture, and other key figures. Other ministers may be moved in and out of the formal Cabinet depending on how much focus there is on their sphere of activity. For example, the Minister for Fuel and Power was dropped from the Cabinet in 1947 after the nationalization of the coal mines had been carried through.

Another feature of Cabinet formation is the frequent reshuffling of offices, a practice that reflects the prime minister's sense for gaining effective teamwork but also tends to increase the influence in government departments of the top permanent officials. Only twelve of the twenty-three members of the Cabinet that fought the election in 1966 still held places in Wilson's 1970 Cabinet. Only four, including the prime minister, still held the same offices as in 1964. Nine of the new members had worked their way up from junior ministerial posts, and only two had been drawn from the backbenches. The first Heath Cabinet in 1970 included only nine members of the previous Conservative Cabinet.

It is uncommon for a parliamentary newcomer to be brought immediately into the Cabinet. A Wilson experiment in this regard made Frank Cousins, General Secretary of the Transport and General Workers' Union, Minister of Technology in 1964 on entering the Commons. Cousins subsequently voted against the government's prices and incomes policies and soon resigned. The Heath equivalent to the Cousins appointment was that of John Davies, who was made Secretary of State for Trade and Industry. Heath also appointed Peter Walker, a self-made millionaire, Secretary of State for the Environment, although he had no previous ministerial experience. In addition, he appointed a somewhat obscure backbencher who is a transportation expert, John Peyton, as senior minister responsible for transportation in the Department for the Environment. Thus Heath demonstrated his concern for technical experience and efficiency. It appears, however, that the general practice holds of drawing Cabinet members from among those with experience in Parliament and as a junior minister.

THE FUNCTIONS OF THE CABINET AND THEIR COORDINATION

The Cabinet has three major functions: to make the final determination on policy to be submitted to Parliament; to control the national executive in accordance with policies approved by Parliament; and to maintain continuous coordination and delimitation of the work of the many departments of state.

To fulfill these vast responsibilities, various organizational arrangements have been attempted. Prime Minister Churchill introduced the practice of coordinating ministers or "overlords" who supervised the work of several min-

---

[1] The Crichel Down case, which became a by-word throughout Great Britain, concerned an estate in Dorset that had been requisitioned by the government in 1937 as a bombing site. When it was no longer needed for this purpose, its hereditary owners tried to buy it back, but their offer was curtly rejected by the Ministry of Agriculture, which planned to use the area as a model farm. Only because of remarkable persistence and vigor were the former owners finally able to secure a public hearing of the issue, and only thereafter were they allowed to regain their land. See R. Douglas Brown, *The Battle of Crichel Down*.

istries, but sharp Labor criticism that such a development undercut ministerial responsibility led to the end of the experiment in 1953. From 1947 to 1964, however, the Admiralty, War Office, and Air Ministry were coordinated under the Minister of Defense who, unlike the "overlords," had statutory authority. More successful has been the regrouping of ministries, the use of Cabinet committees, and the expansion of the staff and role of the Cabinet Secretariat.

Regrouping of ministries

The Wilson government undertook a systematic regrouping of ministries. The separate defense departments were replaced in 1964 by a single Ministry of Defense, the Ministries of Pensions and National Insurance were merged in 1966 into the Ministry of Social Security, the Department of Foreign and Commonwealth Affairs combined in 1968 the responsibilities of the Foreign Office and Commonwealth Relations Office (which had previously taken over those of the Colonial Office), and several other mergers were undertaken. In this period, however, a somewhat controversial new Department of Economic Affairs (DEA) was set up to act as a balance to the traditional coordination of the Treasury, the rationale being that while the latter continued to be responsible for controlling expenditures and for monetary management, the DEA would plan for economic expansion, regional development, and industrial productivity. In 1969, the department was abolished, however, and its planning function was returned to the Treasury (see Chapter 6, Section 2).

The Heath government plans still further reorganization of government departments and offices. A unified Department of Trade and Industry was early established to combine the traditional functions of the Board of Trade (including those for civil aviation) with those of the Ministry of Technology (except for its aerospace functions). It operates under a secretary of state supported by two ministers who are not in the Cabinet. The Ministries of Housing and Local Government, Public Buildings and Works and Transport were grouped under the Ministry for the Environment. (The Scottish and Welsh Offices continue to play the major roles in these fields for their areas.) In the words of the White Paper on the reorganization of the central government (Cmnd. 4506) of October 1970, the objective of these and subsequent reorganizations is to match "the field of responsibility of government departments to coherent fields of policy and administration," which would be determined functionally.

Cabinet committees

Cabinet or interdepartmental committees, a second major means of coordination and preparation for final decisions, aid the process of collective responsibility by formalizing the interaction of different views held by ministers in overlapping segments of government business. Some of these committees are *ad hoc* to deal with particular problems and others are standing committees concerned with major areas of governmental activity such as foreign affairs, social welfare, public expenditure, and economic policy. Harold Wilson, who greatly expanded the use of Cabinet committees, described them in 1967 as "the Cabinet in microcosm," representative not only in numbers but in "opinions and shades of opinion, so that everyone who is really departmentally concerned and one or two who are not will be involved." [2]

The power of the chairmen of Cabinet committees was also increased under Wilson. He himself chaired the committees on defense and overseas policy, and on economic policy, while other senior ministers chaired those particularly relevant to their concerns. The Wilson view was that if the committee reached a clear decision that satisfied its chairman, the matter was then settled. Thus, the older system under which a junior minister could "reserve his position" and have the matter referred to the full Cabinet was replaced by the much more ticklish process of a possible appeal to the prime minister, who then decided at his own discretion whether or not to refer the matter to the Cabinet as a whole.

Side by side with this decentralization of many decisions to lower Cabinet levels, Wilson introduced in 1968 a necessary complementary

[2] See Louise W. Holborn, John H. Herz, and Gwendolen M. Carter, *Documents of Major Foreign Powers*, p. 72.

organ called the Parliamentary Committee, which was, in effect, an inner Cabinet. Composed of the prime minister and seven to nine senior Cabinet ministers, this committee met twice a week to consider all issues of genuine political importance. Unlike all other Cabinet committees, each of which is paralleled by an interdepartmental civil service committee representing the same fields, the Parliamentary Committee received its briefings from the Cabinet Secretariat. The decisions of the Parliamentary Committee were referred to the full Cabinet, which usually met every week for coordination.

It appears that Prime Minister Heath returned to the practice of using the larger Cabinet for consideration of policy issues, although he also streamlined the ministry as a whole. By grouping previous departments into one, their numbers have been somewhat reduced. It is noteworthy, however, that the October 1970 White Paper on reorganization of the central government specifically endorsed the flexibility of the existing system of interdepartmental committees.

The Cabinet Secretariat

Underpinning the work of Cabinet committees, of the full Cabinet, and of the prime minister himself is the Cabinet Secretariat, or Cabinet Office. As with the House of Commons, effective staff support is crucial for bringing together the most relevant material on which decisions are to be based. Wilson doubled the numbers in the Cabinet Secretariat to about a hundred civil servants, drawn from regular departments and organized functionally under the Cabinet Secretary and several assistant secretaries into broad divisions to deal with economic affairs, social policy, and overseas policies. He also brought in a number of experts from the universities, including economists, and made the chief scientific adviser to the government a full-time member of the Cabinet Office and chairman of an advisory committee drawn from the universities, industry, and the Royal Society to plan the science and technology budget for government-sponsored research. Moreover, in 1967 the Central Statistical Office, which has always been a part of the Cabinet Office, was reorganized to give it greater scope in monitoring the data-gathering of the departments and to provide long-range projections.

The chief Heath innovation in the Cabinet Office has been to establish a small multidisciplinary central policy review staff. This body, which is designed to aid the Cabinet as a whole, concentrates on aiding ministers in defining the relative priorities in their areas, the strategies for carrying out these priorities, and also in considering possible alternatives where choice exists.

In the light of its importance today, it is hard to realize that the Cabinet acquired a secretariat so late. The effective breakthrough was made at the end of 1916 when Lloyd George took office as prime minister and established the War Cabinet Secretariat. At the end of the war, this precedent led to the establishment of the Cabinet Secretariat as we now know it. Before that time, there was scant preparation for the meetings, no agenda, and inadequate records. In some cases Cabinet members could not even remember what had been decided. Thus Lord Hartington's private secretary once wrote to Gladstone's secretary: "There must have been some decision. . . . My chief has told me to ask you what the devil *was* decided, for he be damned if he knows."

Today, activities are highly organized. The Cabinet Secretariat, or Cabinet Office, under the direction of the relevant chairman or of the prime minister, organizes the agenda for meetings, keeps a careful record of the conclusions, and circulates them to the ministers. A few days before each meeting the agenda must be sent around so that each member will know what is to be discussed. Careful memoranda describing and explaining the measures under consideration are circulated at least two days before proposals are discussed. A short summary familiarizes the minister who is bogged down in departmental duties with the major points in the argument. In addition, copies of Foreign Office telegrams and dispatches are sent to the members of the Cabinet to keep them informed of day-to-day developments in foreign policy. All departments directly concerned in a measure (including the Treasury, if there are financial provisions) are expected to consult with one another and to work out an agreement for presentation to the relevant committee before the matter is placed on the agenda and the memorandum circulated. Once the relevant Cabinet committee has come to an agreement, the matter is settled, as we have seen, or if of special importance, the Cabinet can often dispose of it with comparatively little discussion.

Not only does the Cabinet Secretariat service the Cabinet and its committees, it also acts as the prime minister's personal staff. The permanent secretary of the Cabinet, the Cabinet Secretary, is at the same time the permanent secretary for the prime minister. Each minister, of course, has a permanent secretary as chief adviser as well as head of the civil service of his department. The permanent secretary of the Cabinet provides the same kind of informational and coordinating service for the prime minister in regard to all policy matters related to the general running of the government. Equally, the Cabinet Secretariat's chief scientific adviser is also the prime minister's scientific adviser.

Under Wilson, the Cabinet Secretariat greatly extended its supervision of the workings of the administration. Whereas formerly Treasury or perhaps Foreign Office officials would chair the interdepartmental committees (paralleling those of the Cabinet committees) through which high-ranking civil servants coordinate policies at their own level, the Cabinet Office took over the function of providing most of these chairmen. Thus the Cabinet Secretariat has become a very high-level and high-powered instrument at the disposal of the Cabinet, and particularly of the prime minister, not only for the preparation of the legislative agenda but also for the management of executive business and supervision of the administration.

As far as the staffing of the Cabinet Secretariat is concerned, the tenure of the permanent secretary tends to be very long: Lord Hankey served for twenty-two years and Tom Jones, his deputy, for a substantial period. Since 1963 the office has been held by Sir Burke Trend (sometimes termed, therefore, "the second most powerful man in England"). But Wilson followed his predecessor's example in keeping the tenure of most other members of the Cabinet Secretariat fairly short. In his words: "There is too much danger of their becoming 'ivory tower'; they come from departments and go back to departments." [3]

THE ORGANIZATION OF THE MINISTRY

The Cabinet naturally carries the ultimate responsibility for policy decisions and initiatives, but it is the apex of the very much larger ministry, numbering between eighty-five and over a hundred. Heath pruned the number of ministers below Cabinet rank when he acquired office so that they totaled about twenty less than those serving under Wilson. Questions have been raised, however, both regarding the appropriate numbers for a ministry under modern conditions and the most efficient organization of those below Cabinet rank. The issue is not only one of maintaining traditional Cabinet authority but also of spreading responsibilities for junior ministers down the line. Backbenchers, as we have seen, can play a role in the discussion of party policy but this is far less prized than participation in the actual exercise of governmental responsibilities. Moreover, with the vast scale and complexity of modern government, the range of fields and responsibilities is so great as to demand a substantial spreading of these responsibilities. These responsibilities include not only the massive volume of legislation but also the steady increase in parliamentary questions, the response to the growth of select committees, increasing interaction with constituents, which throws an ever-growing burden on the departments to respond to questions and problems, the persistent activities of "lobbies," and demands of international organizations, all of which in one way or another must be coped with by the ministry in office.

There are currently what approximate to four tiers of ministers: the ministers in the Cabinet; the ministers with Cabinet rank (and salaries) heading departments but not regularly in the Cabinet; the ministers of state (whose salaries vary); and the parliamentary secretaries. The numbers in each rank, and the gap between them, have varied over the years. Where Attlee in 1950 had thirteen depart-

[3] Holborn, Herz, Carter, *Documents of Major Foreign Powers*, p. 64.

mental ministers outside the Cabinet, Wilson in 1970 had only three. But conversely, in place of Attlee's three ministers of state, Wilson ended up with twenty-two, only six less than the number of parliamentary secretaries. Wilson also adopted the unusual practice of publicly specifying responsibilities for certain parliamentary secretaries (e.g., the ebullient Jennie Lee was given the arts, and even before she was raised to the rank of minister of state, she operated directly under the prime minister rather than the Secretary of State for Education). Traditionally, however, parliamentary secretaries are workhorses, serving their minister in the House and in his department but acknowledging the superiority within the latter of the permanent secretary.

There is also another rank, that of parliamentary private secretary (PPS), whose members serve without pay and at the invitation of ministers, but only with the approval of the chief whip's office. Their function has been described as "calculated to lighten the ministerial load," or, more facetiously, as "either to open the door, or if the minister is dry to see that the necessary stimulant is provided." There are twenty-nine private secretaries in the Heath government: there were thirty-seven under Prime Minister Macmillan, but only fifteen prior to World War I. In 1922, Winston Churchill became the first minister to have two PPS's.

This office has both advantages and disadvantages. It provides the first step on the long and uncertain road to promotion. Between 1918 and 1955, 60 percent of parliamentary private secretaries achieved ministerial office: of the Heath Cabinet, only five out of eighteen had been PPS's, but these included Sir Alec Douglas-Home, Anthony Barber, and Peter Walker. A PPS has a ring-side seat to the working of the government. He sits on standing committees; he attends conferences at his ministry. He has become a participant, however lowly, in the making of policy.

The disadvantage of being a PPS is that it inhibits parliamentary performance. A PPS is expected to refrain from requesting a question or speaking on his minister's subject, not to sign Early Day motions or show hostility of any kind to government measures. The dismissal of seven PPS's in 1967 for abstaining on the motion to enter the Common Market has already been mentioned and had an earlier precedent in the dismissal of four PPS's in 1949 for voting against the Labor government.

Every administration works out its own allocation of ministerial responsibilities, and these seem likely to change with experience. Shortly after Heath assumed office, a Labor MP, William Rodgers, proposed a five-tier structure that has interest as a possible model.[4] Recommending that the Cabinet itself be no larger than Wilson's Parliamentary Committee, Rodgers suggested that there also be twelve to fifteen functional departments with clearly defined fields and ministers who were responsible to Parliament, and a new category of "mini-ministers" who work within federally organized departments and should also be answerable to Parliament even though coordinated by a secretary of state. Below them again but recognized as the key middle rank, he put the ministers of state, of whom he thought Wilson's twenty-two were more appropriate than Heath's original twelve. Finally, he suggested using the rank of parliamentary secretary as a probationary grade from which prospects could be moved in and out without disfavor to their chance of later becoming a minister of state. Whether or not such a plan or some of its aspects are adopted, it provides a rational scheme of organization against which existing practices can be tested.

CABINET DICTATORSHIP?

Americans, who endorse the checks and balances of their own system, and who see the legislation that the Cabinet supports being passed by the House of Commons, while legislation that it opposes has no chance to do so, sometimes charge that Great Britain lives under a system of "Cabinet dictatorship." Such a charge is a gross oversimplification, however, for it overlooks the fact that a British government is under constant pressure from the opposition, from its own backbenchers, from the

[4] William Rodgers, "The Case for an Even Smaller Cabinet," *The Times* (July 1, 1970).

press, and from the public when a major issue is under consideration. It is true that at a moment of emergency, as with the bankruptcy of Rolls-Royce, the British Cabinet can move with extraordinary speed to force a decision through Parliament, but such occasions are fortunately rare. While no one can claim that the public is adequately alerted most of the time to the implications of issues that develop after an election campaign has been held, there is normally a process of public information through debates in the House and other means of analyzing and investigating issues that can be exploited.

It is clear that the government may disregard public opinion on a few issues so long as it knows that the public approves its record in general. But if there is widespread public revulsion and heavy backbench pressure the government will almost inevitably make concessions. In addition to all these reasons why the charge of Cabinet "dictatorship" is not justified, the British executive has traditionally acted with admirable restraint in its use of power, recognizing that the key to the successful functioning of the parliamentary system is that the House of Commons should have ample opportunity to criticize its policies, and that, in this sense, the House should be the mouthpiece of public opinion.

In any event, there is a certain superficiality in speaking of responsibility only as the ability of the people to prevent the government from doing what the people do not want it to do. At least as important is the government's ability positively to do what the people want it to do. And here the difference between the two systems is more clearly marked. If the British and the American executives were equally bent on pushing through a policy desired by the majority of the people, the British executive would be far more likely to succeed. Under the American system of separating governmental powers—and checking and balancing them—and with the laxness of party discipline, Congress often responds to the efforts not of a majority of the people, but of a minority. All that a minority group need do to check legislation is to control a single house of Congress or, in some cases, a single committee, in particular the Rules Committee, of the House of Representatives. In Great Britain such a situation would be inconceivable.

The issue may be summarized thus: Is it better to have a government capable of carrying out the will of the people—but also capable of carrying through something the people do not will? Or is it better to have a government so checked and balanced that it is not likely to push through an unpopular program simply because it cannot overcome even minor opposition? In a period of relative calm there may be something to be said for the second alternative as a way of forcing divergent groups to compose their differences and work out a generally acceptable program. But in times of crisis, which these days seem omnipresent, the government that cannot take decisive and prompt action is in danger of losing important opportunities. Ordinarily, when need is great, the American Congress has been willing to support many of the president's measures. The British executive, however, has the great advantage of being able to plan a comprehensive and coherent program and to ensure its enactment under virtually all circumstances, while the American executive not infrequently has his proposals rejected by a Congress unable to develop an integrated and consistent policy of its own.

It used to be thought that the British and American situations were so different, particularly regarding the presence of minorities, race prejudice, discrimination, and regional disparities, that the power of the majority under the British system to push through its program did not offer the kind of threat to minority rights that it would in the United States. In Northern Ireland, however, the Protestant majority has used its dominance in the local legislature to maintain discriminatory provisions adversely affecting the Catholics (see Chapter 8, Section 1). The Parliament at Westminster has been restrained, on the whole, in exercising its power to the disadvantage of minority groups, although some would claim that both Labor and the Conservatives have yielded too much in their immigration legislation to majority pressures. It is apparent, however, that there is an inherent danger in the British system in the lack of effective safeguards for minority and regional interests, which may pose more serious problems in the future.

2 THE PRIME MINISTER

THE PRIME MINISTER AND THE CABINET

It is sometimes charged, particularly by British observers, that if there is no "Cabinet dictatorship" in Great Britain, there is a dictatorship by the prime minister within his Cabinet and even within his party. This too seems a gross exaggeration. While technically the prime minister chooses his associates, many of them choose themselves. Neither Macmillan nor Douglas-Home, for example, could have maintained an administration without the support of R. A. Butler, whom they outdistanced for the prime ministership but with whom they could not dispense. Demands for the resignation of influential Cabinet members, such as Macmillan made in 1962, seriously shake confidence in the party leader. Although Wilson's use of Cabinet committees might have seemed to undercut the authority of the full Cabinet, it permitted thorough discussion of issues by those ministers most affected by them and the association of the senior ministers with the prime minister in decisions on policy. Labor and Conservative backbenchers, as we have seen, are insistent upon being kept informed regarding policy plans and vocal in reacting to them. Even the prime minister's ultimate threat of calling for a dissolution is hedged with practical restraints because it is at least as likely, if not more so, that he will be turned out of office as that his party's MP's with "safe" seats will lose them at the next election.

Although there is no doubt that the prime minister is the most important member of his Cabinet and party, he only remains so as long as he retains the confidence and support of his associates. There are many factors that contribute to such confidence and support: his leadership and particularly, perhaps, his handling of dissension; the caliber and effectiveness of his principal associates in the Cabinet; the situations with which he has to deal, and his policies regarding them; his timing in crises; his ability to infuse public confidence at the right moments. Labor is more constant than are the Tories in support of its leaders, as we have already indicated, but the debates and voting in Labor's annual conferences give indications of continued or lessening popularity. In the end, the success of a party leader depends most of all on his persuasiveness, on confidence in his judgment, and on the sense of cohesion he transmits to those with whom he works.

If one compares the position of the prime minister to that of the president, there are obvious strong features on both sides. The prime minister is far more likely to secure his program intact, although there are instances, as with Labor's Industrial Relations Bill, where it becomes necessary to drop a highly controversial measure. A prime minister never faces the situation of President Nixon's first term in which there was a Democratic majority in Congress, for the essence of Cabinet government, of course, is that the Cabinet and the majority in Parliament are of the same party. On the other hand, the president is master of his cabinet to a degree that no prime minister is. Moreover, the president's guaranteed term of office is something on which no prime minister can depend, even though most of them stay in office at least four years. But both Eden and Macmillan felt obliged to resign because of ill health, although neither had as serious an illness as that which incapacitated Woodrow Wilson without forcing his removal, and no president could have been removed from office as Neville Chamberlain was in 1940. The opposite side of a guaranteed term, however, is that the prime minister can choose the moment at which he wishes to fight the election, which gives him some, although, as Harold Wilson discovered, not enough advantage to win.

In terms of personal staff, the president has a big advantage, for no prime minister can draw on anything like the resources of the White House staff. The prime minister depends on the expert but relatively small Cabinet Secretariat, as we have seen, and also has a still smaller private staff at 10 Downing Street composed of official and political aides. Wilson, who declared that he attached "enormous importance" to his private political secretariat to maintain links with the parliamentary party, the party in the country, and to answer "the thousands of people who write to me," drew into it officials with "earthy" experience, that is, from departments concerned with industry, agriculture, labor, and so forth, as well as the traditional Foreign Office and Treasury personnel.[5] One additional sharp contrast here with the American White House staff is that apart from his press officer and personal secretaries, all the prime minister's aides are drawn from the civil service.

Conservative prime ministers have always been able to draw also on the resources of the Conservative Party Research Department. This body is more professionally staffed than is the research office of the Labor party and is directly responsible to the leader of the Conservative party, who personally appoints the top officials of the Conservative Central Office.

Richard Crossman once declared that the British have "the worst informed government in the world." That it could benefit from a better flow of information and from more coordinated long-range thinking and planning is not unique. The dependence on staff from the departments may well tend to create an overemphasis on particular problems to the detriment of a general overview on current issues and future possibilities. The shadow of impending general elections tends to shorten the perspective of planning, particularly in the latter years of an administration. Some of these difficulties in planning seem inherent in the nature of democratic government but improved sources and use of information and long-range projections would be helpful.

In one other respect, that of training for the job, the prime minister normally has the advantage. No man can step into the post of prime minister who has not served a long apprenticeship in Parliament and in the councils of his party. The man who can sustain the crossfire of parliamentary debate for many years and maintain a leading role before one of the most exacting audiences in the world, who can convince his colleagues, many of whom are no less brilliant and efficient, that his strategy for the party is the best possible one, and who can also appeal effectively to the public is likely to be extremely versatile, as well as able and experienced. In the United States there is no comparable device for the testing and winnowing out of the ablest leaders.

British prime ministers have varied greatly in their presence, characteristics, and ways of acting. Winston Churchill, of course, was forceful, eloquent, and thrived on action and danger. Neville Chamberlain, in contrast, had far less popular appeal and failed the test of wartime organization. Chamberlain's two predecessors, Stanley Baldwin and Ramsay MacDonald, were also very different: Baldwin being less energetic in pushing his personal views and loyal to his associates; MacDonald's brilliance and ambition leading him to break with his party in 1931, an act for which he has never been forgiven by some Laborites. Clement R. Attlee as prime minister aimed to win agreement among his colleagues rather than to impose his own will, but in his sincere, unspectacular way he was usually decisive and, on occasions, ruthless. Macmillan dominated his Cabinet by sheer intellectual capacity but encouraged discussions and yielded gracefully when necessary. Douglas-Home was not an effective prime minister. Wilson's ready tongue (sometimes too sharp for his party's comfort), his energy, ebullience, and forcefulness made him an effective if not always popular leader. Heath's quiet persistence, developing parliamentary flair, and obstinacy under pressure make him yet another type of prime minister. To some degree, as with the presidency, the role of prime minister brings out unexpected qualities and capacities in a man. Both offices keep their holders in a constant blaze of publicity that highlights weaknesses and failures to a degree that might break less confident personalities.

If this concentration on the qualities and role of the prime minister appears to place him in a very special position within the governing structure of Great Britain, it is perhaps necessary to conclude by reemphasizing the fact that British government is party government. A party gains the majority of seats in

---

[5] Holborn, Herz, Carter, *Documents of Major Foreign Powers*, pp. 63–64.

an election less because of the personality and appeal of its leader than because the public prefers its program and potential. Leadership is inevitably a highly significant part of how the party conducts itself. Among the greatest services a party leader can perform is to persuade its members that they must adopt more forward-looking policies, as Macmillan did in educating the Conservatives to the need for Britain to enter the Common Market, and as Gaitskell did in showing the Labor party that it must give up its former rigid emphasis on nationalization. But the character of those elected to a party is an equally important part of its profile as well as of its appeal. Maintaining the confidence and support of the party's elected members is essential to effective government. In the end, party government, whatever its limitations, requires the interrelationship of the electorate, the leadership, and the backbenchers in the working of British government.

3 THE MONARCH

The British monarch is far more conspicuous than powerful. The coronation is an unparalleled public spectacle; and the monarch's drive to the Houses of Parliament to open a new session is lined with throngs of spectators. Indeed, crowds of people will gather to watch any member of the royal family who would scarcely turn their heads (save in time of grave national crisis or during a bitter political campaign) to catch a view of the prime minister. Newspapers and magazines chronicle in detail the activities of royalty: Prince Charles has a birthday, Princess Anne visits the theater, or Queen Elizabeth opens a flower show, and the evening papers give as much room to pictures and descriptions of the event as they would to most political developments abroad. A prime minister may make a significant political decision without one-half the fanfare that accompanies a royal visit to a Welsh or Scottish village.

Yet in spite of the ceremonial and the excitement, the prime minister and the Cabinet rule. The monarch is not devoid of influence, but it tends to be informal, contingent, and often highly speculative. What influence the monarch has, in short, depends on personality rather than on formal power. He has the right to be informed and to be consulted. The prime minister must always tell him of Cabinet decisions and must be ready to explain the reasons for any policy. The monarch can, in the words of Bagehot, encourage and warn; and if he is intelligent, these opportunities may be important.

The monarch has the advantage of continuity. In the course of a normal reign many governments come and go, and there are close contacts with the leading statesmen of the age. It is not difficult as a result to acquire considerable political knowledge and experience. And since the prime minister must discuss his policies with the monarch, speak of new developments, and listen to what he has to say, the latter is in a position to influence the man who is most deeply concerned with policy.

Few people really know, until long after the monarch has died, how much of a part he or she has played in politics. Queen Victoria, for example, was a woman of decided opinions. In the great rivalry between Gladstone and Disraeli, she was heart and soul with Disraeli. Repeatedly she took action behind the scenes to help her political friends and to impede her enemies. Again, in the reign of Edward VII, the king's support of the French alliance was a factor in cementing the *entente cordiale*. George V is reported to have acted as something of a brake on the Liberal government that was in office when he succeeded to the throne. More important, George V, as we know from Harold Nicolson's biography, urged Prime Minister MacDonald, following his resignation in 1931, to form a new Cabinet made up of leaders of the other parties and persuaded the leaders of the other parties to concur. But there is still complaint, particularly from Labor, that the monarch in so doing exceeded his constitutional powers.

It is now difficult to imagine a situation in

which the monarch would exercise independent initiative in a political matter. As long as one party has a clear majority, and that party has an accepted leader, the monarch must ask him to become prime minister. The situation is more difficult if no party has a clear majority in Parliament. In this case the way might seem to be open to the exercise of some discretion by the monarch as to which party leader he should turn to first. The likelihood is, however, that the parties would decide the matter between them.

The recent past has witnessed the awkward situation of Conservative prime ministers resigning through ill health—first Anthony Eden in 1957, and subsequently Harold Macmillan in 1964—without leaving an assured succession. Queen Elizabeth used conventional channels in seeking the advice of elder Conservative statesmen before turning to Macmillan in 1957, and again in 1964 in requesting Douglas-Home to assume the prime ministership. Particularly in the latter case, however, there was sharp criticism of even this degree of royal initiative. Already in 1957 the Labor party had declared publicly that if it were in a similar situation, the monarch should take no action until the parliamentary Labor party had made its own choice of leader. The Conservatives have also now established their own formal method for selecting a new leader, as we have seen (Chapter 3, Section 2), so the monarch will never again be placed in the equivocal position of appearing to favor one person over another.

CONTRIBUTIONS OF THE MONARCHY

What, then, are the contributions of the monarchy to Great Britain? It is apparent that the monarchy can be and is used to further specific national goals, both economic and political. Recently the royal family, particularly its younger members, has been sent abroad as ambassadors of trade. Prince Philip's visit to the United States in 1966 coincided with a new drive for exports; Princess Margaret and her husband appeared at a series of British weeks in American department stores in 1967, and she went to a comparable occasion in Tokyo in 1969; Princess Alexandra performed the same service in Vienna the same year.

More important, constitutional monarchy can help to provide cohesion to a country which is not free from racial or regional strains. The brilliantly staged and strikingly successful installation of Charles as Prince of Wales in 1969 was not unrelated to the rise of Welsh nationalism. Some feel the government might also have made use of royal influence and even presence to try to ameliorate the strained and now explosive situation in Northern Ireland, although the latter's local government may well be reluctant since a brick was thrown at the queen in 1966, the last time she visited that part of the United Kingdom. Another suggestion is that a royal example of racial and color tolerance inside (as so frequently outside) Great Britain might influence those most affected not only by prejudice but also by loyalty and snobbery.

It is noticeable that the more the powers of the monarchy have atrophied, the greater its symbolic significance has become. The open republicanism of the nineteenth century finds no echo today. On the contrary, the monarchy has a special appeal to mass democracy, both as a symbol of national unity and as a source of constant interest. It answers a need for color and drama, for the personification of principles, that is all too often left unsatisfied in modern society. Especially in a time of strain and unsatisfied hopes, the need for diversion and for emotional outlets is a significant one.

The life of the royal family, moreover, provides an element of human interest and warmth that has a wide appeal. The skillfully made moving picture of the everyday affairs of the queen and her family was as popular as the film of the coronation itself. Indeed, there is an insatiable curiosity about the routines as well as the diversions of the royal family, their clothes, their trips, and their romances. Moreover, the queen's close family relations, her charm, and her deep sense of responsibility, paralleled as they are by those of Prince Charles, provide a pattern of life that many seek to emulate.

It is sometimes suggested that in an age of leader-worshipping cults, monarchy may divert potentially dangerous inclinations into harmless channels. Those irrational feelings that occasionally menace democracy may be focused on the monarch to the people's hearts content, for their trust cannot be abused—because the monarch lacks the power as well as the inclination to abuse it.

Above all, perhaps, the fact that the monarch reigns but does not rule means that loyalty is common to both government and opposition. Such a personal focus of loyalty as the Crown provides in a real sense puts and keeps politicians in their proper places not only as rulers but also as public servants.

THE MONARCH AND THE COMMONWEALTH

Whatever one may say of the role of the monarch within Great Britain, there can be no question of its value for the Commonwealth of Nations. For the Crown is the symbol of the reality of that association.

Colonies, of course, can be governed as effectively by a republic as by a monarchy. But the evolution of British colonies from a position of dependence on Great Britain to one of independence within the Commonwealth was greatly facilitated by the fact that there was a monarchy to act both as a formal and a sentimental link between them; for thus, although they had no common parliament or cabinet, they had a common sovereign.

Today the queen of the United Kingdom is at the same time the queen of Canada, Australia, and New Zealand of the older Commonwealth, and, among its postwar members, Ceylon, Sierra Leone, Jamaica, Trinidad and Tobago, Malta, Mauritius, Fiji, and Barbados. Although the other members of the Commonwealth are republics, they acknowledge the Crown as the symbol of the free association of the Commonwealth nations and, in a similarly symbolic sense, the queen as "head of the Commonwealth."

Particularly among some of those of Anglo-Saxon descent in the overseas parts of the Commonwealth, there is a somewhat romantic and emotional, but patriotic and powerful, loyalty to the king or queen that helps to hold these areas close to the people of the United Kingdom. Thus George VI's visit to Canada in 1939 helped to consolidate the sentiment that brought that country united into World War II. The royal tours of unprecedented extent that Elizabeth II and her husband, Prince Philip, have taken to overseas parts of the Commonwealth help to affirm the reality of the relationship. Although much of the attraction is through the pageantry in these visits, they also enhance the still existing sense of loyalty to the monarchy, particularly among older people. The decision to omit the queen's Christmas broadcast one year gave rise to widespread protest overseas and to its reinstatement the following year. The integrative symbolic and personal effect of the monarchy may have a steadily diminishing impact throughout the Commonwealth, but it is far from having vanished.

6

The British administration: national and local

1 THE RANGE OF PUBLIC RESPONSIBILITIES

In the past century no development the world over has been more spectacular than the increase in the scope of government activity. In the early nineteenth century the major responsibilities of government were to provide peace and order and to make it easy for private enterprise to do the rest. But the growth of heavy industry and crowded cities following the industrial revolution created problems of health and exploitation that individual efforts could not solve. One after another, each group in the community turned to the state to provide protection or aid, and each new demand added to the work of government.

Thus in the early nineteenth century the danger of disease and epidemics in Great Britain's overcrowded communities brought a demand for compulsory rules of sanitation and for the establishment of public health services. Public outcry against the widespread use of child labor in cotton mills and coal mines resulted in restrictive legislation while, more positively, the state also assumed responsibility for providing public education. Labor sought protection against dangerous work conditions and later won the right to organize and bargain collectively. Industry, in turn, as it came to be challenged by the competition of other countries, asked protection through tariffs and sought positive public aid in reequipping itself for greater productivity. British farmers, long neglected in the national concentration on industry, ultimately secured benefits of government-sponsored research and price supports. Individuals, at first the aged, the destitute, and the unemployed, and since World War II also the sick, families with more than one dependent child, and, in fact, all those who have exceptional need, receive government support in one form or another. Most recently, and most far-reaching are the responsibilities for the national economy, which involve measures to stimulate growth, ameliorate unemployment, ease regional inequities, and sustain the balance of trade. In all these fields, the state through its central, regional, and local agents increasingly intervenes in the affairs of the community and the lives of individuals.

2 THE STRUCTURE OF ADMINISTRATION

In undertaking such widespread responsibilities, the government has used a variety of instrumentalities. At the center are the regular departments whose structure reflects the growth of functions but whose changing pattern indicates never-ceasing efforts to respond both to concepts of rational organization and to political and personal pressures. The Treasury services and keeps a watchful eye on the departments, maintaining a check on all expenditures and a central policymaking role pervasive throughout the whole administration. Its concern for economic planning will be dealt with in conjunction with other agencies used in that somewhat problematic field. In addition, the relatively new Civil Service Department now exercises overall supervision and direction of staffing, especially at the top levels.

On a somewhat different level, the nationalized industries run by public corporations, which provide services that once were furnished by private enterprise, now account for about one-fifth of all economic activity in Great Britain. Finally, there is a confusing wealth of advisory and *ad hoc* agencies.

These types of instrumentalities will be described one after the other, but it is important to keep in mind that they necessarily and constantly interact. Public administration is not a settled and static series of bureaus, departments, corporations, and agencies but a vast number of functions being carried on by a very large number of persons, almost all of whom belong to the public or civil service. Exactly where within the overall structure of administration these persons carry on their required functions may be less important than the fact that the functions are handled. There have been and continue to be many different ways in which different British governments have tackled the omnipresent problem of administrative organization. It is also true that a variety of factors influence these decisions: coherence of function, response to immediate as compared to long-range needs, coordination, political philosophy, personal prestige and pressures. As the chapter on Parliament pointed out, administration is a highly significant and also highly political activity, as well as one in which popular control is particularly difficult to maintain.

THE MINISTRIES OR DEPARTMENTS

The most important and largest number of functions within the British administration are performed by the regular ministries or departments. The distinctive feature of a ministry is that it is organized hierarchically under a minister who is responsible for answering in Parliament both for the general aspects of departmental policy and for the detailed actions of his subordinates. Most of these ministers hold Cabinet rank, but those in charge of departments who are outside the Cabinet are equally answerable to Parliament. We have already indicated some of the difficulties for parliamentary control that are involved in the doctrines of ministerial and collective responsibility, and we will discuss this issue further below.

The considerable variety in the titles both of the ministries and of those who head them is sometimes confusing. In the United States all administrative departments are created by act of Congress, and each is under a single head known as the secretary (except in the Department of Justice). In Great Britain the ministries have had a variety of origins that is reflected in the variety of their names. Some ministries, such as the Treasury (the descendant of the Exchequer, which evolved from the royal household), stem from great offices of an earlier time; others, such as the Foreign Office, War Office, and Home Office, have evolved from the ancient office of secretary of state (for which reason each is capable legally of performing the duties of all the others, except in cases where special responsibilities have been defined in legislation); only the more recent ministries were created by act of Parliament. In addition, some ministries were established under boards or commissions, as in the cases of the Treasury and the Board of Trade. However, it was discovered in time that such ministries were more efficient if authority were concentrated in a single person. Although there is still a Treasury Board, it never meets; the real head of the Treasury is the Chancellor of the Exchequer (not the prime minister, although he has the title of First Lord of the Treasury). The real head of the Board of Trade, now incorporated in the Department of Trade and Industry (1970), was the president of the Board of Trade, a title now added to that of Secretary of Trade and Industry. Thus, despite seeming differences in organization, each of the British ministries has a single head, although "federal" ministries like the Department of the Environment have ministers in charge of special areas of work under the overall responsibility of the Secretary of State for the Environment.

Because of the frequent changes in areas of responsibility and titles, which can be made smoothly by order-in-council, subject only to negative prayer or appeal against them (see Chapter 4, Section 4), no effort will be made to be exhaustive in listing the central ministries of the British government. They fall into four main categories: defense and external affairs; internal order; economic and social matters; and finance and economic planning. In considering these different fields (as of 1970), only the most striking or broadly characteristic aspects will be described.

The two fields of *defense and external affairs* have been subject in recent times to a consolidation and fusion process. The three former service departments—the Admiralty (traditionally given precedence because of the age-old dependence on the Navy), the War Office (Army), and the Air Ministry—were made integral parts of a single Ministry of Defense in 1964, instead of merely being coordinated by it. In a pattern common to several integrated departments, the Secretary of State for Defense has two ministers of defense under him, one for administration and one for equipment, and three undersecretaries, one for each of the services.

In external affairs, four former departments have been combined: the Colonial Office, which up to 1966 was responsible for Britain's remaining colonies, mostly islands and ministates; the Commonwealth Relations Office, which until 1968 handled relations with members of the Commonwealth and, for historical reasons, those with Ireland and South Africa, although these countries left the Commonwealth in 1949 and 1961, respectively (see Chapter 8, Section 1); the Ministry for Overseas Development, which until 1970 administered Britain's aid program; and the Foreign Office, renamed the Foreign and Commonwealth Office.

The Home Office, which is primarily responsible for *internal law and order*, in as far as these fields are not controlled by local authorities, has been subject to the process both of fusion and of fission. Since all administrative responsibilities that have not been assigned by law or convention to another minister fall under the Home Secretary, it has been common to add new responsibilities to the Home Office as they arose but also to take them away as these functions became large and urgent enough to require separate departments of their own.

At the present time (1970), the Home Office has jurisdiction over the metropolitan police of London, and because of the practice of grants-in-aid the right to establish standards of organization, discipline, and equipment for the police elsewhere; it supervises the treatment of offenders, including juveniles, and the probation service, administers immigration and naturalization legislation, and regulates the conduct of elections, civil defense, and fire services. The Home Office is responsible for the organization of the magistrates' courts, while the Lord Chancellor, an eminent judicial figure who is also Speaker of the House of Lords, controls the personnel and machinery of the courts of law, appoints the justices of the peace, and recommends other appointments to the judiciary in England and Wales. (For a thorough consideration of the courts, see Chapter 7, Section 2.)

The ministries concerned with *economic and social matters* are the most numerous, as can be expected, and the most changeable. The economic ministries, however organized, deal chiefly with industrial and income policies, regional policies, local government, housing, public buildings and works, power, transport, natural resources, technology, relations with the trade unions, and social service payments. Social ministries deal with such subjects as insurance and welfare, health, education, and the arts. We have already described how the Ministries of Housing and Local Government, of Public Building and Works, and of Transport were unified by the Heath government into a single Department of the Environment (see Chapter 5, Section 1). Previously, the Ministry of Housing and Local Government had split off from the Ministry of Health, and much earlier the latter had taken over the powers of the old Local Government Board. While the Department of the Environment was given major responsibility for developing regional policy, industrial development in the regions was vested in the newly fused Department of Trade and Industry. Thus the process of fusion and of fission goes on with its attendant problems of potential overloading, coordination, and parliamentary control.

The most important department responsible for *finance* and *economic planning* and the key administrative agency for *interministerial coordination* is the Treasury. The Treasury was also responsible up to 1968 for the supervision of the civil service, but this function on the advice of the Fulton Committee (see Section 4) was then transferred to a new Civil Service Department. This development left the Treasury still more concentrated than before on its policymaking functions, which lie at the heart of administration organization and coordination. The central role of the Treasury is to control the spending of all government and other public bodies. It is also in charge of international financial negotiations, and it deals with economic management and, since 1969, again with economic planning in the sense of forecasts. It should be noted also that Treasury personnel does not spend all its time in a single office but moves around to other bodies like the Cabinet Office, interdepartmental committees (for which it provided all the chairmen until Wilson inserted more Cabinet Office personnel), the specialized departments, the Bank of England, and so forth, to secure information, give advice, and maintain coordination.

The coordination and control by the Treasury are exercised at every stage of departmental policy. No ministry may make a proposal involving expenditures or present a financial estimate to the Cabinet without first receiving Treasury authorization. Thus, if a ministry wishes to expand its activities, it must persuade the Treasury that such an expansion is necessary and that it does not involve duplication of a task already performed by another agency. Since the Treasury is likely to be far more open to a projected expenditure if the reasons have been carefully explained in advance and if it has been consulted early in the development of the project, there is a strong incentive for representatives of other ministries to keep in constant touch with the Treasury in order to win a sympathetic comprehension of departmental needs. In this way, Treasury officials acquire an overall picture of the plans and activities of all ministries, which is of the greatest assistance in integrating and reconciling their multifarious activities.

All sections of the Treasury are represented, of course, on the top-level committee that prepares the budget, described by Sir Stafford Cripps, Chancellor of the Exchequer in 1950, as "the most important control and the most important instrument for influencing economic policy that is available to the Government."[1] As long as there are no general controls on wages, prices, and flow of goods (rationing), the budget is the major instrument for regulating the operation of the economy through raising or lowering taxes and through checking or expanding government spending. In the United States the president proposes the budget but the Congress disposes of the money, often in a fundamentally different way from what the administration had planned. In Great Britain there is never any doubt that the major recommendations of the budget, which is a closely knit financial plan, will be accepted exactly as proposed. In any case, no estimate for a ministry may be increased by Parliament.

The Treasury also controls the collection and expenditure of public money. All government revenue, which is collected for the Treasury by the Board of Inland Revenue, the Board of Customs and Excise, the Post Office, and the Commissioners of Crown Lands, goes directly into the Consolidated Fund, which is deposited in the Bank of England. About 15 percent of national expenditures fall in the category of permanent charges, which are not voted annually. These include the interest on the national debt, the salaries of judges, and the Civil List, which covers the expenditures of the royal family—all matters that are normally kept out of politics. All other matters, including the expenditures of all ministries, must be authorized by annual statutes, the parliamentary check upon the financial system. This check is reinforced by the semi-independent Exchequer and Audit Department under the Comptroller and Auditor General, an important nonpolitical officer, who is quite independent of the Treasury (although he works closely with it in checking expenditures by the ministries) and who makes an annual report on withdrawals of

---

[1] Quoted in Samuel Brittan, *Steering the Economy: The Role of the Treasury*, p. 38.

public money directly to the highly important parliamentary Public Accounts Committee.

Even after their estimates have been voted, ministries are not free to spend their appropriations as they wish. They can draw their money from the Consolidated Fund only through a requisition by the Treasury, countersigned by the Comptroller and Auditor General, and this is normally issued for only one-quarter of their appropriations at a time. Moreover, any increase in the number or salaries of officials in a ministry has to receive Treasury approval, even if the ministry has enough money on hand to provide for it.

Not surprisingly, such great concentration of power in the hands of a relatively small department—comprising perhaps a thousand members as compared to others, like Defense, which employs well over a hundred thousand—has led to sharp criticism. This criticism was principally leveled at the Treasury's responsibilities for the civil service and for economic planning. The civil service function was finally removed, as already indicated, to a new Civil Service Department established in 1968. A more complicated path was followed in regard to Treasury responsibilities for economic planning.

ECONOMIC PLANNING

The British, in practice, have never wholeheartedly adopted a notion of economic planning to the degree that the French, for example, did after World War II. Nonetheless, the combination of Keynesian economics, that is, the use of fiscal policies to limit trade cycles and unemployment, and to stimulate desirable economic activities, coupled with the experience during World War II of government control over all aspects of economic life led to new commitments to undertake government intervention in the economy on behalf of public welfare. It was a coalition government, headed by Prime Minister Churchill, which declared in a famous 1944 White Paper that "the Government accepts as one of their primary aims and responsibilities the maintenance of a high and stable level of employment after the war." How this objective, which requires economic growth as well as a high and stable balance of payments, is to be secured, however, has led to much discussion and experimentation both in regard to policies and to instrumentalities.

Labor's commitment to democratic socialism naturally made it sympathetic to the extension of public ownership—reflected in large-scale nationalization projects immediately after the war (see below)—economic planning (where it made tentative but not very far-reaching efforts in its first period of office), and controls. The Conservatives, supported by public weariness of postwar restrictions, continued until the late 1950s to believe that competition could be an adequate stimulus to the economy. Faced, however, with the dismal evidence of economic sluggishness, balance-of-payments crises, inadequate infrastructure, and regional imbalances, they established a body in 1962 that was to concern itself with economic planning and longer-range projections: the National Economic Development Council (NEDC, commonly known as "Neddy"), whose developing organization was somewhat patterned on the effective machinery for economic planning that had been set up in France after the war. Thus, as in France, a series of bodies, known as "Little Neddies," were established in 1963 in which representatives of employers, trade unions, and relevant government departments worked out estimates of growth to be combined into a broad plan.

What is called "indicative planning," that is, a projection of what will happen to selected industries and sectors, including the public sector, if certain targets for overall growth are set, was embodied in the NEDC Plan for 1961–66, published by the Conservative government in 1963, and in Labor's National Plan of September 1963, covering the years 1966–70 and mainly prepared by the new Ministry of Economic Affairs. It must be admitted, however, that the expectation that the planning institutions would stimulate the economic growth at which they aimed—for example, the 1961–66 plan specified 4 percent growth—was not realized. The fundamental disequilibrium affecting the British balance of payments, and ultimately forcing (rather too late) the devaluation of the pound in November 1967, spelled the end of the effort at indicative planning. The

Green Paper published early in 1969 on "Economic Assessment to 1972" made its projections as forecasts rather than as instruments of policy.

In the meantime, the controversial Ministry of Economic Affairs had risen and was about to fall. It was established in 1964 to provide for more forceful planning for growth than was expected from "Neddy's" essentially advisory functions and those of the reorganized Treasury. This ministry took over much of the staff of the National Economy Group established in 1962 inside the Treasury, in response to Plowden recommendations to concentrate on economic planning, forecasting, and advising. In 1969, however, the Ministry of Economic Affairs was abolished and the economic planning functions were restored to the Treasury.

The Heath government introduced yet another addition to economic planning. It noted in its October 1970 White Paper on the reorganization of central government (see Chapter 5, Section 1) that the Treasury's "detailed and comprehensive" annual Public Expenditure Surveys, linked as they were to "medium-term economic assessments," provided "one of the basic elements in the information ministers' need to enable them to balance the claims of competing blocks of public expenditure." To fill two remaining gaps, however, it drew on the team of businessmen based in the Civil Service Department to help identify alternative policy options before final decisions were taken. This team now examines the objectives of expenditure against general government strategy and analyzes existing programs and the major policy options on them. Thus the government gains a better notion of desirable objectives in programs expressed as far as possible "in output terms," and it can examine alternative programs before making its final decisions. Considering the tradition of budget secrecy, it remains to be seen whether this information will be transmitted to Parliament for prior debate.

CIVIL SERVANTS AND MINISTERIAL RESPONSIBILITY

The vast responsibilities carried by the administration in any modern state naturally lead to fears that, in practice, it is the nonelected public personnel that operates government, whereas the elected representatives of the people, whether in Parliament or in the ministry, have relatively little influence on ultimate decisions. This concern, as we have seen, underlies much of the malaise in Parliament, and there can be no doubt that the relation between those formally responsible for the political aspects of government and those who are supposed to be apolitical—and hence, civil—is a sensitive but crucial one. More will be said on this issue in the course of the chapter.

Organization of a department

British departments are organized on a hierarchical principle. Immediately below the minister is the permanent secretary, who is both chief adviser to the minister and chief administrative officer of the department. In an American department, the top offices nearly always change hands when a new administration comes into office, but not in the United Kingdom, where experience and continuity are weighted more heavily than is sympathy with a particular political program.

The permanent secretary and the undersecretary, if there is one, must be constantly available for consultation with the minister, particularly when Parliament is in session; thus, the detailed control of administration is mainly in the hands of the assistant secretaries who head the several divisions into which a ministry is divided. Each of these divisions deals with a particular activity or area, and their work is coordinated through the higher officials in the ministry and by use of intra- and interdepartmental committees.

The permanent secretary, as the link between the rest of the ministry and the minister, inevitably has a great deal of discretion, of course, in determining what material to lay before the minister. Even more important is the fact that he may have a much wider range of experience than the minister himself in the subject matter of the ministry, particularly when the minister has recently come into office. In practice, however, the relative importance of the minister and the permanent secretary is likely to be a matter of personality. Inexperienced, weak, and overtaxed ministers may be swayed consistently by their advisers; but a minister who has a definite conception of what he wishes to accomplish can carry it through. A high civil servant may, and should, put before a minister his best arguments in favor of one course of action. If he is overruled, the ethics of the service demand that he carry out his minister's policy loyally and as effectively as possible. And in the end, since it is the minister who must stand before Parliament and assume responsibility for what his department has done, the minister will want to be convinced of the soundness of an important policy before he undertakes to support it publicly.

The minister and his political associates will also want to consider the public reaction to a particular way of handling a problem. If the permanent officials are the experts on the most efficient way of securing a particular purpose, the minister is, or should be, the expert on public opinion in his own party, in Parliament, and in the country. Moreover, a minister may have a broader view of the totality of an issue. R. A. Butler, who for four years was Chancellor of the Exchequer, was not an expert on technical Treasury operations, but Samuel Brittan suggests that it was his "hunches as a political animal that on occasion enabled him to separate bad advice from good" [2] and choose the wiser policy.

Ministerial and collective responsibility

What concerns MP's, however, is that the policies they can debate in Parliament are likely to have been largely settled already or else deal with generalities, whereas policy and administration are made up of vast numbers of specific decisions. It is this problem that has led to the pressure for more specialized committees, for more White Papers that lay out plans before they are formulated in legislation, for the parliamentary commissioner to get inside the workings of a department and identify which particular civil servant has been responsible for an error of judgment or for an inflexible decision that does not take particular human needs into account, and in this and other ways to remove some of the anonymity that shields civil servants.

[2] Brittan, *Steering the Economy*, p. 115.

This raises issues that are hotly debated. Brittan, for example, favors more open government, with the chance for civil servants to explain and defend their policy advice before parliamentary committees, as in the United States, rather than to have to filter it through a ministerial voice. He points out that the convention of a single minister being responsible for all departmental policy hardly stands up in the light of the constant interaction within interdepartmental committees, not to mention those in the Cabinet. He also feels that for the public to know that a variety of opinions has been canvassed before a final decision is reached would strengthen, rather than weaken, the case.[3]

The Fulton Committee on the Civil Service, which made no radical proposals on this issue, admitted that the assumption that a minister has "full detailed knowledge and control of all the activities of his department" is "no longer tenable." The special problem, as A. H. Hanson and M. Walles point out in *Governing Britain*,[4] is not, in fact, that greater openness and less anonymity are not compatible with ministerial responsibility as long as the principle of obedience is maintained, but that the equally important principle of political neutrality might be impaired. Thus, the more individual civil servants are identified with particular lines of policy, the more likely it might be that they would be caught up in actual political strife. And since the permanent tenure of civil servants rests on the assumption that they will not only serve faithfully whatever administration is in office but also not use their privileged position to the detriment of either side, the issue remains a sensitive one, not likely to be resolved in the immediate future.

THE NATIONALIZED ENTERPRISES

Public enterprise is a long-established feature of all modern governments. But its scope, justification, management, pay scales, relation to private enterprise, and articulation with the British representative system of government are once more somewhat in flux. No one could

[3] Brittan, *Steering the Economy*, pp. 34–35.

[4] A. H. Hanson and M. Walles, *Governing Britain*, pp. 145–47.

have anticipated when the Heath government came into office in June 1970 that, despite its broad commitment to stimulating competition and private enterprise, it would have felt impelled in February 1971 to nationalize a major part of Rolls-Royce because of the latter's bankruptcy, and that it would have pushed the nationalization measure through with unprecedented speed in a single evening. Less surprising, although with far-reaching consequences, have been the pressures on nationalized enterprises to divest themselves of at least some of the profitable sidelines they had developed. Wage disputes and strikes against the Electricity Board and the Post Office, the latter newly turned from a government department into a public corporation, strained government, union, and public patience and ingenuity early in 1971. Thus what had come to be thought of as a fairly settled aspect of governmental responsibilities since World War II has once more become a source of debate and controversy.

Labor's nationalization program after World War II had extended public ownership to just under one-fifth of the country's enterprises. To some degree this program, with its strong Fabian overtones, built upon earlier measures, in particular the four large-scale public enterprises that had been established in the interwar period (by Conservative or predominantly Conservative governments): the British Broadcasting Corporation (BBC), which provided British radio and now part of television broadcasting; the Central Electricity Board (now absorbed in the general nationalization of electricity), which built and operated four thousand miles of high-voltage transmission wires, known as the Grid, that cover Great Britain with a network of power; the London Passenger Transport Board (now under the Transport Commission), which operates various forms of transportation in the vast London area; and British Imperial Airways.

Most of the present nationalized enterprises date from the Labor government's first session when it nationalized the Bank of England, the coal mines, and telecommunications and consolidated national control over civil aviation. All electric power supply and transmission were nationalized in 1947. The railroads, road transport, all London transport, docks, and inland waterways came under national control at the beginning of 1948. The nationalization of gas supply and some parts of the iron and steel industry rounded out the program.

The most controversial aspects of the nationalization program were long-distance road haulage and iron and steel, the only two enterprises that were profitable and had not previously been under at least quasi-governmental control. Both were denationalized subsequently by the Conservatives—a process that creates its own confusions—but most of road transport was left under the Transport Commission, and a large measure of public control was retained over the production of iron and steel despite the sale back to private hands by 1955 of more than half of the steel producing concerns. Labor again nationalized steel under the Iron and Steel Corporation in 1967, and the Heath government has not moved to denationalize it again.

The characteristic form of organization for a nationalized enterprise is the *public corporation*,[5] which is designed to combine commercial flexibility with public accountability. Except for public ownership and the consequent necessity of ensuring ultimate ministerial and parliamentary responsibility, such a corporation is organized like a privately owned corporation or joint-stock company. It is a legal entity that can sue and be sued, sell goods and services, make a profit if possible, enter into contracts, and acquire property of its own. Since it is established by statute, however, it is not subject to company law. Although it is owned by the government, up to 49 percent of its equity could be acquired by the public, as is the case with British Petroleum, although in practice few nationalized enterprises are so attractive to private capital.

The public corporation stands outside the departmental structure and is responsible in

---

[5] Public corporations may be said to fall into three types: the industrial or commercial corporation that runs an industry or public utility; the social service corporation, such as the National Assistance Board or the New Town Development Corporation; and the supervisory public corporation, such as the Iron and Steel Board. Only the industrial or commercial corporation is described here, although the BBC is sometimes said to stand in "a sort of no-man's land" between the social service corporations and the nationalized industries. The ordinary social service corporation has less independence than the industrial corporation from ministerial control, because its purpose is to provide a particular social service on behalf of a government department.

its day-to-day operations not to a minister or to Parliament but to a board whose responsibilities are broadly suggested in the statute. Within these limits, this board is empowered to recruit staff and plan the operations of the corporation. The board is appointed, however, by the minister to whom the enterprise is assigned, who also has further significant powers to determine conditions of service, approve raising capital from appropriate sources, be provided with whatever information he requests, and, potentially most far reaching, give "directions of a general character as to the exercise of performance by the Board of their functions in relation to matters appearing to the Minister to affect public interest."

This mating of commercial initiative with ministerial and parliamentary responsibilities is a constructive way of extending public control without bringing public enterprises into the sphere of party politics. But it involves issues that have not yet been satisfactorily resolved. What should be the boundary between commercial autonomy and public supervision and direction? Is ministerial supervision compatible with strong and imaginative direction by the chief operating figure of the corporation, the chairman of its board? Can parliamentary supervision be secured without impairing the drive of the particular enterprise? For while the successful operation of a nationalized industry is dependent to a large degree on the forcefulness and insight of the man placed in charge, the maintenance of public control involves investigation, supervision, and a measure of official direction.

Each of the nationalized industries has been endowed with a somewhat different structure and function. The National Coal Board was established in 1946 to reorganize, consolidate, and modernize one of the largest, oldest, and most depressed of British industries and to run it as a single centralized enterprise. The Gas Council, in contrast, which was set up two years later, merely coordinates a number of area boards that, in turn, took over numerous existing concerns, some of which were municipally owned. The Gas Council concentrates, therefore, on general policy, research, and industrial relations. It is noteworthy that the gas industry is almost unique among nationalized industries in continuing with its original form, whereas coal, inland transport, and electricity have all been subject to subsequent reorganizations seeking more efficient and responsible structures.

To make clear-cut separation of the functions of the boards and their chairmen, on the one hand, and the responsible minister on the other has been found, in practice, to be virtually impossible. In theory, as we have seen, the separation is between day-to-day management and policy, but these spheres interact too much to fit into separate boxes. Moreover, although apart from the Coal Board, which was financed from the start by the Exchequer, the other three industries mentioned were expected originally to secure their finance from the issue of stock; their failure to secure adequate credit led them also to dependence on the Treasury.

The Conservatives tried to make a distinction between "commercial" and "public" responsibilities but with equal lack of success. As the White Paper of 1961 on the financial and economic obligations of the nationalized industries (Cmnd. 1337) pointed out, nationalized concerns have "wider obligations than commercial concerns in the private sector." Setting targets for the returns on their assets, which also take into account their social contribution, was proposed as a means to combine "the maximum contribution to their own development and the well-being of the community as a whole." More sophisticated techniques were added by the 1967 White Paper on the nationalized industries (Cmnd. 3437). But these, like earlier efforts, tended to make the relation between the board and the minister even closer than before.

As long as there is a common, basic philosophy and agreement on long-range plans between the chairman of the board and the minister and, indeed, the government in power, this close association can work well. But when Lord Robens, for ten years the distinguished, effective, and popular chairman of the Coal Board, resigned in January 1971, it was because the Heath government refused to let his nationalized industry decide for itself what fields it should enter. Nationalized industries, in fact, have branched into many lucrative supplementary fields. The Coal Board, for example, makes houses for its employees, leases time on its computers, has developed mining by-products that brings it into the chemical business, and has a share in rich-looking prospects for North Sea gas and oil. British Rail runs a profitable chain of hotels and operates ferries to the Continent. It appears that the Heath government feels that some of these ancillary businesses should be returned to private hands, and that the nationalized industries should not be allowed to cover deficits in one aspect of their work with such profitable ventures. From the other side it is open to question whether a superb and forceful manager of an industrialized enterprise should be prevented from engaging in such imaginative expansion. Lord Robens obviously felt that he did not wish to continue as chairman of the Coal Board if his freedom of initiative was curbed in this fashion.

There appears to be a basic issue of principle involved in this issue that goes deep into the roles of nationalized industries within the national economy and their management. The Conservative Minister of Industry, who has special responsibilities for the nationalized industries, has maintained that "by and large the public sector should be concerned primarily with those activities which cannot sensibly be done by the private sector." Lord Robens, in contrast, stressed the responsibility of nationalized enterprises both to the public and to their own workers. Taking over a depressed industry with a history of severe labor troubles, the Coal Board, under Lord Robens' leadership, managed to preserve the miners' morale in a period of contraction. His resignation indicated his fear that restrictive government policies would impair morale at all levels, as well as possibilities of a viable and independent existence for a public corporation such as he directed.

On another level, the Iron and Steel Corporation, which faced both overall losses and an impending rise in steel prices in 1971 when it was in the process of carrying out a major five-year modernization plan, was threatened with either losing some of its specialized and profitable steel and construction branches or facing the competition of government-financed steel imports from cheaper sources. A proposal by its chairman, Lord Melchett, who was formerly a leading banker, to sell shares to the public up to 49 percent of the equity, is another possible alternative approach to improving the corporation's position in the eyes of the government.

One persistent question regarding the relation between the minister and the chairman of a nationalized enterprise is whether it would not be better to remove the power of appointment from the former and vest it in a small permanent board with its own staff. This committee could examine the whole field of potential candidates, keep permanent records, and thus be better equipped to make proposals for chairmen and board members of particular enterprises. Whether the board should also have the power to review proposals for dismissals—as in the case of Lord Hall, who lost his post as chairman of the new Post Office public corporation in November 1970 on ground of inadequate management of its operations, and at an earlier date the chairmen of British Overseas Airways Corporation and of British Rail for failure to meet their targets—is another question. But lack of any guaranteed term of office, coupled with current inadequate pension arrangements, may make it difficult to recruit the best men for the job.

Not only ministerial but also parliamentary supervision of nationalized enterprises has been a matter of continuing concern. Questions on day-to-day management are clearly ruled out, while opportunities for discussion in Parliament of the annual reports of nationalized industries were found inadequate, when they were held at all. Largely due to backbench pressure, the Select Committee on Nationalized Industries was finally given broad scope in 1956 to examine their reports and accounts and has since produced a series of excellent analyses of both the policy and administration of particular industries. Working in a nonpartisan fashion, taking evidence from related ministries and outside experts, and checking back at intervals to see how its recommendations have been implemented, this select committee has in many ways provided a model for such parliamentary investigations. It is worth noting, however, that Lord Robens favors setting up an independent public accountability commission to ensure that public enterprises are run in the best interests of the public, leaving it to their own chairmen to decide how best to run them in their own interest.

ADVISORY COUNCILS AND GROUP ACTIVITY

Advisory councils and group activity are often two sides of the same interaction between private concerns and the administration. The former operate through formal channels of advice by producers or consumers, for which provision is made in the law; the latter springs from the activities of a group that are directed toward its own interest. But in either case, the interaction is likely to be rewarding from both sides. The public administration, like political parties and, indeed, MP's, needs the specialized, detailed information that interest groups can provide, the more so since so much of their work is concerned these days with highly specific matters. Moreover, administration, like the representative system itself, needs to keep as much aware of public reactions to its measures as is possible. While it may be argued that particular interest groups present very partial views of public concern, their combined impact and illumination can be considerable.

A wide range of advisory committees—of which some five hundred include representatives of producer groups—dot the departments. Some of these committees are highly specialized; others are of more general character. Some have grown up out of convenience; many are required by law. A large complement of advisory committees was established, for example, under the 1947 Agricultural Act, which obliged the minister to "consult with such bodies of persons" as appear to represent "the interests of producers." The purpose of group representation is to assure those who are to be affected by the implementation of legislation that they will be consulted and, if possible, to associate them with the forms adopted. Thus the Ministry of Agriculture not only has its network of advisory committees (both to receive and to give advice), but also may consult the National Farmers' Union either officially or unofficially. Indeed, since the war, agricultural price-fixing has involved annual negotiations with the National Farmers' Union, and these levels are endorsed by that body, although officially announced by the government.

There is also much detailed information of which a department can make use and which it can secure more easily and cheaply through a trade association than by doing its own research. The Ministry of Transport, for example, can secure useful technical information, particularly on minutiae, from the Society of Motor Manufacturers and Traders, as well as through the National Advisory Council for the Motor Manufacturing Industry. The latter has the advantage, however, of including not only representatives of government and employers but also of relevant unions, as well as an independent member. It acts officially as a means of regular consultation on such subjects as "the location of industry, exports, imports, research, design and progress" of the motor industry.

This integration of interest groups into the process of government is not an abdication of responsibility by representative and administrative agencies. It is, rather, a sensible accommodation between those agencies that are responsible for formulating and carrying out public policy and those most intimately affected by such action. As Samuel H. Beer points out in his *British Politics in the Collectivist Age*, interest groups in Great Britain are "domesticated" and tied into normal operations of government, particularly those of the administration. In the United States, the degree of independence in voting of a congressman leads most interest groups to focus their pressures upon the legislature; in Great Britain, party allegiance and discipline are not overriden by group pressures. It is natural, therefore, for interest groups to concentrate on the administration with what is normally mutual advantage.

3 LOCAL AND REGIONAL GOVERNMENT

"Apoplexy at the center; anaemia at the extremities": this is the picture of an over-centralized administration, all too characteristic of modern governments. It is a picture that has given rise to proposals for local government reform ever since World War II. Moreover, the renewed interest in economic planning in the sixties coupled with expressions of Welsh and Scottish nationalism have stimulated thinking about regional decentralization and deconcentration of the functions of government. The urge for reform has even led to the setting up of the Crowther Commission on Constitutional Reform, which is to report in 1972. But in the meantime, the constantly increasing pressures for centralization that are reflected in the vast scope of the responsibilities possessed by the British central administration need to be counterbalanced more adequately by functions that are locally stimulated and performed.

The movement for reform is spurred by both the noticeable apathy regarding local self-government, once the pride of English democracy, and an awareness of how out of date its units, functions, and finances have become. But while most people agree that there is need to relieve the burdens and balance the powers and responsibilities of the central administration, there has been considerable disagreement over what plans should be implemented. The Royal Commission, which met from 1966 to 1969 under the chairmanship of Lord Redcliffe-Maud, carried out the most comprehensive modern scrutiny of local government in England (the area to which its mandate was restricted) and proposed a radical series of changes; the Conservatives produced no less radical but very different proposals in February 1971. Both sets of proposals seek in their different ways to reconcile the twin demands of efficiency and popular participation in such a way that they fit modern conditions, since the existing local government system no longer does.

Local autonomy was established early in England and Wales,[6] but local self-government is relatively recent. From the time of the Tudors, justices of the peace, appointed by the Crown and selected from the local gentry, exercised a benevolent direction as judges, legislators, and executives in county areas, while local oligarchies ruled in the ancient but antiquated boroughs or towns. The dominance of both groups was not undercut until the nineteenth century, when the industrial revolution and the resulting increase in governmental activities laid responsibilities on local areas that they were obviously incapable of handling. The first shift in authority, however, was to a series of boards and commissioners, established one by one as local areas assumed new tasks in regard to public health, highways, public assistance to the poor, and elementary education. Since each of the new authorities was usually provided with a new set of areas within which to carry out its work, England and Wales became a bewildering network of sanitary districts, poor law districts, conservation districts, and so forth, whose boundaries rarely coincided. Only through a series of local government acts, extending to 1894, was order brought out of this chaos. In a parallel development, governing power was transferred gradually to elected councils, first in the boroughs or towns (1835), then in the counties and the newly created county boroughs or cities (1888), and finally in the subdivisions of the counties, the districts and parishes (1894). Thus by the end of the nineteenth century, local self-government had been established as the rule throughout England and Wales.

It has become more difficult, however, to speak of a separate sphere of local action clearly set off from national government. Certain services once looked on as purely local have steadily taken on more national significance. The local school is part of a national educational system; public assistance is no longer

---

[6] There were slight, although not essential, variations in the forms of local government in Scotland and Northern Ireland. The institutions described are those of England and Wales.

a community task but a national responsibility; even gas and electricity, once characteristically municipal services, have now been nationalized. It remains true that there is still considerable local flexibility in these spheres, and that there are possibilities of a local veto or restraint on certain key policy issues, as with Labor's program for comprehensive schools (see Chapter 1, Section 2). But the great expansion in what are essentially local personal services—education, child care, old people's welfare, mental health, and so forth—has necessarily resulted in the establishment of national standards and the need for national financial support.

Facilitating the rapidity of this change is the fact that in Great Britain there is no constitutional division of powers such as that existing between the national and state governments in the United States. There are only two levels of government in Great Britain—national and local—instead of the three levels of government in the United States—national, state, and local. And the British Parliament has authority over both the organization and the powers of local governments in the same way as American state governments have authority over the local governments, like cities and counties, within their boundaries. Thus reform of local government and arrangements for regional deconcentration will be carried through by national legislation.

PROJECTS FOR REFORM

The Redcliffe-Maud Commission proposed replacing the present fragmented system of 1,210 local authorities [7] (not including 7,000 parish councils and London), which reflect a town-country division outmoded by modern means of communication, by a system of metropolitan areas and 58 unitary authorities integrated by 8 new provincial councils and based on continuing local councils at the borough, district, and parish levels, if the people want them. The commission picked out three metropolitan areas, besides Greater London, as satisfactory planning units for which it suggested two-tier systems with services divided between the metropolitan authority and the metropolitan district councils. The most radical part of the proposals was that the existing relations in functions and finance [8] were to be replaced by giving the new authorities freedom to set their own priorities inside broad, national policies, local sources of funding (to flow from gasoline and motor taxes and driving license fees), and general power and discretion in spending these funds.

The elective principle and regionalism both had a place in the Redcliffe-Maud proposals. The commission believed that the authorities for the unitary areas combining town and country districts should consist of up to 75 elected members who would be free to choose their own organization as well as being responsible for decentralizing and consulting about activities within their area. These areas, the commission suggested, would vary widely in size and population, all the way from 195,000 to a million, since it found no appropriate formula for delimiting them.

The eight provincial councils, which would replace the existing regional economic councils, were to be indirectly elected through the directly elected local authorities. Their special responsibility would be to undertake physical and economic planning within their area in consultation with central authorities and to decide the location of special services, like schools for handicapped children. The commission proposed no services for them to run on their own but that they have their own staffs (unlike the existing planning councils) and power to spend money for special projects.

---

[7] The system existing in 1971 included 45 countries, 79 county boroughs (which include all the important cities in the country except London), 227 noncounty boroughs (consisting of towns not big or important enough to rank as county boroughs), 449 urban districts, and 410 rural districts.

[8] The central government contributed 57 percent of all local expenditures in 1970–71. These funds came in the form of *grants-in-aid,* which meet, for example, about half the cost of local police forces and 20 to 75 percent of the cost of roads, and *Exchequer equalization grants,* which are provided on the basis of need to poor areas so that the services they provide do not fall too short of those established by wealthier communities that can afford to add to prescribed standards.

The chief source of local government finance has traditionally been *rates,* or taxes, in proportion to the annual rental value of property in the area; revenue is also gained from rental of municipal property, some license fees, and so forth. It was estimated that if the Redcliffe-Maud proposals for independent sources of income were adopted, the proportion of central government financing would drop to about 14 percent, which would necessarily make a great change in the relation between central and local government.

LOCAL GOVERNMENT AREAS AS PROPOSED BY THE REDCLIFFE-MAUD COMMISSION, 1966–69

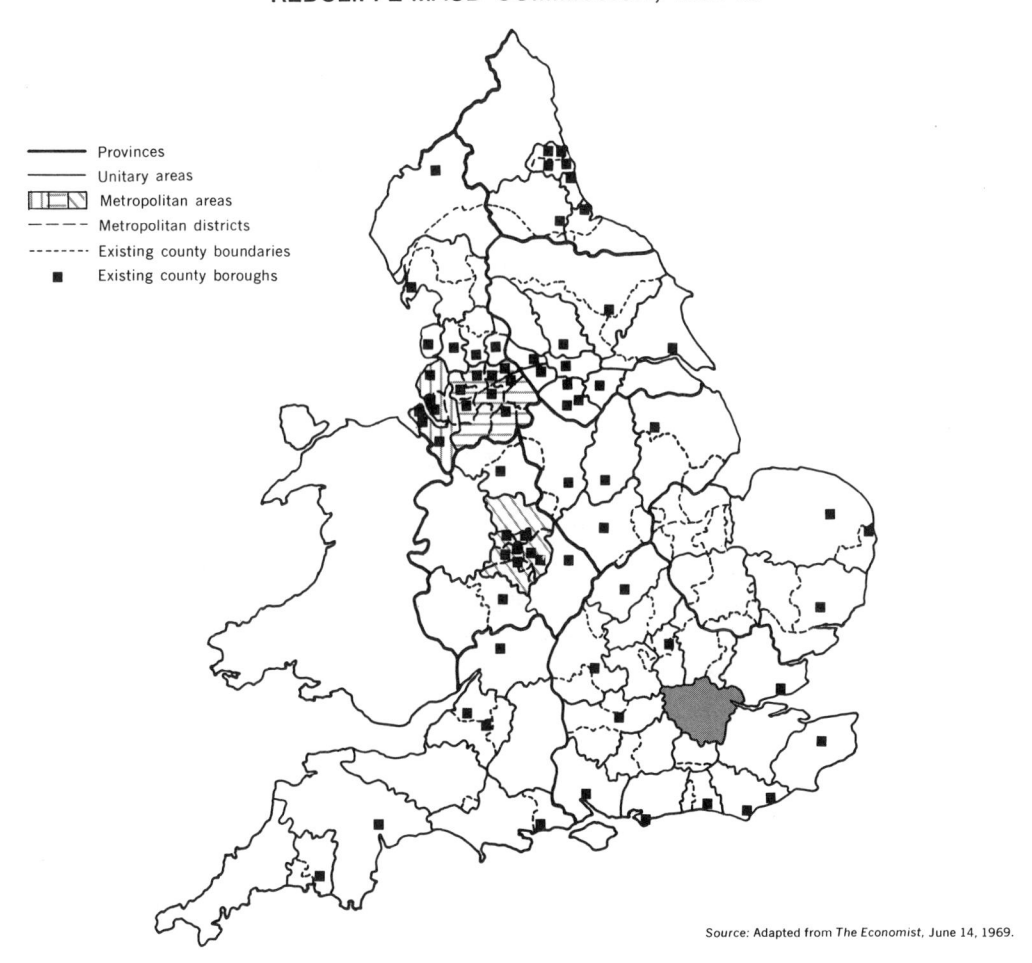

Legend:
- Provinces
- Unitary areas
- Metropolitan areas
- Metropolitan districts
- Existing county boundaries
- ■ Existing county boroughs

Source: Adapted from *The Economist*, June 14, 1969.

Their form, however, was left otherwise blank in anticipation of whatever proposals, if any, will be made on regional government by the Crowther Commission, which reports in 1972. Local councils, as indicated, would exist only where they were wanted. In the words of the report: "The only *duty* of the local council would be to represent local opinion, but it would have the *right* to be consulted on matters of special interest to its inhabitants, and it would have the *power* to do for the local community a number of things done locally."

These proposals were approved with modifications by the Labor government. It suggested, in its February 1970 White Paper, fifty-one instead of fifty-eight unitary authorities, increasing the number of metropolitan authorities to five, and making local councils more effective by some joint memberships between district and unitary authority committees. It rejected the notion, however, that the larger local councils should provide some of the major services such as education. The Wilson administration also refused to commit itself to the suggestion of provincial councils to provide the framework for regional decentralization, preferring to wait for the recommendations of the Crowther Commission on Constitutional Reform.

Although the Heath government is equally committed to local government reform, the pattern proposed by its new Ministry of the Environment is quite a different one. In February 1971, it issued three White Papers on local government reform in Scotland (Cmnd. 4583), Wales (no Cmnd.), and England (Cmnd. 4584). These White Papers outline the major features of what was embodied in legislation in the fall of 1971. On April 1, 1974, 380 new councils in England and 43 in Wales will begin work under the new arrangements. The changeover in Scotland will come a year later.

The Conservative government's plan provided for yet a smaller number of what are still called counties. Thus in place of the existing sixty-two administrative counties (which were often, but not always, identical with historic counties like Devon and Hampshire) and eighty-three county boroughs or the Royal Commission's proposed fifty-eight unitary authorities, there are only thirty counties, some of whose boundaries are necessarily new. To compensate for such large and somewhat remote units, there is a second tier of boroughs and districts. But apart from the six most densely populated areas that are named metropolitan counties and patterned on the structure of Greater London (see below), metropolitan districts, county and municipal boroughs have lost their major powers to the counties, which, as with the Redcliffe-Maud proposals, include town and country areas. While Scotland, which has been provided with eight "regional" authorities, and Wales, with seven new counties, were assigned their numbers and areas of second-tier districts in their White Papers, the exact demarcation of the 360-odd county districts for England, that is, those outside of the metropolitan areas, were determined by a Boundary Commission set up after the legislation was passed. In general, large towns have become districts in their own right but without their previously enjoyed independent status and with reduced functions, while outside of such urban centers, districts include between 40,000 and 100,000 people.

Two much debated features of the White Paper proposals were the allocation of functions between the counties and districts outside the metropolitan areas and the boundaries of the latter. Towns that had enjoyed the status and extended functions of county boroughs protested vigorously. The change, as originally proposed, was indeed radical. Whereas towns had previously had their own schools and libraries, settled their own traffic and highway arrangements, run their own buses and the full range of social services, and done their own planning, they were confronted with the prospect of becoming responsible only for housing, neighborhood improvement, rubbish collection, and local development. Moreover, the inhabitants of those towns not fortunate enough to be selected as the county seat confronted the prospect of having to travel to another town to check administrative policy, for example, with the social-service director, or to lobby the council. Subsequent provision for the delegation of authority by the county to the district, where this did not interfere with county functions, ameliorated the situation somewhat, but it did not wholly ease the strained feelings involved.

The issue of metropolitan boundaries and division of functions was a further source of debate. Some felt that the boundaries of the six metropolitan counties (outside of London) were drawn too tight around their built-up areas to permit a reasonable interaction with their adjoining regions. Others argued, however, that these boundaries were necessary to prevent the unfortunate consequences of "urban sprawl." The metropolitan counties, it should be noted, have fewer powers than those possessed by other counties. Education and social services inside the metropolitan counties are left to the metropolitan districts into which they are divided, which, in some cases—for example, Birmingham, Newcastle, Manchester—are cities in their own right. Strategic planning and transportation, naturally, are metropolitan county functions, but some have felt that housing, which is not, should also be included because of its urgency and close relation to general planning.

The Redcliffe-Maud proposals for a few large all-purpose areas, particularly as formulated by the Labor government, offered a good possibility of strengthening local government by giving it a stronger base and making lines of responsibility clearer. The Conservative two-tier system retains both the overlapping responsibilities and small authorities that weakened local government in the past. Moreover, this system will diminish both the status and responsibility of the cities, the units which were most likely to be able to share power with the central government if their functions had been expanded rather than decreased. The

LOCAL GOVERNMENT AREAS PROPOSED BY CONSERVATIVE GOVERNMENT, FEBRUARY 1971

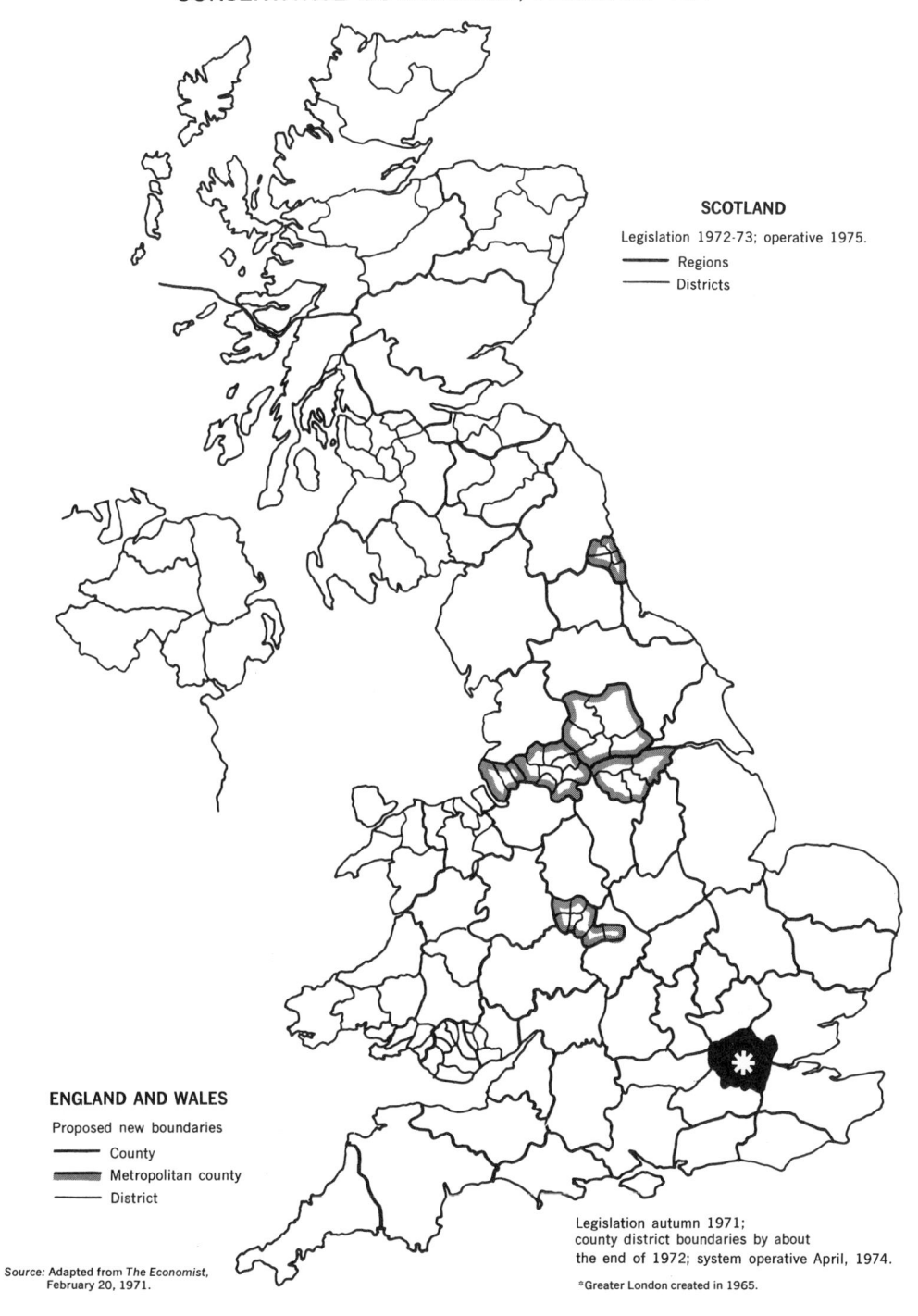

SCOTLAND

Legislation 1972-73; operative 1975.
— Regions
— Districts

ENGLAND AND WALES

Proposed new boundaries
— County
▬ Metropolitan county
— District

Source: Adapted from *The Economist*, February 20, 1971.

Legislation autumn 1971; county district boundaries by about the end of 1972; system operative April, 1974.

*Greater London created in 1965.

county councils, on the other hand, which will become the chief local authority areas, seem unlikely to offer such a workable possibility for effective decentralization of functions and decision-making. The likelihood, therefore, is that the present reorganization of units will do little, if anything, to strengthen the role played by local government or, indeed, to halt its decline.

The whole issue of regional planning is still debated. The closest the British have moved to establishing specific machinery for regional planning is the structure set up by the Labor government in 1964. It consisted of both an executive Planning Board, made up of departmental officials entrusted by central ministries with control of relevant functions in their regions, and an advisory Planning Council, whose members are appointed by the relevant ministry from persons qualified either through expert knowledge or because they represent particular regional interest groups, like businessmen, trade unionists, and members of local government councils. The Conservative White Paper places the responsibility for policy planning on the counties, but the districts are to provide planning permissions, a division that may complicate effective action, as it has tended to do in the past. Districts will be expected to conform to general plans drawn up by their county, but there may be some tensions when the political persuasion of the two bodies is different. Another problem is that some counties, at least, may not provide broad enough areas for planning large-scale development, physical communications, and major land use. Not surprisingly, the government wishes to await the recommendations of the Crowther Commission (as indeed Labor did when in power) before proposing provincial divisions, if it follows the Redcliffe-Maud Royal Commission in that regard. But this hiatus leaves the major units below the central government level with unsuitable boundaries for planning purposes.

THE COUNCILS

Traditionally, the organ of self-government in every unit of local government has been the council, and this continues to be the case for the units of the new scheme. Not only is there far less diversity in the structure of local government in England than in the United States (where county and city governments differ widely in form, and where there are a number of different types of city government), but there is also no separation of powers in English local government such as is common in American city government. Thus the local government council in England has both executive and legislative powers, decides matters of policy, passes ordinances, fixes the budget, considers the way in which programs should be carried out in detail, and selects and works with the permanent officials who run the local services.

Members of a local government council have traditionally been elected for three-year terms; some, called aldermen, were chosen (or, to use a more technical term, co-opted) by the councilors themselves. Since property qualifications for voting in local government elections were swept away in 1945, anyone who can vote in a parliamentary election also has the local franchise. One result is that local elections took on the character of miniature national elections, with Conservatives and Labor working hard to gain control of local councils, both to demonstrate their political strength throughout the country and to consolidate their influence in the organs that administer so many national programs. In general, Labor is strong in urban areas and the Conservatives outside of them, which Labor charged had some bearing on Conservative government proposals for local government reform. On the other hand, England is so strongly urbanized that in practice the new counties, unlike the old ones, may be dominated by townsfolk and not the rural gentry. There will at least have to be a wholly new orientation of party machines to these levels with consequences not yet predictable.

In the past, in any case, once councils had been elected, party politics were less dominant than in the national sphere. Labor has claimed that there is more drive behind programs for social welfare, recreation centers, and housing when Laborites control a council, and the Conservatives have maintained that they are more efficient and financially responsible. Confronted with major responsibilities for most of the public arrangements molding the conditions of life in our complicated and crowded environments, the overriding issue is to get on with the job.

While the council as a whole determines the general outlines of a local program, most council work is administrative and is carried out by committees. These committees function wherever local government has responsibilities. They inspect schools, hire teachers, work on plans for roads, parks, and sewerage systems, or discuss specifications for the units in new housing developments, working closely at all times with the members of their permanent administrative staff. As a result, members of the council acquire a practical experience in governmental problems and administrative work for which members of Parliament have no equivalent. The fact that so much of the work of local government is administrative leads to great dependence on the advice of the local civil service. Moreover, local administration must fit within the overall pattern of central administration. Local government reform seeks to provide some genuine local autonomy within this system.

Local government autonomy, however, depends on more local control of sources of funding and of how these funds are spent. So far the central government has not provided much scope for local judgment. Unless it does so, local authorities will continue to be chiefly agents of the central government rather than of their communities. If this is the case, the hopes of the reformers for more decentralization of decision-making and more citizen participation in local institutions will not be realized.

4 THE PUBLIC SERVICE

The success of any organization depends on the people who do its work. This fact is particularly true of the public service, which demands of its members not only efficiency but also devotion to public purposes. To the extent that the public servant acts in an official capacity, he must be neutral toward the aims of the government. He must be willing to serve with equal energy and devotion the purposes of a Conservative government when it is in power and of a Labor government when it is in power. If his private opinions are opposed to public policy, it is the public policy that he must serve, conscientiously and wholeheartedly.

To state this principle, however, is to open up a whole series of supplementary questions on the best ways of realizing it in practice. Both Great Britain and the United States have had to find practical answers to issues like these: What training and what qualities are most important for the public servant who is to be both expert and responsible? To what extent can public servants be allowed, in private life, to engage in partisan political activity? To what extent may they enjoy the right to strike or (especially in business enterprises run by the government) the right to a closed shop? How representative should the public service be in the sense of having its personnel typify a cross section of the people whom it serves? Is it more desirable for the highest public servants to be professional in the sense of having permanency of tenure or to be active supporters of, and to change office with, the government of the day?

THE CIVIL SERVICE

Great Britain developed one set of answers to these questions in the middle of the nineteenth century that still influences the character of its administration. Reform of its government service arose out of Great Britain's own particular type of spoils system: not, as in the United States, one in which new administrations regularly replaced government officials with their own appointees, but one in which government offices had become the preserve of the sons of noble families who could not make a living elsewhere. Thus the principal need was not, as in the United States, for permanence of tenure, but to secure people of ability and appropriate training.

At that time most government work was paper work—that is, it consisted mainly of collecting material, keeping records, and writing reports for the use of ministers. The work of the public service seemed to fall, therefore, into a great number of routine jobs that could be done by people of average ability, as long as they were careful and well supervised, and a very much smaller number of positions at the top that demanded great insight and judgment. When Lord Macaulay undertook the task of "housecleaning" the service, it was decided that recruitment for both lower and upper positions should be by merit. For the top key group of officials Macaulay had the example of the training instituted somewhat earlier at Haileybury for the recruitment and selection of young men for the Indian service, a selection avowedly designed to secure the type of able, cultured English gentleman who would best maintain British prestige abroad. Such men were the products of the English universities of the day; it was therefore not surprising that the tests designed for recruiting the home civil service were likewise geared to the educational system. Those who wished to become high administrators had to demonstrate their ability through tests similar to comprehensive final examinations at a university, while the army of clerks was recruited on the basis of examinations similar to those in secondary school.

To make sure that the tests were administered fairly, a Civil Service Commission [9] was established in 1855, and, since 1870, open competitions have been the normal means of entry to the British civil service (as contrasted with the political service, i.e., ministers responsible to Parliament). Success in these competitive tests is now necessary both for positions within the United Kingdom and outside. Those who receive a certificate of qualification from the Civil Service Commission are ranked as part of the established civil service and have long enjoyed permanent tenure.

Up to World War I, departments maintained their autonomy in recruitment and promotion, and during the war a vast number of able people were called in to service the war effort. It was only thereafter that decisive changes took place. The civil service became centralized and unified under the Treasury. The permanent secretary of the Treasury was declared to be head of the civil service. The Treasury thus acquired not only effective control over appointments to the departments but by virtue of this strategic position also over promotions. The minister retained a right of veto but not of selection. Along with this decisive change went the long-prized establishment of "general" classes, of which the top administrative class was the one of vital importance for policymaking. The class of technical specialists, which was created later, was looked on as inferior in status and pay to the "generalists," for whom promotion to higher ranks was far better assured. Not surprisingly the nonindustrial service expanded rapidly in response to the increase in duties being assumed by the state. In 1901, it included 116,713 members; in 1939, 374,300; in 1965, 676,900; and, even excluding the transformation of the Post Office into a public corporation, about 475,000 in 1968. The dominant administrative class remained small, although it too grew between 1939 and 1965 from 2,100 to 3,500.

As elsewhere within British government, scrutiny and change are now the order of the day in the civil service. Although changes had been made in recruitment procedures, notably in increased use of the interview for selection and in moving from one grade to another through promotion, the Fulton Report,[10] the most extensive and critical review of the civil service in generations, prefaced its proposals in June 1968 with the somewhat unhistorical comment: "The Home Civil Service today is still fundamentally the product of the nineteenth-century philosophy of the Northcote-Trevelyan Report. [As noted previously, it dates from about 1919.] The tasks it faces are those of the second half of the twentieth century.

---

[9] The British Civil Service Commission is composed of three members who are appointed by the Cabinet. Unlike the United States Civil Service Commission, whose three members are generally chosen from outside the service, the British commissioners are nearly always persons of long experience in the British civil service and hold office until eligible for retirement under regular civil service rules. Since the British commissioners almost never have had active political experience before appointment, there is no rule in Great Britain (in contrast to the United States) that only two of the three members of the commission may belong to the same political party.

[10] The Fulton Committee was appointed by Prime Minister Wilson on February 8, 1966, to examine "the structure, recruitment and management, including training, of the Home Civil Service." The chairman, Lord Fulton, was then vice-chancellor of Sussex University.

This is what we have found; it is what we seek to remedy." Several of the committee's detailed proposals have been already adopted, and the British civil service today is involved in a long process of adjusting to these changes and the new reform philosophy.

The change that may have the most long-range impact is to remove the responsibility for the central management of the civil service from the Treasury to a new Civil Service Department directly under the prime minister. The Fulton Committee rejected the view that "under concentrated control the two functions of controlling expenditure and managing the Service can each be more effectively discharged" and argued that a new system requires a new instrumentality. By making an outstanding and strongly reformist civil servant, Sir William Armstrong, head of the Home Civil Service, and of the Civil Service Department in 1968, and thus giving him supervision of all departments and a decisive voice in all senior appointments, the process of change stimulated by the Fulton Report has been provided with effective leadership.

Regrading the civil service

The Fulton Committee struck hard at the multiplicity of divisions—47 general classes and 1,400 departmental classes—which it felt limited flexibility and movement within the civil service. "All classes," it stated, "should be abolished and replaced by a single, unified grading structure covering all civil servants from top to bottom in the nonindustrial part of the Service," with different levels of pay matching different levels of skill and responsibility. Job classification was looked on as the key to this regrouping, which resembles the personnel divisions of the American civil service with its twenty or so grades regardless of the particular area of operation. This reconstitution of the service was instituted on January 1, 1971, with interim mergers of a number of classes covering about 250,000 of the nonindustrial civil service, and changes affecting some 560 members of the top echelons.

The top division or class of the British civil service prior to January 1, 1971, was called the *administrative class*, sometimes known as "the permanent brain trust" or "mandarins," who carry heavy responsibilities for formulating policy, advising ministers, and controlling and directing departments. Under any scheme of organization these civil servants inevitably have a strong political influence, since ministers, particularly when they come into office but to some extent at all times, depend on them both for information and for the advice that is basic to political decisions and debate. Sir William Armstrong once commented: "The chief danger to which politicians and Ministers are open is not, as is often supposed, that obstructive bureaucrats will drag their feet in implementing their schemes, but that their own optimism will carry them into schemes and policies which will subsequently be seen to fail and which attention to the experience and information available from the Civil Service might have avoided." It is the responsibility of top administrators, and particularly the permanent secretary of a department, to advise and, where necessary, to warn his minister.

The next level used to be known as the *executive class*. It was responsible for specialization in fields like taxation and accountancy, preliminary investigations, answers to parliamentary questions, and, with experience, for important decisions. Mobility from the executive to the administrative class had been considerable well before the Fulton Report and also an indication of the fact that the two might well be merged.

Below these two classes traditionally were the *subclerical* and *clerical services*, comprising more than three-quarters of the established nonindustrial civil service and performing repetitive tasks like typing and working under orders. Little change can occur here.

Selecting the upper civil servants

The characteristics and selection of those clearly destined for top roles in the civil service have been the most controversial aspects of recruitment. A social survey prepared under the direction of two social scientists for the Fulton Committee indicated that the administrative class was disproportionately composed of individuals from "privileged" social and educational backgrounds, two-thirds of them graduates of Oxford or Cambridge, and 56 percent privately educated.[11] The similarity of this background to that of a large number of MP's, particularly in the Conservative party, and to highly placed executives in commercial and industrial enterprises has often led to accusations that, in practice, Great Britain is dominated by a relatively small elite whose associations in the same schools, universities, and clubs have formed them into a self-perpetuating clique with class-centered interests rather than directed for the national good. This accusation, however unjustified, has been a major factor in the demands for a change in the selection procedures for the administrative class.

The focus of criticism in the selection process was placed on the so-called country-house technique of a whole battery of tests conducted over two or three days for a group of about twenty candidates who had already been winnowed from other contestants by their demonstrated academic excellence and achievements in the prescribed qualifying written examination. This technique had already been sharply castigated as early as 1959 in an essay entitled "The Apotheosis of the Dilettante" by Dr. Thomas Balogh (who was subsequently, from 1964 to 1967, economic adviser to the Cabinet). His charge was that by giving greater weight to the interview, "the safeguards against class-prejudice and nepotism established by the anonymity of the written examination were considerably weakened." [12]

To investigate whether the "country-house" technique—known as Method II—unduly weighted the selection process toward those from a particular background and educational stream, the Labor government established yet another committee, this time under J. G. W. Davies, assistant to the governor of the Bank of England.[13] This committee, which also examined the Halsey-Crewe survey, concentrated its attention on current selection procedures rather than on those persons already in the service, noted a broadening in the pattern of recruitment in the previous five years, but concluded that the social background of those who applied still remained too narrow. In general, however, the committee concluded that the main method for recruiting the hundred future policymakers who are chosen annually from the seven hundred contestants was "something to which the public service can point with pride" for achieving a more complete picture of the individual at the moment of selection than either the American or the French civil services secure. At the same time it recommended—and the government approved—lessening the rigidity of academic requirements (by substituting an honors degree for the first- or second-class honors previously demanded) enroute to ultimately dropping formal academic qualifications for eligibility. Moreover, all candidates, including those with first-class honors, who had previously been exempted, were henceforth to take the written qualifying examination, which was recast in 1971 to prevent any undue advantage to candidates with arts degrees.

The Fulton Committee had proposed either to abolish the final selection board that conducts the "country-house" tests or to instruct the board only to add a fixed mark to those received from the two previous stages of examination. The government decided on the Davies Committee recommendation to retain the board but to increase its representation of outside interests by including two non-civil service examiners instead of one.

The effect on the composition of Britain's top civil servants of these changes will only be perceptible a long time hence. It will become apparent first at the level of assistant secretary, where most civil servants achieve their highest rank. This rank is crucial for the effective administration of the department, but it is not involved directly in policymaking. Only relatively few are promoted to the level above assistant secretary to that of undersecretary, which marks the decisive move into the upper civil service. It is these persons that the Civil Service Department watches carefully for the talent to fill top jobs in ministries throughout the service.

One of the major differences between the British and American civil services lies in the fact that the former is a career service in which the members of the administrative class have a

---

[11] A. H. Halsey and I. M. Crewe, "The Civil Service," *Social Survey of the Civil Service*, 3 (1) (1969).

[12] Reprinted in *Crisis in the Civil Service*, ed. by Hugh Thomas, p. 19.

[13] *Report of the Committee of Inquiry into the Method II System of Selection*, 1969.

chance for promotion to the highest administrative positions in the department, whereas in the United States the top departmental offices nearly always change hands when a new administration comes into office—not simply, as critics sometimes suggest, in order to provide political spoils for the electoral victor, but because of the belief that the policies of the new administration will be carried out most effectively if those responsible for their administration are actively in sympathy with them. The vigor and imagination with which some political appointees tackle their jobs give support to this view, and some observers have suggested that the British system, by forcing a high civil servant to subject his own political beliefs and prejudices to those of the government that happens to be in power at a given time, may well substitute experience for a dynamic enthusiasm. The British view, however, is that men of the highest caliber will not enter the civil service unless they can look forward to positions of great responsibility in which they will share in the making of policy.

It is worth noting the training and experience of the thirty top civil servants who were permanent secretaries in 1971. Twenty-six of them had gone to Oxford or Cambridge; two to the London School of Economics; one to Glasgow University; and one, exceptionally, had not gone to the university at all. Only eleven had gone to public schools (i.e., to one of the great private boarding schools), one of them to Eton and one to Harrow; the rest came from grammar schools, except for one educated in New Zealand. Most of them had worked their way up through the service, but a few had also had experience outside Whitehall: Sir Arnold France, the one permanent secretary who did not go to the university, spent eleven years in the District Bank; another worked in a large brokerage firm; a third in Transport House. Their changes of career, however, were due to the war and, as the Fulton Committee pointed out, it had become very difficult for a man of experience to enter the service in middle age, one of the particular advantages of the American system.

The Fulton Committee had also criticized what it considered an exaggerated stress on the "generalist," and felt that scientists, engineers, and other specialists had not been given either the opportunities for advancement or the authority they should possess. The Committee charged as well that too few civil servants were "skilled managers," that there was too little career planning and management and not enough contact between the civil service and the community it exists to serve. In general, it felt there should be "greater professionalism," with the specialists getting more training in management and the administrators more specialized training in either social administration or economic and financial administration. All civil servants, it urged, should have some knowledge of and experience with quantitative techniques (not yet widely taught in the English educational system).

Some of these criticisms, particularly the lack of "professionalism," were much resented by the civil service and, indeed, were probably based on lack of understanding of the intricacy of the tasks of the upper civil service and the competence with which it carries its responsibilities. It was also felt that the committee had an inadequate appreciation of the service's ability to accommodate and even promote change. But some of its suggestions—for example, the proposals for more flexible interchange with outside professions—have been endorsed by Sir William Armstrong himself. As early as 1965 in giving evidence to the Estimates Committee, Sir William had stressed the value of young administrators—in his words, "the top end of the assistant principals and the junior principals, people round about 28 to 30"—going into industry or banking for about a year, so they would get the "feel" of how these enterprises work as well as the experience of another type of administration. He also urged continued training and research on the special problems of government administration.

Neither Wilson nor Heath, however, was satisfied to depend wholly on the resources of the civil service for implementing their policies. Wilson turned in 1964 to two economists, Thomas Balogh and Nicholas Kaldor. The latter was brought into the Treasury as special adviser to the chancellor on taxation and introduced corporation, capital gains, and selective employment taxes—not all of which were welcomed by that department. Heath brought into the same role F. A. Cockfield, who had become Commissioner of Internal Revenue in 1951 at age thirty-one, and moved in 1953 to be finance director, and subsequently managing director of Boots Pure Drugs (a massive concern spread throughout England). After resigning in 1967 he had become president of the Royal Statistical Society and a tax adviser to the Conservative party. An advocate of low tax rates and low government expenditures, his advice, like that of Kaldor, seemed likely to conflict with orthodox Treasury views with unpredictable effects on budgetmaking.

More widely publicized, although possibly less influential, were the fifteen or so businessmen, including a top executive from Britain's most efficiently run chain store, Marks and Spencer, who were brought in to advise on civil service management. They were recruited with the objective of securing the massive economies in both men and money to which the Conservatives are dedicated. Whether they succeed in transforming the bureaucratic process or are swallowed up by it is as yet uncertain.

Training civil servants

The third, and easiest, Fulton reform to adopt was to establish a Civil Service College. In the past the civil service had done relatively little to provide systematic training for its members, a very serious lack because in general, as we have seen, recruitment has been based on ability rather than experience. The French have a well-planned three-year course for those wishing to enter the public service, a course that includes both study, with a heavy legal emphasis, and experience in different branches of the administration. The new British Civil Service College concentrates on postentry training and builds on the experience of the Center for Administrative Studies (established in 1963), which provided training for specialists and administrators in their third year of service. It is too early to evaluate as yet the role and effect of the Civil Service College and of the recommendations regarding opportunities for specialists and for better career planning. In general, however, there has appeared to be some disillusionment among specialists regarding the effect of Fulton recommendations on their behalf.

Redundancy and pay scales

Not only is the civil service sensitive regarding the recent spate of criticism to which it has been subjected, but it has also been alarmed over plans for reductions in its numbers and the impact on its pay scales of the new grading system. At the opening of the Civil Service College in June 1970 shortly after the general election, Prime Minister Heath warned of his plans to reduce the total number and cost of civil servants, following reduction in their functions and commitments, for he admitted that savings by rationalization and improved organization were limited. A major step in streamlining the government superstructure was taken early in January 1971 by eliminating more than three hundred advisory committees providing services to farmers, and cutting the number of civil servants in the Ministry of Agriculture by fifteen hundred persons, that is, by 10 percent of its staff (Cmnd. 4564, 1971). The impact is most likely to fall on small farmers who make up about 70 percent of the holdings and to lead to demands for increased prices. Not surprisingly, it also led to protests by the Institution of Professional Civil Service hoping to deter other ministers from similar cuts.

As Heath had warned, however, the civil service is likely to face continued reduction in size. The Labor government had added sixty-five thousand civil servants between 1964 and June 1970, and theoretically these could all have been in danger. The greatest risk, however, was faced by senior civil servants, particularly the three hundred undersecretaries, of whom sixty-five were combined in the merger of the Board of Trade and the Ministry of Technology into the Department of Trade and Industry. Redundancy discussions between the government and civil service staff unions and associations suggested premature retirement as "desirable in the public interest" for a considerable number at the top. Such a development would be watched with particular interest by the younger members of the First Division Association, which represents the top ranks at

Whitehall, since it might reduce their otherwise long waits for promotion.

At least the Conservative government decided in August 1970 to implement the recommendations of the Plowden Committee on pay levels in the higher civil service. These involved paying the balance of salary increases recommended a year before and accepted in principle by the Labor government. As of January 1, 1971, permanent secretaries received £14,000 ($33,600); the top three, £15,000 ($36,000), much more than the Cabinet ministers they serve, who get £8,500 ($20,400); deputy secretaries, £9,000 ($21,600); undersecretaries, £6,750 ($14,200); and assistant secretaries from £4,390 to £5,640 ($10,536 to $13,536), the latter comprising 8.5 percent increases. Other pay requests are being pressed through established channels.

EMPLOYER-EMPLOYEE RELATIONS

As an employer, government faces many of the same issues in labor relations that private business confronts. Government employees below the administrative rank have never been restricted either in Great Britain or the United States in their right to form unions. Moreover, in both countries, civil service unions have been allowed to affiliate with ordinary industrial unions since 1946, when Labor repealed the ban on affiliation which had been imposed by the Conservatives following the General Strike of 1926.

Traditionally, however, strikes by civil servants, although not illegal (they are punishable in the United States under the Taft-Hartley Act, 1947), have not been considered an acceptable form of pressure. But the National Union of Teachers and the National Local Government Officers' Association early in 1970 both approved the first strikes since their formation, a possible harbinger of things to come.

Moreover, it was not clear in the early stages of the Industrial Relations Bill whether it would include the civil service in its provisions. The service was not specifically excluded, as were members of the armed forces and the police, nor included in the consultative document, but the subsequent bill appeared to cover them. If it were made subject to the legislation, the staff side of the National Whitley Council declared in November 1970 that it would not hesitate to sue the government as employer for any breach of contract. From the side of the government, it might be difficult to ignore government employees when it was trying to enforce legal requirements elsewhere. But in the light of the successes of the Whitley method of negotiating, evolved over half a century, it seems unlikely that it will be superceded by a more legalistic framework.

Whitley Councils

The normal channel for consideration of all questions affecting employment in the civil service is the Whitley Council, a joint negotiation board on which members of the higher civil service and representatives of civil service unions are represented equally. Their joint considerations are expected to end with a general agreement acceptable to both sides.

Organized on every level of the civil service, Whitley Councils act on problems appropriate to their various spheres. The National Whitley Council consists of fifty-four members, of whom the twenty-seven official members are appointed by the Chancellor of the Exchequer (evidence of Treasury financial control), while the twenty-seven staff members include leading officials of various civil service associations, many of them professional, full-time trade union workers. It lays down the general principles governing conditions of service and proposes legislation affecting the conditions of civil servants. About seventy autonomous councils operate on the department level and are concerned with the application of particular rules. In some cases there are also district and local Whitley Councils, and every ministry with a large number of industrial employees, like the Ministry of the Environment, has a Joint Industrial Council that deals with any matters outside wages and trade questions.

Some of the most important reports on which changes in the civil service have been based (including recruitment after World War II and equal pay for men and women in the nonindustrial civil service) have been drafted by the National Whitley Council. Nonetheless, many staff members feel that they have too little influence on decisions at the national level. This is hardly surprising, for the official members of the National Whitley Council can only meet staff demands within the limits established by the Treasury and ministers. A public recommendation by the National Whitley Council means in fact a policy already approved by the Cabinet.

Whitley Councils have much to commend them. They regularize contacts between higher and lower civil servants and provide for frank exchanges of views; they help employees to see the purpose of new plans and training programs; and they help employers to understand better the effect of what they do. The councils cannot provide for joint management of the ministries, for the latter are not business enterprises but the staffs of politically responsible ministers. But the councils do a great deal to fit rules to individual situations and to stimulate good relations.

As far as salaries and wages are concerned, the Treasury negotiates with the staff associations, or trade unions, to try to find a settlement satisfactory to both sides. If this is not possible, however, the government long ago committed itself to the principle of arbitration. For nonindustrial civil servants, the Civil Service Arbitration Tribunal (of which the Treasury names one member, the unions another, and the Minister of Labor the chairman) provides awards that the government accepts as binding under normal circumstances. But when during 1949–50, the tribunal, despite its sympathy with the claims presented to it, refused to adjudicate because the government had declared a national wage freeze, both the service and many outside considered the principle of arbitration had been seriously violated. In 1961, a pay pause, involving a pay standstill in the public sector and alteration of terms under which disputed claims could be taken to arbitration, evoked widespread protests and ultimately forced restoration of normal arbitration procedures. But in a period of staff reductions, rampant inflation, and widespread strikes in industry and nationalized enterprises to force pay increases, the Civil Service Arbitration Tribunal will be under very heavy pressure to satisfy the demands placed upon it. The same is true for the Industrial Court, which is made up in a comparable manner to the Civil Service Arbitration Board and deals with disputes affecting industrial personnel. The best that can be said for both is that they provide a primary court of reference for pay disputes, which, unlike the Whitley Councils, stands higher than either the staff or the government.

Employer-employee relations in the nationalized industries

No such provisions for arbitration over wage disputes exist for the nationalized industries. This lack was particularly serious in the prolonged strike early in 1971 by postal workers, whose recent transfer from civil service rules and facilities to those of a nationalized enterprise left them, they maintained, with no other means to exert pressure on the government. In the slightly earlier strike by workers in the nationalized electrical industry, the Heath government had subsequently turned to a court of inquiry set up especially to consider the wage dispute and this precedent was also adopted after the postmen went back to work, despite the public dismay at the size of the pay increase the earlier tribunal had proposed. Thus it appears that each nationalized enterprise will have to work out its own procedures in attempting to forestall or deal with such serious interruptions of vital public services and the government will have to continue to confront wage pressures.

Workers in nationalized industries occupy a half-way position between those in the civil service and in private industry. They are not recruited under civil service provisions nor have the nationalized industries yet developed their own formal merit systems as, for example, has the American TVA. The preponderance of technical personnel in some public enterprises, plus the similarity of their work to that of private industry, makes it necessary, according to their officials, to compete flexibly for staff with pay rates and working conditions comparable to those of the market place. But since the government is better able to control the budgets and pay scales of public enterprises than those of private industry and commerce, there remain serious strains that are felt most acutely in a period of governmental retrenchment.

Employees in nationalized industries must belong to a union, in accordance with the insistence of the Trades Union Congress, but not necessarily a single one for the whole industry, for such a ruling might have destroyed certain existing unions. From the side of the government, however, it is much more satisfactory if it can negotiate with a single union rather than several.

The position of unions inside nationalized enterprises is a complicated one. Restrictive practices (such as limiting the production of any single worker, requiring the employment of a minimum number of workers on certain types of jobs, or rigidly imposing limitations on the work a particular employee may perform) that developed to prevent employers from exploiting their workers and to spread employment around seem much less justified when the employer is the government and the service is for the community. But the habits of many years are hard to change, and inflation bites as hard on the workers in public as in private enterprises.

THE OVERSEAS SERVICE

What has been written so far has been concerned mainly with the Home Civil Service, but comparable scrutiny, criticism, and recommendations for adjustments and cuts have also been made in regard to the British Diplomatic Service. As did the Fulton Report, the Duncan Review Committee on Overseas Representation [14] recommended merging the administrative and executive classes and also proposed freer and permanent movement between the Diplomatic Service and other professions, including the Home Civil Service. This proposal, not yet fully implemented, aimed at reversing, in the interests of rationalization and reduced personnel, the earlier process of separation between the overseas and home services.

While it had not been until 1943 that the official separation of the Foreign Service and the Home Civil Service had been decreed, the two had long possessed different channels of recruitment and thus characteristics. With its emphasis on competitive examinations, the Home Civil Service had never been the preserve of the wealthy and aristocratic, while the opposite had been true for the Foreign Service. Not until the consolidation in 1943 of the four overseas services—the Foreign Office, the Diplomatic Service, the Commercial Diplomatic Service, and the Consular Service—were the requirements dropped that a candidate had to satisfy a board of selection before being allowed to sit for the written examinations (greatly curbing henceforth the Secretary of State's age-long power of patronage), and also possess a private income. The next step in consolidation followed the 1964 report of the Plowden Committee,[15] which recommended amalgamating the Foreign Office and Commonwealth Relations Office (finally consummated in 1968) and bringing their staffs into a comparable system of organization to that of the Home Civil Service. From there the proposals of the Duncan Committee for steps to integrate these two services would seem to follow logically.

Some of the more policy-oriented proposals of the Duncan Committee, however, were greeted with severe criticism, in particular its proposed division of British representation abroad between "comprehensive" missions with full political and commercial staffs—to be restricted, in its view, to Great Britain's "area of concentration": Western Europe, North America, the Soviet bloc, China, and "certain other countries in the outer area"—and "selective" missions in the rest that would normally have only a basic strength of three "United Kingdom-based officers." The committee also envisaged commercial work as the most urgent task of British overseas representatives. Finally, it wounded many sensibilities by declaring brusquely that "information services should project Britain as a trading partner with a great culture and democratic tradition, rather than as a world power of the first order." Not surprisingly, the Labor government's response to the report was noncommittal and included only an assurance that no area of the world would be diplomatically neglected. As Great Britain progressively withdraws from active involvement in different parts of the world (see Chap-

---

[14] *Report of the Review Committee on Overseas Representation 1968–1969* (Cmnd. 4107), 1969.

[15] *Report of the Committee on Representational Services Overseas, 1962–63* (Cmnd. 2276), 1964.

ter 8, Section 2), however, the impact on the overseas service will not be unlike what the Duncan Report recommended.

INTERNAL SECURITY IN THE CIVIL SERVICE

Perhaps the most difficult and certainly the most delicate problem faced in recent years within the British civil service has been to establish an adequate program of internal security in a climate of opinion that abhorred the excesses of McCarthyism in the United States. It has been the misfortune of both the Labor and the Conservative governments to find out too late that valuable information had been transmitted to the Soviet Union by supposedly responsible government servants. The Profumo case that rocked the Macmillan government had strong implications for security as well as morality. Thus, a progressively tighter security program has been instituted within the service, although without changing its essential features.

The British security program aims at excluding possibly disloyal persons (that is, with either Communist or fascist associations) from sensitive areas; it operates without publicity; and as far as possible people are transferred within the service rather than discharged. All civil servants engaged in work related to defense contracts are required to state specifically whether they fall within the purview of the security program, and they are automatically disqualified for security posts if they acknowledge having had such connections. Moreover, in certain sensitive areas investigation is automatic. Although the investigations of the security services necessarily remain confidential, a civil servant under suspicion receives full opportunity to reply to the charges of unreliability and, if he so desires, to have a personal interview with his immediate superior, with the minister, and with a specially constituted advisory body of three eminent retired civil servants known as the Three Advisers.

The British have handled their security program with quietness and without disrupting the morale of the service. But periodically cases have arisen, such as the Vassall spy case in 1962 or the still more serious case of Maclean and Burgess in 1951. Both Maclean and Burgess were members of the British Foreign Service who had been under surveillance by security services but who nonetheless were able to flee to Moscow after transmitting secret information to the Soviet Union. Such cases have raised grave questions regarding the adequacy of security arrangements.

The series of bodies that have investigated security arrangements in the civil service have focused on a number of different points for concern. The Conference of seven Privy Councillors set up in 1955 following the Maclean-Burgess affair warned particularly about the risks presented by Communists and by those subject to Communist influence or possessing character defects such as drunkenness, addiction of drugs, homosexuality, or "any loose living that may seriously affect a man's reliability."[16] Contrary to general practice, it advised in these "borderline cases" to "continue tilting the balance in favour of offering greater protection to the security of the State rather than in the direction of safeguarding the rights of the individual." In 1962, the Redcliffe-Maud Commission[17] warned about the number of Communists and Communist sympathizers who held positions in staff associations and trade unions. In 1964, following the Vassall case of espionage by an admiralty clerk at the Naval Attache's Office in Moscow, a Standing Security Commission was set up, under the chairmanship of a High Court judge, that, in addition to its investigation of specific cases,[18] recommended an educational campaign to stimulate awareness among middle and lower grades of their responsibilities in regard to security matters. The Duncan Report, however, suggested there could be savings in overseas security arrangements.

As the Profumo case illustrated, laxness in security-mindedness is not restricted to the civil service. Yet there are inevitably so many matters of importance to security in such agencies as the Foreign and Commonwealth Office, the Defense Department, and the Atomic Energy

---

[16] *Statement on the Findings of the Conference of Privy Councillors on Security* (Cmnd. 9715), 1956.

[17] White Paper, *Security Procedures in the Public Service* (Cmnd. 1681), 1962.

[18] *Report of the Standing Security Commission, June, 1965* (Cmnd. 2722), 1965.

Organization that it is natural for attention to center upon their members. No system can be wholly assured against security leaks, but on the whole both the handling of such issues and their infrequency are tributes to the service.

LOCAL GOVERNMENT OFFICIALS

Local government, as we have seen, has long carried a substantial part of the responsibility for administration at the local level and will continue to do so under the new structure. In their work, the local councils depend not on nationally appointed public servants but on officials selected and paid for by themselves. In fact, local government authorities in normal times employ more people than the national government, about one-quarter of whom are teachers, and a considerable proportion do administrative, technical, and clerical work. Much of the importance of local governments, in their day-to-day working with the national government, arises from this control of their own officials. If local councils gain more independent sources of finance to underpin their functions, these officials may find themselves under new strains between their local masters and national plans.

On the whole, the highest local officials are of outstanding ability, partly because the national government has established standards for most professional positions, and partly because of the high professional ideals maintained by the National Association of Local Government Officers, a voluntary organization with steadily increasing influence, particularly after its successful 1970 strike. In contrast to the general practice in the national administration, the permanent heads of departments in local governments are chosen because of their special training in health, housing, road building, and so forth, and are trained doctors, engineers, or other experts, not general administrators. Some observers consider this unfortunate, believing that it often turns a good doctor into a bad administrator, and that local government would be better advised to recruit general administrators from the universities, as is done in the national government. But there are others who feel that local government could teach the national government a good deal about the administrative usefulness of the expert. Newcastle's innovation in 1965 in making a former Ford executive Britain's first city manager (thereby adopting an American device) may also carry useful lessons.

At least there is general self-congratulation that the English local government service escaped the spoils system that has haunted so many American cities and counties. Nor have there been experiments in electing local government officials, and thus there has been no counterweight to the authority of the council. In fact, English government officials, on the whole, are loyal to their councils to a fault, even when their own farsighted plans are crippled by too parsimonious councilors.

The major problems in local government service are found at the lower levels. Emphasis on professional qualifications for high officials means that opportunities for promotion from lower (and less specialized) levels are much more restricted than in the national civil service. In addition, local councils often try to balance the cost of hiring well-trained professional men by employing inadequately trained people in lower positions. Until after World War II, junior clerks were sometimes brought into the service at an immature age and without good records in secondary education. Training plans were lacking. Only recently have Whitley Councils become common at every level of local government service. Thus there is still much to be done to develop the uniformly high standards in the service on which the excellence of local government programs must depend.

HOW SATISFACTORY IS THE CIVIL SERVICE?

Although the British have engaged recently in an unprecedented spate of criticisms of their civil service, on the whole it commands respect and possesses far higher prestige than the American civil service. The average member of the upper civil service is neither a "philosopher king" nor a daring innovator, but he is competent, wide awake, and responsible. He enters the service through tests that emphasize clear, logical thinking and expression and ability to view situations objectively. In the service he works on important problems during most of his life. Moreover, he is schooled throughout his career in its professional ethics, according to which he must put public interest above personal advantage.

The civil servant is expressly forbidden to put himself in a position where duty and interests conflict. "The public expects from them a standard of integrity and conduct not only inflexible but fastidious," stated a report of 1928. The permanent secretary of the Air Ministry was dismissed in 1936 for using his knowledge of public negotiations for his own private advantage, a rare example of violation of the primary rule of the civil service code.

The second major rule in the civil service code of ethics is the ban on direct political activity. "The step from the civil service politician to the politicized civil servant is but a short one," a Royal Commission warned. Although other elements of the code are embodied in Treasury minutes or departmental codes or enshrined in custom, this prohibition is embodied in legislation.

Yet while ministers and the Cabinet must assume the formal responsibility for policy, there can be little doubt that high civil servants inevitably have a significant influence on its formation. In a period when issues are vastly complicated and the flow of information overwhelming, the resources and experience of top civil servants and the financial advice, not to say warnings, of the Treasury are apt to be weighted heavily and be possibly conclusive.

It is this realization that has spurred proposals for more use of technical personnel and especially of trained and experienced economists to analyze the many issues impinging on their expertise. It has even been proposed that ministers should bring with them into the departments their own personal staffs, as French ministers do, not only to reinforce their positions but also to make it unnecessary for high civil servants to appear to be supporting policies that, in fact, they oppose. Under such conditions it might be possible to remove some of the cloaks of anonymity that most high civil servants wrap around themselves in accordance with constitutional principles and allow Parliament and the public to gain better perspectives on the reasons for and against a particular policy.

High civil servants are sometimes spoken of as "statesmen in disguise." But in addition to their sophistication and smooth handling of day-to-day affairs (in which the most searching questions and sharpest controversies are all too often smothered in generalities and good fellowship) is the need for energetic innovation. The machinery is in process of reorganization, the pressing issues of a time of crisis are constantly to the fore. No one doubts the almost uniquely high standards of probity, impressive neutrality, and ability of the British civil service. But much will depend in the future on whether it also brings imagination, originality, and perception to bear on the tasks of government.

7
English law and courts

1 ENGLISH COMMON LAW

The traditional association of law and liberty is so intimate that, particularly in Anglo-Saxon countries, what is called "the rule of law" is looked on as the essence of free government (see Chapter 2, Section 2). According to this concept, every individual in the community has certain rights that should not be infringed upon by other individuals or by government officials. Independent courts are available to which he may appeal if there is any interference with these rights. The rule of law means too that if an individual is accused of failing to do his duty or of committing an injustice, he cannot be punished until after he has had a public hearing in the courts and a formal verdict, based on a specific and known body of law, has been made against him.

Certain additional features of the rule of law are equally important as safeguards of individual liberty. Thus the rule of law (sometimes spoken of as "government under law") implies that the powers of the government can be extended or changed only through regular and accepted political processes that result in publicly known legislation. This is particularly important at a time when government is assuming so many new responsibilities that directly affect the community, for otherwise people might not know rights that they possess or might be punished under rules of which they were unaware, as was true in Nazi Germany and has been so in the Soviet Union. In Anglo-Saxon countries the rights and duties of the government and the relations between the government and private individuals within the state are defined in what is called *public law*. Because the powers of government are defined, government officials are limited to those actions for which they have specific authority, and a private individual can check a particular action by asking the courts to determine whether it is justified by the provisions of the law under which the official is acting.

The law (which may be defined broadly as a known body of rules related to general principles that the courts use in deciding specific cases referred to them) and independent, impartial courts are as important in ordinary social relations within the community as they are in preventing arbitrary action by the government and its agents. By defining individual rights and duties the law removes uncertainties regarding the rules governing daily conduct and renders unnecessary recourse to violence to settle disputes. *Private law* is concerned with the relations between private persons (for example, husband and wife or partners) and with questions relating to private property or to one's own person, such as contracts and torts (for example, slander, trespass, and assault).

Most of private law falls into the category of *civil law*,[1] which concerns itself with the rights of individuals looked on merely as individuals. In civil law, individuals have to take the responsibility for bringing cases before the courts. But if the violation of the rights of one individual by another is considered to be a threat to public order the case comes under *criminal law*, which is public law and for which the government assumes responsibility. While trespass, for example, is a civil offense because it affects only the person whose property has been interfered with, murder is a criminal offense because it robs the community of one of its members and, by example, may threaten the security of others. Other acts that violate certain standards or rules established by the government may also be prosecuted under criminal law.

The exact content and relationship of the various bodies of law change and develop with changing conditions. Otherwise they would put society in a strait jacket. The economic and social needs of society have been affected so vastly by industrialization, for example, that what was once considered to be a matter that only affected the individuals immediately concerned (for example, child labor) has become a matter of concern to society as a whole. Moreover, as some individual rights are curtailed (for example, that of employers to determine the conditions of work for their employees), new rights, such as the right to benefits under social security and workmen's compensation for injuries, are extended.

Ideally, therefore, the law should meet two criteria. It should be certain and precise so that it provides known standards for action. At the same time, it should be flexible enough to meet new conditions.

The peculiar pride of the Anglo-American legal system lies in its ability to combine a high degree of certainty as to legal rules with striking adaptability to changing conditions. This characteristic has been demonstrated in the long continuity of the English common law, extending over eight hundred years. During this time the English have developed a national system of law characterized by a complex interweaving of written statutes and unwritten custom and precedent. The adaptability of this system of law has been demonstrated not only in England but, under different conditions, in most English-speaking countries, including many of the newer members of the Commonwealth.[2] While the United States diverged sharply from English practices in establishing its political institutions, the American legal system was built directly on English legal rules, practices, and institutions. And although American law and courts have developed their own distinctive features, it is still true that precedents are occasionally exchanged across the Atlantic.

THE STRANDS OF ENGLISH LAW

The characteristic features of the English common law system were molded by experience and can scarcely be understood apart from their historical development. The legal system of England and Wales,[3] although well integrated, developed historically out of three strands: *common law, equity*, and *statute law*. Although all three have long merged to form a single system of law, common law, equity, and statute have had separate roots and arose out of particular circumstances and needs.

Common law and equity are sometimes, although inaccurately, spoken of as "unwritten law," because they developed out of the decisions of judges; statute law is thought of as "written law," because it results from the legislative process. Many of the rules that developed from the historic common law and equity have been embodied in legislation, but there are also certain customary procedures and rights that come from the past and are valid in courts of law without legislative formulation.

Historically, the *common law* dates back to

---

[1] The term *civil law* is also used in quite a different sense to distinguish jurisprudence based on Roman sources from the jurisprudence of Anglo-American countries, which has its roots in common law. For the former, see Chapter 7 in the section on France and Chapter 6 in the section on Germany.

[2] Ceylon has Roman-Dutch law, for historical reasons, as do Rhodesia and South Africa, formerly in the Commonwealth.

[3] Scotland and Northern Ireland have their own legal rules and institutions, which differ in part from those of England and Wales. Scottish law, in particular, has been more strongly affected by Roman law than has English law. They also have separate court systems and slight differences in their legal professions. Everything in this chapter, therefore, refers only to England and Wales.

the twelfth and thirteenth centuries when traveling royal judges, sent out in the interests of centralizing authority, forged a law "common" to the whole kingdom out of the cases and customs of local communities and their own knowledge and judgment. This "common" law was then used as the basis for decisions in the new royal courts at Westminster: King's Bench, Exchequer, and Common Pleas. This law was both stable and adaptable. It was stable because the rule of precedent was soon adopted that ensured that once a decision has been reached in a particular type of case, subsequent cases of a similar kind should be decided by the same rule. It was adaptable because every case has individual features, and there were, and are usually, a number of precedents on which to draw. Even so, as feudalism gave place to a moneyed economy, and new needs developed, the common law was found inadequate to deal with all cases. Thus developed the second historical strand in English law: equity.

Equity was rooted not in custom but in conscience. Where the common law courts did not provide a just redress of grievances, an appeal could be made through the king to the chancellor, "the keeper of the King's conscience," who after investigation could issue a special writ ordering performance of the act necessary to secure justice. Equity, for example, could force performance of a contract, whereas common law could only give damages for its breach. Moreover the chancellor, like a modern court, could issue a writ of equity to prevent a house from being destroyed to make way for a public road until after the need for the action had been investigated, whereas common law could only provide damages if the destruction were proved unnecessary.

Another characteristic and important provision of equity was, and is, the "trust." Under common law, property transferred to another person became his own, even though he might be administering it for the benefit of a third person—for example, the infant child of the original owner. Under equity the chancellor could not take away the right of ownership from the person to whom the property had been transferred, but he could order that person to use it for the purpose for which it had been given to him—that is, for the benefit of the child. Thus equity did not abolish rights that existed under common law but insisted that they be used in a just or equitable way. This notion of a trust has had many applications. In the form of settlements under wills or of charitable organizations the trust became a central institution of English and American property law.

Common law and equity were shaped by judges to fit the needs of the periods in which they were formed. Common law provided a basic system of law that built on local customs but shaped them in terms of the new centralized royal authority. Equity supplemented its rules to add what one authority has called "the practice of the 'good citizen,' i.e., the really upright and conscientious person." Gradually equity, too, became a system bound by precedent. In the eighteenth century, a great chancellor declared that the doctrines of equity "ought to be as well settled and made as uniform as those of the Common Law."

The third, and now most important as well as massive, strand in English law is "written" or *statute* law—that is, legislation passed by Parliament or statutory instruments enacted by any one of the subordinate bodies to which Parliament has delegated lawmaking powers. Until the nineteenth century, however, almost all private law, as well as almost all criminal law, was common law or equity. Even when the criminal law was embodied in statutes in the nineteenth and twentieth centuries, as was most of the law governing trusts, partnerships, bills of exchange, and sales of goods and lands, it retained some principles of common law. In this sense, in the fields of private and criminal law, statute law, like equity, is complementary to common law.

There is a fundamental difference, however, between the relation of common law and equity and that between common law and statute law. Equity does not contradict common law but mitigates it or meets its deficiencies. Statute law overrides common law. In fact, the main reason for passing statutes in the field of private law has been to alter rules that had become established by judicial decision but no longer fitted community standards, such as regulating the relations between parent and child. When common law and equity are inadequate or do not meet contemporary needs, recourse must be made to statute.

SHOULD CIVIL LIBERTIES BE PROTECTED BY STATUTE LAW?

The English are seriously considering today whether they should have recourse to statute law to protect their cherished civil liberties more adequately. Historically, their right to personal liberty (although ensured in one important regard by the writ of habeas corpus), or to hold public meetings, engage in free speech, maintain a free press, and otherwise to act independently outside of government regulations could be said, as did A. V. Dicey in his classic statement of the rule of law, to depend on judicial decisions in particular cases brought by private persons. It is true that there are, in practice, legal and parliamentary safeguards for civil liberties, and that the Bill of Rights of 1689 is not only important historically but has also been quoted in modern courts of law in cases concerned with freedom of speech. At the same time, there is not a single modern document listing these rights that would be comparable to the Bill of Rights that amends the Constitution of the United States or to those adopted by members of the Commonwealth of Nations, including India, Malaysia, and, through a postwar addition to its constitution, Canada. Great Britain is a party, however, to the European Convention of Human Rights of 1950, and has accepted the jurisdiction of the European Court of Human Rights, to which individuals can take well-authenticated cases in which a state has violated their rights.

Delivering the Haldane Lecture at London University in December 1970, Lord Justice Salmon extended his support to the widespread demands for a modern bill of rights to provide judges with the power to declare certain repressive measures illegal and thus help to check the ever-increasing number of restrictions to which individuals are subjected. He thus called attention to the crucial point that judges are circumscribed in what they can achieve by the law that they administer. Suggesting that a modern bill of rights might be entrenched by requiring a 75 percent majority of both Houses of Parliament for its repeal, Lord Justice Salmon endorsed yet a more radical break from the traditional practice of passing measures of constitutional significance by simple legislation (see Chapter 2, Section 2). But whether entrenched or not, a British bill of rights might have a major impact, both in reinforcing the ability of the courts to defend individual rights from encroachments and by turning the focus of public attention upon the significance of civil liberties and the potential danger to them.

2 JUDGES, JURIES, AND OFFICIALS

No one can overlook the importance of the judge for the development of the English common law system. Courts are judges sitting in their official capacities to consider and pass judgment in particular cases that have been referred to them. On the judges' knowledge, judgment, integrity, and independence depends the quality of the legal decisions that not only settle particular cases but also decide precedents for the future.

One of the great struggles for individual liberty in England centered upon the independence of the judiciary. The royal courts were originally set up by order of the king, but they quickly acquired a large measure of autonomy.

Nonetheless, since the judges were appointed and dismissed at royal pleasure, the king possessed powerful weapons if he wished to bend the administration of justice to his purposes. Moreover, the king was the ultimate "fount of justice," and Stuart kings maintained that this gave them the right to override the customary rules of law. As great a Lord Chancellor as Francis Bacon declared that judges should be "lions under the throne." But the judges of the seventeenth century resisted royal efforts to make their decisions serve royal purposes. The Act of Settlement, 1701, put the judiciary beyond fear of government pressure. Accordingly, English judges, although appointed by the government, came to hold office for life or until retirement, in the same way as do American federal judges.[4]

In addition to safeguarding the independence of their judiciary, the English put a high premium on specialized legal knowledge and experience. All English judges are drawn from the legal profession, so that, unlike the Continental system in which judges and lawyers belong to two separate, although similar, professions, English judges have a long background as practicing members of the Bar. Americans, too, draw their judges mainly from the legal profession; but in England there has long been a further restriction on the selection of judges unknown in the United States: English judges have come traditionally from that part of the legal profession whose members are known as barristers.

THE LEGAL PROFESSION

The distinctive feature of the English legal profession has long been its division into two separate groups: solicitors and barristers. Insofar as this division finds a parallel in the United States, it is in the distinction between the office lawyer who prepares cases and the court lawyer who argues them. But in England the distinction has been so great that solicitors and barristers receive their credentials from their own separate societies and until recently solicitors could not easily qualify for admission to the Bar.

Solicitors are the workhorses of the legal profession. They deal directly with clients, undertake all routine legal office work, and work on the briefs to be argued by barristers in the higher courts. The preparation for this profession does not necessarily involve university training (although nearly half of the seventeen thousand or so solicitors have university degrees), but the ability and knowledge to pass a number of special professional examinations. It is also necessary to be "articled," that is, apprenticed, to a solicitor for a specified length of time: five years if without a university degree; three years if the degree is in a subject other than law; and two years if a law degree is possessed. Once accepted as a "Solicitor of the Supreme Court," a solicitor begins his career, probably also joining the Law Society, which is a voluntary association of solicitors that possesses certain statutory powers.

Barristers, in contrast, possess a high degree of legal specialization and their under twenty-five hundred members comprise the country's best-known legal talent. Their chief functions are to provide solicitors with legal advice, either in general or in preparation for a trial, and to conduct cases, particularly before the higher courts. They depend on solicitors for their work rather than dealing directly with clients.

All barristers are members of one of the four Inns of Court, which are long-established, self-governing voluntary organizations providing a corporate life for their members in historic buildings. The Inns of Court combine the training and examination functions of a law school with the perpetual upholding of standards of a professional association. Acting together, the Inns of Court form the Bar.

Barristers are themselves divided between "Junior Barristers" and "Queen's Counsel" (QC's), the latter known colloquially as "Silks," since they, unlike the Juniors, are entitled to wear silk gowns. QC's become such on recommendation of the Lord Chancellor, a distinction usually extended when a barrister reaches the top of his profession. They are limited by rules to certain types of work, mainly pleading in open court, and cannot appear without a Junior, but they get higher fees than do the latter. It is from the ranks of the QC's that judges are commonly chosen.

The English court system, however, is badly clogged with cases, and barristers' fees are high. For these reasons, and because solicitors have long desired a larger role in the English legal system, proposals have been made that there should be fewer restrictions on their right to plead in the new circuit crown courts set up under the 1971 Court Act and, more novel,

---

[4] Most American states, in contrast to the British system of appointment, select the judges for the state judiciaries through direct election or election by the legislature. One argument in support of election is that the practice of judicial review gives the judges a political function, and that therefore they should be kept responsive to public opinion. It is generally acknowledged, however, that the caliber of elected judges is less high than that of appointed judges.

that they should be eligible for judicial appointments. Prior to the new act, solicitors were allowed to sit as the chairman and deputy chairman of county quarter sessions (see below), and some who have so acted might be promoted. In any case, to remove the ban on appointing a solicitor to a judicial position would provide the Lord Chancellor with some flexibility in filling openings at the high court level.

Moreover, in the long run (and perhaps some barristers fear this), more solicitors might be appointed to the bench if more were allowed the experience of pleading in court. Solicitors have long been allowed to appear in magistrates' and county courts, and the Lord Chief Justice supported a proposal in the House of Lords during discussion of the Court Bill that they be allowed to plead in the circuit courts when a case comes for sentencing after being tried in a lower court.

Proposals have been made for radical changes in the English legal system aimed at unification both of training and functions. The Committee on Legal Education composed of judges and lawyers under the chairmanship of Justice Ormrod made the controversial recommendation in March 1971 (Cmnd. 4595) that both branches of the profession should be brought together and trained through the universities instead of their own professional bodies. Following an obligatory university law degree, all aspirants would join legal firms for practical experience before taking qualifying examinations to admit them to the Bar or as solicitors. Subsequently, a solicitor would work for three years as an assistant solicitor under a practicing one. Barristers would serve a period as pupils in chambers to secure their experience. In working out the details of training, the committee recommended establishing an advisory committee on legal education to give advice on setting up the necessary courses at the universities, and it also proposed setting up an institute of professional legal studies.

Such a major change, which is dependent on the agreement of the existing professional institutions, may well not be accepted. Yet the situation confronting the court system is an urgent one. Solicitors charged, even before the new Court Act was implemented, that they were facing intolerable difficulties in assuring their clients adequate legal support in court. Since barristers are paid by the number of cases in which they appear, it has been to their interest to handle as many as possible in the same place and on the same day to the consequent neglect of more isolated cases. The restrictions regarding the roles of QC's and Juniors add further complications. But what has been the most forceful spur to reconsideration of the situation of the legal profession has been the new demand under the 1971 Court Act that established a new crown court in place of quarter sessions and assizes (see below) and required some forty additional judges immediately, and ultimately another thirty. The majority of the Royal Commission on Quarter Sessions and Assizes under Lord Beeching's chairmanship, whose 1969 report led to the 1971 Court Bill, had rather hesitatingly recommended that appointments to "circuit judges" be open to solicitors; the Court Bill restricted them to barristers of at least ten years' experience. But something will have to give.

THE QUALITIES OF THE JUDICIARY

Drawing the English judiciary solely from among barristers has had certain consequences. For one, it has meant that English judges combined great ability and experience in interpreting the law with high standards of personal integrity. No suspicion of corruption touches even the lower levels of the judiciary, and much of the innate respect for the law in England comes from the distinguished service of generations of judges.

At the same time, judges have traditionally been drawn from the wealthy and privileged classes of society; as a result, the judicial system in England is occasionally stigmatized as a class system. Young barristers, since they depend on the work that solicitors give them, often have difficulty in earning enough to support themselves in their early years of practice. Thus, few enter the profession unless they have some outside support. But once they start earning, successful barristers receive some of the largest incomes in England. Thus the barrister is likely to belong to a well-to-do family and to have acquired large personal means and social prestige before he is invited to become a judge.

The old socialist charges that as long as English judges were drawn from the ruling class, labor would find that the courts, far from protecting their liberties, would in practice connive against them, have fallen away. The class character of the English judiciary, in fact, is far less marked now than in the past. Yet it would seem that there is much to be said for extending the range of choice far more widely. The Beeching Commission found that nearly 70 percent of people awaiting trial at the central criminal court (commonly known as Old Bailey) had to wait longer than the eight weeks recommended as a maximum by the Streatfield Committee in 1961. Public sentiment is clearly behind swifter justice, and the bottleneck is due to the lack of an adequate number of judges.

THE JUSTICES OF THE PEACE

At one place in the English judicial system professional judges give way for the most part to "amateurs," the justices of the peace. Apart from the full-time, paid judges who hold court in larger towns, the justices of the peace staff the local petty sessions courts of criminal jurisdiction, where all but 2 or 3 percent of criminal cases are settled. Justices are selected on the basis of personal qualities from among the local inhabitants of a district, receive a short course of training before starting their work, and serve without pay. The justices of the peace were originally (under an act of 1361) the king's agents in maintaining peace in the counties and were usually drawn from "the gentry." Their responsibilities are now limited to minor criminal cases, but having J.P. after one's name still carries considerable prestige.

Throughout England and Wales there were 19,250 persons staffing the lowest criminal courts in 1971, of whom only the 47 stipendiary magistrates (37 of whom are in London) can sit alone in trying a case. (In matrimonial cases, the magistrates sit with two lay justices of the peace.) J.P.'s never act alone, except in granting minor appeals for bail. Because younger people can rarely afford to give so much time without pay,[5] most of the justices of the peace are well over fifty. Following the recommendation of a Royal Commission in 1948, there is now an age limit of seventy-five (sixty-five on the juvenile court bench), which is gradually being reduced. It is sometimes charged that the privileged position of J.P.'s makes them unsympathetic to those whose offenses they judge and that they depend too much on the testimony of the local police. But the system has many advantages. The use of so many unpaid officials keeps the costs of criminal jurisdiction low. In the small cases with which they are mainly concerned, the local knowledge of the justices may enable them to impose particularly appropriate penalties or to temper justice with mercy. Perhaps the best feature of the system is that it strengthens the tradition that justice belongs to the people and is their responsibility.

THE JURY

Another use of amateurs in the judicial process is the jury. Traditionally, one of the most important rights of an Englishman or an American is trial by his peers. Taken together with the writ of habeas corpus, under which a person accused of a crime must be brought to trial or released within a limited period of time, the right to demand jury trial has long been looked on in Anglo-Saxon countries as a basic safeguard of individual liberty.

Jury trial has become far less common, however, than it was in the past. This is particularly the case in England, although it is also happening in the United States. The grand jury, still used in the United States to determine whether the prosecution has enough evidence to proceed with a trial, was abolished in England in 1933. The petty, or ordinary, jury

---

[5] The Heath government approved loss-of-earnings allowances and new subsistence payments to justices of the peace starting early in 1971–72. It also agreed to pay subsistence allowances to magistrates within three miles of their homes, thereby eliminating an earlier irritating restriction. The ten stipendiary magistrates outside London serve in cities like Birmingham and Manchester and one or two smaller centers. While their power to decide cases by themselves is called "indefensible," it is too popular to change. They correspond to the police magistrates found in every American city.

of "twelve good men and true" is still used invariably in both countries in trying the most serious criminal offenses, such as rape, kidnaping, and murder. The jury makes the vital decision whether the defendant is guilty or innocent, and under the 1967 Criminal Justice Act, majority verdicts—ten to two, eleven to one, or ten to one—are permitted, although unanimity is required if the jury numbers nine or fewer. The judge, of course, decides the actual sentence. But jury trial is rare in English civil cases, much less common than in American courts. Still more surprising is the relatively small use by the English of juries in minor criminal cases. Barely 10 percent of those who could have a jury trial choose to do so.

Part of the reason for not using juries in civil cases is that the litigants must pay the jury's fees. Defendants may decide against jury trial in lesser criminal cases because jury service, in practice, is mainly restricted to the well-to-do, who cannot be expected to have great insight into the problems of the poor. The most important reasons for the decline in the use of juries, however, seem to be the desire for speedy trials and the belief that—apart from cases involving public morality, such as libel— the jury's injection of its own sense of justice into a case is not needed as a safeguard for the rights of the defendant.

THE JUDICIAL ADMINISTRATIVE SYSTEM

English judges have traditionally had a very large degree of independence in running the courts, for there is no central administrative department such as the Ministry of Justice in France. The Lord Chancellor is largely responsible for ensuring a smoothly working judicial system. The power to make appointments, draft rules, direct cases from one court to another, and maintain general supervision of all court business provides considerable authority, but there is a strong feeling that a more efficient structure is now needed. The Lord Chancellor, who is always chosen by the prime minister from among distinguished senior barristers of his party, has only a small office, which is heavily overburdened and ill equipped to oversee the reorganization of the courts. The Beeching Commission had proposed that the Lord Chancellor be given responsibility for the whole judicial system— except for magistrates' courts—and that a senior officer, to be called circuit administrator, be appointed for each geographical group of courts. The natural corollary would seem to be the establishment of a government department that the Lord Chancellor would head.

No one person in the United States combines so many judicial offices and functions as does the Lord Chancellor. He presides over the House of Lords,[6] and is a member of the Cabinet. He appoints all the justices of the peace, county court justices, and judges to the central courts, except for two—the Lord Chief Justice and the Master of the Rolls—who are appointed by the prime minister. He is expected to keep the court structure efficient, up to date, and abreast of its work, a task for which he obviously needs more administrative support.

Most judges have life tenure (county court judges retire at seventy-two or may be dismissed, but this is very rare), and many remain in the same post to which they were originally appointed. Most administrative officials hold office under civil service rulings. Most court rules are traditional. But in a time of change when a basic reorganization of the court system is taking place, the old assumption that it can be mainly self-operating no longer holds.

There is no real parallel in England to the American offices of federal and state district attorneys. The Director of Public Prosecutions in Britain only intervenes in cases where the detailed services of his office are required, for example, because of complexity or national interest. In 1969, for instance, he undertook prosecutions in only 2,014 cases, of which 1,255 concerned indictable offenses and 759 nonindictable ones. All these interventions were at the request of a public agency although private individuals could also have appealed to him. Otherwise criminal prosecutions are conducted by private barristers retained by the state for

---

[6] The attorney general and his chief assistant, the solicitor general, who give legal advice to ministries and represent the Crown in cases in which its interests are concerned, are members of the House of Commons.

that purpose or in the magistrates courts by police officers who are usually assigned full time to this responsibility. As far as the records of the case are concerned, the policeman appears in his private capacity, e.g., Smith v. X. Any individual has the right to prosecute personally but few do so.

Although the number of serious crimes in England has increased substantially over the past few years, it is still considerably lower than in the United States. Thus the burden on the English court system, particularly above the lowest level of criminal courts, is proportionately smaller than in this country. But the same problems of over-crowded dockets and long delays exist in both countries. Thus neither in England nor in the United States does the court system fulfill its function of providing swift impartial justice in defense of public order and individual or group rights.

3 THE COURTS

The central institutions of the judicial system are the courts. Courts can decide only those cases that are brought before them either by a private individual or a public officer. No matter how unjust a situation may be, the courts have no means of interfering unless a specific complaint is filed. But the character and accessibility of the courts have a good deal to do with the frequency with which they are used. If justice is to be easily available to all people, there must be local courts as well as national, their procedures must not be too technical, and the cost must be within the reach of persons of average means.

A century ago the English court system was a bewildering collection of separate courts. The royal central courts had been superimposed on the local courts. Different sets of courts administered common law and equity, and there was a constant struggle among and within the systems to acquire cases and thus the fees that litigants paid. Conflicts of jurisdiction were frequent, and the litigant who made a mistake about the court in which to start his case might find himself forced to begin all over again in another court after a long and expensive process in the first one. In addition, there was little uniformity of procedure. The complexity of court organization defeated the purpose of making justice easily available.

A determined effort to tackle this problem and bring uniformity into the court structure was made through the Judicature Acts between 1873 and 1876. The distinction between common law and equity courts was swept away, and all courts received the right, where necessary, to use both kinds of law. The central courts were combined technically into the High Court of Justice and the Supreme Court of Judicature, which, although they are only symbols of unity and not courts that ever meet, serve the purpose of preventing conflicts of jurisdiction among the separate central courts of which they are composed. As the chart on page 196 makes clear, each of the three divisions of the High Court of Justice specializes in a particular subject matter (rearranged under the Administration of Justice Act of 1970), but the fiction of maintaining that they are part of the High Court of Justice simplifies the transfer of cases from one to another if necessary.

The Court Act of 1971 instituted the second major reorganization of the courts. It was based on the recommendations of the Royal Commission on Quarter Sessions and Assizes, under Lord Beeching, which extended its originally narrow terms of reference to take in the whole court system. The rationalization and decentralization of the court structure it proposed sought to rearrange the whole judicial system under effective and responsible administration so as to make the courts more geographically and functionally suited to their tasks.

The specific proposal for the higher courts, implemented in the Court Act, was to set up a new type of court, the Crown Court, to sit in a large number of urban centers to deal with all the more serious criminal cases. The Crown Court absorbed the criminal jurisdiction of the previously existing fifty-eight courts of quarter session, and the ninety-three borough sessions,

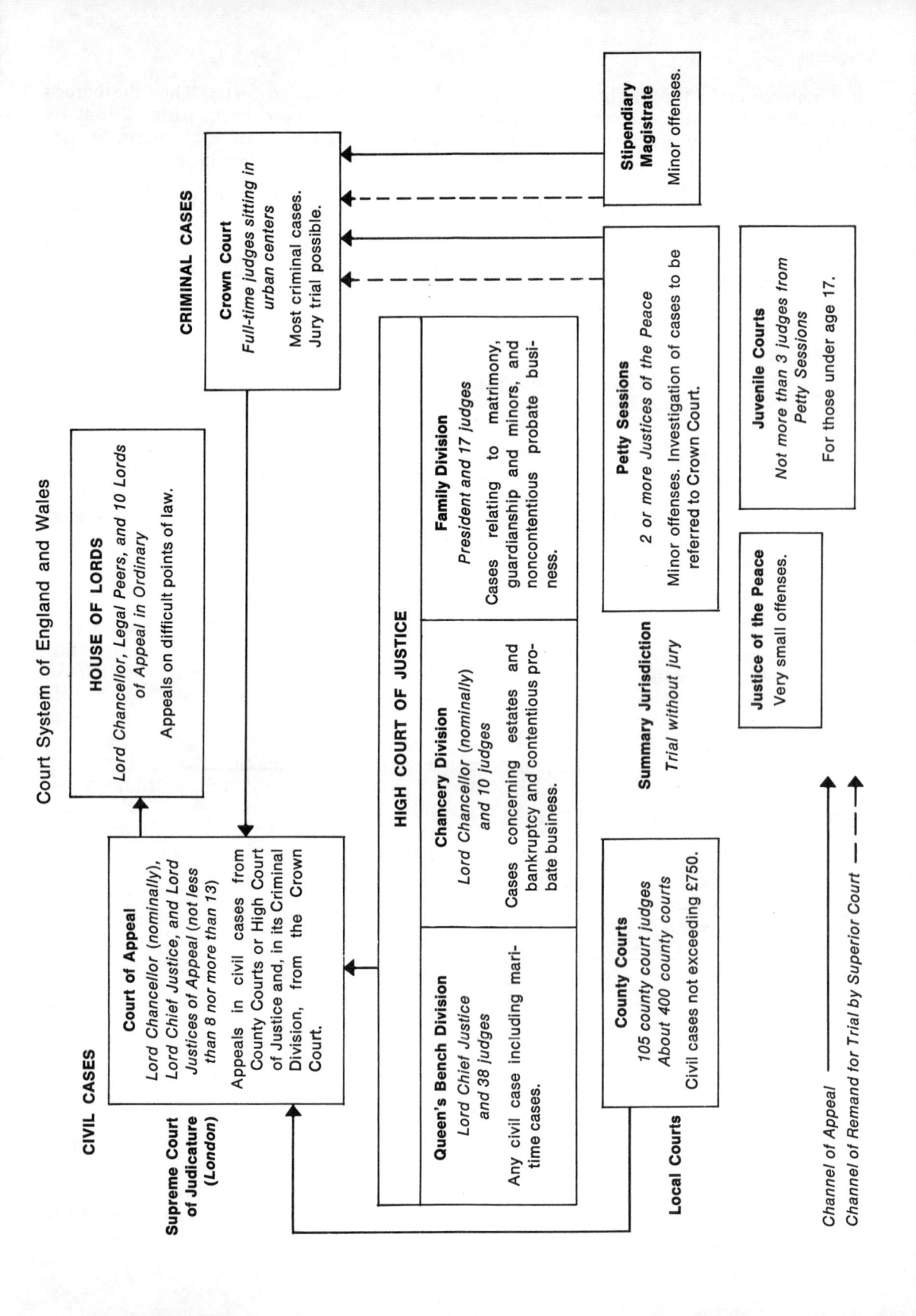

Court System of England and Wales

CIVIL CASES

HOUSE OF LORDS
Lord Chancellor, Legal Peers, and 10 Lords of Appeal in Ordinary

Appeals on difficult points of law.

CRIMINAL CASES

Supreme Court of Judicature (London)

Court of Appeal
Lord Chancellor (nominally), Lord Chief Justice, and Lord Justices of Appeal (not less than 8 nor more than 13)

Appeals in civil cases from County Courts or High Court of Justice and, in its Criminal Division, from the Crown Court.

Crown Court
Full-time judges sitting in urban centers

Most criminal cases. Jury trial possible.

HIGH COURT OF JUSTICE

Queen's Bench Division
Lord Chief Justice and 38 judges
Any civil case including maritime cases.

Chancery Division
Lord Chancellor (nominally) and 10 judges
Cases concerning estates and bankruptcy and contentious probate business.

Family Division
President and 17 judges
Cases relating to matrimony, guardianship and minors, and noncontentious probate business.

Local Courts

County Courts
105 county court judges
About 400 county courts
Civil cases not exceeding £750.

Summary Jurisdiction
Trial without jury

Petty Sessions
2 or more Justices of the Peace. Investigation of cases to be referred to Crown Court.

Justice of the Peace
Very small offenses.

Stipendiary Magistrate
Minor offenses.

Juvenile Courts
Not more than 3 judges from Petty Sessions

For those under age 17.

Channel of Appeal →
Channel of Remand for Trial by Superior Court ⇢

the central criminal court (i.e., Old Bailey), and the assize courts. Courts of quarter session dealt with cases like assault, stealing, or housebreaking where specialized judicial knowledge was not essential. The traveling assize judge, who periodically held court in at least one assize town in every county, could handle serious offenses, including murder and treason, and also had civil jurisdiction. In place of these two sets of courts, the Beeching Commission suggested that about twenty towns outside of London should be centers for both the High Court—to deal with civil cases that the assize courts had inadequately handled—and the most serious criminal cases in the Crown Court, and another eighty towns should be centers for the Crown Court alone. Even this latter number, it believed, could be sharply reduced as soon as more courts are established in the main towns.

To staff the new structure, the Beeching Commission's report envisaged a new bench of judges known as "circuit judges," consisting of the 105 county court judges and all full-time judges, other than High Court judges, who were in the higher criminal courts. These circuit judges would be expected to specialize, for while most county court judges could handle criminal cases, judges who are experienced only with criminal cases rarely are capable of dealing with civil cases. A special problem involved in the reorganization was that a large proportion, about three hundred members of the criminal judiciary, were part-time judges who also carried on their professions as barristers and would thus be eliminated. The change meant, therefore, the appointment of about forty new judges, as discussed above, with probably another thirty to follow.

The commission further recommended reducing the civil work of the High Court by increasing the jurisdiction of the county courts in both contract and tort cases from its existing limit of £700 to £1,000. Moreover, the jurisdiction of county court registrars, whose courts provide the only reasonably inexpensive remedies for small claims, should be raised, it felt, from £30 to £100.

While the 1971 Court Act did not implement the full range of proposals of the Beeching Commission, it established the Crown Court in place of quarter sessions and assizes, and introduced the process of reorganization to which the commission's report had pointed. By thus decentralizing the structure, the Court Act moved the English judicial system close to a simple hierarchy of courts within which there is no duplication of work. Such a degree of unification fills American observers with envy.[7]

DIFFERENCES BETWEEN CIVIL AND CRIMINAL CASES

The basic division in the English court system between civil and criminal cases builds on the distinction made in the first section of this chapter. Civil law, as we have seen, is concerned with the relations between individuals when no element of public security is involved. Disputes over contracts, boundaries, wills, the payment of debts, or suits for divorce are all typical subjects for civil courts. The person seeking redress institutes an *action* to right whatever wrong has been committed and often, in addition, to force the payment of a fine to the injured person.

Civil cases are expensive, especially for the loser. Since they are for the benefit of individuals, the government takes no responsibility for paying their cost, apart from the salary of the judge and the basic maintenance of the court. To meet the additional expenses of running the courts, litigants pay fees that are often quite high. Frequently these costs are added to the damages imposed, thereby making unsuccessful litigation an extremely costly process.

There are a number of ways in which criminal cases differ from civil cases. Since criminal cases involve acts that affect public order, they begin through *prosecutions*, instituted in the name of the Crown.

Further, because criminal jurisdiction is concerned with acts that affect society as a whole, the costs of a criminal trial may be borne by

---

[7] There are fifty-two hierarchies of courts in the United States, since each state and the District of Columbia has one, and there is also the federal structure. The federal courts are well unified, much better than most state court systems. In general, there is little overlapping between the two systems, since the federal courts handle cases involving federal laws and the state courts those involving state laws. If the litigants are from two different states, however, they have the choice of bringing the case before a state court or a federal court, the latter being permitted on ground of "diversity of citizenship."

the public, although the defendant in a criminal case can be made to pay all or part of what are sometimes very high costs of the proceedings, if the court thinks fit. Any fines imposed go into the public treasury. In such cases as assault, damages may also be awarded to an injured person; those damages are, however, usually collected through a civil suit conducted parallel to the criminal prosecution.

In both civil and criminal cases it is possible to appeal from the judgment of a lower court if permission is granted by the higher court. Only in exceptional cases, however, are appeals permitted on the ground that the facts elucidated by the lower court are in question—a rather common practice in the United States. In England, appeals are generally restricted to cases where the interpretation of law by the lower court is challenged.

THE STRUCTURE OF THE COURTS

The separation between the civil and the criminal courts is most clearly marked at the local level. There are two sets of courts and no exchange of personnel between them.[8] The county courts deal only with civil cases. The magistrates' courts and petty sessions, staffed by justices of the peace, deal with minor criminal cases, juvenile hearings, and matrimonial disputes (but not divorce). Appeals in family matters go, however, to the Family Division of the High Court.

The higher courts are also clearly separated between those that handle civil and those that handle criminal cases. Their personnel, however, is not separated so distinctly. Judges for the higher criminal courts are drawn from courts in the civil hierarchy. The only place where hierarchies of civil and criminal courts officially merge is at the very apex, where the Court of Appeal and the House of Lords provide the final source of appeal for both.

---

[8] This practice of having separate courts for civil and criminal cases finds no parallel in the United States. American county courts, for example, have extensive criminal as well as civil jurisdiction and are found in almost every one of the 3,050 counties into which the United States is divided. Many American states have a maze of local courts, in none of which is there so clear a separation of function as between the English county courts and courts of the justices of the peace.

The House of Lords

It may seem odd that the highest court of appeal in England is the House of Lords. This court is a classic example of the continuity of English institutions: the historic right of the House of Lords to hear appeals dates back to the days of the *Magnum Concilium* of Norman times. But no less is this a classic example of the ability of the English to alter practice while retaining form: for more than a century it has not been the House of Lords as a whole that acts as a court but a very select group of its members, a group, in fact, that is elevated to the peerage for the sole purpose of performing this judicial function. In 1876, provision was made for the appointment of seven (now nine) Lords of Appeal in Ordinary (commonly known as Law Lords) who are paid professional judges with life peerages. Together with the Lord Chancellor and those peers who hold or have held high judicial office (such as former Lord Chancellors), they form the actual court of appeal. Thus, as other peers are excluded from participation, the appellate jurisdiction of the House of Lords in practice is that of a small group of highly trained legal experts. In a surprising "practice direction" of July 1966, these judges declared they would not be bound by precedent if it hampered them in taking contemporary conditions into account in making a judgment. In only one instance, however, have they overruled an earlier decision.

The existence of this second appeal court is an expensive anomaly and its value and conservative orientation have been challenged. At least it is used sparingly. Its chief function is to elucidate particularly difficult points of law, and it rarely hears more than fifty cases a year, of which very few are criminal cases. The House of Lords is the highest court not only for England and Wales but for Scotland and Northern Ireland as well; in this way it performs a distinctive function by providing a certain unification for the three judicial systems.

The Judicial Committee of the Privy Council

There is one other appeal body, the Judicial Committee of the Privy Council, which, strictly speaking, does not belong in the English judicial hierarchy, because it reviews cases appealed from courts in various parts of the British Commonwealth and empire outside Great Britain itself. Technically the Judicial Committee is not a court that renders decisions but a body that gives advice to the monarch on cases referred to it; in practice, however, the distinction is unimportant. Although the jurisdiction of the Judicial Committee of the Privy Council is very different from that of the House of Lords, its personnel is almost identical because, at the time when the Law Lords were created as salaried life peers, it was decided that they could carry the bulk of work in both bodies. Moreover, whoever else participates in the judicial work of the House of Lords is almost always a privy councilor and thus entitled to be a member of the Judicial Committee of the Privy Council. The main difference in the membership of the two bodies is due to the practice of adding, on occasion, one or more judges from the Commonwealth overseas to the Judicial Committee, particularly when a case affecting a particular area is under consideration. Any independent Commonwealth country may eliminate or restrict the right of appeal to the Judicial Committee of the Privy Council, and several of them, including Canada, have done so. It still serves, however, as the final source of appeal for British territories that have not acquired full rights of self-government.

EVALUATION OF THE ENGLISH COURT SYSTEM

The court system in England and Wales is well organized to handle different types of cases according to their degree of severity and to permit appeals so that there can be a check on the judgment and reasoning of the judges in lower courts. The independence of the judiciary and the courts ensures freedom from political influence. But there are other questions that must be raised in determining whether or not English courts are adequate to their responsibilities. What is the atmosphere of the courts? Do the courts provide an opportunity for all aspects of a situation to be explored? Do they give private persons adequate protection in criminal cases when the resources of the government are behind the prosecution? Do the courts provide speedy, effective means of settling disputes? Is justice, in practice, open to all on equal terms?

Visitors to English courts are impressed by the solemnity of the proceedings. Even lower courts have a dignity and formality that in the United States is almost wholly confined to the higher courts. Arrayed in wig and gown, the judge or judges sit above and apart from the rest of the court. The lawyers, also gowned, present the circumstances of the case and reply to each other's arguments in a restrained way that contrasts with the vehemence so often displayed by American lawyers. Witnesses are brought forward and questioned as to the facts, but there is no "bullying." The defendant and plaintiff may present their views. The judge listens attentively, giving the impression that every fact is important in making his final decision. Spectators are not permitted to make a noise or to indicate their sympathies. The atmosphere is that of a learned debate. There may be drama in a great lawyer's brilliant presentation of a case or in the manner in which he draws the facts from an unwilling witness. But the appeal is not to the spectators in the courtroom: it is to the judge, or jury and judge, who will make the decision. The presentation may be eloquent but to be effective it must be logical and based on a wide knowledge of legal practices.

The distinctive feature of a trial in an English or an American court, as compared with a trial in a Continental court, is that in the Anglo-Saxon system the judge looks on himself as an umpire before whom a case is argued, not as an investigator seeking to determine guilt or innocence. The English or American judge makes little effort to speed the proceedings. He leaves the major responsibility for bringing out the facts to the interested parties. During the trial the judge does not assume an active role in cross-questioning, as does a Continental judge, although English judges are apt to play a more decisive part in bringing out relevant facts than are American judges. The English judge makes sure that irrelevant material is excluded from consideration and that full opportunity is given to all sides to present their case. It is left to the parties, at least in a civil case, to make use of their chance.

The notion that a trial is a contest in which both sides should have an equal chance is maintained also in criminal cases, although here the prosecution, with the resources of the government behind it, has an obvious advantage. Much is done, therefore, to afford protection to the defendant. A person accused by the police of a breach of law must be immediately warned that anything he says may be taken down and used in evidence. Furthermore, in the trial, witnesses may not be asked leading questions (for example, not "Did you see a revolver in his hand?" but "Did you see anything in his hand?" and "What was it?"). Nor may evidence be introduced of previous misdoing calculated to prejudice opinion against the defendant.

Other safeguards guarantee that there can be no arrest without a warrant; crimes must be known to the law, that is, there can be no prosecution for an act that had not been declared to be a crime at the time it was committed; ignorance of fact is a complete defense—for example, in a case for bigamy, ignorance of the fact of a previous marriage. By these means the individual is given protection from arbitrary state action.

The Criminal Justice Act of 1967 sought to make criminal procedures more efficient and quicker and finally to replace the old concept of retribution with the modern view that criminal jurisdiction aims not only at protecting the community from its dangerous members but also to reform the latter. Written testimony now has equal validity with spoken evidence; juries can give weighted majority verdicts (a controversial move aimed at securing more convictions); suspended sentences were introduced for less serious crimes, although not those involving personal violence, and the Home Secretary was empowered to release all except lifers after serving one-third of their sentences if no public danger was involved; and increasingly severe fines are used with greater frequency in place of imprisonment as another approach to lowering the prison population. Beating of delinquent prisoners was finally abolished. Strict licensing of pistols and rifles already existed before the 1967 act, but tighter controls on shotguns now require securing a license from the police for this weapon.

The problem of overcrowded dockets and jails still remained in 1969, however, as evidenced by the strictures of the Beeching Commission. The 1971 Court Act is obviously directed toward streamlining the structure for criminal justice and increasing the number of judges. The 1972 Criminal Justice Act permits some form of community service to be substituted for a prison sentence. To curb the rising crime rate, the government has invested heavily in new equipment and raised police rates of pay, but crime detection is still plagued by short-handedness, which is intensified by difficulty in recruiting and by the numbers of men leaving the police force. Although the upper ranks of the police support the abolition of the death penalty, the lower ranks understandably would like it reinstated for murdering a policeman. But despite slogans of "law and order," and concern at certain inadequacies in law enforcement, the courts maintain their elaborate protection of the rights of the accused to give him the maximum chance to defend himself.

On the whole, English legal procedures are not encumbered by technicalities, as happens so often in the United States where the rules are generally the result of legislative activity and frequently unsuited to their avowed purpose of aiding the execution of justice. English rules governing the giving of evidence, pleading, and so forth are drafted by the Rules Committee under the Lord Chancellor, and are so simple, straightforward, and effective that it is rare to have a decision reversed in England on a question of procedure, in marked contrast to the frequency with which this happens in the United States.

The high cost of legal aid and the centralization of the appeal courts for civil cases are the most serious inadequacies of the English court system. Technically, of course, the courts are open to all on equal terms. But in practice it is like saying that everyone has a right to buy a Cadillac. Court and lawyers' fees are so high in England (as well as in the United States) that people of moderate means cannot view the prospect of civil litigation without concern. Moreover, although court fees are not necessarily imposed in criminal cases, legal aid is as expensive in this field as in civil cases.

The most substantial attempt in English legal history to meet the charge that the court system unduly handicaps poor litigants was made by the Legal Aid Act of 1949. Although since 1926 there had been an enlarged program of free legal aid for people who were entirely without means, the system had suffered from various defects, such as lack of publicity, no provision of aid in the county courts, and lack of relevance to the problems confronting those of moderate income. The Legal Aid Act of 1949 covers representation in all the regular courts and, in effect, provides that the very poor pay nothing for legal aid and that those of moderate income pay what they can afford. The Law Society and Bar Council administer the system of legal aid; the Ministry of Social Security investigates the question of means (a fact that restrains many people from applying for aid); and the Treasury finances the plan. Certain types of action, notably those that are open to abuse, such as suits for libel, are not covered by the act.

Many people feel, however, that provisions of the 1949 act do not sufficiently meet the criticism that the English court system unduly favors the wealthy. They advocate a national legal service, comparable to the National Health Service, under which lawyers would be organized for the service of the community. As in the United States, it is doubtful whether the poor have an adequate awareness of those provisions of the law that could be used to their advantage. The next step, therefore, would seem to be to approach the problems of legal aid from that perspective, to make justice a positive benefit to all.

4 JUDICIAL CONTROL OF GOVERNMENT OFFICIALS

To judge the acts of government officials by the same rules of law and by the same courts as the acts of ordinary citizens has long been considered a major safeguard of liberty in Anglo-Saxon countries. One of the characteristic features of the "rule of law," declared A. V. Dicey, a great nineteenth-century commentator on the British constitution, is that "every man, whatever be his rank or condition, is subject to the ordinary law of the realm and amenable to the jurisdiction of the ordinary tribunals"; and he drove this point home by declaring that "every official, from the Prime Minister down to a constable or a collector of taxes, is under the same responsibility for every act done without legal justification as any other citizen." Thus an official is no more above the law than anyone else and is equally responsible for justifying his actions in regular court proceedings.

Great Britain and the United States both continue to uphold the general rule expressed by Dicey and, in consequence, despite considerable contemporary urging of its necessity, do not follow the Continental practice of having a separate system of administrative law to cover the relations between government officials and private individuals and a separate system of administrative courts for such cases. Nevertheless, there have been certain modifications of the rigid interpretation of the view expressed by Dicey. Thus in both the United States and Great Britain today there are a number of administrative tribunals that deal with certain types of complaints against official actions. Moreover, in the interest both of forceful governmental action and of effective recompense to individuals injured by the action of state officials, there have also been gradual modifications of the rule that government officials are personally liable for acts committed without legal authority.

Part of the reason for this latter development lies in the danger that an official may not perform his duty according to his best judgment for fear of a personal suit for damages as the result of a decision taken in an official capacity. Or it could happen that the citizen who had been injured might well find himself unable to collect adequate recompense from the official personally.

Take, for example, the case of a sanitary inspector who believes he detects foot-and-mouth disease in a cow at the stockyards. He orders the animal to be killed at once. Subsequently it is found that the animal was not suffering from the disease. The owner attempts to get redress through the courts. If the judge agrees that the action of the inspector did not fall under the authority of the law, the inspector becomes personally liable for damages. On the other hand, if the judge finds the inspector justified in his action because the law provides him with a wide range of discretion, the owner of the cow is left without redress, so long as the state refuses to assume responsibility.

To meet such problems, both the courts and the government have gradually modified their stands. English and American courts usually uphold a government official in a private damage suit as long as there is no proof of negligence. In addition, both the British and American governments have made it easier to enter suit against the government itself in many types of cases.

It is still true that when the government is providing its basic services, such as maintenance of order, conduct of foreign affairs, and operations of the army and navy, it is not subject to suit. (But a bystander injured by a policeman in pursuit of a murderer may seek compensation from the Criminal Injuries Compensation Board.) Since the Crown Proceedings Act of 1947, it has been relatively easy to get redress for injuries suffered by individuals in the course of the non-law-enforcing operations of government.

The Crown Proceedings Act enables ordinary citizens for the first time to bring suit against the government in the same courts (for example, the county court) and in the same way "as if the Crown were a fellow citizen." Thus in the case of the sanitary inspector mentioned above, the owner of the cow could now collect damages from the state, while the inspector himself would be free from responsibility as long as there was no negligence involved. Moreover, the act makes government departments responsible not only for statutory duties but also for the common law duties imposed on ordinary employers, owners, and so forth.

At a time when the state is acquiring such extended functions of regulation, control, and operation of services, little could be more important than to establish the right of individuals freely to sue government agencies in case of injuries. In the words of an attorney general, this act ensures that "the rights of the little man are just as mighty, and are entitled to just the same protection, as the rights of the mighty state." What it recognizes, in fact, is that the principle of equality before the law requires new procedures to protect the citizen in his relations with the modern administrative state.

Still a further means of safeguarding the interests of the citizen in relation to administrative actions is provided by the Parliamentary Commissioner for Administration (see Chapter 4, Section 4), to whom MP's can refer complaints of personal injustice or misuse of power for his investigation. Although this office is far from achieving the range of activities of the Scandinavian ombudsman, on which it was supposed to be modeled, it adds one more instrument for investigating complaints against administrative arbitrariness or incompetence.

ADMINISTRATIVE TRIBUNALS

Although supporters of the Anglo-American system oppose setting up a separate system of administrative courts for dealing with official acts, it has been found useful, both in the United States and Great Britain, to set up what are called administrative tribunals. These tribunals share the characteristic features of courts of law: independence of the executive, the application of known rules, a certain formality in procedure, and binding decisions not subject to ministerial review or rejection. They are administrative only in that they are composed of administrators, not judges, and that they handle cases and questions arising out of administrative regulations.

In both countries there have long been commissions to consider railway rates and tax and patent appeals. Great Britain has special tribunals, both regular and *ad hoc* (that is, set up for a particular case), to which employers and employees may by agreement refer industrial disputes. Moreover, several British ministries have special bodies to deal with appeals on their handling of their particular responsibilities, among the most valuable of which are the local appeals tribunals on social insurance legislation and benefits, which are representative of the public, employers, and employees, and which provide a much needed human touch in a complex system.

There are several justifications for this development. In the first place, procedure in these administrative tribunals is direct, speedy, cheap, and easy for a layman to understand. Workmen's compensation cases, for example, used to be referred in England to the county courts where the procedure was time-consuming, tedious, and costly; now they are handled by an administrative tribunal that can adjust its procedure to the particular case, is not bound by rigid precedents, and yet strives to provide uniform rulings. In fact, just because there is a single central tribunal, there is more apt to be consistency of treatment and coordination of results. Further, administrative tribunals are staffed by experts who deal with subjects, for example, patents, that require technical knowledge. Administrative tribunals can be particularly useful in setting up new standards in a previously unexplored field, for example, town and country planning, which challenge private property rights, traditionally protected by the common law.

Following the Franks Committee Report on Administrative Tribunals and Procedures, the Tribunals and Inquiries Act of 1958 set up the Council on Tribunals, which is charged with general supervision of all British administrative tribunals and with presenting an annual report to Parliament on their workings. Moreover, the decisions of administrative tribunals can be examined by the law courts through appeal on a point of law and through the general right of review by higher courts over the decisions of all lower courts, including administrative tribunals. While administrative tribunals are likely to be the best judges of the relevant facts, for example, the safety devices in a factory in a workmen's compensation case, the courts make the final decision on whether the tribunal was acting within its powers as defined by statute and following prescribed procedures.

Courts, as we have seen, do not provide the only restraint on the public administration. The Cabinet, individual ministers, and parliamentary instruments, in particular the specialized committees and the parliamentary commissioner, attempt to supervise the functioning of the administration. But the task is an overwhelming one and beyond the capacity of political figures. It is for this reason that there have recently been proposals in Great Britain to establish a comprehensive system of administrative law and courts comparable to that which operates so smoothly and efficiently in France. To do so would be to break finally with a historic tradition, but the need is pressing for more comprehensive, swift, and inexpensive means of dealing with complaints of administrative abuse or excessive use of power. By providing such means, the British might also relieve some of the pressures both on the law courts and on Parliament to safeguard the interests of individual citizens.

8

Great Britain and the world

By geography, Great Britain is a European country; through history it became a world power. In the nineteenth century it held a dominant international position by virtue of its industrial leadership, financial power, and naval supremacy. But today Great Britain is no longer preeminent in any of these fields. Moreover, as we have seen, its domestic economic problems are of grave dimensions. Thus the British face agonizing dilemmas over how far their international commitments should still extend and what role they should now pursue in world affairs.

In each of the three great intersecting spheres of the Western world—the Atlantic community, Western Europe, and the Commonwealth of Nations—Great Britain possesses or seeks a distinctive position. The Commonwealth group of thirty-one independent states, with some forty dependencies (twenty-two of them a British responsibility), scattered throughout the continents of the world, total 900 million people, one-quarter of the world's population, occupying 19 percent of its surface.

Within this group, Great Britain, as the senior partner, enjoys a unique relationship based on history, interest, and a common acceptance of the Crown as the symbol of their unity. In the Atlantic community, Great Britain and the United States have an unshakable, although not uncritical alignment. Only in Western Europe had the British failed to achieve the integrated role that many felt should form the core of its economic relationships and political associations. Although British entry into the Common Market is now assured, divisions of opinion within Britain over the advisability of this move complicate the adjustments that are necessarily involved. Moreover, the British have still to work out in practice how best to interrelate their new position in Western Europe with their other associations.

Before we attempt to analyze more fully the competing claims of Britain's relationship to the Commonwealth, to the United States, and to Western Europe, we must consider in more detail the characteristics of the Commonwealth.

1 THE COMMONWEALTH OF NATIONS

The Commonwealth of Nations[1] has long been a remarkable and unique international grouping. Although France has remained even more influential in most of its former African colonies than Britain is in any Commonwealth country, a result in the main of the extent of

---

[1] The older name "British Commonwealth of Nations" has generally been replaced by "Commonwealth of Nations" since 1949, when it was formally recognized that the accession of the Asian Dominions meant that the proportion of British within the Commonwealth was, in fact, small. French-Canadians and Afrikaners always resented the prefix "British." It is still used in Great Britain, however, and also in Australia and New Zealand.

French aid programs, control of trade and tariffs, and educational and technical experts abroad, it was unable to sustain the Franco-African Community for which the constitution of the Fifth Republic provided in 1958. But in a much earlier period, Great Britain succeeded in transforming the colonial relation of those overseas areas that contained predominantly white populations into a distinctive international relation without any intervening stage of separation. Moreover, it subsequently fostered the same transition for other colonies in Africa, Asia, and the Caribbean. Since the Commonwealth of Nations thus provides an example of close cooperation between countries of equal status but widely differing strength, some observers have called it a model for international associations.

The Commonwealth of Nations consists of Great Britain and those former members of the British empire that have acquired full control over every aspect of their internal and external policies but choose to retain a special relationship with Great Britain and other members of the Commonwealth. The relationship was developed historically by Canada, Australia, New Zealand, and South Africa; it was extended in 1947 and 1948 to India, Pakistan (the Muslim part of the Indian subcontinent), and Ceylon; and from 1957 on it was extended to Ghana, Malaysia, Nigeria, Cyprus, Sierra Leone, Tanzania (the union of Tanganyika and Zanzibar), Kenya, Uganda, Jamaica, Malawi, Zambia, Gambia, Malta, Singapore, Trinidad and Tobago, Guyana, Botswana (formerly Bechuanaland), Lesotho (formerly Basutoland), Barbados, Swaziland, Fiji, Mauritius, Tonga, and Western Samoa. In a time when the international trend has been toward nationalism and separatism, these countries of widely differing geographical position, size, natural environment, racial composition, and political power have distinctive political and economic relations within the Commonwealth of Nations.

The strength of the Commonwealth is the strength of the relationship existing between these countries and Great Britain. To understand the present bonds uniting the Commonwealth, we must see how Canada, Australia, New Zealand, and South Africa passed from a position of dependence to one of equality of status with Great Britain without an intervening stage of separation. It is necessary, also, to see why the other countries chose to be members of the Commonwealth when they acquired independence of Great Britain. The bonds of the Commonwealth come not only out of history but also out of present circumstances.

THE EVOLUTION OF COMMONWEALTH STATUS

The original overseas members of the Commonwealth, Canada, Australia, New Zealand, and South Africa, were British "colonies of settlement," although the original settlers in Canada were French and in South Africa (until 1961 a Commonwealth member) they were Afrikaners. (The Afrikaners outnumber those of British extraction, and both are far outnumbered by the local Africans, Indians, and Colored.) But British institutions and traditions had a strong formative influence in these countries, leading to a feeling of loyalty and common purpose with Great Britain, at least among those of British descent. Moreover, in its era of undisputed naval, economic, and financial dominance, Great Britain provided them with notable benefits. The British Navy (to which the colonies contributed nothing except port facilities) ensured their defense. Free of the crippling burdens of armaments, the small populations of these huge areas could concentrate on developing their own resources. Great Britain was both their major market and source of capital.

But loyalty and material benefit would not have been enough to maintain the British connection if political aspirations had been disregarded. The reason the second British empire did not go the way of the first British empire, which split asunder in the American War of Independence, was that a way was found to enable colonies to develop self-government without ceasing to be British. This way was called *responsible government*, which stemmed from the famous report of Lord Durham who was sent to Canada following a rebellion in 1837. Durham recommended that locally elected representatives be empowered to make their own decisions in matters of internal policy, a right soon stretched to include tariffs and immigration regulations. When small scattered colonies

THE COMMONWEALTH OF NATIONS

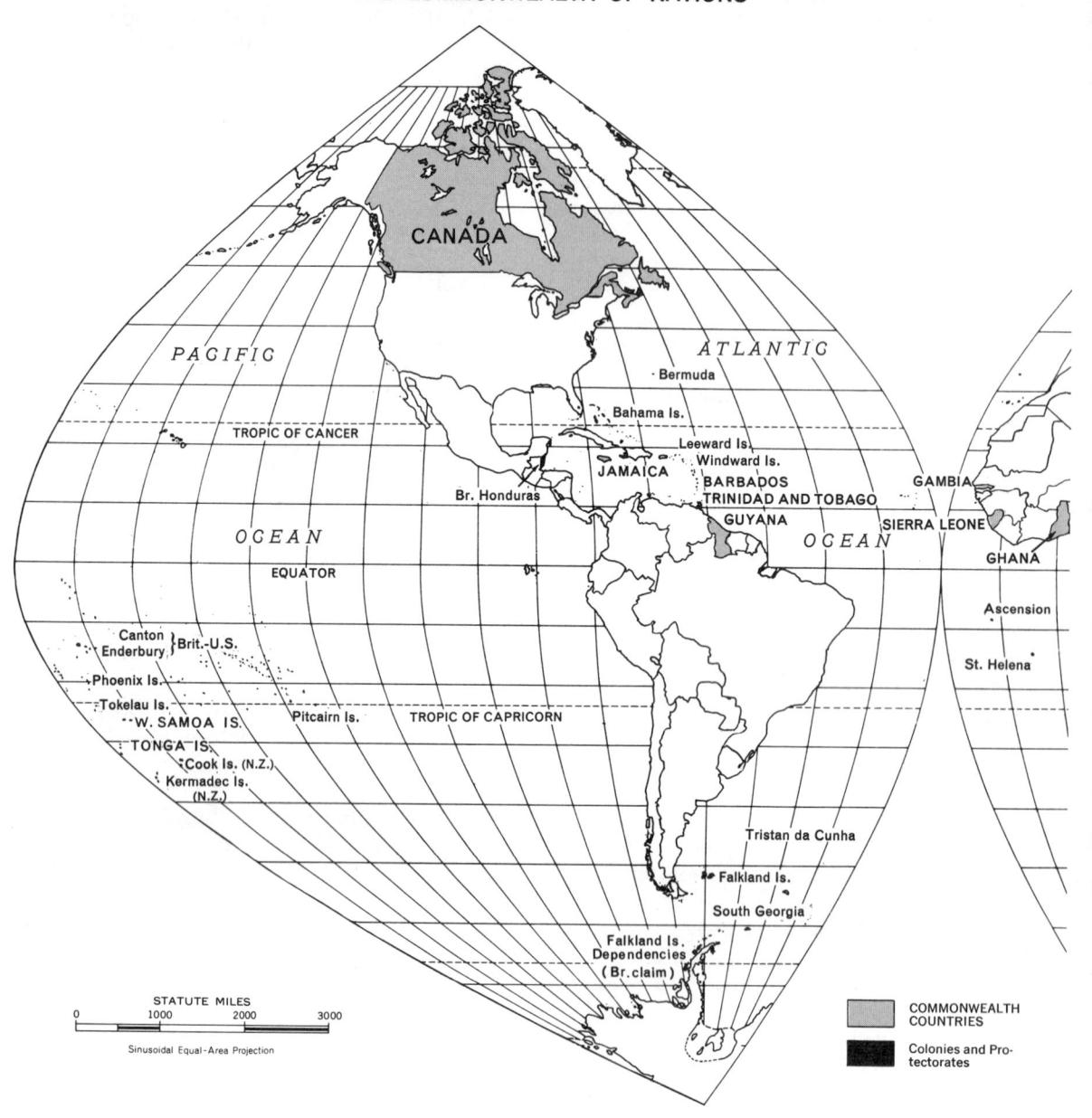

were consolidated into the larger units of Canada, Australia, New Zealand, and South Africa, the constitutional right to control their own affairs was called "dominion status."[2]

[2] The name "dominion" was first used at the time of Canada's Confederation in 1867. It was derived from the Biblical phrase, "Thy dominion shall stretch from sea to sea." It was long used to refer to any of the self-governing overseas members of the Commonwealth and took its mean-

Before 1914 Great Britain maintained ultimate control of foreign relations, and in World War I it declared war for the Dominions as well as for the empire. But the great wartime

ing from whatever status Canada or Australia possessed at a given time. Thus it had no fixed connotation that could limit their development to full independence. Except for New Zealand, "dominion" is not an official part of the name of any Commonwealth country.

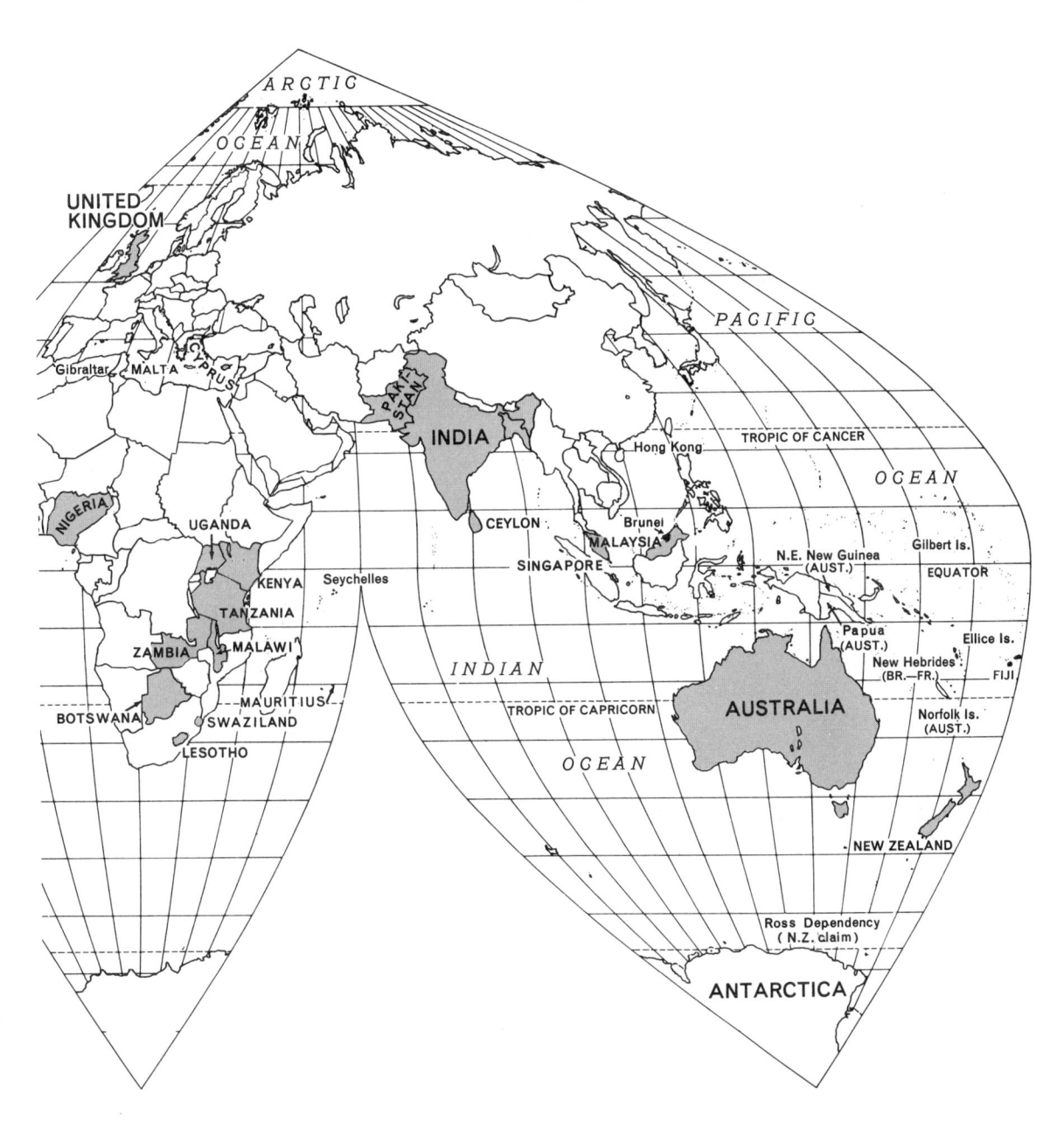

contributions freely made by Canada (which with only eight and a half million people lost more soldiers in the war than did the United States) and by Australia, New Zealand, and South Africa justified their claims to independence of action in this sphere as well as in internal matters.

In the interwar period, traditional forms were brought into line with political realities. The Dominions became separate members of the League of Nations. Equality of status was recognized in the Balfour Report of the Imperial Conference of 1926, which declared Great Britain and the Dominions to be "autonomous communities within the British empire, equal in status, in no way subordinate one to another in any aspect of their domestic or external affairs, though united by a common allegiance to the Crown, and freely associated as members of the British Commonwealth of Nations." The Statute of Westminster, 1931, drafted after consideration by political leaders from all parts of the Commonwealth, brought legal forms into harmony with long-existing constitutional conventions by opening the way for Dominion parliaments to become formally supreme in their own jurisdictions.

The Statute of Westminster, 1931

The Statute of Westminster declares that no British law shall henceforth have effect in a Commonwealth country except on request of that country, that British laws already having effect within it can be repealed by the legislature of that country, and that no power to disallow a statute inheres in the British government. The Statute of Westminster thus made it possible to abolish appeals to the Judicial Committee of the Privy Council (see Chapter 7, Section 3), which traditionally had been the final court of appeal of all British subjects outside Great Britain. Ireland and Canada began the process of abolishing the right to appeal to the Judicial Committee, and appeals now come only from dependent territories and a few Commonwealth countries. The Statute of Westminster also made it possible for the legislation of overseas Commonwealth members to have extraterritorial effect, that is, outside the particular country, for example, over its own merchant shipping.

The Statute of Westminster is often termed the Magna Charta of the Commonwealth. Although informal constitutional arrangements had long approximated the legal position made possible by the Statute, it was welcomed enthusiastically by Ireland, South Africa, and Canada. The latter was able to adopt it, however, only after provisions were inserted at the insistence of its provinces to make sure that the act could not be used to change the balance of the federal system without their consent. Australia and New Zealand were more reluctant to bring the provisions of the act into effect, and they did not do so until 1942 and 1947, respectively. Subsequent members of the Commonwealth inherited it automatically.

Independent policies and ultimate unity

During the interwar period, legal and constitutional issues within the Commonwealth were satisfactorily solved. It was less easy to evolve a workable basis for policy that would harmonize the strictly limited interests of individual Dominions with the worldwide commitments of Great Britain. The basis finally reached combined a constant flow of information and much informal consultation among the different members of the Commonwealth with ultimate freedom of action on the part of each individual member. Such freedom of action was limited in practice by the recognition that, should trouble arise, only popular policies would be supported by other members of the Commonwealth. In the 1920s, for instance, Canada and South Africa disassociated themselves from British Middle East policies and at all times were less ready for commitments to Great Britain than were Australia and New Zealand. The Irish Free State, or Eire, comprising twenty-six of the thirty-two counties of Ireland,[3] a reluctant postwar addition, withdrew from the Commonwealth in 1936. But from 1937 on, the threat of Germany and Japan drew the remaining members of the Commonwealth together. When war broke out in September 1939, Canada, Australia, New Zealand, and South Africa by their own acts entered the conflict in support of Great Britain and in opposition to aggression.

At the end of the war many people expected that the weakened position of Great Britain

---

[3] The partition of Ireland took place in 1921 following a civil war in which its predominantly Catholic and Gaelic areas sought independence. In the island's six northeastern counties, known as Ulster, however, the predominantly Protestant descendants of the Scottish and English settlers who had colonized that area in the seventeenth century clung to their union with Britain. Ulster was provided, therefore, with its own local parliament in Belfast as well as representation in the British Parliament. This status was further guaranteed in the Ireland Act of 1949. But Protestant discrimination against the large Catholic minority in Ulster has intensified the pressures for a united Ireland. Communal violence broke out in Belfast in August 1969, and British troops have patrolled disturbed areas since. The illegal Irish Republican Army continues to press terrorist attacks across the border. Although the Belfast government, under urging from London, has introduced an extensive program of social and political reform to reduce segregation and discrimination, the situation in Ulster remains tense and a particular source of concern to the British government.

would lead to the breakup of the Commonwealth. On the contrary, the association has steadily expanded. As Great Britain's numerous colonies have achieved independence, most of them have chosen to be members of the Commonwealth. Burma and Sudan decided not to do so when they became independent in 1948 and 1956, respectively. British and Italian Somaliland joined to form the Somali Republic in 1960 and the Southern Cameroons became part of the Cameroon Republic in 1961. (Northern Cameroons became part of Nigeria.) Otherwise, as the dependent empire has diminished in size, so the Commonwealth has grown.

Republics in the Commonwealth

The importance of the Crown for the Commonwealth has already been emphasized. Yet beginning with India in 1949, many Commonwealth countries have decided to become republics. Nothing illustrates better the pragmatic flexibility of the association than the ease with which a satisfactory resolution of this situation was devised. When a state becomes a republic it must make a formal request to a Commonwealth conference to be allowed to remain within the Commonwealth and, except in regard to South Africa, no objection has ever been raised. The latter, smarting from criticism of its discriminatory racial policies, withdrew its 1961 request to be accepted as a republic and left the Commonwealth. All the others have been welcomed as members of the Commonwealth and have accepted the Crown "as the symbol of the free association" of the independent countries that compose it and, in a similarly symbolic spirit, the queen as "the head of the Commonwealth."

Commonwealth institutions

The Commonwealth has relatively little political machinery. As recently as 1965, the first Commonwealth secretariat was set up in London under a Canadian secretary general, Arnold Smith. Since then the agenda and arrangements for the Commonwealth's most important institution for formal exchange of views, the *Conference of Prime Ministers* (or Imperial Conference, as it used to be called), are in the hands of a body that is drawn not only from the British civil service, as used to be the case, but from the Commonwealth at large. Moreover, increasingly, meetings of the conference are held in different parts of the Commonwealth, such as Lagos, Nigeria, in 1965, and Singapore, Malaysia, in 1971.

Numerous other Commonwealth meetings have dealt with subjects such as trade, the convertibility of sterling, and economic aid to developing countries. There are also *ad hoc* conferences in many other fields of mutual interest, such as welfare, agriculture, and technology; constant exchanges among "opposite numbers" in particular Commonwealth countries; and meetings of Commonwealth representatives to the United Nations and other international gatherings.

THE BONDS AND STRAINS IN THE COMMONWEALTH

It may well be asked: Why does the Commonwealth hold together? The machinery it has evolved for purposes of consultation does not bind individual members to a particular course of action. The symbol of a common Crown is not enough to determine policy. In practice, its members quite often differ from each other in international conferences.

That the Commonwealth is not an exclusive group is demonstrated by the close defensive arrangements existing between Canada and the United States. But this very lack of exclusiveness is itself a source of strength to the Commonwealth. Membership in that body does not prevent a country from pursuing policies conducive to its particular interests. The only agreed-upon limitation is that it shall notify the other members before it undertakes such action. Thus Commonwealth membership involves few sacrifices except in moments of supreme crisis. On the other hand, it provides a number of advantages both to Great Britain and to its partners.

Strategic ties

For Great Britain, the most important consideration is that twice in a generation the prompt and voluntary support of the older

Commonwealth members has been a major element in supporting a British struggle for survival. During the year from the fall of France to the Nazi attack on the Soviet Union, Canada was Great Britain's strongest ally.

For the Commonwealth at large, however, there is no longer a defensive unity. Since World War II, the defense of the North Atlantic has become an international responsibility (safeguarded by the North Atlantic Treaty Organization) and no longer, as before World War II, chiefly a British responsibility. In the Pacific and Southeast Asia it is the United States on which Commonwealth members—particularly Australia and New Zealand—must depend, a fact reflected in Australia's token participation in Vietnam.

It must not be forgotten, however, that there were some two hundred thousand Commonwealth troops, mostly British, fighting guerrillas in Malaya from 1948 to 1960 when the crisis ended. The Wilson government began the substantial withdrawal of British troops from Singapore and Malaysia, which left only thirty-five thousand there in 1971, and the Heath government can be expected to continue the reduction. Nonetheless, it has agreed to be an equal partner with Australia and New Zealand in the five-member Southeast Asia Treaty Organization, which also includes Singapore and Malaysia. Reluctantly, other British military responsibilities "east of Suez" are being phased out so the western Indian Ocean, long looked on as "a British lake," now lacks defensive strength. In this situation, the factors that have strategic significance are chiefly Britain's willingness to make arms available to Commonwealth members under external attack (as, for example, to India in 1962 when it was attacked by China and to Malaysia against Indonesia), the potentialities of the scattered staging posts of the Royal Navy and Air Force, and the sense of responsibility toward Britain itself that the older Commonwealth members have. Yet it is not unimportant that the Declaration of Principles of the 1971 Prime Minister's Conference asserted that "the security of each member state from external aggression is a matter of concern to all members."

Economic relations

The most important material advantages of the Commonwealth relation have been economic. Except for Canada, whose dollar is linked to the American, all the members of the Commonwealth are part (and by far the most important part) of the *sterling area*, made up of those countries within which the pound sterling rather than the dollar is the principal unit of exchange. The thirty-one Commonwealth countries apart from Canada, and eight non-Commonwealth countries including South Africa and Jordan, keep their foreign currency assets, private and public, in London. In January 1971, these assets totaled more than £3.5 billion, of which more than 1 billion are held as official reserves. It is through these funds that Commonwealth members, other than Canada, largely finance their international trade and float their loans. In 1968, members contracted through the Basle agreement to keep a certain proportion of their reserves in London in return for a dollar guarantee of their worth. Even should a Commonwealth member decide to withdraw from the association, it is hardly likely to withdraw its reserves, particularly since Britain pays high interest rates on them, unless for punitive reasons. Normally, financial policies are closely coordinated between Commonwealth members. One of the most important annual Commonwealth conferences is the gathering of their finance ministers before the meeting of the International Monetary Fund (IMF). For the developing countries there is special urgency to the use of IMF special drawing rights to increase the flow of development aid.

Intra-Commonwealth trade was long encouraged by *imperial preference* under which Commonwealth countries extended to each other lower tariff rates than most favored-nation agreements provided. Such preferences were originally extended by the older overseas Commonwealth members in return for defense. In 1932, when they were formalized, Britain was taking a third of Commonwealth exports, and Commonwealth countries bought a third of British exports. But the Commonwealth was never used to develop the kind of closed trading units the French, Dutch, and

Belgium empires established. Moreover, since changes in the global tariff structure—the General Agreement on Tariffs and Trade and the Kennedy round cuts—preference continues largely only through bilateral agreements initiated by Britain itself.

The Commonwealth is thus no longer a *trading block*, for although its members and their associated states account for one-fifth of the world's trade, only one-quarter of it is among themselves. For some Commonwealth countries, however, like New Zealand, Tanzania, and Malawi, intra-Commonwealth trade is more than half their total, most of it either directly with Great Britain or with immediate neighbors.

Great Britain's Common Market negotiations take these facts into consideration. Two of the most difficult situations were those of New Zealand's dairy products, of which 80 to 90 percent of exports go to Great Britain, and Britain's guaranteed market for sugar from the major Commonwealth producing countries in the West Indies, Fiji, Mauritius, Australia, Swaziland, and a few others. But mutually satisfactory agreements were reached in mid-1971.

The European Economic Community has offered associate status to nine African Commonwealth members, comparable to that enjoyed by the eighteen African countries (mostly former French colonies or trust territories) already securing both favorable conditions for their exports and financial aid through the Yaoundé Convention. The EEC is also considering associate membership for the three Commonwealth members in southern Africa—Botswana, Lesotho, and Swaziland—despite their customs union with South Africa. Two other possibilities for the latter countries would be to adopt a more limited arrangement such as Kenya, Uganda, and Tanzania secured with the Common Market in 1970, or simply to conclude a trade agreement.

There may be advantages, therefore, as well as problems for Commonwealth countries due to Britain's membership in the Common Market. In 1971, the Common Market countries were only taking 5 percent of their imports from the Commonwealth, apart from Great Britain and Canada. British entry might encourage greater access for Commonwealth goods, except from Canada. The latter is seeking market diversification and, in the process, is increasing its sales to Great Britain and the EEC countries. Canada is somewhat apprehensive, therefore, lest an enlarged Common Market might become a more exclusive trading block, with current Canadian exports of minerals to the Continent edged out by the advantages extended to African Commonwealth countries through associate status. No one can tell at this point, in fact, what the trends will be or their ultimate impact on Commonwealth countries and the economic ties of that association.

British overseas *aid*, particularly but not exclusively to its own former colonies, has at last come close to the 1 percent of its gross national product that it had pledged. (American foreign aid is well below this percentage of GNP.) In 1950, a special Commonwealth program of economic aid and technical assistance for India, Pakistan, and Ceylon was launched under the name of the *Colombo Plan*. Subsequently extended to other southern and southeast Asian countries and with substantial support from the United States (now larger than Commonwealth contributions) and Japan, the Colombo Plan has achieved excellent results. Great Britain and Canada have provided financial, economic, technical, and educational aid to developing African and West Indian Commonwealth countries. In 1970, Britain gave £157 million (approximately $376.8 million) in bilateral aid to developing countries in the Commonwealth, approximately 90 percent of its aid total. Canada gave $350 million in aid, 80 percent to Commonwealth countries, in particular India and the West Indies.

Seventeen thousand Commonwealth students were studying in Britain in 1971, forty-five hundred of them postgraduates. Both Britain and Canada, it may be noted, also have programs for volunteers overseas somewhat comparable to the Peace Corps, although concentrating on more specialized personnel. There are also two general Commonwealth aid agencies, the Commonwealth Development Corporation, with borrowing powers of £225 million ($540 million), and the Commonwealth Development Finance Company, with funds of £40 million ($96 million), which particularly but not exclusively service developing Commonwealth countries. The 1971 Commonwealth Development Fund is intended to supplement multilateral aid. The special interest of these and other British aid programs in the developing Commonwealth countries makes them an additional reinforcement of the Commonwealth relation.

Citizenship and immigration

A serious blow to the Commonwealth relationship has resulted from the use made in recent years by Asian and Caribbean citizens of the historic right of entry and settlement in Britain of persons from Commonwealth countries and the resulting restrictions which now differ little from those imposed on aliens. As recently as 1948, the British Nationality Act had declared that any citizen of the United Kingdom, its colonies, or a Commonwealth country was a "British subject" or "Commonwealth citizen" (the terms being interchangeable) and thereby possessed the right to enter Great Britain at any time, to qualify for the franchise, to be a member of Parliament or of the civil service (except in wartime). But accelerated immigration from the newer Commonwealth countries, notably India, Pakistan, and the West Indies, led to local internal tensions (see Chapter 1, Section 1) and progressively restrictive measures.

The first of these measures, the Commonwealth Immigrants Act, passed by the Conservative government in 1962, set no specific limits to Commonwealth immigration but required labor permits for entry, thereby facilitating administrative control. Labor, initially hostile to this legislation, found itself forced by public opinion to renew the act's provisions in 1964. The following year, as we have seen, it introduced an act prohibiting racial discrimination in "places of public resort," but it also formally reduced the number of labor vouchers to 8,500 (of which 1,000 were reserved for Malta), abolished entry of unskilled workers, and extended the power of the Home Secretary to repatriate. In 1968, panic over the possibility of massive emigration of Kenya Asians squeezed out by Africanization and possessing British citizenship led to the openly discriminatory Commonwealth Immigrants Act providing controls over their entry into Great Britain. This measure was only partially counterbalanced by a somewhat strengthened Race Relations Act supervised by the Race Relations Board and a select committee.

In 1971, the Conservative government introduced yet another Immigration Bill, which placed all persons seeking work on the same footing, whether they come from a Commonwealth country or not, and required renewal of the original work permit after a year.

The 1971 legislation also introduced the controversial distinction of "patriality," limiting full freedom to come and go as desired to citizens of the United Kingdom and colonies who had themselves or their parents or grandparents been born in Great Britain or who had settled in Great Britain for five years, as well as Commonwealth citizens whose father, mother, or grandparent had been born in Great Britain. Commonwealth citizens resident in Great Britain for five years remain free to stay unconditionally, to vote, and to participate freely in political life. Citizenship is necessary, however, for a complete safeguard against deportation, and the provisions for aiding voluntary repatriation have also caused some alarm.

These progressive restrictions on the earlier right of entry to Great Britain from Commonwealth countries and of securing work on the same terms as local residents only bring British provisions to a situation comparable to those long existing in most other Commonwealth countries. Moreover, British emigration, especially to the older Commonwealth members, is in fact considerably more substantial than immigration to Britain from them. But since many of the British now associate the Commonwealth with Britain's "color problem," the latter has caused considerable revulsion against the association. Moreover, in the Caribbean, in particular, and among West Indians and Asians resident in Britain, the immigration restrictions so clearly slanted against the colored from the Commonwealth have aroused apprehensions and bitterness. Thus, this particular "bond of Commonwealth" has turned into a source of strain.

The Commonwealth stance on southern Africa

There is yet one further issue that strains the Commonwealth relationship, that is, its policies toward southern Africa. Until 1961, when it withdrew from the Commonwealth, South Africa's legislatively enforced color discrimination was a constant affront to the Commonwealth's multiracialism and particularly to its Asian, African, and West Indian members. Fortunately for its continued cohesion, the sharp criticism of South Africa's racial policies that led it to leave the Commonwealth came from Canada as much as from newer Commonwealth members. Moreover, when Rhodesia made its unilateral and unconstitutional declaration of independence in 1965, the Commonwealth as a whole united behind Prime Minister Wilson's request for United Nations sanctions, which attempted, although unsuccessfully, to force Rhodesia's small, white, ruling minority to agree to the progressive extension of the franchise to the African majority. But Prime Minister Heath's decision to sell arms to South Africa, despite the forceful opposition of Prime Minister Trudeau of Canada and leaders of the postwar Commonwealth countries at the Singapore Conference of Prime Ministers in January 1971, threatened the association as no previous British external action had done. Although Heath maintained that Britain had an obligation to supply seven Wasp helicopters under the Simonstown agreement, which provides berths in South Africa for the British Navy, the fact that he announced the decision to send them without waiting for the first meeting of the Commonwealth committee of eight, set up at Singapore to consider the issue, added yet another source of friction.

WILL THE COMMONWEALTH CONTINUE?

Cooperation in the Commonwealth rests on the willingness to work for and the understanding of common purposes. Sentiment, traditional ties, a common heritage of laws and institutions, shared experiences, all play their role in maintaining the relationship, particularly among the old Commonwealth members. Practical economic advantages are influential with the newer members and their Commonwealth relation will help them to secure associate membership in the Common Market. Technical and professional cooperation extended on a broad scale is of particular importance to the developing members of the Commonwealth. Although the first drafts of the Declaration of Principles at Singapore strongly and directly condemned South African apartheid practices, the final statement, drafted by President Kenneth Kaunda of Zambia, did so by implication. The Declaration of Principles adopted on January 22, 1971, by the leaders of the thirty-one Commonwealth states at the Singapore Conference of Prime Ministers [4] begins:

> The Commonwealth of Nations is a voluntary association of independent sovereign states, each responsible for its own policies, consulting and cooperating in the common interests of their peoples and in the promotion of international understanding and world peace.

It asserts that "the Commonwealth is one of the most fruitful associations" for removing the causes of war, promoting toleration, combating injustice, and securing development. It also includes, as a distinct innovation in Commonwealth statements, a formulation of "certain principles" held "in common." These principles include "the liberty of the individual," "equal rights for all citizens regardless of race, colour, creed or political belief," and "their inalienable right to participate by means of free

---

[4] The member countries of the Commonwealth at the Singapore meeting were: Australia, Barbados, Botswana, Canada, Ceylon, Cyprus, Fiji, Gambia, Ghana, Guyana, India, Jamaica, Kenya, Lesotho, Malawi, Malaysia, Malta, Mauritius, New Zealand, Nigeria, Pakistan, Sierra Leone, Singapore, Swaziland, Tanzania, Tonga, Trinidad and Tobago, Uganda, United Kingdom, Western Samoa, Zambia. Additionally, the Republic of Nauru in the Pacific is a special member, and the Associated States of the Eastern Caribbean participate in Commonwealth meetings, but not in the heads-of-government sessions. The West Indies Associated States, which are self-governing but for which Great Britain retains responsibility for foreign affairs and defense, are as follows: Antigua, Dominica, Grenada, St. Christopher-Nevis-Anguilla, St. Lucia, and St. Vincent. These and other small unviable islands scattered throughout the oceans of the world (see map in this chapter) provide a continuing problem for Great Britain because no special status has been evolved for them short of an unrealistic independence, and many are now proving to be significant strategically in the light of Soviet and Chinese expansion.

and democratic processes in framing the society in which they live."

More distinctive and directly related to the concerns of the newer Commonwealth members are the paragraphs referring to racial prejudice and discrimination that start: "We recognize racial prejudice as a dangerous sickness threatening the healthy development of the human race and racial discrimination as an unmitigated evil of society." Then in a sentence obviously meant to relate to the British intention of selling arms to South Africa, it added: "No country will afford to regimes which practise racial discrimination assistance which in its own judgment directly contributes to the pursuit or consolidation of this evil policy."

Well before South Africa left the Commonwealth, nonracial policies were said to be the key to the continued existence of the multiracial Commonwealth. This could still be the case.

2 INTERNATIONAL RELATIONS

The Commonwealth was long considered the inner area of British international relations, providing built-in opportunities for influence and trade. But Great Britain's foreign policy is concerned more deeply now with its relations with the United States and Western Europe. In addition, Britain seeks good economic and political relations with the Soviet Union and Eastern Europe and has tried to retain its influence with the Arab countries, without impairing its links with Israel.

If all these areas were friendly with one another, the historic position of the British in regard to each might provide them with unparalleled opportunities to act as a center of unity. But the harsh fact is that jealousy, rivalries, divisions, and even aggression between and within blocs have been more common in the postwar world than have friendship and cooperation. Moreover, Britain has sometimes exacerbated its own problem by dealing with each of its associations separately and failing to fit the different parts of its foreign policy into a coherent whole.

Britain's most difficult problem has been its relation with Western Europe. It is drawn impellingly to that area by geography, military strategy, and, increasingly, by economic interest. Yet there are barriers of culture, language, and, most fundamentally, attitude that have made association difficult for both sides. The French, particularly under de Gaulle, sought a dominant position in Western Europe that they could hardly maintain if Britain were an active participant in all its programs. Moreover, they were suspicious of the role and intentions of the United States in Europe. The British, in contrast, wished to associate the Atlantic alliance wherever possible with any strategic commitments they made on the Continent. In addition, as far as economic relations are concerned, influential groups within Great Britain pressed the possibility that either the older Atlantic Commonwealth relation or a pan-European one would be more to British interests than merging itself in a purely Western European group. Thus, although the French and British have now agreed on British entry into the Common Market, there remain sharp divisions in Great Britain itself over whether the move will be to the country's own advantage.

In the field of strategy and defense the British early committed themselves to a solely European grouping, but with the ultimate objective of associating the United States and Canada with it. Thus the British gave the lead to the Brussels Treaty of 1948 that pledged political, economic, and cultural cooperation among Great Britain, France, and the Low Countries—Belgium, Holland, and Luxembourg—and joint military action in case of attack. The consummation of Britain's general strategic objectives, however, was the North Atlantic Treaty Organization (NATO), established in 1949, in which the United States and Canada associated themselves in a vast system of mutual defense with the five Brussels Treaty powers, as well as Norway, Denmark, Iceland, Portugal, and Italy, and, after 1951, Greece and

Turkey. NATO achieved two major British strategic objectives; a continued United States military presence in Europe, and, after further British guarantees through the Assembly of Western European Union to allay French apprehensions, the admission into NATO of newly sovereign and rearmed West Germany.

But NATO was organized in a period when the Soviet Union lacked nuclear weapons, and thereafter de Gaulle grew increasingly dissatisfied with what he considered a static strategic concept (instead of a more mobile nuclear-powered one) and with the integrated military command under an American commander. Thus in the late 1960s de Gaulle forced American troops and installations out of France, thereby impairing what unity NATO had achieved.

By the early 1970s, new situations were evolving. The American military presence in Europe, at least in its current dimensions, was being questioned by Americans themselves as well as by many Europeans. The new *Ostpolitik* of seeking a *détente* with the Soviet Union had been inaugurated by Chancellor Willy Brandt. While not seeking to take West Germany out of its Western alignment, this policy opened avenues for progressive and constructive interactions between East and West. At the same time, the focus of attention for Great Britain had settled firmly upon its economic relations with Western Europe.

In the immediate postwar period, the British had taken the lead in organizing the plans for European self-help incorporated in the requests for American aid under the Marshall Plan. They strongly backed the European Payments Union, established in 1950, to aid the freer flow of trade and payments throughout the portion of Europe not dominated by the Soviet Union. They participated vigorously in the Organization for European Economic Cooperation (OEEC) and its 1962 successor, the Organization for Economic Cooperation and Development (OECD), both concerned with development aid and trade policies, and they did so more enthusiastically after 1951 when both the United States and Canada became associated. But the British stood aloof from the process of Western European integration that began that latter year with the establishment of the European Coal and Steel Community (ECSC).

The Conservative government felt at that time that the ECSC free trade market for coal, iron ore, steel, and scrap, under an institutional structure, would not last long. They justified their refusal to participate by maintaining that membership would encroach on their sovereignty and be incompatible with Commonwealth arrangements. They viewed with considerable suspicion, as a possible threat to their own interests, the second of the specialized Western European agencies, Euratom, which established an atomic energy pool and shared the costs of nuclear research among its members. Most significant was the initial refusal to sign the Rome Treaty, which envisaged gradual removal of restrictions on trade between its six members—France, West Germany, Italy, Holland, Belgium, and Luxembourg—and the establishment of a common external tariff. Thus Great Britain stood outside the European Economic Community, generally known as the Common Market, which came into existence on January 1, 1958, and missed the opportunity to mold the character of that association in liberal directions during its most formative years.

The British made proposals shortly thereafter for a wider free trade area in Europe, and even for one that would also include the Commonwealth, but these plans would clearly have brought Great Britain itself into the key position within whatever grouping was established, and they were rejected as threats to the nascent EEC. Embittered by this failure, the British took the lead in establishing in 1959, largely as a bargaining counter, the much less promising association known as the European Free Trade Association (EFTA), which included Norway, Sweden, Denmark, Switzerland, Austria, and Portugal. But by 1961, the Conservative government decided to seek membership in the increasingly prosperous Common Market, a process that, despite two intervening vetos on British membership by President de Gaulle in 1963 and again in 1967, began once again in 1970, and seemed assured by late 1971.

Many issues are raised by British membership in the Common Market and in the two other Communities, Coal and Steel, and Euratom. The initial hurdle that dominated the first period of negotiations was the financial contributions the British government was willing to make both in the interim period of adjustment and thereafter. But there were still more serious problems. The potential impact of Common Market membership on its Commonwealth partners has already been indicated. Internally, agriculture offers a delicate and controversial issue. The common agricultural policy of the Six has been hammered out with particular difficulty and exactness. Its key feature is to maintain farmers' incomes out of market sales and to manipulate the market by high price guarantees and a system of variable levies to keep the cost of agricultural imports at a comparable or higher level. The British, in contrast, permit the relatively free importation of agricultural produce and maintain farmers' incomes through a deficiency payments scheme for farmers and annual price reviews. Participation in the Common Market means that the cost of British food will rise substantially, probably the most effective argument used by anti-Marketeers. The British also give subsidies to specialized groups like the hill-sheep farmers and to sensitive sections of British farming, like horticulture, as a means of maintaining their competitiveness.

British participation in the Common Market, on the other hand, opens industrial opportunities in a market of nearly 300 million people, larger than that of the United States. This circumstance was cited frequently in favor of entry. Closer technological cooperation may well help to overcome the "technological gap" between European (including British) and American production. Whether economic planning for so large and diverse a grouping is feasible is open to question, but its importance for exploiting the advantages of so large a market is obvious.

Other special issues have included the persistent British balance-of-payments problem, with its relation to the position of sterling either as a reserve currency or absorbed in a possibly stronger European reserve currency; the necessity for Great Britain to accept the EEC's value-added tax (i.e., a production tax that is applied successively to each stage of a product at which "value" is added) as the major form of indirect taxation; and the impact on social security benefits of higher food prices and the value-added tax. The White Paper, "Britain and the European Communities: An Economic Assessment" (Cmnd. 4289, 1970), distinguished between the "impact effects" and the "dynamic effects" of entry into the Communities, suggesting that the latter could be expected in the long run to offset the obvious cost of such changes as would be involved in the new agricultural policies and their financing. Heath said in February 1971 that "we must find arrangements for our entry into the Community which are tolerable in the short run and clearly and visibly beneficial in the long run." That negotiations on all these points had been concluded satisfactorily by late June 1971 was a tribute to all parties concerned.

British membership in the European Economic Community has political as well as economic consequences. There are at present four rather little-known European parliamentary institutions, in the first three of which the British already participated: the semiofficial NATO conference of parliamentarians who debate but do not decide policy; the Assembly of Western European Union, whose members are appointed by national governments and which discusses defense issues in its meetings twice a year, although it has no executive powers; the Council of Europe, set up by treaty in 1949 with eighteen European member states, which can discuss anything except defense, but also has no executive powers; and the European parliament, called officially the Assembly of European Communities, one of the integral institutions set up under the Treaty of Rome for the six members of the Common Market, which is also advisory in functions and without executive powers. The last named institution commonly meets in Strasbourg for five-day sessions about ten times a year (its secretariat, however, is in Luxembourg). Its 142 members are appointed by their respective governments on the basis of proportional strength (except for the Communists) in their own assemblies, and they sit in Strasbourg by parties, not by national groupings. One question is: With what parties will the British Labor party associate itself? More importantly: Will the European parliament become more clearly representative and effective with British membership in the EEC?

Meeting with members of European parliaments in February 1971, Prime Minister Heath declared that the argument between federation and confederation was "sterile and unworthy" and called for new institutions to suit the needs of the European community. President Pompidou has spoken of advancing "step by step, toward a union, which when it has sufficiently become so, both in fact and in the minds of the peoples—and only then—will be able to have its own policy, its own independence, its own role in the world." The parliamentarians to whom Heath spoke went so far as to declare it "essential to accelerate the creation of an economically and politically united Europe, embracing all European countries which accept the obligations involved," and to propose that the functions of the European Economic Community be extended "and should in particular embrace foreign policy and defence." Whatever the road and the speed, political implications are involved.

These political implications were used by opponents of entry to bolster their case. Enoch Powell exploited the concerns of the Tory rightist anti-Marketeers who, as we have seen (Chapter 4, Section 6), had used parliamentary tactics in 1962 to express their concern over British terms for entry into the Common Market. Richard Crossman used the *New Statesman*, which he edits, to suggest that Labor had no commitment to entry and printed cogent warnings by Nicholas Kaldor. Jo Grimond, former leader of the Liberal party, had also reversed his former stand in favor of entry.

Harold Wilson determined his stand on entry by his sense for how best to maintain the unity of the Labor party, whose trade union affiliates, in particular, were almost unanimously opposed to membership in the EEC on grounds of higher costs of food and stiff industrial competition. Although the parliamentary Conservative party also split on the issue of entry, its constituency organizations strongly backed membership. Late in 1971, Parliament approved entering the Common Market by a decisive majority that cut across party lines, but there remain grave doubts and opposition among substantial portions of the population.

Much remains in flux in Great Britain's role in international affairs. The adjustments to its membership in the European Economic Community and European parliament will absorb much of its attention in the coming years. Yet Britain must also work out how best to interrelate this new association with its historic, although much weakened, ties with the Commonwealth and with its traditional alignment with the United States in a time when the latter is reconsidering its international commitments. Since Britain is still eager to maintain a significant role in other areas, there are also strains to face in its Middle East policies and relations with the Soviet Union. How successfully Britain deals with these complex issues will determine its future standing and influence on the world scene.

Conclusion

The British are at a particularly difficult point in their history. They are torn between their desire to maintain themselves as a world power and their more inward-looking, and perhaps more constructive, awareness of the pressing nature of the many needs at home. This overriding issue of priorities is bound up with the basic questioning of values as well as possibilities that pervade so many aspects of British life today. So too is the more detailed consideration of the implications of diverse approaches to pressing internal and external problems.

Although Great Britain has decided to join the European Economic Community and its associated organizations and thus has moved decisively toward a Western European orientation, its people and government are determined to maintain their distinctiveness in character and policies within this entity as they have done in the past with other relationships. This distinctiveness arises from a blend of tradition and modernity. Thus it builds on the past, and often retains those forms, but is responsive in action to the perceived needs of the present and the future.

The British cherish their parliamentary procedures, but they also seek to make them more responsive and responsible to those inside as well as outside the chambers. They are attacking some of the last traditional strongholds of privilege in education, the civil service, and the administration of the law, to make them more democratic in membership and function. They are expanding the range of social services to meet more adequately the needs of the disabled and the elderly. They are making belated but far-reaching efforts to improve the environment of cities and countryside alike, efforts such as those virtually eliminating fog from London, refurbishing formerly grimy Midland towns, and landscaping highways, which go far beyond what has yet been accomplished in the United States.

Britain's economic problems, however, remain pervasive and worrisome. Its membership in the Common Market raises new and difficult questions. Will this participation provide the necessary stimulus to challenge both British workers and management to more effective efforts and a new awareness of their mutual dependence? Or will the efficiency of Continental enterprises and the lower pay of many Continental workers obviate the advantages of the larger market for British manufactures? Will the cost-of-living rise much higher because of guaranteed agricultural prices within the Common Market? And will this rise more than offset what additional prosperity can be expected from industrial expansion? These issues are crucial whatever general lines of policy are followed, for they cut to the heart of what Britain is able to provide for its people.

Whatever developments take place in Great Britain, they will be of great importance to the United States. Membership in the Common Market may somewhat change but will not in any sense destroy their close relations of the past. It is possible that far from drawing Britain away from the United States, the effect of its membership in the EEC may be to associate our country more closely with Western Europe. Moreover, a more prosperous Britain would be a more effective ally. As the United States itself begins to diminish the scope of its international activities and responsibilities and turn more attention to what needs to be done at home, there is much it can learn from how the British are adjusting to their changed role in international affairs. Although Great Britain is far from having found solutions to its "color" problems or to many of the other ills of a modern industrial society, the efforts it is making are well worth our careful consideration, as we too try to find solutions for these omnipresent and demanding problems.

Bibliography

Prepared by
LOUISE W. HOLBORN
Radcliffe Institute, Cambridge, Mass.

The steady output of new books on many aspects of the governments and politics of the major foreign powers has made it necessary to cull with care those listed in the previous bibliographies. A high proportion of the books included in this bibliography were published from 1965 on; books that appeared earlier are not listed unless they are of particular importance. Articles have been included only when they form a major source of information on a particular subject.

For those who want a more detailed survey of earlier material, attention is drawn to the comprehensive bibliographies in earlier editions of *Major Foreign Powers*.

In keeping with the practice in earlier bibliographies, this compilation has been confined to publications in English. The wealth of material on foreign governments available in this language is a reflection of the vastly increased concern of the English-speaking world to understand the peoples and policies of other countries.

ABBREVIATIONS

BBC: British Broadcasting Corporation, London.
Cmnd.: *Command Paper*, HMSO, London.
COI: Central Office of Information, London.
For. Lang. Pub.: Foreign Language Publications, Moscow.
Hansard: Hansard Society for Parliamentary Affairs, London.
HMSO: Her Majesty's Stationery Office, London.
Inst.: Institute.
Int.: International.
J: *Journal*.
Lib.: Library.
Lib. Cong.: Library of Congress, Washington, D.C.
LJ: *Law Journal*.
LR: *Law Review*.
MIT: Massachusetts Institute of Technology, Cambridge, Mass.
P: Press.
PEP: Political and Economic Planning, London.
Pbk: Paperback.
Pub.: Publisher.
Publ.: Publication.
Pub. Aff.: Public Affairs Press, Washington, D.C.
Q: *Quarterly*.
R: *Review*.
Ref. Pamph.: Reference Pamphlet.
RIIA: Royal Institute of International Affairs, London.
Trans.: Translation.
TUC: Trade Union Congress.
U: University.
USGPO: United States Government Printing Office, Washington, D.C.

COMPARATIVE MATERIAL

1. Periodicals

AJCL: *American Journal of Comparative Law*, Ann Arbor, Mich., quarterly.
AJS: *American Journal of Sociology*, Chicago, bi-monthly.
APSR: *American Political Science Review*, Washington, D.C., quarterly.
Aussenpolitik [*German Foreign Affairs Review*], Hamburg, quarterly.
BJPS: *British Journal of Political Science*, Cambridge UP, quarterly.
BJS: *British Journal of Sociology*, London, quarterly.
CEH: *Central European History*, Emory UP, Atlanta, Ga., quarterly.
CG: *Comparative Government*.
CJEPS: *Canadian Journal of Economic and Political Science*, Toronto, quarterly.
Comp. Pol.: *Comparative Politics*, Chicago, quarterly.
CPF: *Comparative Political Finance*.
CPS: *Comparative Political Studies*, Beverly Hills, Calif.
CS: *Commonwealth Survey*, London, fortnightly.
CSSH: *Comparative Studies in Society and History*, The Hague, quarterly.
E: *The Economist*, London, weekly.
ESR: *European Studies Review*, U Lancaster, Macmillan, London, first issue, Jan. 1971.
FA: *Foreign Affairs*, New York, quarterly.
GFP: *German Foreign Policy*, Institute for International Relations, VEB Deutscher Verlag der Wissenschaften, Berlin, German Democratic Republic.
Gov. & Opp.: *Government and Opposition*, London, first issue, 1966, quarterly.
HLR: *Harvard Law Review*, Cambridge, Mass., monthly (Nov–June).
IA: *International Affairs*, London, monthly.
IC: *International Conciliation*, New York, monthly.
ICLQ: *International and Comparative Law Quarterly*, London.
IJ: *International Journal*, Toronto, quarterly.
IJP: *International Journal of Politics*, Journal of Translations from Worldwide Sources, New York, first issue, Winter 1969–70.
IO: *International Organization*, Boston, quarterly.
IPSA: *International Political Science Abstracts*, Oxford, quarterly.

ISSJ: International Social Science Journal, Paris, quarterly.
JCEA: Journal of Central European Affairs, Boulder, Colo., quarterly.
JCH: Journal of Contemporary History, London, quarterly.
JCPS: Journal of Commonwealth Political Studies, Leicester UP, monthly (Nov–June).
JHI: Journal of Historical Ideas.
JIA: Journal of International Affairs, Columbia U, New York.
JICJ: Journal of International Commission of Jurists, Geneva, monthly.
JMH: Journal of Modern History, Chicago, quarterly.
JP: The Journal of Politics, Gainesville, Fla., quarterly.
MJPS: Midwest Journal of Political Science, Wayne State UP, Detroit, quarterly.
Parl. Aff.: Parliamentary Affairs, London, quarterly.
The Parliamentarian, Journal of the Parliaments of the Commonwealth, ed. by Commonwealth Parliamentary Association, House of Parliament, quarterly.
PQ: Political Quarterly, London.
PS: Political Studies, Oxford, three issues annually.
PSQ: Political Science Quarterly, New York.
Pub. Ad.: Public Administration, London, quarterly.
Pub. Law: The Constitutional and Administrative Law of the Commonwealth, London, quarterly.
Race Today, Institute of Race Relations, London, monthly.
Round Table: The Commonwealth, London, quarterly.
SR: Social Research, New York, quarterly.
WP: World Politics, Princeton, N.J., quarterly.
WPQ: The Western Political Quarterly, Salt Lake City, Utah, quarterly.
WT: The World Today, London, monthly.
YLJ: Yale Law Journal, New Haven, Conn., monthly (Nov–June).
YR: Yale Review, New Haven, Conn., quarterly.

2. Books

Abraham, Henry J., *The Judicial Process, An Introductory Analysis of the Courts of the United States, England, and France*, 2nd ed., Oxford UP, 1968, 502 pp, pbk.
Agricultural Policies in Europe and the Soviet Union, Dept. of Agriculture, Economic Research Service, 1968, 59 pp.
Albinski, Henry S. and Lawrence K. Pettit, eds., *European Political Processes: Essays and Readings*, Allyn and Bacon, 1968, 448 pp, pbk.
Almond, Gabriel A. and James S. Coleman, eds., *The Politics of the Developing Areas*, Princeton UP, 1960, 591 pp.
────── and G. Bingham Powell, Sr., *Comparative Politics: A Developmental Approach*, Little, Brown, 1966, 348 pp.
────── and Sidney Verba, *The Civic Culture: Political Attitudes and Democracy in Five Nations*, Little, Brown, 1965, 379 pp, pbk.
Anderson, Charles W., Fred R. von der Mehden, and Crawford Young, *Issues of Political Development*, Prentice-Hall, 1967, 248 pp.
Andrews, William G., ed., *Constitutions and Constitutionalism*, 3rd ed., Van Nostrand, 1968, 240 pp, pbk.

Andrews, William G., ed., *European Politics II: The Dynamics of Change*, Van Nostrand Reinhold, 1969, 278 pp, pbk.
────── and Uri Ra'anan, eds., *The Politics of the Coup D'Etat: Five Case Studies*, Van Nostrand Reinhold, 1969, 153 pp, pbk.
Arendt, Hannah, *The Origins of Totalitarianism*, new rev. ed., Harcourt Brace Jovanovich, 1966, 526 pp.
Bachrach, P., *The Theory of Democratic Elitism: A Critique*, Little, Brown, 1967, 109 pp.
Barry, Brian, *Political Argument*, Humanities Press, 1965, 364 pp.
Bayley, David H., *Public Liberties in the New States*, Rand McNally, 1964, 152 pp, pbk.
Black, Cyril E., *The Dynamics of Modernization: A Study in Comparative History*, Harper, 1966, 207 pp.
Blondel, Jean, *Comparative Government: A Reader*, Doubleday, 1969, 270 pp, pbk.
──────, *An Introduction to Comparative Government*, Praeger, 1970, 557 pp, pbk.
Bloom, Bridget, *Parliaments and Electoral Systems: A World Handbook*, Institute of Electoral Research, London, 1962, 128 pp.
Braibanti, Ralph, "Comparative Political Analytics Reconsidered," *JP*, Feb. 1968:25–65.
Brogan, Sir Denis W., *Worlds in Conflict*, Harper, 1967, 133 pp.
────── and Douglas V. Verney, *Political Patterns in Today's World*, 2nd ed., Harcourt Brace Jovanovich, 1968, 278 pp, pbk.
Bruce, Maurice, *The Coming of the Welfare State*, rev. ed., Schocken Books, 1966, 308 pp.
Bryce, Viscount James, *Modern Democracies*, Macmillan, 1924, 2 vols, 567 and 757 pp.
Brzezinski, Zbigniew and Samuel P. Huntington, *Political Power, USA/USSR: Similarities and Contrasts, Convergence or Evolution*, Viking, 1964, 461 pp.
Bunn, Ronald F. and William G. Andrews, eds., *Politics and Civil Liberties in Europe: Four Case Studies*, Van Nostrand, 1968, 221 pp, pbk.
Burin, Frederick S. and Kurt Shell, eds., *Politics, Law and Social Change: Selected Essays of Otto Kirchheimer*, Columbia UP, 1969, 483 pp.
Burns, Sir Alan, ed., *Parliament as an Export*, Allen & Unwin, London, 1966, 271 pp.
Butler, David E., ed., *Elections Abroad*, St. Martin's, 1959, 280 pp.
Campbell, Angus, P. E. Converse, W. E. Miller, and D. E. Stokes, *Elections and the Political Order*, John Wiley & Sons, 1966, 385 pp.
Campion, Lord and D. W. S. Lidderdale, *European Parliamentary Procedure: A Comparative Handbook*, Allen & Unwin, London, 1955, 270 pp.
Carter, Gwendolen M., ed., *National Unity and Regionalism in Eight African States*, Cornell UP, 1966, 565 pp.
──────, ed., *Politics in Africa: Seven Cases*, Harcourt Brace Jovanovich, 1966, 283 pp, pbk.
────── and John H. Herz, *Government and Politics in the Twentieth Century*, rev. enl. ed., Praeger, 1965, 231 pp, pbk.
────── and Alan F. Westin, eds., *Politics in Europe: 5 Cases in European Government*, Harcourt Brace Jovanovich, 1965, 205 pp.

Castberg, Freda, *Freedom of Speech in the West: A Comparative Study of Public Law in France, the United States and Germany*, Allen & Unwin, London, 1961, 475 pp.

Castles, Francis G., *Pressure Groups and Political Culture: A Comparative Study*, Routledge, London, 1967, 112 pp.

Chapman, Brian, *The Profession of Government: The Public Service in Europe*, 3rd ed., Allen & Unwin, London, 1966, 352 pp.

Christoph, James B. and Bernard E. Brown, *Cases in Comparative Politics*, 2nd ed., Little, Brown, 1969, 301 pp, pbk.

Cole, George D. H., *A History of Socialist Thought*, St. Martin's, 5 vols: *The Forerunners, 1789–1850*, 1953, 345 pp; *Marxism and Anarchism, 1850–1890*, 1954, 481 pp; *The Second International, 1889–1914*, 1956, 1,042 pp; *Communism and Social Democracy, 1914–1931*, 1959, 940 pp; *Socialism and Fascism, 1931–1939*, 1960, 350 pp.

Coleman, James S., ed., *Studies in Political Development*, Princeton UP, 1965, 620 pp.

Curtis, Michael, *Comparative Government and Politics: An Introductory Essay in Political Science*, Harper, 1968, 266 pp.

Dahl, Robert A., *After the Revolution? Authority in a Good Society*, Yale UP, 1970, 172 pp, pbk.

———, ed., *Political Opposition in Western Democracies*, Yale UP, 1968, 458 pp, pbk.

———, *Polyarchy*, Yale UP, 1970, 200 pp.

David, René, *Major Legal Systems in the World Today: An Introduction to the Comparative Study of Law*, trans. John E. C. Brierley, Stevens, London, 1968, 203 pp, pbk.

Dawson, Richard E. and Kenneth Prewitt, *Political Socialization*, Little, Brown, 1969, 226 pp.

Denton, Geoffrey, Murray Forsyth, and Malcolm MacLennan, *Economic Planning and Policies in Britain, France and Germany*, Praeger, 1969, 424 pp.

Duchacek, Ivo D., *Comparative Federalism: The Territorial Dimension of Politics*, Holt, 1970, 370 pp.

Duverger, Maurice, *Political Parties: Their Organization and Activity in the Modern State*, trans. Barbara and Robert North, Wiley, 1954, 439 pp.

———, *The Political Role of Women*, UNESCO, Paris, 1955, 221 pp.

Edinger, Lewis J., ed., *Political Leadership in Industrialized Societies: Studies in Comparative Analysis*, Wiley, 1967, 376 pp, pbk.

Ehrmann, Henry W., ed., *Democracy in a Changing Society*, Praeger, 1964, 210 pp, pbk.

———, ed., *Interest Groups on Four Continents*, Pittsburgh UP, 1958, 316 pp.

Epstein, Leon D., *Political Parties in Western Democracies*, Praeger, 1967, 374 pp.

Fagen, Richard R., *Politics and Communication*, Little, Brown, 1966, 162 pp, pbk.

Fairlie, Henry, *The Life of Politics*, Basic, 1968, 271 pp.

Farrell, R. Barry, ed., *Approaches to Comparative and International Politics*, Northwestern UP, 1966, 368 pp.

Field, G. Lowell, *Comparative Political Development: The Precedent of the West*, Routledge, London, 1968, 247 pp.

Finer, Herman, *The Theory and Practice of Modern Government*, 4th ed., Methuen, London, 1961, 982 pp.

Finer, S. E., *Comparative Government*, Penguin, 1970, 615 pp.

———, *The Man on Horseback: The Role of the Military in Politics*, Pall Mall, London, 1962, 268 pp.

——— and Gabriel A. Almond, "Polemics in Comparative Politics," *Gov. & Opp.*, 5(1), Winter 1969–70: 3–40.

Fogarty, Michael P., *Christian Democracy in Western Europe, 1820–1953*, Notre Dame UP, 1957, 461 pp.

Francis-Williams, Baron Edward, *The Right to Know: The Rise of the World Press*, Longmans, London, 1969, 336 pp.

Fried, Robert C., *Comparative Political Institutions*, Macmillan, 1966, 152 pp, pbk.

Friedmann, Wolfgang and J. F. Garner, eds., *Government Enterprise: A Comparative Study*, Stevens, London, 1970, 351 pp.

Friedrich, Carl J., *Constitutional Government and Democracy*, 4th ed., Blaisdell, 1968, 728 pp.

———, *The Impact of American Constitutionalism Abroad*, Boston UP, 1968, 112 pp.

——— and Zbigniew K. Brzezinski, *Totalitarian Dictatorship and Autocracy*, 2nd rev. ed., Praeger, 1966, 427 pp, pbk.

Gellhorn, Walter, *Ombudsmen and Others: Citizens' Protectors in Nine Countries*, Harvard UP, 1966, 448 pp.

Gurr, Ted, *Why Men Rebel*, Princeton UP, 1970, 421 pp.

Heady, Ferrel, *Public Administration: A Comparative Perspective*, Prentice-Hall, 1966, 115 pp, pbk.

Heidenheimer, Arnold J., ed., *Political Corruption: Readings in Comparative Analysis*, Holt, 1970, 582 pp, pbk.

Hennig, Stanley and John Ander, eds., *European Political Parties*, Praeger, 1970, 565 pp.

Herz, John H., *International Politics in the Atomic Age*, Columbia UP, 1962, 360 pp, pbk.

———, *Political Realism and Political Idealism: A Study in Theories and Realities*, Chicago UP, 1951, 275 pp.

Hoch, Paul, *Academic Freedom in Action*, Sheed & Ward, London, 1970, 212 pp.

Holborn, Louise W., John H. Herz, and Gwendolen M. Carter, eds., *Documents of Major Foreign Powers: A Sourcebook on Great Britain, France, Germany and the Soviet Union*, Harcourt Brace Jovanovich, 1968, 381 pp, pbk.

Holt, Robert and John Turner, *The Political Basis of Economic Development: An Exploration in Comparative Political Analysis*, Van Nostrand, 1966, 410 pp, pbk.

Huntington, Samuel P., *Political Order in Changing Societies*, Yale UP, 1968, 488 pp.

Ionescu, G., *The Politics of the European Communist States*, Weidenfeld & Nicolson, London, 1967, 304 pp.

IPI Survey, *The Press in Authoritarian Countries*, Int. Press Inst., Zurich, 1959, 201 pp.

Jacob, Charles E., *Policy and Bureaucracy*, Van Nostrand, 1965, 217 pp.

Jones, Roy E., *The Functional Analysis of Politics: An*

Introductory Discussion, Humanities Press, 1967, 101 pp.

Kersell, John E., *Parliamentary Supervision of Delegated Legislation: The United Kingdom, Australia, New Zealand and Canada*, Stevens, London, 1960, 178 pp.

King, Edmund J., *Comparative Studies and Educational Decision*, Methuen, London, 1968, 182 pp.

Kirchheimer, Otto, *Political Justice: The Use of Legal Procedure for Political Ends*, Princeton UP, 1961, 452 pp.

Kolarz, Walter, *Communism and Colonialism*, St. Martin's, 1964, 147 pp.

La Palombara, Joseph, ed., *Bureaucracy and Political Development*, Princeton UP, 1963, 487 pp.

—— and Myron Weiner, eds., *Political Parties and Political Development*, Princeton UP, 1966, 495 pp.

Lerner, Daniel and Morton Gordon, *Euratlantica: The Changing Perspectives of the European Elites*, MIT Press, 1969, 416 pp.

Lindsay, Alexander D., *The Modern Democratic State*, Oxford UP, Vol 1, 1943, 286 pp.

Lipset, Seymour M., ed., *Party Systems and Voter Alignments: Cross National Perspectives*, Free Press, 1967, 554 pp.

London, Kurt, *The Making of Foreign Policy: East and West*, Lippincott, 1965, 368 pp, pbk.

Lorwin, Lewis L., *The International Labor Movement: History, Policies, Outlook*, Harper, 1953, 366 pp.

Mackenzie, W. J. M., *Free Elections*, Rinehart, 1958, 184 pp.

——, *Politics and Social Science*, Penguin, 1967, 424 pp.

Macridis, Roy C., ed., *Political Parties: Contemporary Trends and Ideas*, Harper, 1967, 268 pp, pbk.

—— and Bernard E. Brown, *Comparative Politics: Notes and Readings*, 3rd ed., Dorsey, 1968, 660 pp, pbk.

Marshall, Arthur H., *Local Government in the Modern World*, Athlone Press, London, 1965, 38 pp.

Mayer, J. de, et al., *Elections in the Countries of the European Communities and in the United Kingdom*, De Tempel, Bruges, 1967, 378 pp.

Merkl, Peter H., *Modern Comparative Politics*, Holt, 1970, 416 pp, pbk.

Merkl, Peter H., *Political Continuity and Change*, Harper, 1967, 606 pp.

Miller, John D., *The Politics of the Third World*, Oxford UP, 1967, 126 pp, pbk.

Milnor, Andrew, *Elections and Political Stability*, Little, Brown, 1969, 224 pp, pbk.

Mitchell, Joan, *Groundwork to Economic Planning*, Secker and Warburg, London, 1966, 316 pp.

Mueller, Bernard, *Western Europe, Canada and the United States: A Statistical Handbook of the North Atlantic Area*, Twentieth Century, 1965, 239 pp.

Munger, Frank, ed., *Studies in Comparative Politics*, Crowell, 1967, 313 pp.

Neumann, Sigmund, ed., *Modern Political Parties: Approaches to Comparative Politics*, Chicago UP, 1956, 460 pp.

Nolte, Ernst, *Three Faces of Fascism: Action Française, Italian Fascism, National Socialism*, Holt, 1966, 561 pp, pbk.

Normanton, E. L., *The Accountability and Audit of Government*, Praeger, 1966, 470 pp.

Northedge, Frederick S., ed., *The Foreign Politics of the Powers*, Praeger, 1969, 299 pp, pbk.

Parry, Geraint, *Political Elites*, Praeger, 1969, 169 pp.

Peaslee, Amos J., *Constitutions of the Nations*, 4 vols, rev. 3rd ed., Nijhoff, The Hague, 1965, 2,752 pp.

Pesonen, Pertti, ed., *Scandinavian Political Studies*: Vols 1 & 2, Columbia UP, 1966, 341 pp.

Plamenatz, John, *On Alien Rule and Self-Government*, Longmans, London, 1960, 224 pp.

Political Handbook of the World, ed. Walter H. Mallory, Harper, publ. annually.

Preston, Nathaniel S., *Politics, Economics, and Power: Ideology and Practice Under Capitalism, Socialism, Communism, and Fascism*, Macmillan, 1967, 242 pp, pbk.

Pye, Lucien W., *Aspects of Political Development: An Analytic Study*, Little, Brown, 1966, 205 pp.

——, ed., *Communications and Political Development*, Princeton UP, 1963, 381 pp.

—— and Sidney Verba, *Political Culture and Political Development*, Princeton UP, 1965, 584 pp.

Radice, Giles, *Democratic Socialism*, Longmans, London, 1970, 164 pp.

Rae, Douglas W., *The Political Consequences of Electoral Laws*, Yale UP, 1967, 173 pp.

Rasmussen, Jorgen S., *The Process of Politics: A Comparative Approach*, Atherton, 1969, 225 pp, pbk.

Richardson, G. Henry, *Economic and Financial Aspects of Social Security: An International Survey*, Allen & Unwin, London, 1960, 270 pp.

Rogger, Hans and Eugen Weber, eds., *The European Right: A Historical Profile*, California UP, 1965, 589 pp.

Rokkan, S. and J. Meyriat, eds., *International Guide to Electoral Statistics*, Humanities Press, 1969, 351 pp.

Ross, Murray G., ed., *New Universities in the Modern World*, St. Martin's, 1966, 190 pp.

Rowat, Donald C., ed., *The Ombudsman: Citizen's Defender*, Allen & Unwin, London, 1965, 348 pp, pbk.

Sampson, Anthony, *The New Europeans: A Guide to the Workings, Institutions and Character of Contemporary Western Europe*, Hodder & Stoughton, London, 1968, 462 pp.

Schwartz, Bernard, ed., *The Code Napoleon and the Common-Law World*, New York UP, 1956, 448 pp.

Seidman, Harold, *Politics, Position and Power: The Dynamics of Federal Organization*, Oxford UP, 1970, 311 pp.

Sigmund, Paul E., ed., *The Ideologies of the Developing Nations*, rev. ed., Praeger, 1967, 428 pp.

Smith, Bruce L. R. and D. C. Hague, eds., *The Dilemma of Accountability in Modern Government*, Macmillan, 1971, 391 pp.

Stebbins, Richard P., ed., *Political Handbook and Atlas of the World*, Simon and Schuster, 1970.

Stewart, Michael, *Modern Forms of Government: A Comparative Study*, 3rd ed., Allen & Unwin, London, 1964, 284 pp.

Strauss, E., *The Ruling Servants: Bureaucracy in Russia, France and Britain*, Praeger, 1961, 308 pp.
Strong, C. F., *A History of Modern Political Constitutions: An Introduction to Comparative Study of Their History and Existing Form*, Capricorn, 1964, 389 pp, pbk.
Thompson, James D., ed., *Comparative Studies in Administration*, Pittsburgh UP, 1960; 224 pp.
Ulich, Robert, *The Education of Nations: A Comparison in Historical Perspective*, rev. ed., Harvard UP, 1967, 365 pp.
Walsh, Annmarie H., *The Urban Challenge to Government: An International Comparison of Thirteen Cities*, Praeger, 1969, 294 pp.
———, *Urban Government for the Paris Region*, Praeger, 1967, 217 pp.
Wheare, Kenneth C., *Federal Government*, 4th ed., Oxford UP, 1964, 266 pp, pbk.

Jones, Grace, *Legislatures*, 2nd ed., Oxford UP, 1968, 166 pp, pbk.
———, *Modern Constitutions*, 2nd ed., Oxford UP, 1966, 150 pp, pbk.
Wheeler-Bennett, John W., *A Wreath to Clio: Studies in British, American and German Affairs*, St. Martin's, 1967, 224 pp.
Willis, Roy F., *France, Germany, and the New Europe 1945–1967*, rev. ed., Stanford UP, 1968, 431 pp.
Wiseman, H. Victor, *Political Systems: Some Sociological Approaches*, Praeger, 1966, 254 pp, pbk.
Wolf-Phillips, Leslie, *Constitutions of Modern States*, Praeger, 1967, 274 pp, pbk.
Woolf, S. J., ed., *European Fascism*, Weidenfeld & Nicolson, London, 1968, 386 pp.
Zolberg, Aristide R., *Creating Political Order*, Rand McNally, 1966, 168 pp, pbk.

GREAT BRITAIN

GENERAL WORKS

Bailey, Sidney D., *British Parliamentary Democracy*, 3rd ed., Houghton, Mifflin, 1971, 281 pp, pbk.
Birch, A. H., *The British System of Government*, Allen & Unwin, London, 1967, 284 pp, pbk.
Booker, Christopher, *The Neophiliacs: A Study of the Revolution of English Life in the Fifties and Sixties*, Collins, London, 1969, 381 pp.
Brasher, N. H., *Studies in British Government*, 2nd ed., St. Martin's, 1971, 224 pp.
Bray, Jeremy, *Decision in Government*, Gollancz, London, 1970, 320 pp.
Britain 1971: An Official Handbook, HMSO, 1971, 522 pp. (annual)
Butler, David E. and J. Freeman, *British Political Facts, 1900–67*, 2nd ed., St. Martin's, 1968, 314 pp.
——— and Donald Stokes, *Political Change in Britain*, Penguin, 1971, 80 pp.
Calleo, David P., *Britain's Future*, Hodder & Stoughton, London, 1968, 252 pp.
Caves, Richard E. et al., *Britain's Economic Prospects*, Brookings Inst., 1968, 510 pp.
Crick, Bernard, ed., *Essays on Reform, 1967: A Centenary Tribute*, Oxford UP, 1967, 222 pp.
———, "The 1970's in Retrospect," *Parl. Aff.*, 41(1), Jan–Mar. 1970:106–14.
——— and William A. Robson, *Protest and Discontent*, Penguin, 1970, 220 pp.
Crosland, Anthony, *A Social Democratic Britain*, Fabian Tract 404, London, 1970–71, 16 pp.
Fairlie, H., *The Life of Politics*, Methuen, London, 1968, 271 pp.
Great Britain Central Statistical Office: Social Trends No. 1, HMSO, 1970, 184 pp.
Hanson, A. H. and M. Walles, *Governing Britain*, Fontana, London, 1970, 304 pp, pbk.
Jay, Douglas, *After the Common Market: A Better Alternative for Britain*, Penguin, 1968, 126 pp.
Jennings, Sir Ivor, *The Queen's Government*, rev. ed., Pelican, 1967, 164 pp.
Jones, Grace, *The Political Structure*, Longmans, London, 1969, 110 pp, pbk.

Lapping, Brian, *The Labour Government 1964–1970*, Penguin, 1970, 219 pp.
Levin, Bernard, *The Pendulum Years: Britain and the Sixties*, Cape, London, 1970, 451 pp.
Mackintosh, John P., *The Government and Politics of Britain*, Hutchinson, London, 1970, 206 pp.
Mathiot, André, *The British Political System*, trans. Jennifer S. Hines, Stanford UP, 1967, 352 pp, pbk.
Moorhouse, Geoffrey, *Britain in the Sixties: The Other England*, Penguin, 1964, 189 pp.
Morrison, Lord of Lambeth, Herbert Stanley, *Government and Parliament: A Survey from the Inside*, 3rd ed., Oxford UP, 1964, 386 pp, pbk.
Nicholson, Edward M., *The System*, Hodder, London, 1967, 525 pp.
Oakley, R. and P. Rose, *The Political Year, 1970*, Pitman, London, 1970, 250 pp. (to be issued annually)
Pollard, Sidney and David W. Crossley, *The Wealth of Britain 1085–1966*, Batsford, London, 1968, 303 pp.
Popham, C. T., *Government in Britain*, Pergamon, London, 1969, 268 pp, pbk.
Punnett, Robert M., *British Government and Politics*, Heinemann, London, 1968, 488 pp.
Reynolds, E. E. and N. H. Brasher, *Britain in the Twentieth Century, 1900–1964*, Cambridge UP, 1966, 375 pp, pbk.
Robson, William A., *Politics and Government At Home and Abroad*, Allen & Unwin, London, 1967, 299 pp.
Rose, Richard, *People in Politics: Observations Across the Atlantic*, Faber, London, 1969, 251 pp.
———, ed., *Policy-Making in Britain: A Reader in Government*, Macmillan, 1969, 375 pp.
———, *Politics in England: An Interpretation*, Little, Brown, 1964, 266 pp, pbk.
———, ed., *Studies in British Politics: A Reader in Political Sociology*, 2nd rev. ed., Macmillan, London, 1969, 428 pp.
Sampson, Anthony, *The New Anatomy of Britain*, Stein & Day, 1972, 733 pp.

Stacey, Frank, *The Government of Modern Britain*, Oxford UP, 1968, 500 pp, pbk.
Stankiewicz, W. J., *Crisis in British Government: The Need for Reform*, Collier-Macmillan, London, 1967, 410 pp.
Stewart, Michael, *The British Approach to Politics*, 5th ed., Allen & Unwin, London, 1966, 310 pp, pbk.
Summerskill, Edith, *A Woman's World*, Heinemann, London, 1967, 258 pp.
Vig, Norman J., *Science and Technology in British Politics*, Pergamon, London, 1968, 190 pp.
Whitaker, Ben, ed., *A Radical Future*, Cape, London, 1967, 223 pp.
Wiseman, H. Victor, *Politics in Everyday Life*, Blackwell, Oxford, 1966, 222 pp.
Woodhouse, C. M., *Post-War Britain*, Bodley Head, London, 1966, 94 pp.
Wootton, Barbara, *In a World I Never Made*, Allen & Unwin, London, 1967, 283 pp.

Chapter 1. THE BRITISH PEOPLE AND THEIR POLITICS

1. LAND, PEOPLE, SOCIETY, AND ECONOMY

Adams, Walter, ed., *The Brain Drain*, Collier-Macmillan, 1968, 273 pp.
Benewick, Robert, *Political Violence and Public Order: A Study of British Fascism*, Penguin, 1969, 340 pp.
Bottomore, Thomas B., *Elites and Society*, Penguin, 1966, 160 pp.
Bruce, Maurice, *The Coming of the Welfare State*, 4th ed., Batsford, London, 1961, 374 pp.
Cairncross, Sir Alec, ed., *Britain's Economic Prospects Reconsidered*, Allen & Unwin, London, 1971, 244 pp, pbk.
Cole, George D. H. and Raymond Postgate, *The British Common People*, Barnes & Noble, 1961, 742 pp, pbk.
Coupland, Sir Reginald, *Welsh and Scottish Nationalism*, Collins, London, 1954, 448 pp.
Gilbert, Bentley B., *British Social Policy, 1914–1939*, Batsford, London, 1971, 343 pp.
Gregg, Pauline, *The Welfare State*, Harrap, London, 1967, 400 pp.
Guttsman, Wilhelm L., *The British Political Elite*, Basic Books, 1964, 398 pp.
——, ed., *The English Ruling Class: Readings in Politics and Society*, Weidenfeld & Nicolson, London, 1969, 310 pp.
Hackett, John W. and A. M. Hackett, *The British Economy: Problems and Prospects*, Allen & Unwin, London, 1967, 221 pp.
Harris, John S., *Government Patronage of the Arts in Great Britain*, Chicago UP, 1970, 341 pp.
Henderson, Patrick D., ed., *Economic Growth in Britain*, Weidenfeld & Nicolson, London, 1966, 296 pp.
Hutchinson, T. W., *Economics and Economic Policy in Britain, 1946–1966: Some Aspects of Their Interrelations*, Allen & Unwin, London, 1968, 307 pp.
Jackson, Brian, *Working Class Community: Some General Notions Raised by a Series of Studies in Northern England*, Routledge, London, 1968, 191 pp.

Jackson, J. A., ed., *Social Stratification*, Cambridge UP, 1968, 238 pp.
Kaufman, G., ed., *The Left: A Symposium* (The Great Society series), Blond, London, 1967, 184 pp, pbk.
Leach, Gerald, *The Brocrats*, Cape, London, 1970, 317 pp.
Lewis, Roy and Angus Maude, *The English Middle Classes*, Knopf, 1950, 386 pp.
Mabey, R., ed., *Class: A Symposium* (The Great Society series), Blond, London, 1967, 176 pp, pbk.
McGregor, O. R., Louis Blom-Cooper, and Colin Gibson, *Separated Spouses*, Duckworth, London, 1971, 281 pp.
MacNeil, Robert, *The People Machine*, Eyre & Spottiswoode, London, 1970, 364 pp.
Miller, S. M., *Social Class and Social Policy*, Basic Books, 1968, 336 pp.
Parkin, Frank, *Middle Class Radicalism*, Manchester UP, 1968, 207 pp.
"Protest and Discontent," special issue, *PQ*, 40(4), Oct–Dec. 1969.
Raynor, John, *The Middle Classes*, Longmans, London, 1969, 125 pp, pbk.
Roberts, Robert, *The Classic Slum*, Manchester UP, 1971, 219 pp.
Rose, Gordon, *The Working Class*, Longmans, London, 1968, 151 pp.
Schorr, Alvin, *Explorations in Social Policy*, Basic Books, 1968, 308 pp.
Seabrook, Jeremy, *The City Close-Up*, Penguin, 1971, 283 pp.
Shonfield, Andrew, *Modern Capitalism: The Changing Balance of Public and Private Power*, Oxford UP, 1969, 456 pp, pbk.
Stamp, Lawrence D., *The Land of Britain: Its Use and Misuse*, 3rd ed., Longmans, London, 1962, 546 pp.
—— and S. H. Beaver, *The British Isles: A Geographic and Economic Survey*, 5th ed., Longmans, London, 1964, 820 pp.
Thompson, E. P., *The Making of the English Working Class*, Pantheon, 1964, 845 pp.
Willmott, Peter and Michael Young, *Family and Class in a London Suburb*, Humanities Press, 1960, 187 pp.

2. NORTHERN IRELAND

DePoor, Liam, *Divided Ulster*, Penguin, 1970, 208 pp.
Devlin, Bernadette, *The Price of My Soul*, Deutsch/Pan, London, 1969, 206 pp.
Hastings, Max, *Ulster 1969: The Fight for Civil Rights in Northern Ireland*, Gollancz, London, 1970, 203 pp.
Lawrence, R. J., *The Government of Northern Ireland: Public Finance and Public Services 1921–1964*, Clarendon Press, Oxford, 1965, 198 pp.
Rose, Richard, *Governing Without Consensus: An Irish Perspective*, Faber, London, 1971, 567 pp.
Wilson, Thomas, ed., *Ulster Under Home Rule: A Study of the Political and Economic Problems of Northern Ireland*, Oxford UP, 1956, 253 pp.

3. CHURCHES

Grubb, Sir Kenneth, *Crypts of Power*, Hodder, London, 1971.

Heubel, E. J., "Church and State in England: The Price of Establishment," WPQ, 18(3), Sept. 1965: 646-55.
Hill, Clifford S., West Indian Migrants and the London Churches, Oxford UP, 1963, 89 pp.
Hunter, Leslie S., The English Church: A New Look, Penguin, 1966, 176 pp.
Mayfield, Guy, The Church of England: Its Members and Its Business, 2nd ed., Oxford UP, 1963, 211 pp.

4. IMMIGRATION AND RACE RELATIONS

Ambalavaner, S., Coloured Immigrants in Britain: Selected Bibliography, 2nd ed., Inst. for Race Relations, London, 1968, 82 pp.
Banton, Michael, Race Relations, Tavistock, London, 1967, 434 pp.
———, White and Coloured: The Behavior of British People Toward Coloured Immigrants, Cape, London, 1959, 223 pp.
Brockway, Fenner and Norman Pannell, Immigration: What Is the Answer? Two Opposing Views, Routledge, London, 1965, 120 pp, pbk.
Davison, R. B., Commonwealth Immigrants, Oxford UP, 1964, 87 pp.
Deakin, Nicholas, ed., Colour and the British Electorate, 1964: Six Case Studies, Pall Mall, London, 1965, 172 pp.
Economic Issues in Immigration, Inst. of Economic Affairs, London, 1970, 180 pp.
Facts Paper on the United Kingdom, 1970-71, Inst. for Race Relations, London, 1970, 48 pp.
Foot, Paul, Immigration and Race in British Politics, Penguin Special, 1965, 254 pp.
Freedman, Maurice, ed., A Minority in Britain: Social Studies of the Anglo-Jewish Community, Mitchell, London, 1955, 304 pp.
Garrard, John A., The English and Immigration, 1880-1910, Oxford UP, 1971, 244 pp.
Glass, Ruth and Harold Pollins, London's Newcomers: The West Indian Migrants, Harvard UP, 1961, 278 pp.
Hepple, Bob, Race, Jobs, and the Law in Britain, Allen Lane, London, 1968, 256 pp.
Hill, Clifford, Immigration and Integration, Pergamon, 1970, 224 pp.
Hiro, Dilip, Black British, White British, Eyre & Spottiswoode, London, 1971.
Hooper, Richard, ed., Colour in Britain, BBC, London, 1965, 239 pp.
Huxley, Elspeth, Back Street New Worlds: A Look at Immigrants in Britain, Morrow, 1965, 190 pp.
Isaac, Julius, British Postwar Migration, Cambridge UP, 1955, 329 pp.
Jones, K. and A. D. Smith, The Economic Impact of Commonwealth Immigration, Cambridge UP, 1970, 186 pp.
Lewin, Julius, The Struggle for Racial Equality, Longmans, London, 1967, 191 pp.
Mandle, W. F., Anti-Semitism and the British Union of Fascists, Longmans, London, 1968, 78 pp.
Patterson, Sheila, Immigration and Race Relations in Britain, 1960-67, Oxford UP, 1969, 460 pp.
Peach, Ceri, West Indian Migration to Britain: A Social Geography, Oxford UP, 1968, 122 pp.
Rose, Eliot J. B. et al., Colour and Citizenship: A Report on British Race Relations, Oxford UP, 1969, 815 pp. (Updated and abridged by Nicholas Deakin, Colour, Citizenship and British Society, Panther, London, 1970)
Smithies, Billy and Peter Fiddick, Enoch Powell on Immigration: An Analysis, Sphere, London, 1969, 158 pp.
Steel, David M. S., No Entry: The Background and Implications of the Commonwealth Immigrants Act 1968, Hurst, London, 1969, 263 pp.
Zubaida, Sami, ed., Race and Racialism, Tavistock, London, 1970, 185 pp.

5. EDUCATION

Armytage, Walter H. G., Four Hundred Years of English Education, Cambridge UP, 1964, 353 pp, pbk.
Ashby, Sir Eric and Mary Anderson, The Rise of the Student Estate in Britain, Macmillan, 1970, 186 pp, pbk.
Avorn, Jerry L. et al., University in Revolt, Macdonald, London, 1969, 307 pp.
Baron, George A., A Bibliographical Guide to the English Educational System, enl. ed., Athlone, London, 1960, 97 pp.
Beloff, Michael, The Plateglass Universities, Secker & Warburg, London, 1968, 208 pp.
Blackstone, Tessa, Kathleen Gales, Roger Hadley, and Wyn Lewis, Students in Conflict, Weidenfeld & Nicolson, London, 1970, 384 pp.
Butler, Lord, The Education Act of 1944 and After, Longmans, London, 1966, 24 pp.
Caine, Sir Sydney, British Universities: Purpose and Prospects, Bodley Head, London, 1969, 272 pp.
Cockburn, Alexander and Robin Blackburn, eds., Student Power: Problems, Diagnosis, Action, Penguin, 1969, 378 pp.
Crawley, Harriet, A Degree of Defiance: Students in England and Europe Now, Weidenfeld & Nicolson, London, 1969, 207 pp.
Crouch, Colin, The Student Revolt, Bodley Head, London, 1970, 251 pp.
Dent, Harold C., British Education, rev. ed., Longmans, London, 1966, 70 pp.
Dent, Harold C., The Educational System of England and Wales, London UP, 1961, 224 pp.
Dodd, H. W., L. M. Hacker, and L. Rogers, Government Assistance to the Universities in Great Britain, Columbia UP, 1952, 133 pp.
Douglas, James W. B., J. M. Ross, and H. R. Simpson, All Our Future: A Longitudinal Study of Secondary Education, Peter Davies, London, 1968, 255 pp.
Driver, Christopher, The Exploding University, Hodder & Stoughton, London, 1971.
15 to 18: Report of the Central Advisory Council for Education in England, The Crowther Report, 2 vols, HMSO, 1959 (reprinted 1962), 759 pp.
Gosden, P. H., The Development of Educational Administration in England and Wales, Blackwell, Oxford, 1966, 228 pp.
Half Our Future: Report of the Central Advisory Council for Education in England, The Newsom Report, HMSO, Aug. 1963, 299 pp.

Halsey, A. H. and Martin Trow, *The British Academics*, Faber, London, 1971, 560 pp.

Higher Education: Government Statement on the Robbins Report, Cmd. 2165, HMSO, 1963, 5 pp.

Higher Education: The Robbins Report, Cmd. 2154, HMSO, Oct. 1963, 335 pp.

House of Commons, *Report from the Select Committee on Education and Science*, Session 1968–69, Student Relations, HC 449, Vol. I–VII, HMSO, 1969, 201 pp. (With six volumes of evidence, etc.)

———, *Second Report from the Committee of Privileges*, Session 1968–69, Events Attending Visit of Subcommittee B Appointed by the Select Committee on Education and Science to the U of Essex, HC 308, HMSO, 1969, 44 pp.

Illingworth, Sir Charles, *University Statesman: Sir Hector Hetherington*, George Outram, Glasgow, 1971.

Kamm, Josephine, *Hope Deferred: Girls' Education in English History*, Methuen, London, 1964, 332 pp.

Kelly, Thomas, *A History of Adult Education in Great Britain*, Liverpool UP, 1962, 352 pp.

Kidd, Harry, *The Trouble at LSE: 1966–67*, Oxford UP, 1969, 199 pp.

Lester-Smith, William O., *Education in Great Britain*, 5th ed., Oxford UP, 1968, 167 pp.

Lowndes, G. A. N., *The British Educational System*, Hutchinson, London, 1960, 183 pp.

McGuigan, Gerald F. et al., *Student Protest*, Methuen, Canada, 1968, 285 pp.

Manzer, Ronald A., *Teachers and Politics in England and Wales*, Manchester UP, 1970, 164 pp.

Mountford, Sir James F., *British Universities*, Oxford UP, 1966, 180 pp.

Nagel, Julian, ed., *Student Power*, Merlin Press, London, 1969, 235 pp.

Parkinson, Michael, *The Labour Party and the Reorganisation of Secondary Education, 1918–1965*, Routledge, London, 1970, 139 pp.

Partridge, John, *Middle School: The Secondary Modern School*, Gollancz, London, 1966, 176 pp.

Payne, George Louis, *Britain's Scientific and Technological Manpower*, Stanford UP, 1960, 466 pp.

Pedley, Robin, *The Comprehensive School*, Penguin, 1963, 222 pp.

Peterson, Paul E., "British Interest Group Theory Reexamined: The Politics of Comprehensive Education in Three British Cases," *Comp. Pol.*, 3(3), April 1971:381–402.

Robbins, Lord, *The University in the Modern World*, Macmillan, 1966, 170 pp.

Rudd, Ernest and Stephen Hatch, *Graduate Study and After*, Weidenfeld & Nicolson, London, 1968, 229 pp.

Spender, Stephen, *The Year of the Young Rebels*, Weidenfeld & Nicolson, London, 1969, 186 pp.

Students and Staff of the Hornsey College of Art, *The Hornsey Affair*, Penguin, 1969, 220 pp.

Wakeford, John, *The Cloistered Elite: A Sociological Analysis of the English Boarding School*, Macmillan, 1969, 269 pp.

Wilkinson, Rupert Hugh, *The Prefects: British Leadership and the Public School Tradition*, Oxford UP, 1963, 243 pp.

The Years of Crisis: Report of the Labour Party's Study Group on Higher Education, Transport House, 1963, 47 pp.

6. SOCIAL SERVICES

Abel-Smith, Brian and Kathleen Gales, *British Doctors at Home and Abroad*, Codicote, Herts, 1964, 64 pp.

The Beveridge Report: Social Insurance and Allied Services, Cmd. 6404, Macmillan, 1942, 249 pp.

Brain, Lord, *Medicine and Government*, Tavistock, London, 1967, 21 pp.

Brand, Jeanne L., *Doctors and the State: The British Medical Profession and Government Action in Public Health, 1870–1912*, Johns Hopkins UP, 1965, 307 pp.

Brown, Muriel, *Introduction to Social Administration in Great Britain*, Hutchinson, London, 1969, 208 pp, pbk.

Cartwright, Ann, *Human Relations and Hospital Care*, Routledge, London, 1964, 272 pp.

Eckstein, Harry, *The English Health Service: Its Origins, Structure and Achievements*, Harvard UP, 1959, 289 pp.

Farndale, W. A. J., *Trends in the National Health Service*, Pergamon, London, 1964, 423 pp.

Freeman, Hugh and W. A. J. Farndale, eds., *New Aspects of the Mental Health Services*, Pergamon, London, 1967, 776 pp.

"The Future of the Social Services," special issue, *PQ*, 40(1), Jan–Mar. 1969.

George, V. N., *Social Security: Beveridge and After*, Routledge, London, 1968, 258 pp.

Gilbert, Bentley, *British Social Policy*, Batsford, London, 1971, 343 pp.

———, *The Evolution of National Insurance in Great Britain: The Origins of the Welfare State*, Joseph, London, 1966, 498 pp.

Harris, Robert W., *National Health Insurance in Great Britain, 1911–1946*, Allen & Unwin, London, 1946, 224 pp.

Jefferys, Margot, *An Anatomy of Social Welfare Services*, Joseph, London, 1966, 371 pp.

Lindsey, Almont, *Socialized Medicine in England and Wales: The National Health Service, 1948–1961*, North Carolina UP, 1963, 561 pp.

Marmor, Theodor R., *The Politics of Medicare*, Routledge, 1970, 146 pp.

Marshall, T. H., *Social Policy*, 2nd ed., Hutchinson, London, 1970, 200 pp.

Morris, Mary, *Voluntary Work in the Welfare State*, Routledge, London, 1969, 279 pp.

National Health Service: The "Guillebaud" Report, Cmd. 9963, HMSO, 1956.

Owen, David, ed., *A Unified Health Service*, Pergamon, London, 1968, 148 pp.

Powell, Enoch, *A New Look at Medicine and Politics*, Pitman, London, 1966, 74 pp.

Robson, W. A., *The Future of the Social Services*, Pelican, 1970, 206 pp.

Rowntree, B. Seebohm and G. R. Lavers, *Poverty and the Welfare State*, Longmans, London, 1951, 104 pp.

Slack, Kathleen M., *Social Administration and the Citizen*, 2nd rev. ed., Joseph, 1969, 269 pp.

Stevens, Rosemary, *Medical Practice in Modern England: The Impact of Specialization and State Medicine*, Yale UP, 1966, 413 pp.
Strategy for Pensions, Cmnd. 4755, HMSO, 1971.
Titmuss, Richard M., *Commitment to Welfare*, Allen & Unwin, 1968, 272 pp.
Willcocks, Arthur J., *The Creation of the National Health Service: A Study of Pressure Groups and a Major Social Policy*, Humanities Press, 1967, 118 pp.
Williams, Lady Gertrude, *The Coming of the Welfare State*, Allen & Unwin, London, 1967, 120 pp.
Young, A. F., *Social Services in British Industry*, Routledge, London, 1968, 258 pp.

7. TRADE UNIONS AND INDUSTRIAL RELATIONS

Bain, G. S., *The Growth of White Collar Unionism*, Oxford UP, 1970, 233 pp.
Blackburn, Robin and A. Cockburn, eds., *The Incompatibles: Trade Union Militancy and the Consensus*, Penguin, 1967, 281 pp.
Brown, E. H. Phelps, *The Growth of British Industrial Relations*, Macmillan, 1960, 451 pp.
Citrine, Lord, *Men and Work: Autobiography*, Hutchinson, London, 1964, 384 pp.
Clegg, H. A., *The System of Industrial Relations in Great Britain*, Blackwell, Oxford, 1970, 484 pp.
Fay, Stephen, *Measure for Measure: Reforming the Trade Unions*, Chatto & Windus, London, 1970, 131 pp.
Flanders, Allan, *Trade Unions*, 7th rev. ed., Hutchinson, London, 1968, 212 pp, pbk.
Goldthorpe, John H. et al., *The Affluent Worker in the Class Structure*, Cambridge UP, London, 1969, 246 pp, pbk.
Hobsbawn, Eric J., *Labouring Men: Studies in the History of Labour*, Weidenfeld & Nicolson, London, 1964, 401 pp.
Hughes, John, *The TUC: A Plan for the 1970's*, Fabian, London, 1969, 36 pp.
In Place of Strife: A Policy for Industrial Relations, Cmnd. 3888, HMSO, 1969.
Kilroy-Silk, Robert, "Legislating on Industrial Relations," *Parl. Aff.*, 22(3), Summer 1969:250–57.
Lowell, John and B. L. Roberts, *A Short History of the TUC*, Macmillan, 1968, 200 pp.
Paynter, Will, *British Trade Unions and the Problem of Change*, Allen & Unwin, London, 1970, 172 pp.
Pollard, Sidney, *Cooperatives at the Crossroads*, Fabian, London, 1965, 44 pp.
Report of the Royal Commission on Trade Unions and Employers' Associations 1965–68, Cmnd. 3623 (Donovan), HMSO, 1968.
Trades Union Congress, *Action on Donovan, Interim Statement by the TUC General Council Response to the Report of the Royal Commission on TU and Employment Associations*, TUC, London, 1968, 40 pp.
———, General Council, *Industrial Relations: Program for Action*, TUC, London, 1969.
Turner, Herbert A., *Is Britain Really Strike-Prone? A Review of the Incidence, Character and Costs of Industrial Conflict*, Cambridge UP, 1969, 48 pp.
Wigham, Eric L., *Trade Unions*, 2nd ed., Oxford UP, 1969, 189 pp.

Wilson, Charles, *Unilever, 1945–1965: Challenge and Response in the Post-War Industrial Revolution*, Cassell, London, 1968, 299 pp.
Zweig, Ferdynand, *The Worker in an Affluent Society: Family Life and Industry*, Heinemann, London, 1961, 268 pp.

8. PRESSURE GROUPS

Castles, F. G., *Pressure Groups and Political Culture: A Comparative Study*, Routledge, London, 1967, 112 pp, pbk.
Christoph, James B., *Capital Punishment and British Politics: The British Movement to Abolish the Death Penalty, 1955–1957*, Allen & Unwin, London, 1962, 202 pp.
Eckstein, Harry, *Pressure Group Politics: The Case of the British Medical Association*, Allen & Unwin, London, 1960, 168 pp.
Finer, S. E., *Anonymous Empire: A Study of the Lobby in Great Britain*, 2nd rev. ed., Pall Mall, London, 1966, 173 pp, pbk.
Howarth, Richard W., "The Political Strength of British Agriculture," *PS*, 17(4), Dec. 1969:458–69.
Moodie, G. C. and G. Studdert-Kennedy, *Opinions, Publics and Pressure Groups*, Allen & Unwin, London, 1970, 115 pp.
Potter, A. M., *Organised Groups in British National Politics*, Faber, London, 1961, 396 pp.
Roberts, G. K., *Political Parties and Pressure Groups in Britain*, Weidenfeld & Nicolson, London, 1970, 203 pp.
Self, Peter and Herbert J. Storing, *The State and the Farmer*, Allen & Unwin, London, 1962, 251 pp.
Stewart, J. D., *British Pressure Groups: Their Role in Relation to the House of Commons*, Oxford UP, 1958, 273 pp.
Swartz, Marvin, *The Union of Democratic Control in British Politics During the First World War*, Oxford UP, 1971, 281 pp.
Wilson, H. H., *Pressure Group: The Campaign for Commercial Television*, Secker & Warburg, London, 1961, 232 pp.
Wootton, Graham, *The Politics of Influence: British Ex-Servicemen, Cabinet Decisions and Cultural Change, 1917–1957*, Routledge, London, 1963, 301 pp.

9. PRESS, BROADCASTING, AND TELEVISION

Andrews, Sir Linton, *The Autobiography of a Journalist*, Benn, London, 1964, 262 pp.
Annual Reports and Accounts of the British Broadcasting Corporation, HMSO.
Annual Reports and Accounts of the Independent Television Authority, HMSO.
Ayerst, David, *Guardian: Biography of a Newspaper*, Collins, London, 1971, 702 pp.
BBC Handbook, BBC, London, published annually.
Blumler, Jay G. and Denis McQuail, *Television in Politics: Its Uses and Influence*, Faber, London, 1968, 379 pp.
Braddon, Russell, *Roy Thomson of Fleet Street*, Collins, London, 1965, 396 pp.
Briggs, Asa, *The History of Broadcasting in the United Kingdom*, Oxford UP, 3 vols: *The Birth of Broad-*

casting, 1961, 415 pp; *The Golden Age of Wireless*, 1965, 688 pp; *The War of Words*, 1970, 784 pp.

The British Broadcasting Corporation Act, Cmnd. 9138 and Cmnd. 9196, HMSO, 1954.

Cudlipp, Hugh, *At Your Peril*, Weidenfeld & Nicolson, London, 1963, 400 pp.

The "D" Notice System, Cmnd. 3312, HMSO, 1967, 16 pp. (Government reply to the Radcliffe Report)

Francis-Williams, Baron, *Nothing So Strange*, Cassell, London, 1970, 354 pp.

Gannon, Franklin R., *The British Press and Germany, 1936–39*, Oxford UP, 1971, 328 pp.

General Council of the Press, *Annual Reports*, since Oct. 1954, The Council, London.

Greene, Sir Hugh, *The Third Floor Front: A View of Broadcasting in the Sixties*, Bodley Head, London, 1969, 144 pp.

Halloran, James, Philip Elliott, and Graham Murdock, *Demonstrations and Communication: A Case Study*, Penguin Special, 1970, 334 pp.

Hedley, Peter and C. Aynsley, *The "D" Notice Affair*, Joseph, London, 1968, 144 pp.

Hopkinson, Tom, ed., *Picture Post, 1938–50*, Penguin, 1970, 288 pp, pbk.

Howard, Peter, *Beaverbrook: A Study of Max the Unknown*, Hutchinson, London, 1964, 164 pp.

Independent Television Authority, *ITV, A Guide to Independent Television*, ITA, 1970, 241 pp.

King, Cecil H., *Strictly Personal: Some Memoirs of Cecil H. King*, Weidenfeld & Nicolson, London, 1969, 240 pp.

———, *With Malice Toward None: A War Diary*, Sidgwick & Jackson, London, 1970, 343 pp.

Levy, Herman P., *The Press Council: History Procedure and Cases*, Macmillan, 1967, 505 pp.

McLachlan, Donald, *In the Chair: Barrington-Ward of the Times*, Weidenfeld & Nicolson, London, 1971, 319 pp.

Report of the Broadcasting Committee, 1949 (Beveridge Committee), Cmnd. 8116, HMSO, 1951, 327 pp.

Report of the Royal Commission on the Press, 1947–1949, Cmnd. 7700, HMSO, 1949, 363 pp.

Robson, W. A., ed., *The Political Quarterly in the Thirties*, Penguin, 1971, 250 pp, pbk.

Seymour-Ure, Colin, *The Press, Politics and the Public: An Essay on the Role of the National Press in the British Political System*, Methuen, London, 1968, 328 pp.

Trenaman, Joseph and Denis McQuail, *Television and the Political Image: A Study of the Impact of Television on the 1959 General Election*, Methuen, London, 1961, 287 pp.

Tunstall, Jeremy, *The Westminster Lobby Correspondents: A Sociological Study of National Political Journalism*, Routledge, London, 1970, 142 pp.

Wedell, Eberhard G., *Broadcasting and Public Policy*, Joseph, London, 1968, 370 pp.

———, *Structures of Broadcasting: A Symposium*, Manchester UP, 1970, 108 pp.

Whale, John, *The Half-Shut Eye: Television and Politics in Britain and America*, Macmillan, 1969, 219 pp.

Wilson, Trevor, ed., *The Political Diaries of C. P. Scott 1911–1928*, Collins, London, 1970, 509 pp.

Windlesham, Lord David, *Communication and Political Power*, Cape, London, 1966, 288 pp.

Chapter 2. THE BRITISH POLITICAL HERITAGE

1. HISTORY AND CONSTITUTION

Amery, Leopold, *Thoughts on the Constitution*, 2nd ed., Oxford UP, 1964, 195 pp, pbk.

Anson, Sir William R., *Law and Custom of the Constitution*, 4th ed., 2 vols, Oxford UP, 1922–35, 404 pp.

Bagehot, Walter, *The English Constitution*, Cornell UP, 1966, 310 pp.

Birch, A. H., *Representative and Responsible Government*, Allen & Unwin, London, 1964, 252 pp.

Blake, Robert, *Disraeli*, St. Martin's, 1966, 819 pp.

Brose, Olive J., *Church and Parliament: The Reshaping of the Church of England, 1828–1960*, Stanford UP, 1959, 239 pp.

Churchill, Sir Winston S., *The Great Democracies: A History of the English-Speaking Peoples*, Dodd, Mead, 4 vols: *The Birth of Britain* (to 1485), 1956, 521 pp; *The New World* (1485–1688), 1956, 433 pp; *The Age of Revolution* (1688–1815), 1957, 402 pp; *The Great Democracies* (1815–1900), 1958, 403 pp.

Clark, Sir George, *English History: A Survey*, Clarendon Press, Oxford, 1971, 567 pp.

Clarke, P. F., *Lancashire and the New Liberalism*, Cambridge UP, 1971, 481 pp.

Critchley, Thomas A., *The Conquest of Violence: Order and Liberty in Britain*, Constable, London, 1970, 226 pp.

Dicey, Albert V., *Introduction to the Study of the Law of the Constitution*, 10th ed., Macmillan, 1959, 837 pp, 1961, 535 pp, pbk.

Gregory, Roy, *The Miners and British Politics, 1906–1914*, Oxford UP, 1968, 215 pp.

Harvey, Jack and L. Bather, *The British Constitution*, St. Martin's, 1964, 572 pp.

Jennings, Sir Ivor, *The British Constitution*, 5th rev. ed., Cambridge UP, 1966, 210 pp, pbk.

———, *Magna Carta and Its Influence in the World Today*, HMSO, 1965, 43 pp.

Kidd, Ronald, *British Liberty in Danger: An Introduction to the Study of Civil Rights*, Lawrence & Wishart, London, 1941, 270 pp.

Maitland, Frederic W., *The Constitutional History of England*, Macmillan, 1961, 548 pp, pbk.

Marshall, Geoffrey and Graeme C. Moodie, *Some Problems of the Constitution*, rev. ed., Hutchinson, London, 1961, 201 pp.

Pallister, Anne, *Magna Charta: The Heritage of Liberty*, Oxford UP, 1971, 131 pp.

Pollard, Sidney, intro., *The Sheffield Outrages*, Adams & Dart, London, 1971, 468 pp.

Sedgwick, Romney, *The House of Commons, 1715–1754*, HMSO, 1970, 2 vols: I. 633 pp; II. 571 pp.

Smellie, Kingsley, *Great Britain Since 1688*, Michigan UP, 1964, 488 pp.

Smith, F. B., *The Making of the Second Reform Bill*, Cambridge UP, 1966, 297 pp.

Street, Harry, *Civil Liberties*, Pelican, 1964, 316 pp.
Taylor, Alan J. P., *English History, 1914–1945*, Oxford UP, 1965, 736 pp.
Thomson, David, *England in the Nineteenth Century, 1815–1914*, rev. ed., Penguin, 1964, 251 pp.
———, *England in the Twentieth Century*, Penguin, 1965, 304 pp.
Trevelyan, George M., *Illustrated History of England*, Longmans, London, 1956, 758 pp.
Vile, M. J. C., *Constitutionalism and the Separation of Powers*, Oxford UP, 1967, 359 pp.
Vincent, John, *The Formation of the Liberal Party 1875 to 1868*, Constable, London, 1966, 281 pp.
Williams, Lord Francis, *A Pattern of Rulers*, Longmans, London, 1965, 272 pp.
Woodward, E. L., *History of England*, Methuen, London,. 1948, 273 pp.

2. POLITICAL IDEAS

Anderson, Perry and Robin Blackburn, eds., *Towards Socialism*, Cornell UP, 1966, 397 pp.
Autobiography of John Stuart Mill, Dolphin, Oxford, 1962, 240 pp, pbk.
Bennett, George, ed., *The Concept of Empire: Burke to Attlee, 1774–1947*, Black, London, 1953, 434 pp.
Brinton, Crane, *English Political Thought in the Nineteenth Century*, Benn, London, 1933, 311 pp.
Cecil, Lord Hugh, *Conservatism*, Butterworth, London, 1912, 254 pp.
Coates, Ken, *The Crisis of British Socialism*, Spokesman, London, 1971.
Cobban, Alfred, *Edmund Burke and the Revolt Against the Eighteenth Century*, Allen & Unwin, London, 1960, 280 pp.
Cole, Margaret, *The Story of Fabian Socialism*, Stanford UP, 1962, 366 pp.
Davidson, W. L., *Political Thought in England, The Utilitarians from Bentham to J. S. Mill*, Oxford UP, 1947, 196 pp.
Fremantle, Anne, *This Little Band of Prophets: The British Fabians*, Mentor, 1960, 320 pp, pbk.
Gooch, G. P., *Political Thought in England: Bacon to Halifax*, Oxford UP, 1946, 108 pp.
Hearnshaw, F. J. C., *Conservatism in England: An Analytical, Historical and Political Survey*, Macmillan, 1935, 322 pp.
Hobhouse, Leonard T., *Liberalism*, Holt, 1911, 254 pp.
Hulse, James W., *Revolutionists in London: A Study of Five Unorthodox Socialists*, Oxford UP, London, 1970, 246 pp.
Kendall, Walter, *The Revolutionary Movement in Britain: 1900–21, The Origins of British Communism*, Weidenfeld & Nicolson, London, 1969, 465 pp.
Letwin, Shirley R., *The Pursuit of Certainty: David Hume, Jeremy Bentham, John Stuart Mill, Beatrice Webb*, Cambridge UP, 1965, 391 pp.
Lichtheim, George, *A Short History of Socialism*, Weidenfeld & Nicolson, London, 1970, 362 pp.
McDowell, R. R., *British Conservatism, 1832–1914*, Faber, London, 1960, 191 pp.
MacKenzie, Norman, *Socialism: A Short History*, Hutchinson, London, 1966, 192 pp, pbk.
Morris, C., *Political Thought in England: Tyndale to Hooker*, Oxford UP, 1953, 220 pp.
Plamenatz, J. P., *Consent, Freedom and Political Obligation*, 2nd ed., Oxford UP, 1968, 182 pp, pbk.
———, *The English Utilitarians*, Macmillan, 1949, 228 pp.
Thompson, Laurence, *The Enthusiasts*, Gollancz, London, 1971, 256 pp.
Tsuzuki, Chüshichi, *H. M. Hyndman and British Socialism*, Oxford UP, 1961, 304 pp.
Ulam, Adam B., *Philosophical Foundations of English Socialism*, Harvard UP, 1951, 173 pp.

Chapter 3. BRITISH PARTIES AND ELECTIONS

To obtain material on the British parties, the following addresses in the United Kingdom are useful:

Conservative Party: Conservative and Unionist Central Office, 32 Smith Square, Westminster, London, S.W. 1; Bow Group, 60 Berners Street, London, W. 1.
Labour Party: The Labour Party, Transport House, Smith Square, London, S.W. 1; Fabian Society, 11 Dartmouth Street, London, S.W. 1.
Liberal Party: The Liberal Party, 36 Smith Square, London, S.W. 1.

1. GENERAL

Beattie, Alan, ed., *English Party Politics and Society*, Vol. I: 1660–1906, Vol. II: 1906–1970, Weidenfeld & Nicolson, 1970, 219 pp, 638 pp, pbk.
Beer, Samuel H., *British Politics in the Collectivist Age*, Knopf, 1964, 384 pp.
Berry, David, *The Sociology of Grass Roots Politics: A Study of Party Membership*, St. Martin's, 1970, 155 pp.
Blondel, Jean, *Voters, Parties, and Leaders: The Social Fabric of British Politics*, Penguin, 1963, 272 pp, pbk.
Budge, Ian and D. W. Urwin, *Scottish Political Behaviour: A Case Study in British Homogeneity*, Barnes & Noble, 1966, 148 pp.
Bulmer-Thomas, Ivor, *The Growth of the British Party System*, Humanities Press, 1966, 2 vols: I, 344 pp; II, 328 pp.
———, *The Party System in Great Britain*, Macmillan, 1953, 328 pp.
Cross, Colin, *The Fascists in Britain*, St. Martin's, 1963, 214 pp.
Jackson, Robert J., *Rebels and Whips: An Analysis of Dissension, Discipline and Cohesion in British Political Parties Since 1945*, St. Martin's, 1968, 346 pp.
Jennings, Sir Ivor, *Party Politics*, Cambridge UP, 3 vols: *Appeal to the People*, 1960, 387 pp; *The Growth of Parties*, 1961, 404 pp; *The Stuff of Politics*, 1962, 504 pp.
King, Anthony, ed., *British Politics: People, Parties and Parliament*, Heath, 1966, 180 pp.
McKenzie, Robert T., *British Political Parties: The Distribution of Power Within the Conservative and Labour Parties*, 2nd ed., Praeger, 1963, 694 pp, pbk.
Mayhew, Christopher, *Party Games*, Hutchinson, London, 1969, 176 pp.

Pulzer, Peter G. J., *Political Representation and Elections: Parties and Voting in Great Britain*, Praeger, 1968, 168 pp.

Thayer, George, *The British Political Fringe*, Blond, London, 1965, 256 pp.

2. CONSERVATIVE PARTY

Birch, Nigel, *The Conservative Party*, Collins, London, 1949, 49 pp.

Blake, R., *The Conservative Party from Peel to Churchill*, Eyre & Spottiswoode, London, 1970, 317 pp.

Dickie, John, *The Uncommon Commoner: A Study of Sir Alec Douglas-Home*, Praeger, 1964, 224 pp.

Hailsham, Viscount (Quintin M. Hogg), *The Conservative Case*, Penguin, 1959, 176 pp.

Hoffman, J. D., *The Conservative Party in Opposition, 1945–51*, MacGibbon & Kee, London, 1964, 288 pp.

McKenzie, Robert and Allan Silver, *Angels in Marble: Working Class Conservatives in Urban England*, Heinemann, London, 1968, 295 pp.

Maude, A., *The Common Problem*, Constable, London, 1969, 307 pp.

Nordlinger, Eric A., *The Working Class Tories: Authority, Deference, and Stable Democracy*, California UP, 1967, 276 pp.

Petrie, Sir Charles, *The Carlton Club*, Eyre & Spottiswoode, London, 1955, 221 pp.

Raison, Timothy, *Why Conservative?* Penguin, 1964, 144 pp.

Roth, Andrew, *Enoch Powell: Tory Tribune*, Macdonald, London, 1970, 393 pp.

Sparrow, Gerald, *Rab, Study of a Statesman: The Career of Baron Butler of Saffron Walden*, Odhams, London, 1965, 253 pp.

Thomson, Neville, *Silent Minority*, Oxford UP, 1971, 256 pp.

Utley, T. E., *Enoch Powell: The Man and His Thinking*, Kimber, London, 1968, 190 pp.

White, Reginald James, ed., *The Conservative Tradition*, 2nd ed., Black, London, 1964, 256 pp.

3. LABOR PARTY

Abrams, Mark and Richard Rose, *Must Labour Lose?* Penguin, 1960, 127 pp.

Attlee, Clement Richard, 1st Earl, *The Labour Party in Perspective, and Twelve Years Later*, Longmans, London, 1949, 199 pp.

Bealey, Frank, ed., *The Social and Political Thought of the British Labour Party*, Weidenfeld & Nicolson, London, 1970, 233 pp.

Brand, Carl F., *The British Labour Party: A Short History*, Stanford UP, 1964, 340 pp.

Briggs, Asa and John Saville, eds., *Essays in Labour History, 1886–1923*, Macmillan, 1971, 368 pp.

Burgess, Tyrell, *Matters of Principle: Labour's Last Chance*, Penguin, 1968, 128 pp, pbk.

"Cassandra" (William Connor), *George Brown: A Profile*, Pergamon, London, 1964, 96 pp.

Collins, Henry and Chimer Abramsky, *Karl Marx and the British Labour Movement: Years of the First International*, Macmillan, 1965, 356 pp.

Cowling, Maurice, *The Impact of Labour, 1920–1924*, Cambridge UP, 1971, 579 pp.

Crosland, C. A. R., *The Conservative Enemy: A Programme of Radical Reform for the 1960's*, Cape, London, 1963, 251 pp.

Crossman, Richard H. S., ed., *New Fabian Essays*, republ. with new intro., Dent, London, 1970, 215 pp.

——, *The Politics of Socialism*, Atheneum, 1965, 252 pp.

Fabian Essays in Socialism, 6th ed., Allen & Unwin, London, 1962, 322 pp.

Gregory, Roy, *The Miners and British Politics: 1906–1914*, Oxford UP, 1969, 215 pp.

Hall, Peter Geoffrey, *Labour's New Frontiers*, Deutsche, London, 1964, 180 pp, pbk.

Harrison, Martin, *Trade Unions and the Labour Party Since 1945*, Wayne State UP, 1960, 360 pp.

Howard, Anthony and Richard West, *The Road to Number 10*, Macmillan, 1965, 317 pp.

Janosik, E. G., *Constituency Labour Parties in Britain*, Pall Mall, London, 1968, 222 pp.

Jay, Douglas, *Socialism in the New Society*, Longmans, London, 1962, 358 pp.

Jenkins, Roy, *The Labour Case*, Penguin, 1959, 146 pp.

Labour Party, *Bibliography of Labour Party Publications*, London, 1968, 95 pp.

Middlemas, Robert Keith, *The Clydesiders: A Left Wing Struggle for Parliamentary Power*, Hutchinson, London, 1965, 307 pp.

Miliband, Ralph, *Parliamentary Socialism: A Study in the Politics of the Labour Party*, Merlin, London, 1964, 356 pp, pbk.

Northcott, Jim, *Why Labour?* Penguin, 1964, 192 pp.

Phillips, Morgan, *Labour in the Sixties*, Labour Party, London, 1960, 24 pp.

Poirier, Philip P., *The Advent of the British Labour Party*, Columbia UP, 1958, 288 pp.

Rodgers, W. T., ed., *Hugh Gaitskell 1906–1963*, Thames & Hudson, London, 1964, 167 pp.

—— and Bernard Donoughue, *The People into Parliament: A Concise History of the Labour Movement in Britain*, Viking, 1966, 191 pp.

Tawney, R. H., *The Radical Tradition*, Allen & Unwin, London, 1964, 240 pp.

Towards Socialism: Essays, Fontana Lib., 1965, 397 pp, pbk.

Worsthorne, Peregrine, *The Socialist Myth*, Cassell, London, 1971, 256 pp.

Young, James D., "A Survey of Some Recent Literature on the Labour Movement," *PQ*, 39(2), Apr–June 1968:205–14.

4. LIBERAL PARTY

Butler, Jeffrey, *The Liberal Party and the Jameson Raid*, Oxford UP, 1968, 336 pp.

Cowie, Harry, *Why Liberal?* Penguin, 1964, 155 pp.

Cross, Colin, *The Liberals in Power, 1905–1914*, Barrie & Rockliff, London, 1963, 198 pp.

Douglas, Roy, *The History of the Liberal Party, 1895–1970*, Sidgwick and Jackson, London, 1971, 331 pp, pbk.

Foord, A. S., "Whigs into Liberals," *Gov. & Opp.*, 3(2), Spring 1968:243–48.

Fulford, Roger, *The Liberal Case*, Penguin, 1959, 175 pp.
Grimond, Joseph, *The Liberal Challenge: Democracy Through Participation*, Hollis & Carter, London, 1965, 320 pp.
Rasmussen, Jorgen S., *Retrenchment and Revival: A Study of the Contemporary British Liberal Party*, Arizona UP, 1964, 285 pp.
Vincent, John, *The Formation of the Liberal Party, 1857–1868*, Constable, 1966, 316 pp.
Watkins, Alan, *The Liberal Dilemma*, MacGibbon & Kee, London, 1966, 158 pp.
Watson, George, ed., *Radical Alternative: Essays in Liberalism by the Oxford Liberal Group*, Eyre & Spottiswoode, London, 1962, 190 pp.
Wilson, Trevor, *The Downfall of the Liberal Party, 1914–1935*, Cornell UP, 1966, 416 pp.

5. COMMUNIST PARTY

Darke, Bob, *The Communist Technique in Britain*, Penguin, 1952, 159 pp.
Gallacher, William, *The Case for Communism*, Penguin, 1949, 208 pp.
MacFarlane, L. J., *The British Communist Party: Its Origin and Development Until 1929*, MacGibbon & Kee, London, 1966, 338 pp.
Martin, Roderick, *Communism and the British Trade Union, 1924–1933: A Study of the National Minority Movement*, Clarendon Press, Oxford, 1969, 209 pp.
Newton, Kenneth, *The Sociology of British Communism*, Allen Lane, 1969, 214 pp.
Pelling, Henry, *The British Communist Party: A Historical Profile*, Macmillan, 1958, 204 pp.
Wood, Neal, *Communism and British Intellectuals*, Columbia UP, 1959, 256 pp.

6. ELECTIONS

Allen, A. J., *The English Voter*, English UP, London, 1964, 258 pp, pbk.
Bealey, Frank, J. Blondel, and W. P. McCann, *Constituency Politics: A Study of Newcastle-Under-Lyme*, Faber, London, 1965, 440 pp.
Benney, Mark et al., *How People Vote: A Study of Electoral Behaviour in Greenwich*, Routledge, London, 1956, 227 pp.
Birch, A. H., *Small-Town Politics, A Study of Political Life in Glossop*, Oxford UP, 1959, 199 pp.
Bonham, John, *The Middle Class Vote*, Faber, London, 1954, 210 pp.
Butler, David E., *The British General Election of 1951*, Macmillan, 1952, 288 pp.
——, *The British General Election of 1955*, Macmillan, 1956, 236 pp.
——, *The Electoral System in Britain Since 1918*, 2nd ed., Clarendon Press, Oxford, 1963, 232 pp.
—— and Anthony King, *The British General Election of 1964*, St. Martin's, 1965, 410 pp.
—— and Anthony King, *The British General Election of 1966*, St. Martin's, 1967, 320 pp.
—— and Michael Pinto-Duschinsky, *The British General Election of 1970*, St. Martin's, 1971, 493 pp.
Butler, David E. and Richard Rose, *The British General Election of 1959*, St. Martin's, 1960, 203 pp.
—— and Donald Stokes, *Political Change in Britain: Factors Shaping Electoral Choice*, St. Martin's, 1969, 516 pp.
Campbell, Angus et al., *Elections and the Political Order*, Wiley, 1966, 385 pp.
Comfort, George O., *Professional Politicians: A Study of British Party Agents*, Pub. Aff., 1958, 69 pp.
Conclusions on Review of the Law Relating to Parliamentary Elections, Cmnd. 3717, HMSO, 1968. (Labor government proposals)
Conference on Electoral Law: Final Report, Cmnd. 3550, HMSO, 1968.
Craig, F. W. S., ed., *British General Election Manifestos 1918–1966*, Pol. Ref. Pubs., London, 1970, 303 pp.
——, comp. and ed., *British Parliamentary Election Results*, Vol. I. 1918–1949, Pol. Ref. Pubs., London, 1969, 760 pp.
——, ed., *British Parliamentary Election Statistics 1918–1970*, Pol. Ref. Pubs., 1971, 110 pp.
Daudt, H., *Floating Voters and the Floating Vote: A Critical Analysis of American and English Election Studies*, Stenfert Kroise, N.V., Leyden, 1961, 171 pp.
Deakin, Nicholas and Jenny Bourne, "Powell, The Minorities, and the 1970 Election," *PQ*, 41(4), Oct–Dec. 1970:399–415.
Fletcher, Peter, "An Explanation of Variations in 'Turnout' in Local Elections," *PS*, 17(4), Dec. 1969: 495–502.
Fulford, R., *Votes for Women: The Story of a Struggle*, Faber, London, 1957, 343 pp.
Hanham, H. J., *Elections and Party Management*, Longmans, London, 1959, 485 pp.
Hodder-Williams, Richard, *Public Opinion Polls and British Politics*, Routledge, London, 1970, 103 pp.
Holt, Robert T. and John E. Turner, *Political Parties in Action: The Battle of Barons Court*, Collier-Macmillan, 1968, 311 pp.
Kavanagh, Dennis, *Constituency Electioneering in Britain*, Longmans, London, 1970, 118 pp.
Kinnear, Michael, *The British Voter: An Atlas and Survey Since 1885*, Cornell UP, 1968, 160 pp.
Leonard, R., *Elections in Britain*, Van Nostrand, 1968, 192 pp.
McCallum, Ronald B. and Alison Readman, *The British General Election of 1945*, Oxford UP, 1947, 311 pp.
McKie, David and Chris Cook, *Election '70*, The Guardian/Panther, London, 1971, 204 pp.
Martin, Laurence W., "The Bournemouth Affair: Britain's First Primary Election," *JP*, 22(4), Nov. 1960:654–81.
Milne, R. S. and H. C. MacKenzie, *Marginal Seat, 1955: A Study of Voting Behaviour in the Constituency of Bristol North-East at the General Election of 1955*, Hansard, London, 1958, 210 pp.
——, *Straight Fight: A Study of Voting Behaviour in the Constituency of Bristol North-East at the General Election of 1951*, Hansard, London, 1954, 174 pp.
Mitchell, Brian R. and Klaus Boehm, *British Parlia-*

mentary Election Results, 1950–1964, Cambridge UP, 1966, 135 pp.
Nicholas, H. G., The British General Election of 1950, Macmillan, 1951, 353 pp.
1966 Census: General and Parliamentary Constituency Tables, HMSO, 1970.
O'Leary, Cornelius, The Elimination of Corrupt Practices in British Elections, 1868–1911, Oxford UP, 1962, 262 pp.
Paterson, P., The Selectorate, MacGibbon & Kee, London, 1967, 190 pp.
Ranney, Austin, Pathways to Parliament: Candidate Selection in Britain, Wisconsin UP, 1965, 298 pp.
Report of the Committee on the Age of Majority. (Latey), Cmnd. 3342, HMSO, 1967.
Rose, Richard, Influencing Voters: A Study of Campaign Rationality, Faber, London, 1967, 288 pp.
———, ed., The Polls and the 1970 Election, Strathclyde UP, 1971, 67 pp.
Rush, Michael, The Selection of Parliamentary Candidates, Nelson, London, 1969, 307 pp.
Sharpe, Laurence J., ed., Voting in Cities: The 1964 Borough Elections, Macmillan, 1967, 356 pp.
Trenaman, Joseph and D. McQuail, Television and the Political Image: A Study of the Impact of Television on the 1959 General Election, Methuen, London, 1961, 287 pp.
Wood, J., Powell and the 1970 Election, Elliott Right Way Books, London, 1970, 125 pp.

Chapter 4. THE BRITISH PARLIAMENT

Abraham, L. A. and S. C. Hawtrey, A Parliamentary Dictionary, 2nd ed., Butterworth, London, 1965, 241 pp.
Adams, John Clarke, The Quest for Democratic Law: The Role of Parliament in the Legislative Process, Crowell, 1970, 241 pp.
Advisory Committees in British Government: A PEP Report, Allen & Unwin, London, 1960, 228 pp.
Aitken, Jonathan, Officially Secret, Weidenfeld & Nicolson, London, 1971.
Barker, Anthony and Michael Rush, The Member of Parliament and His Information, Allen & Unwin, London, 1970, 443 pp.
Berkeley, Humphry, Crossing the Floor, Allen & Unwin, London, 1971.
Birt, Phyllis and Harry Mitchell, comps., Who Does What in Parliament? Mitchell and Birt, London, 1971, 63 pp. (quarterly)
Bossom, Alfred C., Lord Bossom of Maidstone, Our House: An Introduction to Parliamentary Procedure, rev. ed., Barrie-Rockliff, London, 1965, 207 pp, pbk.
Boulton, C. J., "Recent Developments in House of Commons Procedure," PA, 23(1), Winter 1969–70: 61–71.
Bromhead, Peter A., The House of Lords and Contemporary Politics, 1911–1957, Routledge, London, 1958, 283 pp.
———, Private Members' Bills in the British Parliament, Routledge, London, 1956, 216 pp.
——— and Donald Shell, "The Lords and Their House," PA, 20(4), Autumn 1967:37–49.
Butt, Ronald, The Power of Parliament, Constable, London, 1967, 468 pp.

Campion, Lord, An Introduction to the Procedure of the House of Commons, 3rd ed., St. Martin's, 1958, 350 pp.
Cawthorne, Graham, Mr. Speaker, Sir, Cleaver-Hume, London, 1952, 164 pp.
Chester, D. N. and Nona Bowring, Questions in Parliament, Oxford UP, 1962, 335 pp.
Chubb, Basil, The Control of Public Expenditure: Financial Committees of the House of Commons, Oxford UP, 1952, 291 pp.
Cocks, Sir Barnett, ed., Erskine May's Parliamentary Practice, 18th ed., Butterworth, London, 1971, 1,108 pp.
Conference on the Reform of the Second Chamber, 1918 (The Bryce Report), Cmnd. 9038, HMSO, 1918.
Coombes, David, The Member of Parliament and the Administration: The Case of the Select Committee on Nationalized Industries, Allen & Unwin, London, 1966, 221 pp.
Crick, Bernard, The Reform of Parliament, rev. ed., Weidenfeld & Nicolson, London, 1968, 325 pp.
Denning, Lord, The Profumo-Christine Keeler Affair: Report to Parliament, Popular Lib., 1963, 174 pp, pbk.
Eaves, John, Jr., Emergency Powers and the Parliamentary Watchdog: Parliament and the Executive in Great Britain, 1939–1951, Hansard, London, 1957, 208 pp.
Finer, S. E., H. B. Bennington, and D. V. Bartholomew, Backbench Opinion in the House of Commons, 1955–1959, Pergamon, London, 1961, 219 pp.
Ford, P. and G. Ford, A Breviate of Parliamentary Papers, Blackwell, Oxford. 3 vols: The Foundation of the Welfare State, 1900–1916, 1957, 470 pp; Inter-War Period, 1917–1939, 1951, 571 pp; War and Reconstruction, 1940–1954, 1961, 515 pp.
Ford, P. and G. Ford, A Guide to Parliamentary Papers: What They Are, How to Find Them, How to Use Them, new ed., Blackwell, Oxford, 1956, 79 pp.
———, Select List of British Parliamentary Papers, 1833–1899, Blackwell, Oxford, 1953, 165 pp.
Frasure, Robert C., "Constituency, Racial Composition and the Attitudes of British MP's," Comp. Pol., 3(2), Jan. 1971:201–10.
Friedmann, Karl A., "Commons, Complaints and the Ombudsman," PA, 21(1), Winter 1967–68:38–47.
Gordon, Strathearn, Our Parliament, 6th ed., Cassell, London, 1964, 256 pp.
Hanson, A. H., Parliament and Public Ownership, Cassell, London, 1961, 248 pp.
——— and Bernard Crick, eds., The Commons in Transition, Collins, London, 1970, 304 pp, pbk.
Hazlehurst, Cameron, Politicians At War: July, 1914, to May, 1915, Cape, London, 1971, 346 pp.
Heasman, D. J., "Parliamentary Paths to High Office," Parl. Aff., 16(3), Summer 1963:315–30.
Herbert, Sir Alan P., The Ayes Have It, Methuen, London, 1937, 240 pp.
———, Independent Member, Doubleday, 1951, 363 pp.
Hill, Andrew and Anthony Wichelow, What's Wrong with Parliament? Penguin, 1964, 102 pp.

House of Commons, issued after each election, *The Times*, London.
House of Commons, *Select Committee on Broadcasting: First Report*, HC 146, HMSO, 1966, 184 pp.
House of Lords Reform, Cmnd. 3799, HMSO, 1968, 36 pp.
Howarth, Patrick, *Questions in the House: The History of a Unique British Institution*, Lane, London, 1956, 220 pp.
Humberstone, Thomas L., *University Representation*, Hutchinson, London, 1951, 128 pp.
Irving, Clive, Ron Hall, and Jeremy Wallington, *Scandal '63: A Study of the Profumo Affair*, Heinemann, London, 1963, 227 pp, pbk.
Jennings, Sir Ivor, *Parliament*, 2nd ed., Cambridge UP, 1959, 587 pp.
Johnson, Donald, *A Cassandra at Westminster*, Johnson, London, 1967, 239 pp.
Johnson, Nevil, *Parliament and Administration: The Estimates Committee, 1945–1965*, Allen & Unwin, London, 1967, 200 pp.
Justice, *The Citizen and the Administration: The Redress of Grievances* (The Whyatt Report), Stevens, London, 1961, 104 pp.
Kersell, John E., *Parliamentary Supervision of Delegated Legislation*, Stevens, London, 1960, 178 pp.
King, Horace M., *Before Hansard*, Dent, London, 1968, 114 pp.
———, *Parliament and Freedom*, new ed., Murray, London, 1962, 144 pp.
Laundy, Philip, *The Office of Speaker*, Cassell, London, 1964, 488 pp.
Lee, J. M., "Select Committees and the Constitution," *PQ*, 41(2), Apr–June 1970:182–94.
Lindsay, T. F., *Parliament From the Press Gallery*, Macmillan, 1967, 176 pp.
Mann, Jean, *Women in Parliament*, Odhams, London, 1962, 256 pp.
Manual of Procedure in Public Business, 8th ed., HMSO, 1951 (only official work on parliamentary procedure).
Marsden, Philip, *The Officers of the Commons, 1363–1965*, Barrie & Rockliff, London, 1966, 240 pp.
Menhennet, David and John Palmer, *Parliament in Perspective*, Bodley Head, London, 1967, 156 pp.
Morris, Alfred, ed., *The Growth of Parliamentary Scrutiny by Committee*, Pergamon, London, 1970, 156 pp.
Morrison, Lord of Lambeth, Herbert Stanley, *Government and Parliament: A Survey from the Inside*, 3rd ed., Oxford UP, 1964, 384 pp, pbk.
Palmer, John, *Government and Parliament in Britain: A Bibliography*, 2nd rev. ed. and enl., Hansard, London, 1964, 51 pp.
Parliamentary Commissioner for Administration, *Papers on Work since 1967*, HMSO, 1968.
Parliamentary Reforms, *A Survey of Suggested Reforms Covering the Period from 1933–1966*, 2nd ed., Cassell, London, 1968, 208 pp.
"Reforming the Commons by Members of the Study of Parliament Group," *Planning*, 31(491), Oct. 1965: 271–310.
Reid, Gordon, *The Politics of Financial Control: The Role of the House of Commons*, Hutchinson, London, 1966, 176 pp, pbk.
Richards, Peter G., *Honourable Members: A Study of the British Backbencher*, new ed., Faber, London, 1964, 294 pp.
———, *Parliament and Conscience*, Allen & Unwin, London, 1970, 229 pp.
———, *Parliament and Foreign Affairs*, Allen & Unwin, London, 1967, 191 pp.
Roth, Andrew, *The Business Background of MPs: Parliamentary Profiles*, Parl. Profile Serv., London, 1967, 412 pp.
———, *Can Parliament Decide—About Europe or About Anything?* Macdonald, London, 1971.
Rowat, Donald C., *The Ombudsman*, 2nd ed., Allen & Unwin, London, 1968, 384 pp, pbk.
Taylor, Eric, *The House of Commons at Work*, 7th ed., Penguin, 1967, 256 pp.
Walkland, S. A., *The Legislative Process in Great Britain*, Allen & Unwin, London, 1968, 109 pp, pbk.
Weston, Corime C., *English Constitutional Theory and the House of Lords*, Routledge, London, 1965, 304 pp.
Wheare, Kenneth C., *Government by Committee: An Essay on the British Constitution*, Oxford UP, 1955, 264 pp.
Winterton, Lord, *Orders of the Day*, Cassell, London, 1954, 369 pp.
Wiseman, H. V., *Parliament and the Executive: An Analysis with Readings*, Routledge, London, 1966, 271 pp, pbk.
Wymer, Norman G., *Behind the Scenes in Parliament*, Phoenix, London, 1966, 95 pp.
Young, Roland, *The British Parliament*, Faber, London, 1962, 259 pp.
Young, Wayland, *The Profumo Affair: Aspects of Conservatism*, Penguin, 1963, 117 pp.

Chapter 5. THE BRITISH CABINET, PRIME MINISTER, AND MONARCH

1. CABINET AND PRIME MINISTER

Alexander, Andrew and Alan Watkins, *The Making of the Prime Minister 1970*, Macdonald, London, 1970, 218 pp.
Attlee, Clement R., *As It Happened*, Heinemann, London, 1954, 227 pp.
Baldwin, A. W., *My Father: The True Story*, Essential, London, 1956, 360 pp.
Bardens, Dennis, *Portrait of a Statesman: The Personal Life Story of Sir Anthony Eden*, Phil. Lib., 1956, 326 pp.
Benemy, F. W. G., *The Elected Monarch: The Development of the Power of the Prime Minister*, Harrap, London, 1965, 284 pp.
Berkeley, Humphry, *The Power of the Prime Minister*, Allen & Unwin, London, 1968, 128 pp.
Brown, R. Douglas, *The Battle of Crichel Down*, Lane, London, 1955, 192 pp.
Bullock, Alan C., *The Life and Times of Ernest Bevin*, Heinemann, London, 2 vols: *Trade Union Leader 1881–1940*, 1960, 685 pp; Vol. II., 1967, 407 pp.
Butler, R. A., *The Art of the Possible: The Memoirs of Lord Butler*, Hamish Hamilton, London, 1971, 288 pp.

Campbell-Johnson, Alan, *Sir Anthony Eden: A Biography*, McGraw-Hill, 1955, 272 pp.

Carlton, David, *MacDonald versus Henderson*, Macmillan, 1970, 239 pp.

Carter, Byrum E., *The Office of Prime Minister*, Princeton UP, 1956, 364 pp.

Carter, Lady Violet Bonham, *Winston Churchill: An Intimate Portrait*, Harcourt Brace Jovanovich, 1965, 413 pp.

Churchill, Randolph S., *Winston S. Churchill*, Houghton, 2 vols with companion documents: *Youth: 1874–1900*, 1967, 614 pp, 2 companion volumes, 1967, 1,290 pp; *Young Statesman: 1901–1914*, 1967, 775 pp, 3 companion volumes, 1968, 2,159 pp.

Citrine, Walter, McLennan, 1st Baron Citrine, *Memoirs*, Hutchinson, London, 2 vols: *Men at Work*, 1964, 384 pp; *Two Careers*, 1967, 384 pp.

Cross, Colin, *The Eloquent Conventionalist: Philip Snowden*, Barrie & Rockliff, London, 1966, 366 pp.

Cross, J. A. and R. K. Alderman, *The Tactics of Resignation*, Routledge, London, 1967, 88 pp, pbk.

Daalder, Hans, *Cabinet Reform in Britain, 1914–1963*, Stanford UP, 1963, 381 pp.

Dalton, Hugh, *Memoirs*, Muller, London, 3 vols: *Call Back Yesterday, 1887–1931*, 1953, 330 pp; *The Fateful Years, 1931–1945*, 1957, 493 pp; *High Tide and After, 1945–1960*, 1962, 453 pp.

De'ath, Wilfred, *Barbara Castle: A Portrait from Life*, Clifton Books, Brighton, 1970, 126 pp.

Dilks, David, ed., *The Diaries of Sir Alexander Cadogan, 1938–1948*, Cassell, London, 1971.

Eden, Sir Anthony (Earl of Avon), *Memoirs*, Houghton Mifflin, 2 vols: *Full Circle, 1951–1957*, 1960, 676 pp; *The Reckoning*, 1965, 704 pp.

Ehrman, John, *Cabinet Government and War, 1890–1940*, Cambridge UP, 1958, 138 pp.

Feiling, Keith, *The Life of Neville Chamberlain*, Macmillan, 1946, 475 pp.

Foot, Paul, *The Politics of Harold Wilson*, Penguin, 1968, 347 pp, pbk.

Fry, Geoffrey K., "Thoughts on the Present State of the Convention of Ministerial Responsibility," PA, 23(1), Winter 1969–70:10–20.

George-Brown, Lord, *In My Way: The Political Memoirs*, Gollancz, London, 1971, 299 pp.

Gilbert, Martin, *Winston Churchill*, Vol. III. *1914–1916*, Heinemann, London, 1971, 1,025 pp.

Great Britain, Public Record Office, "The Records of the Cabinet Office to 1922," HMSO, 1966 (Public Record Office Handbook no. 11), 60 pp.

Halifax, Earl of, *Fullness of Days*, Collins, London, 1957, 319 pp.

Heath, Edward, *Old World, New Horizons: Britain, Europe, and the Atlantic Alliance*, Harvard UP, 1970, 128 pp.

Hughes, Emrys, *Macmillan: Portrait of a Politician*, Allen & Unwin, London, 1962, 256 pp.

Hutchinson, George, *Edward Heath: A Personal and Political Biography*, Longmans, London, 1970, 229 pp.

James, Robert R., *Churchill: A Study in Failure 1900–1939*, Weidenfeld & Nicolson, London, 1970, 387 pp.

James, Robert R., *Roseberg*, Weidenfeld & Nicolson, London, 1963, 548 pp.

Jenkins, Peter, *The Battle of Downing Street*, Charles Knight, London, 1970, 185 pp, pbk.

Jenkins, Roy, *Asquith: Portrait of a Man and an Era*, Collins, London, 1964, 572 pp.

———, *Mr. Attlee*, Heinemann, London, 1948, 266 pp.

Jennings, Sir Ivor, *Cabinet Government*, 3rd ed., Cambridge UP, 1959, 587 pp.

Jones, Thomas, *A Diary with Letters, 1931–1950*, Oxford UP, 1954, 582 pp.

———, *Lloyd George*, Harvard UP, 1951, 330 pp.

———, *Whitehall Diary*, ed. Keith Middlemas, Oxford UP, 2 vols: I. *1916–1925*, 1969, 382 pp; II. *1926–1930*, 1969, 324 pp.

King, Anthony, ed., *The British Prime Minister: A Reader*, Macmillan, 1969, 221 pp.

King, Mark M., *Aneurin Bevin: Cautious Rebel*, Yoseloff, London, 1961, 316 pp.

Lowenstein, Karl, *British Cabinet Government*, trans. Roger Evans, Oxford UP, 1967, 396 pp, pbk.

Mackintosh, John P., *The British Cabinet*, 2nd ed., Methuen, London, 1968, 651 pp, pbk.

———, "The Prime Minister and the Cabinet," *Parl. Aff.*, 21(1), Winter 1967–68:53–68.

Macleod, Iain, *Neville Chamberlain*, Atheneum, 1962, 319 pp.

Macmillan, Harold, *Memoirs*, Harper, 4 vols: *Winds of Change 1914–1930*, 1966, 584 pp; *The Blast of War 1939–1945*, 1968, 623 pp; *Tides of Fortune 1945–1955*, 1969, 749 pp; *Riding the Storm 1956–1959*, 1971, 686 pp.

Middlemas, Keith and John Barnes, *Baldwin: A Biography*, Weidenfeld & Nicolson, London, 1969, 1,116 pp.

Morrison, Herbert, Lord of Lambeth, *An Autobiography*, Odhams, London, 1960, 336 pp.

Mosley, Richard K., *The Story of the Cabinet Office*, Routledge, London, 1969, 94 pp.

Nicolson, Sir Harold G., *Curzon: The Last Phase, 1919–1925*, Harcourt Brace Jovanovich, 1939, 416 pp.

Nicolson, Nigel, ed., *Harold Nicolson: Diaries and Letters*, Atheneum, London, 3 vols: I. *1930–1939*, 1966, 446 pp; II. *1939–1945*, 1967, 511 pp; III. *1945–1962*, 1968, 448 pp.

Noel, G. E., *Harold Wilson and the "New Britain," The Making of a Modern Prime Minister*, Gollancz, London, 1964, 143 pp.

Norwich, Alfred Duff Cooper, Viscount, *Old Men Forget: An Autobiography*, Hart-Davis, London, 1953, 399 pp.

Owen, Frank, *Tempestuous Journey: Lloyd George, His Life and Times*, McGraw-Hill, 1955, 756 pp.

Red, Bruce and Geoffrey Williams, *Dennis Healey and the Policies of Power*, Sidgwick & Jackson, London, 1971, 288 pp.

Report of the Machinery of Government Committee (Haldane), Cmnd. 9230, HMSO, 1918.

Robbins, Keith, *Sir Edward Grey: A Biography of Lord Grey of Fallodon*, Cassell, London, 1971, 438 pp.

Roskill, Stephen, *Hankey: Man of Secrets*, Vol. I. *1877–1918*, Collins, London, 1970, 672 pp.

Sampson, Anthony, *Macmillan: A Study in Ambiguity*, Penguin, 1968, 271 pp.
Shrimsley, Anthony, *The First Hundred Days of Harold Wilson*, Praeger, 1965, 162 pp.
Skidelsky, Robert, *Politicians and the Slump: The Labour Government of 1929–1931*, Humanities Press, 1967, 431 pp.
Smith, Dudley, *Harold Wilson: A Critical Biography*, Hale, London, 1964, 224 pp.
Smith, Leslie, *Harold Wilson: The Authentic Portrait*, Scribner's, 1965, 231 pp.
Southgate, Donald, "The Most English Prime Minister," *The Policies and Politics of Palmerston*, Macmillan, 1966, 647 pp.
Stevenson, Frances, *Lloyd George: A Diary*, Hutchinson, London, 1971, 338 pp.
Taylor, Alan J. P., ed., *Lloyd George: Twelve Essays*, Hamish Hamilton, London, 1971, 393 pp.
Turner, Duncan R., *The Shadow Cabinet in British Politics*, Routledge, London, 1969, 106 pp.
Walker, Patrick G., *The Cabinet*, Cape, London, 1970, 190 pp.
Williams, Sir Francis, *A Prime Minister Remembers: The War and Post-War Memoirs of the Rt. Hon. Earl Attlee*, Heinemann, London, 1961, 264 pp.
Wilson, Harold, *The Labour Government 1964–1970: A Personal Record*, Weidenfeld & Nicolson, London, 1971, 855 pp.
———, *The New Britain, Labour's Plan: Selected Speeches 1964*, Penguin, 1964, 134 pp.
———, *Purpose in Politics: Selected Speeches, 1956–1963*, Weidenfeld & Nicolson, London, 1964, 270 pp.
———, *The Relevance of British Socialism*, Weidenfeld & Nicolson, London, 1964, 115 pp.
Young, Kenneth, *Arthur James Balfour*, Bell, London, 1963, 542 pp.
———, *Churchill and Beaverbrook: A Study in Friendship and Politics*, Eyre & Spottiswoode, London, 1966, 349 pp.
———, *Sir Alec Douglas-Home*, Dent, London, 1970, 282 pp.

2. THE MONARCHY

Beaverbrook, Lord, *The Abdication of King Edward VIII*, ed. Allan J. P. Taylor, Hamilton, London, 1966, 122 pp.
Benemy, F. W. G., *The Queen Reigns, She Does Not Rule*, Harrap, London, 1963, 182 pp.
Boothroyd, Basil, *Philip*, Longmans, London, 1971, 238 pp.
Duncan, Andrew, *The Reality of Monarchy*, Heinemann, London, 1970, 387 pp.
Hardie, Frank, *The Political Influence of the British Monarchy, 1868–1952*, Batsford, London, 1970, 224 pp.
Magnus, Philip, *King Edward the Seventh*, Dutton, 1964, 528 pp.
Martin, Kingsley, *The Crown and the Establishment*, rev. ed., Penguin, 1965, 192 pp.
Morrah, Dermont, *The Work of the Queen*, Kimber, London, 1958, 191 pp.
Murray-Brown, Jeremy, ed., *The Monarchy and the Future*, Allen & Unwin, London, 1969, 227 pp.

Nicolson, Sir Harold G., *King George the Fifth: His Life and Reign*, Doubleday, 1953, 570 pp.
———, *Monarchy*, Weidenfeld & Nicolson, London, 1962, 335 pp.
Petrie, Sir Charles Alexander, *The Modern British Monarchy*, Eyre & Spottiswoode, London, 1961, 228 pp.
Pope-Hennessey, James, *Queen Mary*, Allen & Unwin, London, 1960, 685 pp.
Ratcliff, Edward C., *The Coronation Service of Her Majesty Queen Elizabeth II*, Cambridge UP, 1953, 79 pp.
Wheeler-Bennett, Sir John W., *King George VI: His Life and Reign*, Macmillan, 1958, 891 pp.

Chapter 6. THE BRITISH ADMINISTRATION: NATIONAL AND LOCAL

1. NATIONAL ADMINISTRATION AND ECONOMIC POLICY

Barnes, Robert J., *Central Government in Britain*, 2nd rev. ed., Butterworth, London, 1969, 169 pp.
Beer, Samuel H., *British Politics in the Collectivist Age*, Knopf, 1965, 384 pp.
———, *Treasury Control: The Coordination of Financial and Economic Policy in Great Britain*, 2nd ed., Oxford UP, 1957, 138 pp.
Beveridge, Sir William H., *Full Employment in a Free Society*, Norton, 1945, 429 pp.
Brandon, Henry, *In the Red: The Struggle for Sterling, 1964–66*, Deutsch, London, 1966, 125 pp.
Brittan, Samuel, *Government and the Economic Market Economy*, Hobart, London, 1971, 93 pp, pbk.
———, *Steering the Economy: The Role of the Treasury*, Secker & Warburg, London, 1969, 360 pp.
Brown, Rupert G. S., *The Administrative Process in Britain*, Methuen, London, 1970, 349 pp.
Chester, D. N. and F. M. G. Willson, eds., *The Organization of British Central Government 1914–1964*, 2nd rev. ed., Allen & Unwin, London, 1968, 521 pp.
Clarke, John J., *Outlines of Central Government, Including the Judicial System of England*, 14th ed., Pitman, London, 1965, 275 pp.
Coatman, John, *Police*, Oxford UP, 1959, 248 pp.
Control of Public Expenditure (Plowden Report), Cmnd. 1432, HMSO, June 9, 1961.
Critchley, T. A., *A History of Police in England and Wales 900–1966*, Constable, London, 1969, 347 pp.
Cullingworth, J. B., *Town and Country Planning in England and Wales*, 3rd rev. ed., Allen & Unwin, London, 1967, 341 pp.
Davis, William, *Three Years Hard Labour: The Road to Devaluation*, Deutsch, London, 1968, 224 pp.
Economic Survey, Cmnd., HMSO (annual since 1947).
Fedden, Robin, *The Continuing Purpose: A History of the National Trust, Its Aims and Work*, Longmans, London, 1968, 226 pp.
Gladden, Edgar N., *The Essentials of Public Administration*, 3rd ed., Staples, London, 1964, 288 pp.
———, *An Introduction to Public Administration*, 4th ed., 1966, 260 pp.
Hagen, Everett E. and S. F. T. White, *Great Britain: Quiet Revolution in Planning*, Syracuse UP, 1966, 180 pp.

Heap, Desmond, *An Outline of Planning Law*, 5th ed., Sweet & Maxwell, London, 1969, 299 pp.

Jay, the Rt. Hon. Douglas, M. P., "Government Control of the Economy: Defects in the Machinery," *PQ*, 39(2), Apr–June 1968:134–44.

Jewkes, John, *The New Ordeal by Planning: The Experience of the Forties and Sixties*, Macmillan, 1968, 240 pp.

Johnson, Franklyn A., *Defence by Committee: The British Committee of Imperial Defence, 1885–1959*, Oxford UP, 1960, 416 pp.

Lewis, W. Arthur, *Development Planning*, Allen & Unwin, London, 1966, 278 pp, pbk.

"The Machinery for Economic Planning," *Pub. Ad.*, 44, Spring 1966:1–72.

Marshall, G., *Police and Government*, Methuen, London, 1967, 168 pp, pbk.

Martin, J. P. and Gail Wilson, *The Police: A Study in Manpower*, Heinemann, London, 1969, 296 pp.

Meyers, P., *An Introduction to Public Administration*, Butterworth, London, 1971, 226 pp.

Peacock, Alan T. and Jack Wiseman, *The Growth of Public Expenditure in the United Kingdom*, Princeton UP, 1962, 244 pp.

Political and Economic Planning, *Advisory Committees in British Government*, Allen & Unwin, London, 1960, 228 pp.

Productivity, Prices and Incomes Policy in 1968 and 1969, Cmnd. 3590, HMSO, 1968.

Productivity, Prices and Incomes Policy after 1969, Cmnd. 4237, HMSO, 1969.

Robertson, James, *Reform of British Central Government*, Chatto & Windus, London, 1971.

Roseveare, Henry, *The Treasury: The Evolution of a British Institution*, Allen Lane, London, 1969, 406 pp.

Rowley, C. K., *The British Monopolies Commission*, Allen & Unwin, London, 1966, 394 pp.

Sabine, B. E. V., *British Budgets in Peace and War, 1932–1945*, Allen & Unwin, London, 1970, 336 pp.

Schaffer, F., *The New Town Story*, McGibbon & Kee, London, 1970, 342 pp.

Shonfield, Andrew, *British Economic Policy Since the War*, Penguin, 1958, 288 pp.

Williams, Alan, *Public Finance and Budgetary Policy*, Allen & Unwin, London, 1963, 283 pp, pbk.

Wiseman, H. Victor, *The Organisation of British Central Government, 1914–64*, 2nd ed., Allen & Unwin, London, 1968, 251 pp.

New Whitehall Series, under the auspices of the RIPA, studies of individual departments by senior civil servants, Allen & Unwin, London:

> *The Colonial Office*, Sir Charles Jeffries, 1956, 222 pp.
> *The Department of Scientific and Industrial Research*, Sir Harry Melville, 1962, 196 pp.
> *The Foreign Office*, Lord Strang, 1955, 226 pp.
> *Her Majesty's Customs and Excise*, Sir James Crombie, 1962, 208 pp.
> *The Home Office*, Sir Frank Newsam, 1954, 224 pp.
> *The Inland Revenue*, Alexander Johnston, 1965, 201 pp.
> *The Ministry of Agriculture, Fisheries and Food*, Sir John Winnifrith, 1962, 224 pp.
> *The Ministry of Housing and Local Government*, Evelyn Sharp, 1969, 253 pp.
> *The Ministry of Labour and National Service*, Sir Godfrey Ince, 1960, 215 pp.
> *The Ministry of Pensions and National Insurance*, Sir Geoffrey King, 1958, 163 pp.
> *The Ministry of Transport and Civil Aviation*, Sir Gilmour Jenkins, 1959, 231 pp.
> *The Ministry of Works*, Sir Harold Emmerson, 1956, 171 pp.
> *The Scottish Office and Other Scottish Government Departments*, Sir David Milne, 1957, 232 pp.
> *The Treasury*, Lord Bridges, 2nd ed., 1967, 248 pp.

2. PUBLIC ENTERPRISE AND INDUSTRIAL POLICY

Barry, Eldon E., *British Economic Policy Since 1951*, Penguin, 1971.

———, *Nationalization in British Politics: The Historical Background*, Stanford UP, 1965, 396 pp.

Broadway, Frank E., *State Intervention in British Industry, 1964–68*, Kaye & Ward, London, 1969, 191 pp.

Dow, J. C. R., *The Management of the British Economy, 1945–1960*, Cambridge UP, 1966, 462 pp.

Grove, J. W., *Government and Industry in Britain*, Longmans, London, 1962, 514 pp.

Hanson, A. H., *Parliament and Public Ownership*, 2nd ed., Cassell, London, 1962, 248 pp.

House of Commons, Select Committee on Nationalized Industries, Sess. 1967–68, Report: *Ministerial Control of the Nationalised Industries*, HC371–I, 235 pp; *Minutes of Evidence*, HC371–II, 730 pp; *Appendices and Index*, 267 pp; HMSO, 1968.

Jewkes, John, *Public and Private Enterprise*, Routledge, London, 1965, 94 pp.

Keeling, B. S. and A. E. G. Wright, *The Development of the Modern British Steel Industry*, Longmans, London, 1965, 210 pp.

Kelf-Cohen, Reuben, *Twenty Years of Nationalisation: The British Experience, 1947–1968*, Macmillan, 1969, 339 pp.

Moonman, Eric, *Reluctant Partnership: A Critical Study of the Relationship between Government and Industry*, Gollancz, London, 1971, 224 pp.

Nationalised Industry, Nos. 1–12, ed. G. R. Taylor, Acton Society, London, 1950–52.

Robson, William A., *Nationalized Industry and Public Ownership*, rev. ed., Allen & Unwin, London, 1962, 567 pp.

Shanks, Michael F., *The Innovators: The Economics of Technology*, Penguin, 1967, 294 pp.

———, ed., *Lessons of Public Enterprise*, Fabian, London, 1963, 314 pp.

Thornhill, W., *The Nationalized Industries*, Nelson, London, 1968, 248 pp.

Tivey, Leonard J., *Nationalization in British Industry*, Cape, London, 1966, 219 pp.

3. LOCAL GOVERNMENT

Birch, A. H., *Small-Town Politics*, Oxford UP, 1959, 199 pp.

Bulpitt, J. G., *Party Politics in English Local Government*, Longmans, London, 1967, 133 pp.

Burney, Elizabeth, *Housing on Trial: A Study of Immigrants in Local Government*, Oxford UP, 1967, 267 pp.

Buxton, R. J., *Local Government*, Penguin, 1970, 287 pp, pbk.

Clarke, John J., *Outlines of Local Government of the United Kingdom*, 20th ed., Pitman, London, 1969, 245 pp.

Clements, Roger V., *Local Notables and the City Council*, Macmillan, 1969, 207 pp.

Cullingworth, J. B., *Housing and Local Government*, Allen & Unwin, London, 1966, 275 pp.

Donnison, D. V., *The Government of Housing*, Penguin, 1967, 397 pp.

Griffith, J. A. G., *Central Departments and Local Authorities*, Allen & Unwin, London, 1966, 574 pp.

Hampton, William, *Democracy and Community*, Oxford UP, 1970, 349 pp.

Hart, Sir William O., *Introduction to the Law of Local Government and Administration*, 8th rev. ed., Butterworth, London, 1968, 784 pp.

Headrick, T. E., *The Town Clerk in English Local Government*, Allen & Unwin, London, 1962, 232 pp.

Jackson, Richard M., *The Machinery of Local Government*, Macmillan, 1968, 390 pp.

Jackson, William E., *Achievement: A Short History of the London County Council*, Longmans, London, 1965, 304 pp.

———, *Local Government in England and Wales*, 3rd ed., Pelican, 1963, 222 pp.

Jewell, R. E. C., *Central and Local Government*, Charles Knight, London, 1966, 295 pp.

Jones, G. W., *Borough Politics: A Study of the Wolverhampton Borough Council, 1888–1964*, Macmillan, 1969, 404 pp.

McCrone, Gavin, *Regional Policy in Britain*, Allen & Unwin, London, 1969, 277 pp.

Mackintosh, John P., *The Devolution of Power: Local Democracy, Regionalism, and Nationalism*, Penguin, 1968, 207 pp.

Redlich, Josef and Francis W. Hirst, *The History of Local Government in England*, ed. Brian Keith-Lucas, St. Martin's, 1970, 284 pp.

Rees, Joan B., *Government by Community*, Charles Knight, London, 1971, 256 pp.

Reform of Local Government in England (Labour Govt. proposals for reform), Cmnd. 4276, HMSO, 1970, 40 pp.

Report of Royal Commission on Local Government in England, 1966–1969 (Redcliffe-Maud), Cmnd. 4040, HMSO, 1969, 388 pp (short version, Cmnd. 4039).

Report of Royal Commission on Local Government in Greater London, Cmnd. 1164, HMSO, 1960.

Report of Royal Commission on Local Government in Scotland, 1966–1969 (Wheatley), Cmnd. 4150, HMSO, 1969, 320 pp (appendices 130 pp.).

Rhodes, Gerald, *The Government of London: The Struggle for Reform*, Weidenfeld & Nicolson, London, 1970, 320 pp.

——— and Sydney K. Ruth, *The Government of Greater London*, Allen & Unwin, London, 1970, 197 pp.

Richards, Peter G., *The New Local Government System*, Allen & Unwin, London, 1968, 192 pp.

Ripley, Brian J., *Administration in Local Authorities*, Butterworth, London, 1970, 157 pp, pbk.

Robson, William A., *Local Government in Crisis*, Allen & Unwin, London, 1966, 160 pp, pbk.

Salter, James A., 1st Baron Salter, *Slave of the Lamp*, Weidenfeld & Nicolson, London, 1967, 301 pp.

Smallwood, Frank, *Greater London: The Politics of Metropolitan Reform*, Bobbs-Merrill, 1965, 324 pp, pbk.

Smellie, K. B., *A History of Local Government*, 4th ed., Allen & Unwin, London, 1968, 176 pp.

Stanyer, Jeffrey, *County Government in England and Wales*, Routledge, London, 1967, 116 pp, pbk.

Steed, Michael, Bryan Keith-Lucas, and Peter Hall, *The Maud Report*, New Society Pub., 1969, 20 pp.

Townsend, Peter et al., *The Fifth Social Service*, Fabian Society, London, 1970, 160 pp, pbk.

Wiseman, H. Victor, *Local Government at Work: A Case Study of a County Borough*, Routledge, London, 1967, 116 pp, pbk.

———, ed., *Local Government in England 1958–69*, Routledge, London, 1970, 206 pp.

4. PUBLIC SERVICE

Abramovitz, Moses and Vera Eliasberg, *The Growth of Public Employment in Great Britain*, Princeton UP, 1957, 151 pp.

Balogh, Thomas, *The Civil Service: Whitehall Appraised*, Blond, London, 1967, 128 pp, pbk.

———, R. Opie, and H. Thomas, *The Civil Service: An Enquiry*, Blond, London, 1968, 141 pp.

Campbell, G. A., *The Civil Service in Britain*, 2nd ed., Duckworth, London, 1965, 256 pp.

Chapman, R. A., *The Higher Civil Service in Britain*, Constable, London, 1970, 194 pp.

Foot, M. R. D., *SOE in France*, HMSO, 1966, 578 pp.

Fry, Geoffrey K., "Some Weaknesses in the Fulton Report on the British Home Civil Service," *PS*, 17(4), Dec. 1969:484–94.

———, *Statesmen in Disguise: The Changing Role of the Administrative Class of the British Home Civil Service, 1853–1966*, Macmillan, 1969, 479 pp.

Gladden, Edgar N., *Civil Services in the United Kingdom, 1853–1970*, 3rd rev. ed., Frank Cass, 1967, 289 pp.

Heussler, Robert, *Yesterday's Rulers: The Making of the British Colonial Service*, Syracuse UP, 1963, 260 pp.

Hough, Richard, *First Sea Lord: An Authorized Biography of Admiral Lord Fisher*, Allen & Unwin, London, 1969, 372 pp.

Keeling, Desmond, "The Development of Central Training in the Civil Service, 1963–70," *Pub. Ad.*, 49, Spring 1971:51–72.

Kingsley, John D., *Representative Bureaucracy: An Interpretation of the British Civil Service*, Allen & Unwin, London, 1938, 218 pp.

Mallaby, Sir George, *From My Level: Unwritten Minutes*, Hutchinson, London, 1965, 222 pp.

Ministry of Agriculture and Fisheries, *Public Inquiry into the Disposal of Land at Crichel Down*, Cmnd. 176, HMSO, 1954, 33 pp.

Parris, Henry, *Constitutional Bureaucracy: The Development of British Central Administration Since the Eighteenth Century*, Allen & Unwin, London, 1969, 324 pp, pbk.

Report of the Committee on the Civil Service, 1966-68 (Fulton), Cmnd. 3638, HMSO, 1968, 3 vols: 1. 206 pp; 2. 115 pp; 3. (surveys and investigations), 465 pp.

Report of the Review Committee on Overseas Representation 1968-1969 (Duncan), Cmnd. 4107, HMSO, 1969, 204 pp.

Richards, Peter G., *Patronage in British Government*, Toronto UP, 1963, 285 pp.

Ridley, F. F., *Specialists and Generalists: A Comparative Study of the Professional Civil Servant at Home and Abroad*, Allen & Unwin, London, 1968, 213 pp.

Robinton, Madeline R., "The Lynskey Tribunal: The British Method of Dealing with Political Corruption," *PSQ*, 68(1), Mar. 1953:109-24.

Robson, William A., "The Fulton Report on the Civil Service," *PQ*, Oct-Dec. 1968:397-414.

Salter, Lord, *Memoirs of a Public Servant*, Faber, London, 1961, 355 pp.

Stack, Freida, "Civil Service Associations and the Whitley Report of 1917," *PQ*, 40(3), July-Sept. 1969:283-95.

Strong, Kenneth, *Intelligence At The Top: The Recollection of an Intelligence Officer*, Cassell, London, 1968, 284 pp.

Thomas, Hugh S., ed., *Crisis in the Civil Service*, Blond, London, 1968, 141 pp.

Walker, N., *Morale in the Civil Service, A Study of the Desk Worker*, Edinburgh UP, 1961, 302 pp.

Wilson, H. H., *The Problem of Internal Security in Great Britain, 1948-1953*, Doubleday, 1954, 86 pp.

Wright, Maurice, *Treasury Control of the Civil Service, 1854-1874*, Oxford UP, 1969, 441 pp.

Chapter 7. ENGLISH LAW AND COURTS

1. THE LAW

Allen, Sir Carleton Kemp, *Common and Statute Law in the Making*, 7th ed., Oxford UP, 1964, 649 pp.

Cross, Rupert and P. Asterley Jones, *An Introduction to the Criminal Law*, 6th rev. ed., Butterworth, London, 1968, 366 pp.

Dicey, Albert V., *Law and Public Opinion in England*, Macmillan, 1962, 600 pp, pbk.

Gatley, John C. C., *Libel and Slander*, 6th ed., rev. R. L. McEwen and P. S. C. Lewis, Sweet & Maxwell, London, 1967, 768 pp.

Geldart, William M., *Elements of English Law*, 7th ed., prepared D. C. M. Yardley, Oxford UP, 1966, 182 pp.

Giles, Francis T., *Criminal Law: A Short Introduction*, 3rd ed., Penguin, 1963, 300 pp.

Ginsberg, Morris, ed., *Law and Opinion in England in the Twentieth Century*, Stevens, London, 1959, 407 pp.

Jacobs, Francis, *Criminal Responsibility in English Law*, Weidenfeld & Nicolson, London, 1971, 224 pp.

Keeton, George W. and G. Schwarzenberger, eds., *Current Legal Problems*, Stevens, London (published annually).

Keir, D. L. and F. H. Lawson, *Cases in Constitutional Law*, 5th rev. ed., Oxford UP, 1967, 559 pp.

Street, Harry, *Freedom, the Individual and the Law*, 2nd ed., Penguin, 1967, 335 pp.

———, *Justice in the Welfare State*, Stevens, London, 1968, 130 pp, pbk.

Wade, E. C. S. and G. Godfrey Phillips, *Constitutional Law: An Outline of the Law and Practice of the Constitution, Including Central and Local Government and the Constitutional Relations of the British Commonwealth*, 8th ed., Longmans, London, 1967, 767 pp.

Yardley, David C. M., *Introduction to British Constitutional Law*, 3rd rev. ed., Butterworth, London, 1969, 157 pp.

2. JUDGES AND THE COURT SYSTEM

Abel-Smith, Brian and Robert Stevens, *In Search of Justice: Society and the Legal System*, Allen Lane, London, 1968, 384 pp.

———, *Lawyers and the Courts: A Sociological Study of the English Legal System, 1750-1965*, Heinemann, London, 1967, 518 pp.

Cornish, William R., *The Jury*, Allen Lane, London, 1968, 298 pp.

Devlin, Lord Patrick, *The Criminal Prosecution in England*, Yale UP, 1958, 150 pp.

———, *Trial by Jury*, Stevens, London, 1956, 187 pp.

Drewry, Gavin, "The House of Lords as a Final Court of Appeal," *BJS*, 19, Dec. 1968:445-52.

——— and Jenny Morgan, "Law Lords as Legislators," *Parl. Aff.*, 22(3), Summer 1969:226-39.

Edwards, J. L. J., *The Law Officers of the Crown: A Study of the Offices of Attorney-General and Solicitor-General of England with an Account of the Office of the Director of Public Prosecutions of England*, Sweet & Maxwell, London, 1964, 425 pp.

Fellman, David, *The Defendant's Rights Under English Law*, Wisconsin UP, 1966, 137 pp.

Giles, Francis T., *The Juvenile Courts: Their Work and Problems*, Allen & Unwin, London, 1946, 131 pp.

———, *The Magistrate Courts: What They Do, How They Do It and Why*, new ed., Stevens, London, 1963, 250 pp.

Hanbury, Harold G., *English Courts of Law*, 4th ed., Oxford UP, 1967, 152 pp.

Heuston, R. F. V., *Lives of the Lord Chancellors, 1885-1940*, Oxford UP, 1964, 632 pp.

Hyde, H. Montgomery, *Lord Justice: The Life and Times of Lord Birkett of Ulverston*, Random House, 1965, 683 pp.

Jackson, Richard M., *The Machinery of Justice in England*, 6th ed., Cambridge UP, 1972, 455 pp.

McClean, John D. and J. C. Wood, *Criminal Justice and the Treatment of Offenders*, Sweet & Maxwell, London, 1969, 327 pp.

Page, Leo, *Justice of the Peace*, 3rd ed., Faber, London, 1967, 278 pp.

Radcliffe, G. R. Y. and Geoffrey Cross, *The English Legal System*, 4th ed., Butterworth, London, 1964, 460 pp.

Watson, John, *Which is the Justice?* Allen & Unwin, London, 1969, 242 pp.

Williams, Glanville, *The Proof of Guilt: A Study of the English Criminal Trial*, Stevens, London, 1958, 326 pp.

Zander, Michael, *Lawyers and the Public Interest*, Weidenfeld & Nicolson, London, 1968, 342 pp.

3. ADMINISTRATIVE LAW AND TRIBUNALS

Allen, Sir Carleton Kemp, *Law and Orders: An Inquiry into the Nature and Scope of Delegated Legislation and Executive Powers in England*, 3rd ed., Stevens, London, 1965, 412 pp.

Garner, J. F., *Administrative Law*, 3rd ed., Butterworth, London, 1970, 473 pp.

Griffith, John A. G. and Harry Street, *Principles of Administrative Law*, 4th rev. ed., Pitman, London, 1967, 339 pp.

Phillips, O. Hood, *Constitutional and Administrative Law*, 4th rev. ed., Sweet & Maxwell, London, 1967, 865 pp.

———, *Leading Cases in Constitutional and Administrative Law*, 3rd rev. ed., Sweet & Maxwell, London, 1967, 452 pp.

Wade, Henry W. R., *Administrative Law*, 2nd rev. ed., Oxford UP, 1967, 338 pp.

Chapter 8. GREAT BRITAIN AND THE WORLD

1. EMPIRE TO COMMONWEALTH

Beloff, Max, *Imperial Sunset*, Vol. 1. *Britain's Liberal Empire, 1897–1921*, Methuen, London, 1969, 387 pp.

Clutterbuck, Richard, *The Long Long War: The Emergency in Malaya, 1948–1960*, Cassell, London, 1967, 220 pp.

Cohen, Sir Andrew, *British Policy in Changing Africa*, Northwestern UP, 1959, 116 pp.

Coupland, R., *The Durham Report: An Abridged Version with an Introduction and Notes*, Oxford UP, 1945, 186 pp.

Cross, Colin, *The Fall of the British Empire, 1918–1968*, Coward-McCann, London, 1969, 359 pp.

Elias, Taslim O., *British Colonial Law*, Stevens & Sons, London, 1962, 323 pp.

Furnivall, J. S., *Colonial Policy and Practice*, New York UP, 1956, 568 pp.

Goldsworthy, D. J., *Colonial Issues in British Politics 1945–1961*, Oxford UP, 1971, 425 pp.

Hancock, William K., *Empire in the Changing World*, Penguin, 1943, 186 pp.

Hollander, Barnett, *Colonial Justice: The Unique Achievement of the Privy Council's Committee of Judges*, Bowes & Bowes, London, 1961, 115 pp.

Jeffries, Sir Charles, *The Transfer of Power: Problems of the Passage to Self-Government*, Pall Mall, London, 1960, 148 pp.

Johnson, Franklyn A., *Defence by Committee: The British Committee of Imperial Defence, 1885–1959*, Oxford UP, 1960, 416 pp.

Jones, Arthur C., ed., *New Fabian Colonial Essays*, Hogarth, London, 1959, 271 pp.

Kirkman, W. P., *Unscrambling an Empire: A Critique of British Colonial Policy, 1956–1966*, Chatto & Windus, London, 1966, 214 pp.

Lee, J. M., *Colonial Development and Good Government: A Study of the Ideas Expressed by the British Official Classes in Planning Decolonialization, 1939–1964*, Oxford UP, 1967, 319 pp.

Morris, James, *Pax-Britannica: The Climax of an Empire*, Harcourt Brace Jovanovich, 1968, 544 pp.

Perham, Dame Margery, ed., *Colonial Government: Annotated Reading List on British Colonial Government with Some General and Comparative Material upon Foreign Empires*, Oxford UP, 1950, 80 pp.

———, *The Colonial Reckoning: The End of Imperial Rule in Africa in the Light of British Experience*, Knopf, 1962, 203 pp.

———, *Colonial Sequence: 1930–1949*, Methuen, London, 1967, 351 pp.

Young, Kenneth, *Rhodesia and Independence: A Study in British Colonial Policy*, 2nd rev. ed., Dent, London, 1969, 581 pp.

2. THE COMMONWEALTH OF NATIONS

Arnold, Guy, *Towards Peace and a Multi-Racial Commonwealth*, Chapman & Hall, London, 1964, 184 pp.

Ball, M. Margaret, *The "Open" Commonwealth*, Duke UP, 1971, 275 pp.

Beaton, Leonard, *Commonwealth in a New Era: Pioneers of an Open World*, Trade Policy Research Center, London, 1969, 32 pp.

Burns, Sir Alan, ed., *Parliament as an Export*, Allen & Unwin, London, 1966, 271 pp.

Caiden, G. E., *The Commonwealth Bureaucracy*, Melbourne UP, 1967, 445 pp.

Caradon, Lord, *Race Relations in the British Commonwealth and The United Nations*, Cambridge UP, 1967, 25 pp.

Carter, Gwendolen M., *The British Commonwealth and International Security: The Role of the Dominions, 1919–1939*, Ryerson, Toronto, 1947, 326 pp.

Carter, Gwendolen M., "The Commonwealth and the United Nations," IO, 4(2), May 1, 1950:247–60.

———, "The Expanding Commonwealth," FA, 35(1), Oct. 1956:131–43.

Commonwealth Prime Ministers' Meeting in London, 7–15 January 1969, Final Communiqué, Cmnd. 3919, HMSO, 1969, 15 pp.

The Commonwealth Relations Conference, 1959, Oxford UP, 1959, 64 pp.

Conservative Political Center, *Wind of Change: The Challenge of the Commonwealth*, London, 1960, 63 pp.

Eayrs, J., ed., *The Commonwealth and Suez: A Documentary Survey*, Oxford UP, 1964, 483 pp.

Hamilton, W. B., Kenneth Robinson, and C. D. W. Goodwin, eds., *A Decade of the Commonwealth 1955–1964*, Duke UP, 1966, 567 pp.

Hancock, William K., *Survey of British Commonwealth Affairs*, Oxford UP, 2 vols in 3 parts: *Problems of Nationality, 1918–1936*, 673 pp; *Problems of Economic Policy, 1918–1939, 1937–1942*, 324 and 355 pp.

Harvey, Heather J., *Consultation and Co-operation in The Commonwealth: A Handbook on Methods and Practice*, Oxford UP, 1951, 411 pp.

Mansergh, Nicholas, *The Commonwealth Experience*, Weidenfeld & Nicolson, London, 1969, 471 pp.

Mansergh, Nicholas, ed., *Documents and Speeches on British Commonwealth Affairs, 1931–1952*, 2 vols, Oxford UP, 1954, 604 and 690 pp; and *1952–1962*, 1963, 775 pp.

——, *Survey of British Commonwealth Affairs*, Oxford UP, 2 vols: *Problems of External Policy, 1931–1939*, 1952, 481 pp; *Problems of Wartime Co-operation and Post-war Change, 1939–1952*, 1958, 469 pp.

Marshall, Geoffrey, *Parliamentary Sovereignty and the Commonwealth*, Oxford UP, 1957, 277 pp.

Mazrui, Ali A., *The Anglo-African Commonwealth: Political Friction and Cultural Fusion*, Pergamon, London, 1967, 163 pp.

Mendelsohn, Ronald, *Social Security in the British Commonwealth*, Athlone, London, 1954, 390 pp.

Millar, Thomas B., *The Commonwealth and the United Nations*, Sydney UP, 1967, 237 pp.

——, "Empire into Commonwealth into History: A Review of Recent Writing on the Commonwealth," IO, 24(1), Winter 1970:93–99.

Miller, J. D. B., *Britain and the Old Dominions*, Chatto & Windus, London, 1966, 286 pp.

Soper, Tom, *Evolving Commonwealth*, Pergamon, London, 1966, 150 pp.

Symonds, Richard, *The British and their Successors: A Study in the Development of the Government Services in the New States*, Faber, London, 1966, 287 pp.

United Kingdom, *Colombo Plan for Cooperative Economic Development in South and Southeast Asia*, Annual Reports of the Consultative Committee, HMSO (annually since 1957).

Watts, Ronald L., *New Federations: Experiments in the Commonwealth*, Oxford UP, 1967, 419 pp.

Wheare, Kenneth C., *The Constitutional Structure of the Commonwealth*, Oxford UP, 1961, 201 pp.

——, *The Statute of Westminster and Dominion Status*, 5th ed., Oxford UP, 1953, 347 pp.

Wiseman, H. V., *Britain and the Commonwealth*, Allen & Unwin, London, 1966, 157 pp, pbk.

——, *The Cabinet in the Commonwealth: Post-War Developments in Africa, The West Indies, and South-East Asia*, Praeger, 1959, 364 pp.

3. BRITAIN AND EUROPE

Allen, Harry C., *The Anglo-American Predicament: the British Commonwealth, the United States and European Unity*, St. Martin's, 1960, 241 pp.

Birch, R. C., *Britain and Europe 1871–1939*, Pergamon, London, 1966, 313 pp.

Britain and the European Communities: An Economic Assessment, Cmnd. 4289, HMSO, 1970, 46 pp.

Camps, Miriam, *Britain and the European Community, 1955–1963*, Princeton UP, 1964, 547 pp.

Carter, W. Horsfall, *Speaking European: The Anglo-Continental Cleavage*, Allen & Unwin, London, 1966, 223 pp.

Coffey, Peter and John R. Presley, *European Monetary Integration*, Macmillan, 1971, 143 pp.

Cosgrove, Carol A., *A Reader's Guide to Britain and The European Communities*, RIIA, London, 1970, 106 pp.

Davidson, Ian, *Britain and the Making of Europe*, Macdonald, London, 1971.

Einzig, Paul, *The Case Against Joining the Common Market*, St. Martin's, 1971, 132 pp.

Gladwyn, Lord, *The European Idea*, Weidenfeld & Nicolson, London, 1966, 171 pp.

Kaiser, Karl and Roger Morgan, eds., *Britain and West Germany: Changing Societies and the Future of Foreign Policy*, Oxford UP, 1971, 294 pp.

Kitzinger, Uwe E., *Britain, Europe and Beyond*, Sijthoff, Leyden, 1965, 222 pp.

——, *The Second Try: Labour and the EEC*, Pergamon, London, 1969, 353 pp.

Lieber, Robert J., *British Politics and European Unity: Parties, Elites and Pressure Groups*, California UP, 1971, 317 pp.

Mally, Gerhard, *Britain and European Unity*, Hansard, London, 1966, 156 pp.

Mandel, Ernest, *Europe versus America? Contradictions of Imperialism*, NLB, London, 1970, 139 pp.

Marsh, John S. and Christopher Ritson, *Agricultural Policy and The Common Market*, RIIA, London, 1971, 199 pp.

Pfaltzgraff, Robert L., Jr., *Britain Faces Europe, 1957–1967*, Pennsylvania UP, 1969, 228 pp.

Pickles, William, *Britain and Europe: How Much Has Changed?* Blackwell, Oxford, 1967, 119 pp, pbk.

Pinder, John, *Britain and the Common Market*, Cresset, London, 1961, 134 pp.

The United Kingdom and European Communities, Cmnd. 4715, HMSO, July 7, 1971.

Watt, D. C., *Britain Looks to Germany: A Study of British Opinion and Policy Towards Germany since 1945*, Wolff, London, 1965, 164 pp.

4. INTERNATIONAL RELATIONS

Barker, A. J., *Suez, The Seven-Day War*, Faber, London, 1964, 223 pp.

Beloff, Max, *The Balance of Power*, Allen & Unwin, 1968, 73 pp.

Beloff, Max, *New Dimensions in Foreign Policy: A Study in British Administrative Experience, 1947–1959*, Macmillan, 1961, 208 pp.

Brown, Neville, *Arms without Empire: British Defense Role in the Modern World*, Penguin, 1967, 169 pp.

Busk, Douglas, *The Craft of Diplomacy: Mechanics and Development of National Representation Overseas*, Pall Mall, London, 1967, 293 pp.

Crosby, Gerda R., *Disarmament and Peace in British Politics, 1914–1919*, Harvard UP, 1957, 192 pp.

Epstein, Leon D., *British Politics in the Suez Crisis*, Illinois UP, 1964, 220 pp.

Fitzsimons, M. A., *The Foreign Policy of the British Labour Government, 1945–1951*, Notre Dame UP, 1953, 182 pp.

Fleming, Danna F., *The Cold War and Its Origins, 1917–1960*, 2 vols, Doubleday, 1961, 1,158 pp.

Gaitskell, Hugh, *The Challenge of Coexistence*, Harvard UP, 1957, 114 pp.

Glubb, John B., *Britain and the Arabs, 1908–1958*, Hodder & Stoughton, London, 1958, 496 pp.

Gordon, Michael R., *Conflict and Consensus in Labour's Foreign Policy, 1914–1965*, Stanford UP, 1969, 333 pp.

Great Britain Foreign Office: *Documents on British Foreign Policy, 1919–1939*, HMSO, London, First Series: 17 vols, 1919 to 1930, 1947–70; Series IA, 3 vols, 1925 to 1929, 1966–70; Second Series, 11 vols, 1930 to March 1938, 1946–70; Third Series, 10 vols, March 1938 to Sept. 1939, 1949–61.

Harvey, John, ed., *The Diplomatic Diaries of Oliver Harvey, 1937–1940*, Collins, London, 1970, 448 pp.

Hawley, Donald, *The Trucial States*, Allen & Unwin, London, 1971, 379 pp.

Hayter, Teresa, *Aid as Imperialism*, Penguin, 1971, 222 pp.

Higgins, Rosalyn, *The Administration of United Kingdom Foreign Policy through the United Nations*, ed. G. J. Mangone, Syracuse UP, 1966, 63 pp.

Luard, Evan, *Britain and China*, Chatto & Windus, London, 1962, 256 pp.

Maclean, Donald, *British Foreign Policy Since Suez*, Hodder & Stoughton, London, 1970, 343 pp.

Medlicott, W. N., *British Foreign Policy Since Versailles 1919–1963*, Methuen, London, 1968, 362 pp.

Meehan, Eugene J., *The British Left Wing and Foreign Policy: A Study of the Influence of Ideology*, Rutgers UP, 1961, 201 pp.

Moncrieff, Anthony, ed., *Suez: Ten Years After*, BBC, London, 1968, 160 pp.

Monroe, Elizabeth, *Britain's Moment in the Middle East, 1914–1956*, Johns Hopkins UP, 1963, 254 pp.

Moulton, James L., *Defence in a Changing World*, Eyre & Spottiswoode, London, 1964, 191 pp.

Naylor, John F., *Labour's International Policy: The Labour Party in the 1930s*, Weidenfeld & Nicolson, London, 1969, 388 pp.

Nicholas, H. G., *Britain and the United States*, Chatto & Windus, London, 1963, 180 pp.

Northedge, F. S., *British Foreign Policy: The Process of Readjustment, 1945–1961*, Allen & Unwin, London, 1962, 341 pp, pbk.

———, *The Troubled Giant: Britain Among the Great Powers, 1916–1939*, Bell, London, 1966, 657 pp.

Nutting, Anthony, *No End of a Lesson*, Constable, London, 1967, 206 pp.

Robertson, Terence, *Crisis: The Inside Story of the Suez Conspiracy*, Hutchinson, London, 1965, 349 pp.

Rosecrance, R. N., *Defense of the Realm: British Strategy in the Nuclear Epoch*, Columbia UP, 1968, 308 pp.

Steiner, Zara S., *The Foreign Office and Foreign Policy, 1898–1914*, Cambridge UP, 1970, 274 pp.

Thomas, H., *The Suez Affair*, Weidenfeld & Nicolson, London, 1967, 243 pp.

Vital, David, *The Making of British Foreign Policy*, Allen & Unwin, London, 1968, 119 pp, pbk.

Waltz, Kenneth N., *Foreign Policy and Democratic Politics: The American and British Experience*, Little, Brown, 1967, 352 pp.

Ward, Barbara and P. T. Bauer, *Two Views on Aid to Developing Countries*, Inst. of Economic Affairs, London, 1966, 58 pp.

Watkins, K. W., *Britain Divided: The Effect of the Spanish Civil War on British Political Opinion*, Nelson, London, 1963, 270 pp.

Watt, Donald Cameron, *Personalities and Policies: Studies in the Formulation of British Foreign Policy in the Twentieth Century*, Longmans, London, 1965, 277 pp.

Woodward, Llewellyn, *British Foreign Policy in the Second World War*, Vol. I, HMSO, 1970, 680 pp.

Younger, Kenneth, *Changing Perspectives in British Foreign Policy*, Oxford UP, 1965, 147 pp.

Index

"Abhorrers," 34, 35
Absolutism, Tudor, 32–33
Act of Settlement (1701), 34, 38, 166
Act of Union (1707), 33
Administration, 134–62; and councils, 150–51; employer-employee relations in, 157–59; local and regional, 145–51, 161; and public service, 151–62; reform of, projects for, 146–50; regional and local, 145–51, 161; structure of, 134–44; *see also* Cabinet, British; Civil service, British; Economic planning, British
Administration of Justice Act (1970), 171
Administrative tribunals, 177, 178–79
Admiralty, 124, 136
Africa, 115; South, *see* South Africa
Afrikaners, 180n, 181
Agricultural Act (1947), 144
Agriculture, 11, 45, 192
Air Ministry, 124, 136, 162
Amalgamated Union of Engineers and Foundrymen (AEF), 65, 66
American Revolution, 46, 48, 181
Anarchism, 51
Angles, 8
Anglican Church, *see* Church of England
Anglo-Saxon Chronicle, The, 30
Anne, Queen (1702–14), 33, 34
Antigua, 189n
Apartheid, 189
"Apotheosis of the Dilettante, The" (Balogh), 154
Appeal courts, 174, 176
Armstrong, William, 153, 155
Arran, Lord, 25
Assize court, 173
Association of British Chambers of Commerce (ABCC), 19
Atomic Energy Organization, 160–61
Attlee, Clement R., 50, 117n, 126, 127, 130
Australia, 4, 5, 47, 133, 182n, 184, 186; and Commonwealth of Nations, 180n, 181, 182, 187, 189n; productivity of labor in, 21; and Statute of Westminster (1931), 184; in World War I, 183; in World War II, 184
Austria, 191
Autobiography (Mill), 49

Bacon, Francis, 166
Bagehot, Walter, 38, 42, 99, 131; quoted, 38
Baldwin, Stanley, 41 and n, 130
Balfour, Arthur James, 10n
Balfour Report of Imperial Conference (1926), 183
Balogh, Thomas, 154, 155
Bank of England, 104, 137, 141, 154

Baptists, 9, 10
Bar Council, 177
Barbados, 133, 181, 189n
Barber, Anthony, 59, 60, 147
Barristers, 167, 168
Bartholomew, D. V., 93n
Basle agreement (1968), 186
Beaverbrook, Lord, 23, 24
Beeching Commission, 168, 169, 170, 171, 173, 176
Beer, Samuel H., 19, 90 and n, 93 and n, 144
Belgium, 21, 190, 191
Benn, Anthony Wedgwood, 118
Bentham, Jeremy, 48, 49
Berrington, H. B., 93n
Bevan, Aneurin, 70
Beveridge, Lord, 50, 119
Beveridge Plan, 13, 50
Bevin, Ernest, 64
Bill of Rights: British, 34, 38, 166; United States, 40, 44, 166
Bismarck, Otto von, 2
Blondel, Jean, 60 and n
Blumler, Jay G., 27 and n, 28
Board of Customs and Excise, 137
Broad of Inland Revenue, 137
Board of Trade, 124, 135, 156
Boots Pure Drugs, 156
Botswana, 181, 187, 189n
Boundary Commission and constituencies, 79
Bow Group in House of Commons, 91
Bowring, Nona, 101n
Brandt, Willy, 191
Britain, *see* Great Britain
British Broadcasting Corporation (BBC), 27, 28, 58, 114, 141 and n
British Commonwealth of Nations, *see* Commonwealth of Nations
British Empire, 181
British Medical Association (BMA), 18
British Nationality Act (1948), 188
British Politics in the Collectivist Age (Beer), 90, 144
British Rail, 143
Brittan, Samuel, 137n, 140 and n
Brown, Douglas Clifton, 96
Brown, George, 62
Brown, R. Douglas, 123n
Bryce, Lord, 118, 119
Budget, 137
Burgess-Maclean spy case, 160
Burke, Edmund, 46
Burma, 185
Butler, David E., 17 and n, 61n
Butler, R. A., 115, 129, 140
Butt, Ronald, 92, 93n, 114 and n, 115, 116

Cabinet, British, 30, 31, 37, 40, 41, 42, 95, 98, 99, 100, 105, 107, 109,

111, 116, 121–28, 135 137, 162; charge of dictatorship by, unjustifiable, 127–28; committees of, 124–25; functions of, and their coordination, 123–26; membership of, 123; and prime minister, 129–31; rise of, 34–35; Secretariat of, 125–26, 129–30; *see also* Administration; Civil service, British; Ministries
Cabinet, United States, 122
Callaghan, James, 92
Cambridge University, 12, 44, 91, 153, 155
Cameroon Republic, 185
Campion, Lord, 101n
Canada, 4, 5, 6, 133, 166, 175, 182n, 184, 186, 187, 189, 190, 191; and Commonwealth of Nations, 181, 182, 189n; and NATO, 190; productivity of labor in, 21; and Statute of Westminster (1931), 184; and United States, 185; in World War I, 183; in World War II, 184, 186
Cape Town, 5
Carlton Club, 35
Carrington, Lord, 118
Carter, Gwendolyn M., 114n, 124n, 126n, 130n
Castle, Barbara, 85, 116
Catholic Church, 9, 32–33, 34
Cavaliers, Anglican, 35
Celts, 8
Censorship, 23, 44
Center for Administrative Studies, 156
Central Electricity Board, 141
Central Office of Conservative party, 59, 60–62
Central Statistical Office, 125
Ceylon, 133, 164n, 181, 187, 189n
Chamberlain, Austen, 62
Chamberlain, Neville, 10n, 41, 62, 129, 130
Chancellor of Exchequer, 111, 123, 135, 137, 140, 157
Charles I (1625–49), 33, 35
Charles II (1660–85), 34, 35
Chartism, 36
Chester, D. N., 101n
China, 159, 194
Church of England, 19–20, 33, 117
Churchill, Winston, 47, 62, 99, 114, 123, 127, 130, 138
Circuit judges, 173
Civil law, 164 and n, 173, 174
Civil List, 137
Civil service, British, 39, 137, 138, 151–62; administrative class of, 153, 159; clerical, 153; employer-employee relations in, 157–58; ethics of, 140, 162; executive class of, 153, 159; Fulton Committee on, 137, 140, 152 and n, 153, 154, 155, 156; internal

Civil service, British (Cont.)
security in, 160–61; overseas, 159–60; pay scales of, 156, 157; redundancy in, 156, 157; regrading, 153; selection process for, 153–56; strikes in, 157; subclerical, 153; training for, 156; unions in, 157; Whitley Councils in, 157–58, 161; *see also* Administration; Cabinet, British; Ministries
Civil service, French, 156
Civil service, United States, 153, 154, 155, 157
Civil Service Arbitration Tribunal, 158
Civil Service College, 156
Civil Service Commission, 152 and *n*
Civil Service Department, 135, 137, 138, 139, 153, 154
Civil War: British (1642–49), 33, 35; United States, 38
Class structure, 11, 12; in period of change, 15–17
Coal Board, 142, 143
Cobbett, William, 106*n*
Cockfield, F. A., 156
Cole, G. D. H., 50
Cole, Margaret, 50
Colombo Plan, 187
Colonial Office, 124, 136
Commercial Diplomatic Service, 159
Commisioners of Crown Lands, 137
Committee of the Whole House, 107, 108
Committee on Agriculture, 104
Committee on Education and Science, 104
Committee on Legal Education, 168
Committee on Nationalized Industries, 103, 104, 107, 114, 143
Committee on Science and Technology, 104
Common law, 39, 43, 163–66
Common Market, *see* European Economic Community
Commons, House of, *see* House of Commons
Commonwealth Development Corporation, 187
Commonwealth Development Finance Company, 187–88
Commonwealth Immigrants Act (1962), 188
Commonwealth Immigration Act (1968), 44, 116, 188
Commonwealth of Nations, 3*n*, 5, 8, 9, 21, 40, 48, 63, 89, 115, 136, 175, 180–90, 191, 192, 193; bonds and strains in, 185–89; and British monarchy, 133; and economic relations, 186–88; evolution of, 181–85; future of, 189–90; and immigration, 188; and independent policies, 184; institutions of, 185; law in, 164, 166; republics in, 185; and South Africa, 181, 182, 185, 189, 190; and Statute of Westminster (1931), 40, 184; strains and bonds in, 185–89; strategic ties in, 185–86
Commonwealth Relations Office, 124, 136, 159
Communist party, 71, 72
Comptroller and Auditor General, 112, 137, 138

Confederation of British Industry, 19
Conference of Prime Ministers and Commonwealth of Nations, 185, 189
Congregationalists, 9, 10
Congress, United States, 89, 92, 105, 111, 128, 135, 137
Connally, John, 122
Conservatism: British, 46–48, 50; United States, 46
Conservative party, 3, 4, 10, 15, 17, 18, 27, 28, 36, 37, 52, 54, 55, 58–63, 72, 86, 114, 131, 132, 154; agents of, for constituencies, 81; annual conference of, 62, 116; Central Office of, 59, 60, 61, 130; and Church of England, 10; economic problems of, 20, 21; and education, 12; funds raised by (1967–69), 59; and housing, 14; machinery of, 59–63; membership of, 57; and National Health Service, 14; parliamentary, 62–63, 115–16; Research Department of, 59, 60, 61, 130; structure of, 58–59, 61; victory by, in 1970 election, 77, 84, 85
Consolidated Fund, 137, 138
Constitution, British, 37–45, 47; and civil liberties, 43–44, 45; conventions of, 40–41; and fusion of powers, 41; and judicial decisions, 39–40; principles of, 41–43; sources of, 38–41; value of, 44–45
Constitution, United States, 37, 38, 39, 40, 41, 45, 74, 166
Consular Service, 159
Cooperative party, 65, 66, 92
Cooperatives, 65–66, 67
Corn Laws, 37
Cornwall, 8
Council of Europe, 192
Council on Tribunals, 179
Court Act (1971), 167, 168, 171, 173, 176
Court of Assize, 173
Court system, 31, 39, 171–79; and civil liberties, 43, 166; and differences between civil and criminal cases, 173–74; evaluation of, 175–77; and judicial control of government officials, 177–79; structure of, 174–77; *see also* Judges; Juries; Law, British
Cousins, Frank, 64, 123
Crewe, I. M., 154 and *n*
Crichel Down case, 102, 122–23, 123*n*
Crick, Bernard, 101*n*, 109 and *n*, 120
Criminal Injuries Compensation Board, 178
Criminal Justice Act: of 1967, 170, 176; of 1972, 176
Criminal law, 164, 173–74
Cripps, Stafford, 137
Cromwell, Oliver, 33
Crossman, Richard, 103, 107, 108, 130, 193
Crown Court, 171, 173
Crown Proceedings Act (1947), 178
Crowther Commission on Constitutional Reform, 72, 145, 147, 150
Cumberland, 8
Curia Regis (Little Council), 30, 31, 121

Curzon, Lord, 41 and *n*
Cyprus, 181, 189*n*

Daily Express, 24, 26, 76
Daily Herald, 23, 25
Daily Mail, 24, 26
Daily Mirror, 24, 25, 26
Daily Sketch, 24
Daily Telegraph, 23, 24, 25, 26, 106
Daily Worker, 23, 24
Dalton, Hugh, 111
Danes, England invaded by, 8
Davies, J. G. W., 154
Davies, John, 123
Davies, S. O., 79*n*
Declaration of Independence, United States, 10, 38, 46, 48
Declaration of Principles (Singapore, 1971), 189
Defence of the Realm Act (1914), 23
De Gaulle, Charles, 63, 115, 190, 191
Democracy, 53; public opinion in, 22
Democratic party, United States, 55, 56
Denmark, 190, 191
Department of Economic Affairs (DEA), 124
Department of Environment, 123, 135, 136
Department of Foreign and Commonwealth Affairs, 124
Department of Trade and Industry, 124, 135, 136, 156
Devlin, Bernadette, 91
Dicey, A. V., 166, 177
Diplomatic Service, 159
Director of Public Prosecutions, 170
Disraeli, Benjamin, 37, 47, 58, 131
Divine right of kings, belief in, 33
Dominica, 189*n*
Douglas-Home, Alec, 41, 62, 118, 127, 129, 130, 132
Dugdale, Thomas, 122–23
Duncan Report, 159, 160
Durham Report, 181
Dutschke, Rudi, 44

Eckstein, Harry, 18 and *n*
Economic planning: British, 138–39; French, 138
Economist, 25
Economist Intelligence Unit, 24
Eden, Anthony, 10, 115, 129, 132
Education: British, 11–13; United States, 12
Edward I (1272–1307), 32, 33*n*
Edward VI (1547–53), 33
Edward VII (1901–10), 131
Egalitarianism, 4, 15, 77
Egypt, 115
Eire, *see* Ireland
Elections, British, 17, 24, 25, 27, 73–85; agents in, 81; campaigning in, 77–78; candidates in, selection of, 79–81; canvassing in, 82; Conservative victory in (1970), 77, 84, 85; and constituencies, 78–79; dates for, 73–75; expenses for, 81–82; geography of (1959), 74; heckling in, 82; map of (1970), 83; national results of (1945–70), 84; and polls, 75–77; postal voting in, 84; tele-

INDEX

vision used in, 82; voters in, 79; see also Party system, British
Elections, United States, 74
Electricity Board, 141
Elizabeth I (1558–1603), 33
Elizabeth II (1953–   ), 132, 133
Emancipation Proclamation, 38
Emergency Powers Act (1939), 23
England, see Great Britain
English Constitution, The (Bagehot), 38
Episcopal Church, United States, 9
Equity (law), 164, 165
Ethiopia, 70, 123
Eton College, 12, 155
Euratom, 191
European Coal and Steel Community (ECSC), 191
European Communities, Assembly of, 192
European Convention of Human Rights (1950), 166
European Economic Community (Common Market), 20, 189; and Great Britain, 2, 3, 9, 21, 63, 67, 70, 103, 113, 115, 116, 127, 131, 180, 187, 190; problems of British entry, 191, 192, 193, 194
European Free Trade Association, 191
European Payments Union, 191
Evening News, 25
Ewing, Winifred, 72
Examiner of Petitions for Private Bills, 108
Exchequer and Audit Department, 137

Fabian Society, 50, 51, 63
Falkland Islands, 5
Family allowances, 14 and *n*
Farming, see Agriculture
Federation of British Industries (FBI), 18, 19
Feudalism, 165
Fifth French Republic, 181
Fiji, 133, 181, 187, 189*n*
Finance Bill, 92, 107, 108
Financial Times, 23, 24, 25, 26
Finer, Samuel E., 93*n*
Foreign and Commonwealth Office, 136
Foreign Office, 124, 125, 130, 135, 136, 159
Foreign policy, 190
Foreign Secretary, 123
France, 5, 9, 11, 21, 30, 39, 54, 66, 179, 180, 190, 191; and NATO, 191; productivity of labor in, 21; social security in, 13–15, 21
France, Arnold, 155
Franks Committee Report on Administrative Tribunals and Procedures, 179
Frasure, Robert C., 93*n*
French Revolution, 46, 48; Reign of Terror during, 48
Fulton Committee on Civil Service, 137, 140, 152 and *n*, 153, 154, 155, 156
Fyfe, Maxwell, 59, 62

Gaitskell, Hugh, 50, 51, 70, 114, 131
Gallup Poll, 75, 76, 77, 82
Gambia, 181 189*n*

Gas Council, 142
Gazette, 108
General Council of the Press, 25
George I (1714–27), 34, 35
George II (1727–60), 34, 35
George III (1760–1820), 34
George V (1910–36), 131
George VI (1936–52), 133
German Federal Republic (West Germany), 9, 191; and NATO, 191; population of, 9; and Soviet Union, 191
Germany, 11, 30, 54, 184; productivity of labor in, 21
Ghana, 181, 189*n*
Gibraltar, 5
Gladstone, William E., 37, 96, 97, 131
Glasgow University, 155
Glorious Revolution (1688), 30, 34, 35, 46, 48
Goldthorpe, John E., 16*n*
Governing Britain (Hanson and Wallace), 140 and *n*
Grand jury, United States, 169
Great Britain, 2, 146, 194; administration of, see Administration; agriculture in, 11; area of, 6; aristocracy in, 11 and *n*; as banking center, 5; birth rates in, 9; and "brain drain," 21; Cabinet in, see Cabinet, British; challenge to, 3–4; civil service in, see Civil service, British; class structure in, see Class structure; climate of, 6; commercial and military position of, 5–6; and Commonwealth of Nations, see Commonwealth of Nations; conservatism in, 46–48, 50; Conservative party of, see Conservative party; constitution of, see Constitution, British; early inhabitants of, 8; economic planning in, 138–39; economic problems of, 19–22; education in, 11–13; elections in, see Elections, British; emigration from, postwar, 9, 188; and European Economic Community, see European Economic Community and Great Britain; foreign trade of, 5, 19; gross national product (GNP) of, 6, 19; history of, 8, 30–37; homogeneity of, 6, 11, 55; housing in, 14–15; immigrants in, 8, 188; importance of, for other countries, 4; industrial revolution in, 5; infant mortality rates in, 14; interest groups in, 17–19; and international relations, 190–93; Labor party of, see Labor party; Liberal party of, see Liberal party; liberalism in, 48–50; local government in, 145–51, 161; maternity death rate in, 14; monarchy in, 121, 131–33, 166; national character of, 8; National Health Service in, 14; nationalization in, 140–44, 158–59; Navy of, 5, 136, 181; Parliament of, see Parliament; party system in, see Party system, British; in period of change, 29; political heritage of, 30–52; political ideas in, see Political ideas, British; population of, 6, 9, 11, 198; pound devalued by (1967), 20; press in, 22–

27, 28, 106; prime minister of, 41, 42, 121, 122, 129–31; Privy Council of, see Privy Council; productivity of labor in, 21; public opinion organs in, 22–29; Race Relations Board in, 9; radio in, 27, 28, 141; religion in, 9–11; social security in, 13–15, 21; socialist movement in, 11, 46, 50–52, 138; taxation in, 17, 20, 21, 63, 78, 155, 156; television in, 17, 24, 27, 28, 106, 114, 141; trade unions in, see Trade unions; unemployment in, 20; and United States, 2, 4, 48, 66, 180, 190, 194; urbanization of, 11, 150; as welfare state, 3, 13, 22, 29, 56; and world, 180–93; see also Commonwealth of Nations; Court system, British; Law, British
Great Reform Act (1832), 36, 38, 56
Greece, 190
Green Paper, 104, 139
Grenada, 189*n*
Grimond, Jo, 71, 120, 193
Guardian, 23, 24, 25, 26, 29
Guillotine resolution in House of Commons, 110
Guyana, 181, 189*n*

Habeas Corpus Act (1679), 43
Halifax, Lord, 41
Hall, Lord, 143
Halsey, A. H., 154 and *n*
Hankey, Lord, 126
Hanover, House of, 34
Hansard record of parliamentary debates, 103, 106*n*
Hanson, A. H., 101*n*, 140 and *n*
Harris Poll, 75, 76, 77
Harrow boys' school, 12, 155
Heath, Edward, 28, 41, 52, 58, 60, 62, 63, 77, 78, 81, 84, 107, 116, 123–27 *passim,* 130, 136, 139, 141, 142, 143, 147, 155, 156, 158, 169*n,* 186, 189, 192, 193
Henry II (1154–89), 31
Henry III (1216–72), 31, 32
Henry V (1413–22), 32
Henry VI (1422–61), 32
Henry VII (1485–1509), 32
Henry VIII (1509–47), 32, 33
Herbert, A. P., 79*n,* 108*n*
Herz, John H., 124*n,* 126*n,* 130*n*
High Court of Justice, 171, 173, 174
Hitler, Adolf, 5
Hoare-Laval pact, 123
Hogg, Quintin, 118
Holborn, Louise W., 124*n,* 126*n,* 130*n*
Holland, 21, 190, 191
Home Civil Service, 152, 153, 159
Home Office, 135, 136
Home Secretary, 44, 123, 136, 176, 188
Hong Kong, 47
House of Commons, 32–37 *passim,* 40, 41, 42, 57, 73, 79, 87, 88, 89, 90, 119, 120, 121, 128; Bow Group in, 91; ceremonials in, 94–95; chamber of, 98–99; closure procedures in, 109, 110; criticism in, procedures for, 100; debates in, 94, 109–10; finance of, 111–13; government bills in, 108;

House of Commons (Cont.)
  informal agreements in, 97; lawmaking by, 106–11; legislation delegated by, 110–11; members of, *see* Members of Parliament; Monday Group in, 91; organization of, 94–99; and press, 106; private bills in, 108; public bills in, 108; question period in, 100–01; Speaker of, 95–97, 98, 100, 101, 109, 110; specialized committees in, after 1966, 104–05; standing committees in, 108–09; Standing Orders of, 111; whips in, 97; work of, 99–106; *see also* Parliament
House of Lords, 32, 36, 40, 41 and *n*, 42, 44, 111, 113, 117–19, 120, 168; composition of, 117–18; as court of appeals, 119, 174, 175; functions of, 118–19; powers of, 118; reform of, 37, 116, 117 and *n*, 120; Speaker of, 136, 170; Standing Order of (1963), 118; and television, 106; *see also* Parliament
Housing, 14–15
Humble Petition and Advice (1656), 33
Hyndman, H. M., 50

Iceland, 190
Immigration Bill (1971), 188
Imperial Airways, 141
Imperialism, 47–48, 66
Income Bill (1966), 114
Independent Labor party, 50, 51
Independent Television Authority (ITA), 27, 28
India, 4, 5, 14*n*, 47, 166, 186, 188; and Commonwealth of Nations, 181, 185, 187, 189*n*
Indian Ocean, 186
Indonesia, 186
Industrial Court, 158
Industrial Relations Act, 22, 97, 110, 116, 129, 157
Industrial revolution, 5, 35, 49
Industry, 5, 19
Inflation, 19, 20, 22
Inns of Court, 167
Institution of Professional Civil Service, 156
Instrument of Government (1653), 33, 34
Insurance, social, *see* Social security
International Monetary Fund (IMF), 186
International Publishing Company (IPC), 23, 25
Ireland, 3*n*, 37, 136, 184 and *n;* partition of, 184*n;* and Statute of Westminster (1931), 184
Iron and Steel Corporation, 141, 143
Israel, 190
Italy, 9, 191; Ethiopia attacked by, 70, 123; and NATO, 190; population of, 9; productivity of labor in, 21

Jamaica, 4, 133, 181, 189*n*
James I (1603–25), 33
James II (1685–88), 34, 35
Japan, 21, 184, 187
Jenkins, Roy, 75
Jewish Socialist Labor party, 64

John, King, of England (1199–1216), 31
Johnson, Lyndon B., 122
Jones, Jack, 64
Jones, Tom, 126
Jordan, 186
Judges, 166–67, 173; and administrative system, 170–71; qualities of, 168–69; *see also* Court system; Juries; Law, British
Judicature Acts (1873–76), 171
Judicial Committee of the Privy Council, 174–75, 184
Juries, 169–70; *see also* Court system; Judges; Law, British
Justices of the peace, 169, 174
Jutes, 8

Kaldor, Nicholas, 155, 156, 193
Kangaroo procedure, House of Commons, 110
Kaunda, Kenneth, 189
Kennedy, John F., 122
Kenya, 4, 116, 181, 187, 188, 189*n*
Keynes, John Maynard, 138
King, Cecil, 25
King, Horace, 96, 97

Labor party, 3, 4, 11, 15, 17, 18, 19, 20, 27, 28, 36, 37, 41 and *n*, 51, 54, 62, 63–64, 72, 105, 113, 114, 131, 132; annual conference of, 67; and cooperatives, 65–66, 67; and education, 12, 13; egalitarianism of, 4, 15, 77; and Fabian Society, 50, 51, 64; head office of, 69–70; and housing, 14; local organization of, 66; machinery of, 67, 69–70; membership of, 57, 64; National Executive Committee (NEC) of, 64, 66, 67, 69, 82, 86; and National Health Service, 14; National Plan of, 138; Nonconformist element in, 10; parliamentary, 67, 70; structure of, 64–66, 68; and trade unions, 64–66, 67, 69, 86
Labor unions, *see* Trade unions
Laissez-faire, 49
Lansbury, George, 70
Laski, Harold, 50
Law, Bonar, 10*n*
Law: civil, 164 and *n*, 173, 174; common, 39, 43, 163–66; criminal, 164, 173–74; defined, 163; private, 163, 164; public, 163, 164; rule of, 43, 163, 166
Law, British: and civil liberties, 43, 166; common, 39, 43, 163–66; and equity, 164, 165; profession of, 167–68; rule of, 43, 163, 166; statute, 164, 165, 166; *see also* Court system, British; Judges, British; Juries, British
Law, United States, 164, 167*n*, 169, 173*n*, 174 and *n*, 176
Law Society, 167, 177
League of Nations, 123, 183
Lee, Jennie, 127
Legal Aid Act (1949), 176, 177
Lesotho, 181, 187, 189*n*
Lewis, Roy, 15 and *n*
Liberal democracy, *see* Democracy

Liberal party, 10, 27, 28, 36, 37, 40, 50, 71, 72, 113; and Nonconformist churches, 10
Liberalism, 46, 48–50
Liberties, basic, *see* Bill of Rights
Life Peerage Act (1958), 118
Lindsay, Lord, 119
Lloyd, Selwyn, 96
Lloyd George, David, 10*n*, 40, 99, 117*n*, 118, 125
Local government, 145–51, 161
Local Government Board, 136
Locke, John, 48
Lockheed Aircraft Corporation, 20
London Cooperative Society (LCS)', 65
London Passenger Transport Board, 141
London School of Economics, 155
London University, 166
Lord Chancellor, 118, 119, 123, 167, 168, 170, 174, 176
Lord Chief Justice, 168, 170
Lords, House of, *see* House of Lords
Lords of Appeal in Ordinary (Law Lords), 119, 174, 175
Luxembourg, 190, 191, 192

Macaulay, T. B., 152
MacDonald, Ramsay, 50, 70, 97, 130, 131
Maclean-Burgess spy case, 160
Macmillan, Harold, 41, 62, 115, 116, 118, 127, 129, 130, 131, 132, 160
McNamara, Robert, 122
McQuail, Denis, 27 and *n*, 28
Magna Charta, 31, 33, 38, 43
Magnum Concilium (Great Council), 30, 31, 174
Malawi, 181, 187, 189*n*
Malaysia, 5, 6, 166, 181, 185, 186, 189*n*
Malta, 133, 181, 188, 189*n*
Manchester Guardian, 25
Mandate convention, 41
Marplan survey, 16, 75, 76
Marples, Ernest, 101
Marshall, Geoffrey, 102*n*
Marshall Plan, 191
Marx, Karl, 50
Mary I (1553–58), 33
Mary II (1662–94), 34, 35
Mass media, 17; *see also* Public opinion organs
Master of the Rolls, 170
Maude, Angus, 15 and *n*
Mauritius, 133, 181, 187, 189*n*
Mediterranean Sea, 5
Melchett, Lord, 143
Members of Parliament, 90–94, 98, 102, 109, 140, 154; bills introduced by, 108; facilities for, 105; occupations of (1970), 92; party discipline of, 56–57, 113–17; role of, 93–94; salary of, 105; *see also* House of Commons; House of Lords
Methodists, 9, 10 and *n*, 11
Middle class, 11, 12, 15, 16, 17, 37, 51, 54*n*, 58
Middle East, 4
Mill, James, 49
Mill, John Stuart, 49, 50

INDEX

Mineworkers, 65
Ministries, 135–38; organization of, 126–27, 139–40; regrouping of, 124; see also Administration; Cabinet, British; Civil service, British
Ministry of Agriculture, 123, 144, 156
Ministry of Defense, 123, 124, 136, 138
Ministry of Economic Affairs, 138, 139
Ministry of Environment, 124, 147, 157
Ministry of Fuel and Power, 123
Ministry of Health, 136
Ministry of Housing and Local Government, 124, 136
Ministry of Labor, 123
Ministry of Overseas Development, 136
Ministry of Pensions and National Insurance, 124
Ministry of Public Buildings and Works, 124, 136
Ministry of Social Security, 124, 177
Ministry of Technology, 123, 124, 156
Ministry of Transport, 124, 136, 144
Model Parliament (1295), 32
Monarchy, 121, 131–33, 166
Monday Group, House of Commons, 91
Monopolies Commission, 24
Montfort, Simon de, 31
Morning Star, 23
Murdoch interests, 25

National Chamber of Trade, 19
National Coal Board, 142, 143
National Council of Labor, 67
National Democratic party, 71, 72
National Economic Development Council (NEDC), 138, 139
National Economy Group, 139
National Farmers' Union, 18, 144
National Front, 71, 72
National Health Service, 14
National Insurance Act (1967), 14
National Local Government Officers' Association, 157, 161
National Opinion Polls (NOP), 75, 76
National party, 71, 72
National Union of Conservative and Unionist Associations, 59–60, 62
National Union of Manufacturers (NUM), 18, 19
National Union of Teachers, 157
National Whitley Council, 157, 158
Nationalization, 140–44, 158–59
Nationalized Industries Committee, 103, 104, 107, 114, 143
Nauru, Republic of, 189*n*
Nazism, 163
New Left, 51
New Statesman, 25, 193
New Zealand, 4, 5, 133, 155, 182*n*, 184, 186; and Commonwealth of Nations, 180*n*, 181, 182, 187, 189*n*; productivity of labor in, 21; and Statute of Westminster (1931), 184; in World War I, 183; in World War II, 184
News of the World, 24
News of the World Organization, 23
Newspapers: British, 23–27; United States, 28; see also Press
Nicholas, Harry, 69
Nicolson, Harold, 131

Nigeria, 5, 106, 181, 185, 189*n*
Nixon, Richard M., 21, 41, 57, 122, 129
Nonconformists 9, 10–11, 34, 35, 37, 50
Norman Conquest (1066), 8, 30
North Atlantic Treaty Organization (NATO), 186, 190, 191, 192
Northcliffe, Lord, 23
Northcote-Trevelyan Report, 152
Northern Ireland, 3*n*, 6, 8, 78, 128, 132, 145*n*, 164*n*, 174, 184*n*
Norway, 105, 190, 191

Observer, 24, 25, 29
Official Secrets Act, 106
Ombudsman, 39, 101–02, 122, 178
On Liberty (Mill), 49
Open University, 13
Opinion polls, 75–77
Opinion Research Center (ORC), 75, 76, 77
Opposition, 99–100, 122, 133
Organization for Economic Cooperation and Development (OECD), 9, 21, 191
Ormrod, Justice, 168
Ostpolitik, 191
Overseas Airways Corporation, 143
Oxford University, 12, 91, 153, 155

Pakistan, 181, 187, 188, 189*n*
Palestine Bill (1948), 114
Parliament, 30–45 *passim,* 89–120, 127, 146; members of, see Members of Parliament; origins of, 30–31; and press, 106; Queen's speech in, 94, 100; reform of, movement for, 102–03, 120; rise of, 31–32; supremacy of, principle of, 42–46; see also House of Commons; House of Lords
Parliamentary Act: of 1911, 37, 38, 118; of 1949, 118
Parliamentary Commissioner for Administration, 178
Parliamentary Committee, 125, 127
Parliamentary Counsel's Office, 119
Parliamentary private secretary (PPS), 127
Party system, British: and aggregates of group demands, 87; character of, 53–57; "collectivist" theory of, 90; discipline in, 56–57, 113–17; effectiveness of, 85–88; and organization, 57–73, 86; and representativeness, 86; rise of, 35–37; see also Conservative party; Labor party; Elections, British
Party system, United States, 54, 55, 56, 57
Pax Britannica, 5
Peel, Robert, 58
Peerage Act (1963), 118
People, 24
Permanent Council, 121
Permanent secretary, 139, 157
Peterson, Paul E., 12*n*
Petition of Right (1628), 33, 38
"Petitioners," 34, 35
Peyton, John, 123
Pinto-Duschinsky, Michael, 61*n*

Plaid Cymru (Welsh political party), 71, 72
Planning, economic, see Economic planning
Plowden Report, 112, 139, 157, 159
"Pocket boroughs," 35, 36
Political culture, 11
Political heritage, 30–52
Political ideas, 46–52; of conservatism, 46–48, 50; of liberalism, 48–50; of socialism, 11, 46, 50–52, 138; of utilitarianism, 48–49
Political party system, British, see Party system, British
Polls, opinion, 75–77
Pompidou, Georges, 193
Portugal, 190, 191
Post Office, 137, 141, 143, 152
Powell, Enoch, 8, 58, 63, 77, 91, 116, 122, 193
Power of Parliament, The (Butt), 114 and *n*
Presbyterians, 9
Press, 22–27, 28, 106
Pressure Group Politics: The Case of the British Medical Association (Eckstein), 18 and *n*
Prime minister, 41, 42, 121, 122, 129–31
Prince of Wales, 132
Private law, 163, 164
Privy Council, 31, 32, 34, 95, 121; Judicial Committee of, 174–75, 184
Procedure Committee in House of Commons, 107
Profumo case, 115, 123, 160
Protestant church, 9; see also Church of England
Prussia, 39
Public Accounts Committee, 112, 138
Public corporation, 141*n*, 141–42, 143, 152
Public Expenditure Surveys, 139
Public law, 163, 164
Public opinion, 22, 128
Public opinion organs, 22–29; see also Mass media
Public service, see Civil service
Puritanism, 33, 35

Race Relations Bill (1965), 98, 188
Radio, 27, 28, 141
Rasmussen, Jorgen, 73*n*
Redcliffe-Maud Commission, 145, 146 and *n*, 147, 148, 150, 160
Reform Act (1832), 36, 38, 56
Reform of Parliament, The (Crick), 120
Reformation Parliament (1529–36), 33
Reign of Terror, French Revolution, 48
Religion, 9–11
Rent Bill, 115
Representation of the People Act (1948), 79, 84
Republican party, United States, 55, 56
Restoration of Charles II, 35
Rhodesia, 63, 116, 164*n*, 189
Rights, see Bill of Rights
Robens, Lord, 142, 143
Rodgers, William, 127 and *n*
Rolls-Royce, bankruptcy of, 20, 128, 141

INDEX

Roman Catholic Church, 9, 32–33, 34
Romans in Great Britain, 18
Roosevelt, Franklin D., 40
Rose, Richard, 27 and *n*
"Rotten boroughs," 35, 36
Roundheads, 35
Royal Arsenal Cooperative Society, 65
Royal Commissions, 103, 145, 148, 162, 168, 169, 171
Royal Statistical Society, 156
Runnymede Trust, 8
Russia, 11, 30; *see also* Soviet Union

St. Christopher-Nevis-Anguilla, 189*n*
St. Lucia, 189*n*
St. Vincent, 189*n*
Salmon, Lord Justice, 166
Salter, Arthur, 79*n*
Samoa, Western, 181, 189*n*
Saxons, 8, 30
Schools, *see* Education
Science, 13
Scotland, 3 and *n*, 6, 8, 15, 33, 35, 59, 71, 72, 78, 81, 109 and *n*, 145 and *n*, 148; as Labor party stronghold, 72; law in, 164*n*, 174; Presbyterians in, 9; urbanization of, 11
Scottish National party (SNP), 71, 72
Scottish Standing Committee, 109
Scrutiny Committee of Parliament, 110
Secretariat of Cabinet, 125–26, 129–30
Secretary of State for Defense, 136
Secretary of State for the Environment, 123, 136
Secretary of State for Trade and Industry, 123, 135
Sedition, 39
Select Committee on Estimates, 112
Select Committee on Expenditure, 104, 112
Select Committee on Parliamentary Privilege, 102, 106
Select Committee on Procedure, 112
Selective employment tax (SET), 20, 21
Seymour-Ure, Colin, 23*n*, 24 and *n*, 25 and *n*
Shaw, George Bernard, 50, 52
Shops Bill, 115
Sierra Leone, 133, 181, 189*n*
Simonstown agreement, 189
Singapore, 5, 181, 185, 186, 189 and *n*
Smith, Adam, 49
Smith, Arnold, 185
Soblen, Robert A., 94
Social Democratic Federation, 36, 50, 51
Social security, 13–15, 21
Socialism, 11, 46, 50–52, 138
Socialist Medical Association, 64
Society, Burke on, 46–47
Solicitors, 167, 168
Somali Republic, 185
South Africa, 5, 10, 58, 71, 87, 116, 136, 164*n*, 182*n*, 184, 186, 187; apartheid in, 189; and Commonwealth of Nations, 181, 182, 185, 189, 190; and Statute of Westminster (1931), 184; in World War I, 183; in World War II, 184
Southeast Asia, 5, 197

Southeast Asia Treaty Organization (SEATO), 186
Soviet Union, 6, 58, 66, 114, 163, 190, 191, 193; *see also* Russia
Spain, 33
Speaker: of House of Commons, 95–97, 98, 100, 101, 109, 110; of House of Lords, 136, 170
Spectator, 25
Standing Orders of House of Commons, 111
Statute law, 164, 165, 166
Statute of Westminster (1931), 40, 184
Sterling area, 186
Stokes, Donald E., 17 and *n*
Streatfield Committee, 169
Strikes, 157, 158
Stuart dynasty, 33, 34, 166
Study of Parliament Group, 107, 120
Suez Canal, 47; and crisis (1956), 10, 100, 115
Suffrage, reform of, 35–36
Sun, 23, 24, 25, 26
Sunday Citizen, 24
Sunday Express, 24
Sunday Mirror, 24
Sunday Telegraph, 24
Sunday Times, 24, 25
Supreme Court of Judicature, 171
Supreme Court, United States, 39, 40, 45
Swaziland, 181, 187, 189*n*
Sweden, 191
Switzerland, 9, 21, 191

Taft-Hartley Act (1947), 157
Tanzania, 181, 187, 189*n*
Tariff structure, global, 187
Tawney, R. H., 50
Taxation, 17, 20, 21, 63, 78, 155, 156
Technology, 13
Television: British, 17, 24, 27, 28, 106, 114, 141; United States, 27
Television in Politics: Its Uses and Influence (Blumler and McQuail), 27 and *n*
Thomas, James, 111
Thomson, Lord, 24, 25
Thorpe, Jeremy, 71, 78
Three Advisers of security services, 160
Times, 15, 23, 24, 25, 26, 29
Tonga, 181, 189*n*
Tories 35, 36; *see also* Conservative party
Trade Disputes Bill (1969), 64, 73, 85
Trade unions, 19, 21, 51, 64–65, 66, 67, 69, 86; civil-service, 158; in nationalized industries, 159
Trades Dispute Act (1927), 65
Trades Union Congress (TUC), 19, 21, 116, 159
Transport and General Workers Union (TGWU), 19, 64, 65, 66, 69
Transport Commission, 141
Transport House, 155
Treasury, 124, 130, 135, 137, 138, 139, 142, 152, 153, 155, 156, 157, 158, 177
Treaty of Berlin (1878), 34*n*
Treaty of Brussels (1948), 190
Treaty of Rome (1958), 191, 192

Trend, Burke, 126
Tribunals and Inquiries Act (1958), 179
Tribune, 25
Trinidad and Tobago, 133, 181, 189*n*
TriStar contract for Rolls-Royce engines, 20
Trudeau, Pierre E., 189
Tudor absolutism, 32–33
Tudor dynasty, 32, 33*n*, 145
Turkey, 191
Two-party system, 37, 54–55, 88

Uganda, 181, 187, 189*n*
Ulster, *see* Northern Ireland
Undersecretaries, 139, 156, 157
Unions, trade, *see* Trade unions
United Kingdom, *see* Great Britain
United Nations, 63, 185, 189
United States, 6, 41, 43, 122; area of, 6; birth rates in, 9; blacks in, 8; and Canada, 185; civil service in, 153, 154, 155, 157; Congress of, 89, 92, 105, 111, 128, 135, 137; conservatism in, 46; Constitution of, *see* Constitution, United States; education in, 12; elections in, 74; and Great Britain, 2, 4, 48, 66, 180, 190, 194; infant mortality rates in, 14; interest groups in, 18; law in, 164, 167*n*, 169, 173*n*, 174 and *n*, 176; maternity death rate in, 14; and NATO, 190, 191; newspapers in, 28; party system in, 54, 55, 56, 57; population of, 11; productivity of labor in, 21; Supreme Court of, 39, 40, 45; television in, 27; unemployment in, 20; urbanization of, 11; and Vietnam, 66, 116; wage-price controls in, 21
Universities, 12, 13
Utilitarianism, 48–49

Value-added tax (VAT), 20–21, 71, 78, 192
Vassall spy case, 25, 160
Victoria, Queen (1837–1901), 38, 47, 131
Vietnam, 66, 116, 186
Voting, *see* Elections

Wage-price controls, United States, 21
Wales, 3 and *n*, 6, 8, 11, 15, 33*n*, 71, 72, 78, 132, 136, 145 and *n*, 148, 164 and *n*, 169, 174, 175; education in, 12; as Labor party stronghold, 72; Nonconformists in, 9; urbanization of, 11
Walker, Patrick Gordon, 122
Walker, Peter, 123, 127
Wallas, Graham, 50
Walles, M., 140 and *n*
Walpole, Robert, 34
War Office, 124, 135, 136
Wars of the Roses, 32, 35
Webb, Beatrice, 50
Webb, Sidney, 50
Welfare state, 3, 13, 22, 29, 55, 56
Wells, H. G., 50
West Indies, 8, 14*n*, 187, 188, 189*n*
Western European Union, 192

Western Samoa, 181, 189n
Westin, Alan F., 114n
Westminster, Statute of (1931), 40, 184
Whigs, 35, 36, 48
White Papers, 107, 112, 116, 117 and n, 119n, 124, 125, 138, 139, 140, 142, 147–48, 150, 192
Whitley Councils, 157–58, 161
William the Conqueror, 30, 31
William III of Orange, 34, 35
Willkie, Wendell, 40

Wilson, H. H., 114n
Wilson, Harold, 28, 50, 51, 55, 62, 63, 64, 66, 67, 69, 70, 71, 75 and n, 77, 78, 84, 114, 116, 123–30 passim, 137, 147, 152n, 155, 186, 189, 193
Wilson, Woodrow, 129
Wilson Report on Labor party's defeat (1955), 65
Witan, 30
Women's suffrage: British, 36; United States, 39

Woolf, Leonard, 50
Working class, 15, 16, 17, 36, 51, 54 and n
World War I, 13, 19, 127, 152, 182
World War II, 5, 8, 29, 90, 133, 138, 141, 161, 184

Yaoundé Convention, 187
Younger, Kenneth, 44

Zambia, 181, 189n